PRAISE FOR

AMERICAN TAPESTRY

"No political [book] has ever looked like this one. . . . Reads like a panorama of black life. . . . There can be little doubt that [Mrs. Obama], and the President, will savor this book."

—*New York Times Book Review*

"Swarns has unearthed and disseminated crucial American history here. . . . A remarkable, only-in-America story that Swarns tells with care and thoughtfulness."   —*Washington Post*

"A meticulous, detailed investigation into Mrs. Obama's family tree. . . . Among the revelations brought to light in *American Tapestry* was the truth about the Great Migration. . . . There's rarely a clear A-to-B path when history's truthful, and Swarns honors this nuance. . . . *American Tapestry* holds rewards."   —*Denver Post*

"A completely fascinating look at the complex ancestry of one family, African Americans, and all Americans."   —*Booklist* (starred review)

"A meticulously researched and eloquently written real-life detective story."   —*Essence*

"Tremendously moving. . . . Swarns provides numerous tales of heartbreak and achievement, many of which essentially make up the American story."   —*Kirkus Reviews*

"A layered, scrupulously researched, and wrenching chronicle."

—*Publishers Weekly*

"The First Family becomes ever more fascinating—and ever more representative of the nation as a whole—in Rachel Swarns's terrific investigation into the roots of Michelle Obama. Reaching back to the Revolutionary War and moving up through the present with rich and illustrative detail, Swarns shows the ways in which Mrs. Obama's family was touched by every major shift in the nation's history. This is a most compelling read and more evidence for our interconnectedness as a people."

—Henry Louis Gates, Jr., Harvard University professor and host and executive producer of PBS's *Finding Your Roots*

"A grand, important book that shows how American bloodlines are rarely wholly black or purely white, neither one race nor another. Nowhere is that more true than in *American Tapestry*, an eloquent history of the First Lady's family." —James McBride, author of the *New York Times* bestseller *The Color of Water*

"Rachel Swarns has not only excavated, with painstaking care, the family tree that is Michelle Obama's, but, with great insight and beautiful prose, has revealed the complex, eye-opening, and disconcerting experiences that are America. This is a work of impressive historical imagination and deep cultural significance."

—Steven Hahn, Pulitzer Prize–winning author of *A Nation Under Our Feet: Black Political Struggles in the Rural South from Slavery to the Great Migration*

"In this tour de force of biological sleuthing, Rachel L. Swarns explodes simplistic notions of life and love in the Old South. She peels back accumulated layers of myth, bigotry, and pure wishful thinking to show us the rich intertwining of white and black families and bloodlines. More than adding fascinating depth to the First Lady's personal family story, Swarns has bestowed upon all Americans a revelatory understanding of our shared racial heritage."

—Fergus M. Bordewich, author of *Bound for Canaan: The Epic Story of the Underground Railroad, America's First Civil Rights Movement*

"Tracing the ancestry of the first African American First Lady from the time of slavery to the present, Swarns excavates the buried truth of mixed-race America. Unforgettable in its sweep and movingly told, *American Tapestry* has the power to reshape our understanding of the phrase 'descended from slaves.' This country has long been more multiracial, Swarns's illuminating book makes clear, than many Americans—white or black—have cared to admit."

—Janny Scott, author of the *New York Times* bestseller *A Singular Woman: The Untold Story of Barack Obama's Mother*

AMERICAN
TAPESTRY

THE STORY
OF THE BLACK, WHITE,
AND
MULTIRACIAL ANCESTORS
OF MICHELLE OBAMA

RACHEL L. SWARNS

Amistad
An Imprint of HarperCollins*Publishers*

S

Grateful acknowledgment is made to Francesca Gray for the photographs that appear on pages 17 and 207 and to Jewell Barclay for the photographs on page 117.

P.S.™ is a trademark of HarperCollins Publishers.

HarperCollins books may be purchased for educational, business, or sales promotional use. For information please write: Special Markets Department, HarperCollins Publishers, 10 East 53rd Street, New York, NY 10022.

A hardcover edition of this book was published in 2012 by Amistad, an imprint of HarperCollins Publishers.

FIRST AMISTAD PAPERBACK EDITION PUBLISHED 2013.

Designed by Suet Yee Chong

Library of Congress Cataloging-in-Publication Data has been applied for.

ISBN 978-0-06-199987-1 (pbk.)

13 14 15 16 17   OV/RRD   10 9 8 7 6 5 4 3 2 1

TO THOSE WHO CAME BEFORE

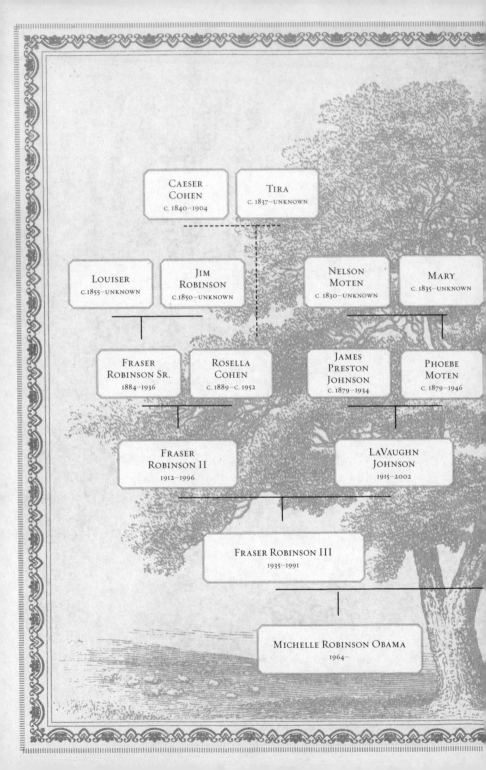

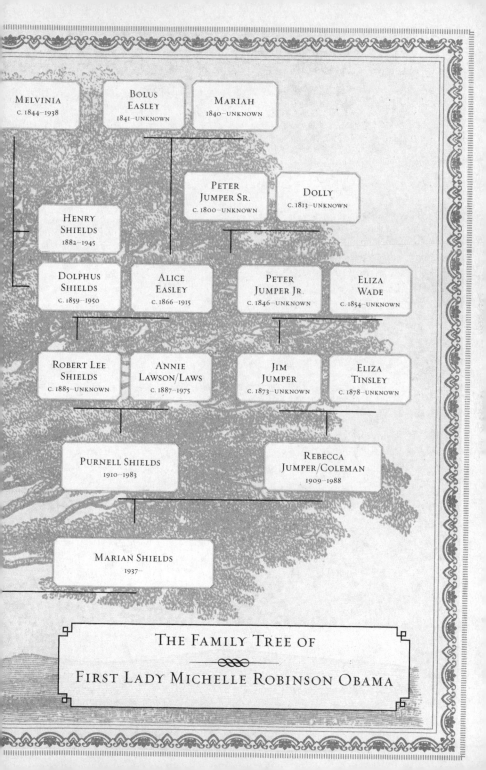

MELVINIA
c. 1844–1938

BOLUS
EASLEY
1841–UNKNOWN

MARIAH
1840–UNKNOWN

PETER
JUMPER SR.
c. 1800–UNKNOWN

DOLLY
c. 1813–UNKNOWN

HENRY
SHIELDS
1882–1945

DOLPHUS
SHIELDS
c. 1859–1950

ALICE
EASLEY
c. 1866–1915

PETER
JUMPER JR.
c. 1846–UNKNOWN

ELIZA
WADE
c. 1854–UNKNOWN

ROBERT LEE
SHIELDS
c. 1885–UNKNOWN

ANNIE
LAWSON/LAWS
c. 1887–1975

JIM
JUMPER
c. 1873–UNKNOWN

ELIZA
TINSLEY
c. 1878–UNKNOWN

PURNELL SHIELDS
1910–1983

REBECCA
JUMPER/COLEMAN
1909–1988

MARIAN SHIELDS
1937–

THE FAMILY TREE OF

FIRST LADY MICHELLE ROBINSON OBAMA

CONTENTS

The Family Tree of
First Lady Michelle Robinson Obama
viii

PROLOGUE:

THE MYSTERY OF MICHELLE OBAMA'S ROOTS

1

PART I
Migration

AMERICAN TAPESTRY

The Mystery of Michelle Obama's Roots

FREEDOM CAME TO JONESBORO, GEORGIA, IN THAT SPRING of 1865, during those hardest of hard times. The town was in ruins, its buildings shattered by cannon fire. The fledgling green fields had been decimated by drought and hunger rippled through the land. Everywhere Southerners turned, people were moving. Many newly freed slaves were dropping their hoes and packing their sparse belongings. They were walking away from the parched earth and the white people who had owned them, overseen them, or marginalized them. Melvinia, a dark-eyed young woman with thick wavy hair and cocoa-colored skin, watched them go. Like all of them, she knew the miseries of slavery. She had toiled in bondage for most of her existence. She had been torn away from her family and friends when she was a little girl. She had been impregnated by a white man when she was as young as fourteen. Yet when the Civil War ended, when she could finally savor her own liberty, she decided to stay. She decided to build a new life right where she was, on the outskirts of that devastated town, on a farm near the white man who had fathered her firstborn son. She was barely in her twenties and silenced by the forced illiteracy of slavery. Even if she had wanted to, she could not have put pen to paper to reveal the name of the father of her child, to spell it out in the permanence of black ink. This was a different kind of affirmation. Her choice was her clue. A census taker would record her address after the war, memorializing her decision in his curly script. His notes would serve as something of a handwritten message that would survive, untouched, for more than one hundred years. It would be the only message Melvinia would ever leave.

Nearly a decade would pass before she gathered up her children and headed north on her own. Black people walked then, sometimes for miles and miles on those dusty, country roads, or squeezed onto the crowded, rattling railroad cars that chugged between small towns in rural, up-country Georgia. Sometime in the 1870s, Melvinia put some sixty miles between herself and her past. And somewhere along the way, she decided to keep the truth about her son's heritage to herself. People who knew her say she never talked about her time in slavery or about the white man who so profoundly shaped her formative years as a teenager and a young mother. She never discussed who he was or what happened between them, whether she was a victim of his brutality or a mistress he treated affectionately or whether she loved and was loved in return. She went her way and he went his, and, just like that, their family split right down the middle. Their children, grandchildren, and great-grandchildren—some black, some white, and some in between—scattered across the country as the decades passed, separated by the color line and the family's fierce determination to step beyond its painful roots in slavery.

Contemporary America emerged from that multiracial stew, a nation peopled by the heirs of that agonizing time who struggled and strived with precious little knowledge of their own origins. Melvinia's descendants would soar to unprecedented heights, climbing from slavery to the pinnacle of American power in five generations. Her great-great-great-granddaughter, Michelle Obama, would become the nation's first African American First Lady. Yet Mrs. Obama would take that momentous step without knowing Melvinia's name or the identity of the white man who was her great-great-great-grandfather. For more than a century, Melvinia's secret held.

On November 4, 2008, some 143 years after Melvinia experienced her first days of freedom in that postwar wasteland, Mrs. Obama stood before a crowd of thousands of roaring, singing, and weeping supporters in Chicago's Grant Park. It was Election Night and her husband had just become the first African American president of the United States. Mrs. Obama was all warm smiles and gracious thank-yous that evening, the poised picture of a sophisticated, self-assured woman prepared to take her place in history. The truth was, though, that she knew very little about her own. The story of her husband's origins had become the powerful narrative that dominated the 2008 presidential campaign. The son of a white woman from Kansas and a black man from Kenya, Barack Obama embodied the hopes of many Americans eager to see an often-divided nation finally come together to fulfill its egalitarian ideals and step beyond its stains of inequality, segregation, and slavery. Mrs. Obama's smooth, chocolate-brown skin seemed to hold few surprises. She was born on the South Side of Chicago, in a working-class corner of the city's storied black community, just like her parents. Like many African Americans, her family had moved north during the Great Migration in the first half of the twentieth century. Mrs. Obama knew her grandparents as a girl, but only bits and pieces about the relatives who came before them. She had grown up hearing whispers about white ancestors in her family tree, but no one knew who they were. Melvinia was gone, buried and forgotten, and her name had long since faded from Mrs. Obama's family memory. The slave girl's legacy may well have remained hidden were it not for two strangers—one black and one white—who happened to be watching Mrs. Obama on that stage on Election Night. The bloodlines of those two women also extended back to that devastated Georgia town. In the 1850s and 1860s, their ancestors—Melvinia, who was black, and Henry Wells Shields, who was white—lived together on a two-hundred-acre farm near Jonesboro where they picked cotton, raised cattle, and harvested bushels of Indian corn and sweet potatoes. Over time, those two women would begin unraveling their shared history and, in the process, the First Lady's as well. But that night, they knew none of it. They watched the Obamas as many of us did, as ordinary Americans eager to witness the moment unfolding before them.

Jewell Barclay, an eighty-year-old elementary-school crossing guard, clapped and cheered as she watched Mrs. Obama and her husband stride across her television screen. Jewell is a former cafeteria aide who went to work straight out of high school. She is a white-haired widow, an African American grandmother who has lived most of her life on a neat, tree-lined block in Cleveland. Schoolchildren and their mothers called to her by name whenever she walked by— "Miss Barclay! Miss Barclay!"—and Jewell, funny and kindhearted, consoled the troubled and cheered the brokenhearted. She thanked Jesus for living long enough to see this first black president and First Lady who looked so in love. In a small town outside of Atlanta, Joan Tribble, a sixty-five-year-old bookkeeper, was watching, too. Joan is a fiercely independent divorcée with blue-gray eyes and an associate's degree, who rarely hesitates to speak her mind. She prides herself on her common sense, her pointed wit, and her beloved grandchildren. She didn't vote for Mr. Obama. "Too young and too inexperienced," she observed during the presidential campaign. She cast her ballot for his rival, John McCain, but admired Mrs. Obama from afar. "A strong woman," she said, nodding approvingly. On Election Night, Joan peered through her wire-rimmed glasses as she tap-tapped the remote control, watching as the tableau of the young president-elect, his wife, and their daughters filled her living room.

The two grandmothers would have scoffed with disbelief that night if anyone had told them that they might have a personal connection to the new First Lady or to each other. They were strangers, after all, three women separated by geography and politics, class and race. For Joan Tribble and Jewell Barclay, Mrs. Obama might as well have lived in another universe. She was a Harvard-educated lawyer, a former hospital executive who had earned a six-figure salary and owned a stately mansion in Chicago. As First Lady, she would dine at Buckingham Palace with the Queen of England, chat with Stevie Wonder, and lead the Obama administration's efforts to combat childhood obesity. Her every public move would be watched by the world. Jewell and Joan, on the other hand, lived ordinary lives, far from the spotlight. But in life, even the most familiar roads sometimes twist and swerve unexpectedly.

The pieces started falling into place in October 2009, during Mrs. Obama's first year in the White House, when she finally learned about Melvinia, the mysterious white man who was her great-great-great-grandfather, and their son, Dolphus. A genealogist, Megan Smolenyak, had discovered the connection and the news broke on the front page of the *New York Times* in an article that I wrote and reported with a colleague. For the first time, Mrs. Obama could identify a slave in her mother's family. For the first time, she could point to a white ancestor in her family tree. Some of the First Lady's friends and colleagues wept when they read about Melvinia, envisioning the young girl so many years ago, and wondering whether she was raped, whether she was loved, whether there was any way to know the truth and the identity of the white man who had impregnated her. Mrs. Obama was so moved that she shared the story with relatives and friends during her first Thanksgiving in the White House that year. They dined on roasted turkey and oyster stuffing, macaroni and cheese, and green bean casserole. And Mrs. Obama, the first descendant of slaves to serve as First Lady, handed out copies of her family tree along with some of the documents that we had uncovered: the obituary of Melvinia's biracial son, Dolphus, and his funeral program, which included a black-and-white photograph of the man himself. There it was, plain as day: the details of her melting pot ancestry, laced with pain and agonizingly unanswered questions. "It was fascinating," said Maya Soetoro-Ng, the president's sister, who was there that night as the nation's most prominent family shared their personal portion of history at the White House, a mansion built, in part, by slaves. A few months later, the First Lady said she was still coming to terms with her newfound knowledge. "We're still very connected to slavery in a way that is powerful," Mrs. Obama told reporters over tea and pastries in the Old Family Dining Room in the White House in January 2010. "Finding out that my great-great-great-grandmother was actually a slave . . . that's my grandfather's grandmother. That's not that far away. I could have known that woman. It just—it makes [slavery] real."

Across the country, Jewell Barclay and Joan Tribble were coming to terms with it, too. I tracked them down after my article appeared in the *New York Times*. I wanted to dig deeper into the First Lady's history and began searching for the descendants of Melvinia and her owner, Henry Wells Shields, who I hoped might help unlock the doors to Mrs. Obama's past. As I explored new branches of the First Lady's family tree, I discovered that Jewell was Melvinia's great-great-granddaughter and Mrs. Obama's second cousin once removed. Joan was Henry's great-great-granddaughter. This, I thought, was a good place to start.

I rang Jewell's doorbell in Cleveland one sunny afternoon in April, armed with a bulging folder full of census records, death certificates, and fading photographs. We sat together at the kitchen table and I walked her through her family line, one ancestor after another, one generation after another, from that slave girl in Georgia to the First Lady in the White House. For a moment, Jewell was speechless. She had never dreamed that she would see a black president in her lifetime, and there I was telling her that she had a cousin in the White House, that she was related to Michelle Obama. "This is something!" she exclaimed. "This is really something!" She had known Melvinia's son, Dolphus, when she was a girl; he was her great-grandfather. Dolphus was also the First Lady's great-great-grandfather, but Mrs. Obama had grown up without knowing about him or about Jewell, her long-lost cousin. "Wouldn't he be so proud?" Jewell marveled, imagining Dolphus's reaction to the astonishing news. But her delight was tempered by the thought of what might have happened to Melvinia on that farm so many decades ago. She hesitated for a moment when I asked what she thought Melvinia might have experienced. Then she shook her head. "Masters messing with those young black girls," she said. "That's what I think happened."

In Atlanta, Joan had to swallow a harder, more difficult truth: that her great-great-grandfather had held the First Lady's ancestors in bondage. Worse still was the possibility that one of her forebears might have raped Melvinia. To be related to the First Lady would have been something to marvel at; to suspect that that family relationship was born of unspeakable violence was something else altogether. "It's horrible," Joan told me when we sat down over a stack of records in the Georgia Archives in Morrow, Georgia, near where her relatives had settled more than a hundred years ago. "You really don't like to face this kind of thing." Some of her elderly cousins wanted to keep quiet about the connection to Mrs. Obama, fearful that the family name would be maligned, that they would be labeled as racists. Other white members of the far-flung Shields family felt a wrenching sorrow as they struggled to reconcile the new information with what they knew about their forebears. Most people in the family had no idea that their ancestors had been slave owners. They knew them as honorable men, hardworking men of simple means who had fought for their country and provided for their families. They worried that all that would be overlooked if a member of the white Shields family was found to be Mrs. Obama's great-great-great-grandfather. But in the end, Joan decided not to follow the lead of her cousins, who wanted to leave their dead to the dead. She wanted to know more, even if that meant more uncertainty and a rethinking of how some viewed her family. Her ancestors were not wealthy people; they did not leave behind any gold coins, trousseaus, or tracts of land. This complicated, unsettling history was her inheritance—and Jewell's and the First Lady's, too. It is, in so many ways, the story of America, in which racial intermingling lingers in the bloodlines of many African Americans, and slavery was the crucible through which many contemporary family lines were forged.

Such forbidden liaisons across the racial divide—they were outlawed in nineteenth-century Georgia—have been open secrets for generations in some families. Rumors about Sally Hemings, the now-famous slave and longtime mistress of Thomas Jefferson, swirled through high-society Virginia during her lifetime, even though they were emphatically denied. Melvinia lived in a world far removed from the elegance of Jefferson's Monticello. Her story is much more reflective of ordinary, day-to-day life in the antebellum South, even though that reality still rarely resonates in the public consciousness. Hemings and Jefferson both occupied elite positions in their respective circles. Jefferson was an American president, a wealthy intellectual, a founder of the Republic who owned scores of slaves and lived on a grand estate. Hemings had a white father, had lived in Paris, and may have spoken some French. She was a house slave, a favored maid. There is no indication that she ever picked cotton or tobacco a day in her life. Melvinia and her owner, on the other hand, were much more typical of the average citizens who became entangled in America's entrenched system of servitude. She was dark skinned and illiterate and no stranger to the backbreaking labor of the fields. Her master, Henry, was a man of modest means whose family was itself only a generation or so removed from illiteracy.

No records have survived, or perhaps ever existed, to indicate whether Henry or one of his sons fathered Melvinia's child, but Joan and Jewell decided to try to find out. The two women had never crossed paths—they did not even know each other's names—but over the next two years, they both pored through their memories and family papers. Jewell dug up the sixty- and seventy-year-old photos that she had tucked away in a manila envelope and reminisced about Melvinia's son, Dolphus, and the widely held belief that he had a white father. Joan went through the old wills, census sheets, and death certificates that she had collected over the years. (The genealogy bug had bitten her long before she learned of her link to the First Lady.) Mrs. Obama, who does not grant interviews for book projects as a matter of policy, declined my request for an interview, as did her mother and brother. But several of her relatives—an aunt, an uncle, two first cousins, a great-aunt, and a great-uncle—agreed to dig through their family records, photographs, and oral histories. While I delved into documents housed in courthouses, libraries, and archives in Georgia, Illinois, Virginia, North Carolina, South Carolina, and Washington, D.C., they talked to me by phone, mailed me old newspaper clippings and family photos, and graciously invited me into their living rooms to share their recollections. Together, we worked to create a detailed portrait of an American family that had emerged from slavery and journeyed north to become one of the nation's most important clans, an intimate saga that had almost completely been lost in the passage of time.

Melvinia and Dolphus were only two of the fascinating and complicated characters that we discovered in Mrs. Obama's lost family tree. As I began digging deeper, the hazy silhouettes of the others slowly came into focus. There were runaways who escaped from servitude in the South and found freedom in the North. There were soldiers who enlisted during perilous times, one who fought during the Revolutionary War, and another who joined the Union Army decades later during its blistering march through the South. In every generation, formidable women stood out. Phoebe Moten Johnson, the wanderer, traveled to four cities by the time she was twenty-eight and was among the first to glimpse the skyscrapers of Chicago. Rebecca Jumper lost her parents and everything she held dear before her tenth birthday, and yet she persevered. And there was Rosella Cohen, who guided her children through the lean, hard years of the Depression and left behind tantalizing hints of a family link to one of the founders of the Jewish Reform movement. There were men who seemed larger than life—irresistible, charismatic, flawed, and vulnerable. Fraser Robinson Sr., a one-armed dynamo, deftly navigated the racial riptides in South Carolina only to leave his oldest son forever burdened with the enormous challenge of emulating his success. Dolphus Shields would become one of the best-known black men in Birmingham, Alabama, while his younger brother, Henry, struggled with all his might to make his mark back home in Georgia. Everyone who knew Dolphus remarked on his light skin and straight hair. He was near white, they said knowingly. But Dolphus was not the only one in the First Lady's family with mixed ancestry. All four of Mrs. Obama's grandparents had multiracial roots, a genetic inheritance that harkened back to the earliest decades of this nation.

In his book *The Souls of Black Folk,* W. E. B. DuBois, the African American intellectual, famously declared that "the problem of the 20th century is the problem of the color line," pointing to the yawning divide between black and white. But in the 1800s, millions of people—including Dolphus, Phoebe, Rebecca's parents, and many others in the First Lady's family tree—occupied a more ambiguous space between those two racial poles. In 1890, census takers counted 1.1 million people of mixed ancestry living in the country. (Mr. Du-Bois, in fact, was among them.) Some were the descendants of white slave owners and African slaves; others were the grandchildren and great-grandchildren of white indentured servants and African slaves or Native Americans. Some were born of unspeakable brutality. Others were the products of liaisons that are harder, in a modern context, to precisely categorize. Not rapes, but not relationships that were entirely free, either. And then there were those who emerged out of love. Some slaves were freed by their masters; others remained enslaved until after the Civil War. Some were so fair skinned that they vanished or "passed" into the white world, but most became part of the multihued African American population. Mrs. Obama's ancestors, who were swept up in some of the most important moments in the nation's history, emerged from this particularly American mélange.

Her forebears would witness the agonies of bondage and the jubilation of Emancipation. They watched the hopes and rights that flowered during Reconstruction quickly fall apart in the racial violence that followed. They joined the vast march of African Americans who moved west and north, transforming themselves from farmers and sharecroppers into city people: carpenters, cobblers, ministers, domestics, coal miners, railroad porters, secretaries, and post office clerks. They built lives in more than a dozen states across the country, from South Carolina to New Jersey, from North Carolina to West Virginia, from Maryland to Michigan, from Louisiana to Kentucky. Their children and grandchildren would be poised to charge through the doors forced open by the civil rights movement. But if Mrs. Obama's relatives were often buffeted by forces beyond their control, they also, whenever possible, took risks and charted their own course. They founded African American churches that still stand today and opened small businesses. They were pioneers, on the forefront of integration, who made themselves at home in predominantly white neighborhoods and studied in predominantly white schools. With their votes, they helped elect the first generation of African American politicians in Illinois. They witnessed bombings and bloody racial violence, and one was shot to death in a quarrel over love. They celebrated marriages and births and mourned their dead. Their lives were sharply constricted by poverty and legalized discrimination, and yet they still clung to the belief that things would get better. "Their American dream was that you dream a little bit at a time," Francesca Gray, Mrs. Obama's aunt, said of the First Lady's forebears and of her own.

And yet as hard as we searched, many of the First Lady's ancestors often seemed like wraiths, elusive shadows who slipped through history, leaving behind few signs that they had existed at all. Barred by law and practice from learning to read and write, Mrs. Obama's enslaved ancestors left behind no letters, journals, or diaries that have emerged thus far. Newspapers and magazines rarely chronicled the lives of ordinary African Americans, deeming their stories unworthy of telling. And even the family stories, the oral histories that passed from parent to child, quietly faded as the decades passed. Some stories were lost on the road as individuals and families uprooted themselves from farming communities, small towns, and Southern cities and boarded crowded, segregated trains and headed north. People married, had children, separated or divorced, and lost touch with the family and friends who knew them back home. Old people died and infants were born and the cycle of life rolled on and on, carrying generations further and further from their origins. Soon all that was left were fragments of their family histories, fading black-and-white photographs of men and women whose names, identities, and origins had been forgotten. It is the kind of quiet, gradual fading of family memory that happens so naturally, so organically, that it is gone before anyone realizes it.

But other memories seem to have been discarded, deliberately cast aside. Some of the descendants of Melvinia's white owners chose not to pass on what they knew about the family's history of slave ownership. And Melvinia's own descendants seemed equally content to let the memories of that time wither. For many members of that first generation to emerge from slavery, the experience of bondage was so shameful and painful that they rarely spoke of it. They focused on moving forward, on moving their children forward. Over and over again, older members of Mrs. Obama's family said that their parents and grandparents and great-grandparents didn't talk about slavery, discrimination, or racial violence or about the provenance of the family's white ancestry. They described an almost willful, collective forgetting, an intentional loss of memory that spanned different communities and encompassed different branches of the family.

The silence pervaded Mrs. Obama's immediate family as well, a sort of burdened inheritance. As a little girl, Mrs. Obama and her brother, Craig Robinson, lived on the South Side of Chicago in a one-bedroom apartment so small that her parents had to partition the living room to create space for her and her brother to sleep. Their home stood within blocks of their four grandparents; they have warm memories of spending time with them at family barbecues and Sunday dinners. But Mrs. Obama and her brother grew up knowing little about how those grandparents ended up on the South Side and virtually nothing about the ancestors who came before them. Mr. Robinson remembers discussing slavery and segregation on a Sunday drive in his parents' Buick Electra 225 when he was about twelve and Michelle was about ten. He and his sister watched the popular and powerful miniseries *Roots,* based on Alex Haley's family's experience in slavery, when they were teenagers. Mrs. Obama, meanwhile, recalls being transfixed by Toni Morrison's *Song of Solomon,* with its powerful evocation of a twentieth-century family still haunted by the old wounds of slavery. She swallowed it whole, reading it all in one day. "That book, it like grabbed me and I just kept reading and kept reading," she told a group of school children last year. During the summers, she and her family often passed by old rice plantations as they visited relatives in South Carolina. But the family never discussed how the plantations might be related to their personal history. Mrs. Obama has said that she talked about almost everything with her parents, but "we didn't talk about that."

The family's conversations about slavery were almost always rooted in discussions about the African American experience in general, rarely about the family's experience in particular. "We were aware that most [African American] families were at some point descended from slaves and we talked about that and kind of understood that was the case in our family," said the First Lady's brother. During Barack Obama's presidential campaign, his aides enlisted a historian to dig into Mrs. Obama's father's line, which also extends back to slavery. But Craig Robinson has said his family knew little beyond that. "We didn't do the whole family tree," he said. "Getting into the nitty-gritty of the genealogy, we didn't do that." Nomenee Robinson, Mrs. Obama's uncle, said that when he tried to dig, he found himself blocked by an impenetrable silence. "All of these elderly people in my family, they would say, 'Boy, I don't know anything about slavery time,'" Mrs. Obama's uncle recalled. "And I kept thinking: 'You mean your mother or grandmother didn't tell you anything about it?' What I think is that they blocked it out."

At the White House, Mrs. Obama used her platform as First Lady to bring some measure of attention to the slavery experience that had shaped her family and the nation. She told students attending a Black History Month program there that slaves had helped build the executive mansion and that the Emancipation Proclamation had been signed there. In the Capitol building, she helped unveil a bust of Sojourner Truth, the slave-turned-abolitionist fought for racial and gender equality, telling the audience of dignitaries that she could almost imagine her looking down from the heavens. "I hope that Sojourner Truth would be proud to see me, a descendant of slaves, serving as the First Lady of the United States," she said. In July 2009, she traveled to Ghana with her husband, their daughters, and her mother and visited Cape Coast Castle, a notorious slave port perched on the windswept sea where Africans were held in dungeons until they were marched in shackles to ships headed for the Americas. In each of the prisons—

there was one for women and one for men—Mrs. Obama and her daughters placed a single red rose. The visit offered the world a public and pointed reminder of what President Obama would later describe as "all the pain and all the hardships, all the injustices and all the indignities on the voyage from slavery to freedom." But outside public view, the impact was also personal and private for a family still wrestling with its own share of this history. "They were visibly shaken," said Fritz Baffour, a member of Ghana's parliament who helped guide the family through the dungeons. "They became quite somber." He said that Mrs. Obama knew that her family could "trace their ancestry to slaves. She wanted the children to be aware of that fact, as part of the family history, to understand what went on." Later that month, the First Lady took her daughters to Monticello, Thomas Jefferson's estate in Virginia, where they could see how the men and women shipped from Africa actually lived as slaves there.

The First Lady wanted her girls to understand their own history, and she wanted to know more about it herself. Mrs. Obama once remarked that she would welcome the truth about her white ancestry. "An important message in this journey is that we're all linked," she said, about a month before she stood on that stage in Chicago on Election Night. "We are, in fact, through our histories of growth and survival in this country. Somewhere there was a slave owner—or a white family . . . that again led to me. So who were those people? I would argue they're just as much a part of my history as my great-grandfather."

Joan Tribble and Jewell Barclay came to the same conclusion. After bracing themselves for what they might learn, they each decided to take a DNA test, to see whether the swipe of a cotton swab could finally lead to the truth, whether twenty-first-century technology could help unravel a nineteenth-century mystery. With luck, the testing would allow them to determine once and for all whether Mrs. Obama's white great-great-great-grandfather belonged to the family that had enslaved Melvinia. Three members of Mrs. Obama's family and three descendants of Melvinia's owner ultimately agreed to take the test, despite objections from their families and the realization that they may have to shoulder the burdens of that painful history. Even Joan and Jewell expressed their own private anxieties. When asked whether she might like to meet the descendants of the man who owned Dolphus, her great-grandfather, should they prove to be her relatives, Jewell agreed immediately. "Oh, yes!" she said. Then she stopped. She could not help but wonder whether the white descendants, even in this day and age, would be willing to embrace her, a black woman, as part of the family. "If they want to meet me," she said, finally. Joan wondered, too, whether Mrs. Obama's family would truly accept any white relatives, particularly if they turned out to be the descendants of a man who might have raped her great-great-great-grandmother. In Mrs. Obama's only public discussion about Melvinia, the First Lady never mentioned her white ancestor, the man who fathered Melvinia's son. "Sometimes I get the idea that she's not, that she'd just as soon not know about the white connection," Joan says.

Even in these contemporary times, when so many Americans embrace their multiracial roots, there are those among the living who would prefer such old secrets to sleep with the dead, to remain untouched, unresolved. It would have been easier for Joan and Jewell not to embark on this journey. They both knew that they might stumble across raw, painful truths, drawing unwanted attention that could disrupt their quiet lives. But they are older now, women who have discovered in their later years a hunger to connect with those who came before them. The only way to do that is to go backward, one generation at a time, peeling back the layers of history to unearth the story of one remarkable family and one singular nation. And so the trail begins with the men and women who were swept north to Chicago. It winds its way back to their parents, those forebears who were shaped by the demise of Reconstruction and the rise of Jim Crow in the South. Then, finally, it brings us back to the beginning, to that Georgia farm where the slave girl and the white man once lived. Let the ancestors tell their stories. Let them speak from beyond the grave, through the yellowing records and photographs they left behind, and through the memories and genetic inheritances of those who still live.

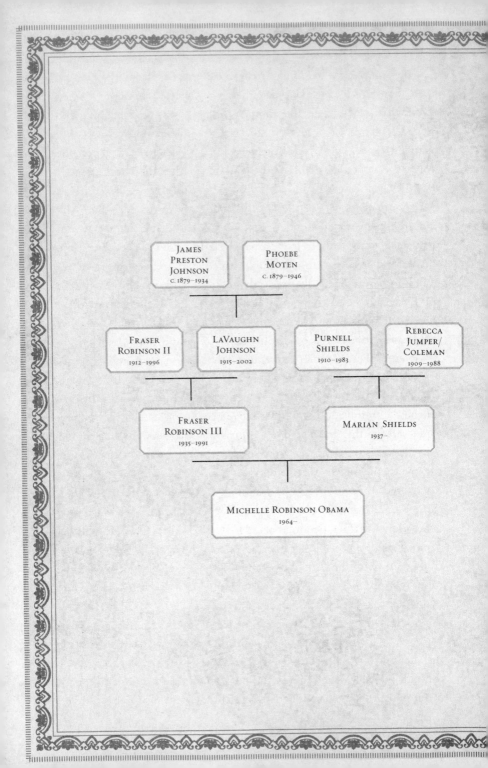

PART I

〰〰〰

Migration

Phoebe Moten Johnson

THE PATERNAL GREAT-GRANDMOTHER
OF MICHELLE OBAMA

ONE

Phoebe, the Wanderer

L ONG BEFORE AFRICAN AMERICANS POURED INTO CHI- cago, before jazz filled the city's dance halls, before the bus- tling black neighborhoods on the South Side became known as the Black Metropolis, Michelle Obama's ancestors staked their claim to Illinois. Big city, twentieth-century Chicago did not exist when her forebears settled in the sleepy, rural, southernmost corner of the state that juts into Kentucky like a pointed finger, the spot where the waters of the Mississippi and Ohio Rivers meet and mix. There, in the late 1800s, more than half a century before Mrs. Obama was born, a young girl with luminous brown eyes and bronze-colored skin labored on a farm, even as she dreamed of a bigger, better life somewhere else. Her name was Phoebe Moten, and she was born on December 17, 1879, just sixteen years after the Civil War. We all have our beginnings, those places where our stories first unfold. Phoebe would take her first steps in Villa Ridge, a tiny hamlet in Pulaski County, Illinois, with rolling green hills and rich black soil, where sweet strawberries ripened in spring and winter wheat sprang from the earth after plantings in the fall. It was a speck of a town, population 1,366 to be precise, the kind of place that people often passed through on their way to somewhere else, with a post office, a sawmill, a Masonic lodge, and a railway station that rarely appeared on state maps. But there was no missing that train when it flew through the center of town. The Illinois Central Railroad was a force of nature, a burst of steel and steam that sent fallen leaves swirling and left grasses trembling in its wake.

Phoebe would grow up watching that train, on its way to and from small towns and big towns, from Cairo to Chicago and from Chicago to Cairo, carrying people and produce to places she had never seen. She was the daughter of poor sharecroppers, former slaves who were still firmly tethered to the earth. At the time, landless black farmers in Villa Ridge were trying to plant their way to prosperity, filling borrowed plots with swaying rows of corn and wheat, tending milk cows and cackling chickens, and sowing and harvesting for their white landlords. Phoebe would work the fields, too, alongside her sisters, but she was young and restless and weary of the relentless, unchanging rhythms of farming life. The sight of that gleaming, modern train would bring to mind other ways of living. By the mid-1890s, its rumble had become the village's background music, as familiar as the songbirds trilling in the hickory trees and the Cache River's gurgling while fireflies hovered and flickered like wandering stars. Phoebe, who was still just a teenager, might have ignored the train's enticing call had she not been struck by a series of calamities that upended her existence and changed her life. Her children and grandchildren marvel now at how the course of the nation's history might have buckled and swerved if Phoebe had stayed put, if she had become a farmer's wife and kept her feet firmly planted in that fertile soil. If she had chosen that path, her great-granddaughter, Michelle Obama, might not have been born.

Phoebe rarely indulged in such musings. She clung to the belief that her steps were divinely ordered, her path purposefully guided. Her destiny was foretold, she believed, long before she or her parents laid eyes on the promised land of Illinois.

Sometime around 1899, on the eve of a new century, Phoebe would say farewell to Villa Ridge. Her children have little doubt as to how she left. One day, they believe, before her twentieth birthday, Phoebe finally took her place on that train. She was heading north. "I don't ever want to go back to the farm," she would say years later.

She had no money to speak of, no property of her own, and no husband. She was a country girl, about five feet five inches tall and just venturing into adulthood. Yet between 1899 and 1908, Phoebe would travel to four different cities, each one a little bigger than the next, each one a little farther north.

She was a pioneer, a member of one of the first waves of African Americans who packed their bags and moved north, paving the way for the southerners who poured into places like Chicago, Detroit, and New York after World War II and transformed America's big cities and the trajectory of millions of black families. That Phoebe began her trek long before the Great Migration got under way in earnest is remarkable enough. What is more striking is that her parents, Mary and Nelson Moten, headed north earlier still. As slaves, the couple accomplished something that most blacks could only dream about: they found their way to the free state of Illinois before the Civil War brought slavery to an end. They arrived around 1863, joining the flood of African Americans streaming into the state. Phoebe's mother, who was born in Missouri, had straight black hair, light-brown eyes, and a complexion that strongly suggested she was biracial. Her descendants believe she had some Cherokee blood running through her veins. Phoebe was born with the telltale markers of mixed ancestry, too. At one point in her life, census takers would call Phoebe mulatto. Others described her as black or Negro. One of her sons was classified as white when he was an infant.

Today, people with multiracial roots often celebrate their blended identities, and Americans like Barack Obama are no longer forced to choose one race or the other. We often think of the late twentieth century and the early twenty-first century as that singular period when the nation, transformed by immigration and intermarriage, stepped beyond simple notions of black and white. But the United States saw itself as a nation of many hues back in the 1800s, populated as it was by Europeans, Africans, Native Americans, and their multicolored progeny. The difference between now and then is that Mr. Obama and others discuss their heritage openly and publicly today, which was rarely the case back then. In those days, sex across the color line was outlawed in most southern states, and babies born in such circumstances were typically the product of either violent or forbidden encounters. The stories of their origins remained shrouded in silence. After the Civil War, biracial children and their descendants, like Mary and Phoebe, stood as the flesh-and-blood symbols of those coerced liaisons and clandestine unions. For decades, the government struggled to figure out how to classify these individuals, settling on one set of labels, then others, before finally, in 1930, deciding to describe them all as black. Some people embraced their multiracial origins; it gave them a leg up in a society that esteemed people with lighter skin. For others, their fair coloring served as a painful reminder of the powerlessness of their mothers and grandmothers and the violence they endured. Phoebe belonged to a new generation, the first generation of African Americans born into freedom, and she was determined to leave those dark days behind. But in her face and in her blood, she would always carry that raw history with her.

She entered the world at a time of great promise. Villa Ridge, with its dense stands of oak, walnut, hickory, and maple trees, was something of an oasis for the hundreds of former slaves who settled there when they were first savoring freedom. It was a place that many old-timers could hardly imagine leaving, particularly around the time that Phoebe was born. In 1880, about five hundred African Americans lived in Villa Ridge, a little more than a third of the settlement's population. Eighty-four black farmers had managed to buy their own land, and their numbers were growing. Congress had passed a federal Civil Rights Act five years earlier that outlawed the practice of denying blacks access to inns, theaters, public conveyances, and restaurants, giving families hope that society was finally opening up. Already, many of the village's black men and women were on the rise. A small but growing number of African Americans in Pulaski County, which included Villa Ridge, had managed to move off the farms, finding work as blacksmiths, cooks, and laborers for the railroad and sawmills. A handful of black professionals—a doctor and two teachers—tended to their ailments and taught basic literacy skills. Eleven ministers nurtured the souls of the growing community. And on Election Day, black farmers, sharecroppers, and artisans alike all lined up to cast their ballots. Some African Americans were even running for office and winning. "Just now our town is one of the liveliest in Southern Illinois," wrote the Pulaski correspondent for the *Argus-Journal* in 1880, capturing the optimism of the time. "It has more saw mills, more flag poles, more stump speakers and more colored voters to the square foot, than any other town in these parts." Blacks in neighboring communities looked on with envy. One man from Alexander County noted admiringly that blacks in Pulaski County were winning elections as county commissioners when African Americans in his community had only "dared to ask for the nomination as Coroner."

It seemed like the ideal place for former slaves who hoped to buy a bit of land and push their children up and out of poverty. But for Phoebe's parents and many others, such dreams would sadly unwind as national and local officials took steps to turn back the clock, erasing many of the gains African Americans had made since Emancipation. In 1883, four years after Phoebe was born, the U.S. Supreme Court struck down the Civil Rights Act. It didn't take long for opportunities to begin narrowing in southern Illinois. By the time Phoebe was a little girl, her aging parents were still too poor to buy their own farm. Blacks who aspired to work outside the fields were struggling to find well-paying jobs. The railroad relegated them to menial labor, if they hired them at all. Some municipalities refused to employ African Americans for public-works projects because white laborers balked at working alongside them. "Our newly instituted dredging system of the Mississippi River, employing nearly 500 men of all nationalities, but the Negro is not found there; can't even get a job as a fireman," one man complained at the time. Some African Americans observed

that the so-called good life in southern Illinois was becoming little
more than a myth. Who was to argue that the South was that much
worse? "The north legislates to keep us from working," one black
writer noted wryly in the *Illinois Record* in 1897, "while the south legislates to keep us from voting."

For Phoebe, the stagnant economic landscape coincided with a
succession of personal tragedies. By the time she turned seven, her
father, Nelson, who spent his entire life working on farms that he
would never own, was dead and buried, around the age of sixty-two.
Her mother, Mary, remarried a man named Jerry Suter, who owned
a farm in Villa Ridge and became like a father to her. But sometime
afterward, between 1887 and 1900, Mary would also die. Phoebe was
forced to navigate the turmoil of adolescence without her beloved
mother to guide her. She found herself orphaned in Villa Ridge with
limited options. The local schools were poorly equipped, poorly attended, and segregated. Still, Phoebe somehow learned to read and
write, in her cramped script, and worked her way through elementary
school, possibly as far as the eighth grade. This was no small achievement for the child of illiterate parents, the descendant of a family that
had endured generations of forced illiteracy during the reign of slavery. At the time, 45 percent of blacks still could not read or write.
Phoebe's accomplishments suggest that her parents, and her stepfather,
prodded her toward finding a way out.

In Villa Ridge, however, Phoebe's prospects were decidedly un-
appealing. Women usually married farmers and worked the land, or
found low-paying jobs cleaning houses or washing clothes for white
families; and even those jobs weren't always easy to find. Phoebe had
sisters and brothers, stepsisters, stepbrothers, and a stepfather in Villa
Ridge, who may have urged her to stay, to put aside her grief and establish roots in the settlement that her parents had made their home.
But Phoebe was weary of the long days working on her stepfather's
farm. Her parents had spent most of their lives laboring on land they
did not own. Phoebe wanted no part of that life. No one knows precisely when she headed out of Villa Ridge, though her children be-

lieve she was a teenager when she stepped aboard that train and left the world of her childhood behind.

Phoebe could have chosen any number of towns or cities along the way. But she was young and new to the notion of faraway places. She headed north and got off the train in a town called Carbondale. By 1899, the place Phoebe now called home—with a population of just under 3,500 people—was more than double the size of Villa Ridge. Carbondale had a university, an electric company, and public water-works. It also had an abundance of jobs available for African Americans hoping to escape the drudgery of sharecropping. Word spread quickly and black people from nearby towns and villages, as well as southern states, started pouring into the city, drawn by plentiful work on the railroad and in local coal mines. Blacks accounted for only about 18 percent of the city's population when Phoebe made her way there, but their numbers were quickly growing.

Phoebe might have left Villa Ridge to join an older sister, who had also moved to Carbondale. By 1905, her sister was living there with her husband, who would become a prominent black minister in town. A man named Elbert Taylor lived there, too. He was a young laborer who had roots in Villa Ridge, just like Phoebe. They both had mixed-race ancestry, and they both had fathers who had worked as sharecroppers. Back in Villa Ridge, their families had been neighbors. Elbert's parents had moved there from Tennessee sometime between 1880 and 1900 and rented a house near the farm owned by Phoebe's stepfather. Phoebe and Elbert very well might have known each other there, exchanging smiles and conversation as they worked in the fields. Perhaps Phoebe decided to follow him to Carbondale, or they stumbled across each other in their newly adopted city. What is certain is that sometime, somewhere, Phoebe and Elbert met and decided to marry. They exchanged wedding vows in Carbondale on December 4, 1899, not long before the birth of a new century, a turning point for many young African Americans like Phoebe and Elbert, who were severing their family's long-standing ties to rural farming life. But they still clung to some traditions that dated back to slavery.

Phoebe decided on a December wedding, just like her older sister and her mother had done before her. It was a custom that dated back to the days before the Civil War, when slaves often married during the weeks before Christmas when their masters were most likely to be generous with gifts of free time and extra food.

Phoebe was nineteen and Elbert was twenty-one when the Reverend A. F. Daniel brought them together in a ceremony held just two weeks before Phoebe's birthday. It should have been one of the biggest moments of Phoebe's young life. Yet in later years, when she was a mother with many children, she chose to keep everything about her wedding day a secret. It is as if she decided to wipe the slate clean, to erase any evidence of the young laborer she had once embraced as her husband. Elbert might as well have been a phantom. No photographs of him are known to have survived. Phoebe's children say their mother never uttered Elbert's name. Some fifty years after Phoebe's death, her youngest son would shake his head in astonishment when he stumbled across her marriage license—and the name Elbert Taylor—as he researched his family tree.

Phoebe and Elbert walked out of that ceremony in 1899 as husband and wife, with the blessings of a man known in those days as a minister of the Gospel. But whatever hopes she and her husband may have nurtured for their future were doomed. Six months after the wedding, Elbert was dead. Phoebe was only twenty years old and already a widow. No one alive today knows what struck Elbert down. His young age suggests a tragic accident, a killing, or a devastating, unexpected illness. A death certificate for him has yet to surface, and there is a good chance that one may not exist. State law at the time required county clerks to be notified of all deaths, but penalties for failing to do so were weak and many deaths were simply never reported. Phoebe's silence about Elbert's life and death may have sprung from memories too unbearable to speak of. There is no doubt that Elbert's premature demise unraveled her plans, at least for a time, of moving north. By June 19, 1900, Phoebe was right back where she started, in Villa Ridge.

Journeys often unfold in fits and starts. So it was for Phoebe and the thousands of black men and women who took to the road after slavery's demise. Some set their sights on the wide-open spaces in Kansas—envisioning the farms they might buy there—and ended up in crowded St. Louis when their pennies could carry them no farther. Some dreamed of New York City but made their peace with Baltimore. For Phoebe, it was a return to her hometown and to square one. It was the kind of devastating setback that could change the course of a life, shaking one's faith in the future and one's trust in God, and forcing a reevaluation of nearly everything that matters. But whatever anguish lingered in Phoebe's heart, she clung tight to her old plans for a new life. She could not control the fates. But she was still intent on making a change, even if it had to come about in Villa Ridge. Determined to avoid farming, Phoebe decided not to live with her stepfather, who still owned the land she had worked on as a teenager. Instead, she moved in down the road with Elbert's family, Jeff and Lina Taylor, who shared a home with their three other children and Jeff's mother. A former sharecropper, Jeff had already made the break from farming, finding work as a laborer for the railroad. Settled into her in-laws' rented house, along with the rest of his extended family, Phoebe finally made that break, too. She took up "housekeeping," which, in the jargon of the time, meant she cleaned houses for white families. Some women turned up their noses at domestic work, being, as it was, positioned on one of the lowest rungs of the job market. But for Phoebe it was a step up. It was inside work, a job that kept her out of the dirt, kept her fingers clean and stinging insects away from limbs that would ache after long days in the fields. It meant that she could stay a little cooler on the hottest days of the year and stay warm when the cold winds blew in from up north.

She could often count on gifts and hand-me-downs from her employers, secondhand furniture that looked nearly as good as new; cast-off clothing with fine stitching; used books and magazines that offered a broader view of the world; and holiday delicacies that were out of reach for most black women. Between 1890 and 1900, the number of African American women who worked as domestics more than doubled in Pulaski County. Black women, even those with some education like Phoebe, had few better options. Still, it was often exhausting, backbreaking work: domestics at the time typically labored from dawn until late at night, cooking, scrubbing, washing, only to return home to start the same routine all over again in their own households. Women like Phoebe had little recourse if their madams refused to pay their wages, abused them, or fired them. The temperaments of their employers varied enormously, with some embracing their employees as invaluable members of the household and others treating them with disdain and abuse. One white woman, the daughter of a grain merchant who lived in southern Illinois, referred affectionately in her diary to her servant girl as "a black angel in calico." Another disparaged the entire class of black female servants, complaining in the *Cairo Bulletin* that "only about one in seventeen knows how to work."

Black women, for their part, learned to placate difficult bosses. They quit when they had better prospects and lodged quiet protests when they didn't, employing work slowdowns and tactical absenteeism to get their grievances across. One group of housekeepers in southern Illinois even formed a union. Mostly, though, they learned to get by. "I have lived in the best families in this town since I have been here, and I have had some good places and some awfully mean ones," one servant wrote to the *Cairo Bulletin*. "I could tell a story of grievances . . . if I tried." Phoebe's decision to give up farming for domestic work would shape the rest of her life. It gave her a source of income and a measure of independence, critical for a young woman whose eyes were still fixed on the road north. Even as she coped with the unexpected loss of her husband and the derailment of life in a big city, she was determined to hold on to her dreams. The move back to Villa Ridge would only be temporary. Somehow, she decided, she would find another way out.

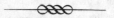

TWO

St. Louis

P HOEBE WOULD NEVER TELL HER CHILDREN WHY SHE SET-
tled here or there. She would not talk about the heartbreak
of leaving family and friends and old graves behind, or about
the heady exhilaration of stepping out of one life and into a new one.
But she would tell her children many stories when they were little,
and her favorites were always about the frontiersmen, the outlaws who
ventured into wild, lawless places and surmounted insurmountable
odds with pistols blazing. The tales of wandering men like Buffalo
Bill and Jesse James fired her imagination. Black women rarely figured
in such lively tales; their adventures were hardly deemed worthy of re-
counting. Still, Phoebe might have seen something of herself in those
men, with their hunger for new places and their determination to
forge ahead, villains and sheriffs (and dead husbands) be damned. Like
them, she also took pains to hide her tracks. Between her nineteenth
and twenty-second birthdays, Phoebe trekked through several cities in
southern Illinois, but her footprints are not easy to find. County officials captured her stop in Carbondale, when they recorded her short-
lived marriage to Elbert in 1899. Census enumerators found her a year
later, when she was a widow living with her in-laws, back home in
Villa Ridge. She told her children, later in life, only bits and pieces

about the detours she made along the way. More than a century has passed since Phoebe left Villa Ridge for the second time, and it often seems as if her footsteps were covered in dust by the relentless winds that blow across the plains. In some places, the road she traveled was inadvertently swept clean by the passing years and the thousands of migrants who came after her. In other places, it seems, she stopped, turned, and deliberately obscured her own trail. No one alive today knows the precise pace or number of stops that she made on her journey. There are gaps in her story, countless unknowns. There are tales that her children have forgotten and tales that she chose not to share.

But one thing is clear: within a year of her husband's death, Phoebe was back on the road. This time, she traveled past Carbondale and headed west. Sometime between June 1900 and April 1901, she stopped in the city of Edwardsville, which sits in the far western corner of Illinois, a stone's throw from the Missouri line. Edwardsville, population 4,157, was the biggest city Phoebe had ever set foot in. In those days, many African Americans from southern Illinois were migrating to northern parts of the state and beyond as they sought better jobs and better opportunities. For Phoebe, Edwardsville would prove to be more than a stepping-stone. It was in that city that she decided to share her life and her travels with the man who would become her second husband and life partner. His name was James Preston Johnson, a twenty-one-year-old itinerant minister, carpenter, railroad worker, and itchy-foot traveler who seemed determined to find his way to a big city, no matter how many miles he had to travel or how many states he had to cross. In Phoebe, it seems, he met his match. No one knows exactly how James, who spent his earliest years in Louisiana, ended up hundreds of miles away in Illinois or how he got to know Phoebe. They may have bumped into each other in Villa Ridge or in Edwardsville or somewhere in between. He was the kind of man who would catch a woman's attention. In one undated black-and-white photograph, James cut something of a dashing figure. He was a quiet man, about six feet tall, mustachioed and formally dressed in a dark jacket, white shirt, and tie. Like Phoebe's first husband, James also had white ancestry and light skin. His father was an illiterate mulatto sharecropper, a former slave who may have been the son of a white man with German ancestry. Born in 1879, James lived for a time in Madison Parish, Louisiana, near the Mississippi border. His mother, who was black, was from Mississippi.

As an adult, James sometimes claimed Vicksburg, Mississippi, which sat just across the Mississippi River from Louisiana, as his hometown. He may well have moved to Vicksburg from Louisiana when he was a little boy. By 1878, with the last of federal troops having left the South, many blacks in Mississippi and in neighboring Louisiana began fleeing as intimidation and racial violence became increasingly widespread. James would join the exodus sometime between 1880 and 1901. His aunt and at least two of his cousins moved north, too, their descendants say. Many African Americans who left were farmers, and they hopscotched across Louisiana, Mississippi, and Kentucky on their way to Illinois and Kansas. James, though, had ambitions far beyond the fields. He dabbled in the ministry, where his deep voice earned him something of a following wherever he went. He wanted to build his own business, to become his own boss, to join the early ranks of African American entrepreneurs.

He also wanted a wife. Phoebe, who was twenty-one, relatively educated, and eager to find a place for herself in one of the nation's growing cities, fit the bill. She was not beautiful, but she had striking dark eyes and a way of making a stranger feel at home. In an undated black-and-white photograph, she stares directly at the camera, eyes wide. She is wearing a blouse with a high collar, adorned by white cloth flowers, and her thick hair is neatly parted and pulled back. A sparkling stone glitters in her right ear. She looks serene, offering little hint of the restlessness that seems to have carried her so far from home. In Phoebe, James found the woman who would accompany him wherever his nomadic dreams might lead. On April 20, 1901, just a month before James's twenty-second birthday, the couple got married before a police magistrate in Edwardsville. It was James's first wedding. Phoebe, who often fell back on her penchant for keeping secrets, claimed that it was her first marriage, too. As a mother, Phoebe would emphasize honesty and the importance of baring one's soul to God and fellow man. But on that day in 1901, she decided to keep the truth, and her deceased first husband, to herself. Maybe it didn't matter whether James knew that his bride had been previously wed. What he was certain of was that he was a man who liked to roam and she was a woman who was determined to find her way to a big, bustling city. Anyone who knew Phoebe and James might have guessed that they wouldn't be long for Edwardsville.

In that corner of Illinois, the big time was St. Louis, Missouri, the nation's fourth-largest city, that vast, congested river metropolis that was drawing thousands of black sharecroppers from across the South. For country girls like Phoebe, St. Louis was nothing short of a marvel. Fifteen- and sixteen-story skyscrapers lined the city's grand avenues. Trolley cars powered by electricity rattled through the streets, carrying well-heeled passengers and workingmen alike. More than eleven thousand people chattered on newfangled telephones, and glimmering electric lights kept the main streets aglow even on the darkest evenings. The city's factories and breweries were churning out beer, shoes, stoves, and wagons. In the saloons and vaudeville theaters, black pianists were pounding out exciting rhythms, a brand-new kind of music called ragtime with a rollicking, syncopated tempo that became St. Louis's signature sound.

Even the poor neighborhoods bustled with more energy than most new arrivals had ever seen, with streetcars rolling and horses and buggies clip-clopping past the teeming brick tenements. There seemed to be no end to the influx of newcomers. Steamboats churned the waters of the Mississippi, carrying migrants into the burgeoning city. And the rattling cars of the Illinois Central Railroad, which coughed up black clouds of smoke as it headed north, discharged a steady stream of wide-eyed passengers from as far south as Mississippi and as close as the small towns of neighboring Illinois. Between 1880 and 1900, the population in St. Louis surged by 61 percent to 575,238. About 6 percent of those residents—some 35,516—were black. Only in Baltimore did African Americans account for a higher percentage of the population in a major city. The black population would continue to surge in St. Louis during the first decade of the twentieth century.

Phoebe and James joined the incoming throngs sometime between 1901 and 1903, moving into an apartment in a downtown neighborhood overcrowded with poor Italian, Polish, and black migrants. The newlyweds unpacked their belongings in a narrow, two-story brick building on North Twelfth Street, where they probably occupied one floor. Their new home stood on an alleyway, between Morgan Street and Franklin Avenue. On balmy spring afternoons, the couple could stroll about a dozen blocks to the shores of the Mississippi River. They lived within walking distance of some of the city's most storied icons, the Wainwright Building and Barr's, a large department store. The city's black aristocrats—the doctors, lawyers, and teachers—would move into tidy houses in a neighborhood called the Ville. But grand St. Louis, even middle-class St. Louis, might as well have been a world away from the impoverished community where Phoebe, James, and other African Americans settled. Their neighborhood had the most dilapidated houses, particularly along Twelfth Street, where Phoebe and James lived, and along nearby Wash and Morgan Streets and Lucas Avenue. Plaster crumbled from the decrepit brick buildings, and frame houses with sunken roofs sagged and shook as the streetcars rumbled by. Families stuffed paper in their windows to keep out the winter chill, but biting winds and vermin still crept through the cracks and holes in the walls and ceilings. A housing survey estimated that about 50 percent of the structures in Phoebe's neighborhood were unfit for habitation. Many streets remained unpaved. Piles of rags, manure, rubbish, and old mattresses towered in the backyards; and even spring breezes could not carry away the stench of filthy backyard toilets. Newspaper accounts from around the turn of the century described the congested black neighborhoods in St. Louis as undesirable slums, places of grinding poverty, crime, and disease.

But Phoebe had finally arrived in a big city, and she made that

brick tenement a home for her growing family. There were some luxuries: garbage was collected twice a week and black schools typically
received nearly as much financing as their white counterparts, something unheard of in southern Illinois. Her building had two windows,
one on each floor. Maybe Phoebe could have even glimpsed, from
that second-floor window or from the roof, the glimmering Mississippi River. It was in that house, on March 25, 1903, that she gave
birth to the couple's first child. She named the boy James Preston,
after her husband. (In their records, city officials described the newborn infant as white.)

Roy Wilkins, one of the leaders of the NAACP, also lived in St.
Louis when Phoebe was exploring her new role as a wife and mother
on North Twelfth Street. His parents, who had fled racial violence
in Mississippi, stepped off the Illinois Central Railroad in St. Louis
in 1901. Mr. Wilkins, who was born in a four-room flat in a narrow row house there in 1902, described the city of his earliest days as
bustling and segregated. It had only one black grocer, and years later
Mr. Wilkins could still remember the smell of sweet molasses, sawdust, and fresh ground coffee that wafted from the man's shop. The
city was almost completely divided along the color line: blacks were
barred from hotels, restaurants, swimming pools, and tennis courts.
The public hospital and public schools were segregated, though blacks
had equal access to the public library and black children competed
with whites in track-and-field events until 1916. Still, African Americans breathed much more freely in St. Louis than they did in the Deep
South, Mr. Wilkins said. White police officers greeted him with casual kindness, he recalled, and he felt little racial tension. "Missouri
was a border state, less virulently racist than Mississippi, and thus I
was able to start life a long leg up on my father and grandfather," Mr.
Wilkins wrote in his memoirs.

Like Mr. Wilkins's father, who worked in a brick kiln, James found
a job as a laborer, too. About a third of the black men in St. Louis did
the same. They cleaned streets, packed and unpacked goods in stores
and warehouses, drove horse-drawn dray wagons, waited tables. Black

women typically cared for children, cleaned houses, or worked as laundresses. The scanty public records available do not indicate whether Phoebe had a job, but she might have done some domestic work to help pay the bills. Rent in those days typically ran about $4 to $9 a month, and many families struggled to pay even that, scrounging for pennies for food, clothing, and streetcar fares. Black families in the neighborhood could send their children to the Dumas Public School, which was an easy stroll, as was St. Elizabeth's Catholic Church, which ministered to a black congregation. John W. Wheeler, the prominent owner of the black newspaper, *Palladium*, urged the city's ordinary black citizens to seize the widening opportunities available and to pull themselves up from poverty. "Organize parents' associations in each school district, to get the idle children in school, to teach cleanliness and manners among them, to break the habit of going from school in droves," Mr. Wheeler wrote in a column on February 14, 1903, entitled, "Something for the Negro to Consider." He continued: "Stop loafing around other men's business places. There are 5,000 colored children in the schools and 5,000 out. Put those out in. That is our work."

In St. Louis, African Americans were actively pushing for increased self-reliance and to preserve and expand their rights. While Phoebe was tending her newborn baby, blacks in her newly adopted city were mounting successful opposition to proposed legislation that would have forced them to sit in segregated railroad cars. In 1904, the year that Phoebe gave birth to her second child, Howard, St. Louis hosted the World's Fair, and a stream of prominent black leaders from across the political spectrum poured into the city. Among them were Booker T. Washington, W. E. B. DuBois, the poet Lawrence Dunbar, and T. Thomas Fortune, a newspaper owner. (Even with such a panoply of luminaries, however, concessionaires still refused to serve black patrons.) Phoebe might have read the interviews with Booker T. Washington's wife that appeared in local newspapers. It was the first time the city's white newspapers, which even published Mrs. Washington's photo, had so prominently depicted a black woman in such a favorable light.

Still, life for ordinary blacks remained a constant struggle. Many barely eked out a living and came home every evening to cramped, dark apartments. Mr. Wilkins, the NAACP leader, remembered that his family's flat was so spare that the only adornments were the bricks his father occasionally brought home from the kiln. His mother would paint them and cover them with colorful cloth. "That was all the interior decorating we could afford," he said. And while there was work to be had for laborers like James and Mr. Wilkins's father, it was often backbreaking and poorly compensated. "Work in the brick kiln soured my father's spirits and he became sterner and more remote," Mr. Wilkins said. "He had the inner resources to make the passage to St. Louis but the spiritual and physical effort of the change seemed to exhaust him. Each morning he picked up his lunch pail and headed to work, and at nightfall he returned with brick dust on his boots and a scowl on his face." By 1907, Mr. Wilkins was moving on, heading north again. His mother had died of consumption, and he and his sister and brother left St. Louis in the care of an aunt who took them to Minnesota.

Phoebe and James began thinking of moving, too. Lynchings and race riots had erupted in two Missouri cities, one in Joplin in 1903 and another in Springfield in 1906, leaving some African Americans unsettled. By the time Phoebe and James's third son, Calio, was born in 1906, Missouri was feeling too much like the Deep South for many blacks. Phoebe may also have had more personal reasons for wanting to leave. Her fourth son, Charlie, who was born the next year, didn't live to see his first birthday. Some relatives believe he suffered from influenza. Charlie was nearly eight months old when he died on January 11, 1908. Phoebe recorded the date, as she did the births and deaths of all her children. She rarely spoke at all about her time in St. Louis, about why she moved there and why she left, at least not to her children. But within months of burying her son, Phoebe and James had decided to try their luck somewhere else. Word was spreading about the opportunities in a city farther north. Blacks could vote and earn better wages there, people said. They could send their children to integrated schools and maybe even flourish in a place where the worst of southern segregation did not exist. For many African Americans at the time, moving north meant progress. It certainly meant that to Phoebe, who was weighing her fifth move in less than a decade. But it also meant separation and dislocation. It was yet another break with the past, another journey that would carry Phoebe still farther from her origins.

She may not have thought very much about the growing distance from her beginnings. Or she may have found some comfort in the widening physical and emotional distance from the deaths of her parents, her first husband, and her baby, Charlie. Phoebe's surviving children would never know the hardships of country living, the inadequacies of segregated, rural schools, or the struggles of transitioning from farming to urban life. And they would never know much about their mother's history, either, about where she got that shimmering brown skin and thick hair, or about the identities of her parents who emerged from the nation's complicated racial mix in the decades before slavery's demise. Villa Ridge would soon become a fading memory, a place consigned to tattered photographs, packed safely out of sight. The Illinois Central Railroad ran several trains through St. Louis every day during those years. Passengers could get on an overnight car at 9:05 P.M. and step off in the biggest city in the Midwest by 6:58 the next morning. Sometime in 1908, Phoebe, her husband, and their three boys packed their bags and said good-bye to St. Louis. By the time the cold winds of winter were lashing, she had stepped eagerly into her new future in Chicago.

THREE

Siren Song of the North

THE GREAT MIGRATION, WHICH CARRIED MILLIONS OF African Americans from the South to the North, conjures up a vision of a single, unremitting flow of multitudes, a relentless stream of men, women, and children in search of another way of living. In reality, there were multiple waves—some smaller, some larger—that ebbed and flowed as determined and dazzled newcomers poured into northern states. Some people moved to escape racial violence and discrimination or dire economic straits. Some moved to find better jobs, better pay, better schools, better opportunities, a place in line at the ballot box. Historians describe it as one of the largest internal mass movements in history: between 1910 and 1970, 6.5 million black people moved north. Mrs. Obama's forebears were in the vanguard of that migration, setting out long before anyone could imagine how completely black southerners would transform the northern American city.

Mass movements rarely burst forth as a torrential flood of humanity. They begin with one person, one family, one emotional swirl of tearful farewells and see-you-real-soons, one rattling train ride north. In North Carolina, where Mrs. Obama's maternal ancestors settled around the turn of the century, it was Carrie Tinsley Coleman who set out first. Around the time that Phoebe was heading to Chicago, Carrie was saying good-bye to her father and her older sister and the town of Leaksville, which was tucked tight along North Carolina's border with Virginia. Carrie was only twenty-three years old. Like Phoebe, she was also a country girl, the daughter of former slaves. Carrie had never learned to read or write, but she had a literate husband and an adventurous spirit and she had already put the farming life behind her. Carrie was working as a maid and her husband, John, was hauling bricks in a brickyard when they fell in love in Leaksville. They decided to head north by 1907, the year that metered taxis started running in New York City and soon before the first electric washing machines went on sale. Most working-class black women would be scrubbing on washboards for years to come. No matter. Carrie knew she would be doing her washing—and her living—in a big city, somewhere up north.

Some historians refer to this early stream of black migrants as "the Migration of the Talented Tenth" because it included prominent ministers, teachers, and businessmen as well as ambitious, less-educated blacks, people like Carrie, Phoebe, and their husbands, who "were not content to live life on southern terms," in the words of historians St. Clair Drake and Horace R. Cayton. (The vast majority of blacks—about 77 percent—still lived in the South in 1940. People started moving in great numbers when World War II created a boom in factory jobs and the mechanization of the cotton picker wiped out thousands of agricultural jobs.) Many members of Carrie's generation had started moving even before they journeyed north, joining the steady stream of African Americans who were leaving small southern towns for larger ones. By 1900, Carrie's family had moved from the farming community of Martinsville, Virginia, to Leaksville, which was an emerging factory town with cotton and tobacco mills. Her father, a sharecropper, would prosper in Leaksville, finding work in a cotton mill and buying his own house. But the siren song of the North was more alluring to young people like Carrie, who dreamed of bigger cities with better-paying jobs and more freedoms. North

Carolina had stripped blacks from the voting rolls and the weight of segregation felt increasingly oppressive, limiting how high black men and women could climb. Carrie, it seems, wanted more from life than Leaksville could offer.

Ancestral lines do not always stick to a straight path, from mother to daughter, from great-grandmother to great-granddaughter. There are curves in every family story, the fateful moments that bend the branches of a family tree and spin out a new destiny for the generations that follow. So it was for Carrie Coleman, Mrs. Obama's great-aunt, who ventured north with her husband in search of something else, something better. On the journey, the couple skipped over Washington, D.C., which was still something of a sleepy backwater. Their destination was forty miles north of the nation's capital, a thriving, humming industrial city with fiery steel mills, rumbling railroads, and a garment district peopled by polyglot workers from around the globe. Their destination? Baltimore. More foreign immigrants poured into Baltimore's port than anywhere else in the country, aside from New York's Ellis Island. And the town claimed such black luminaries as Frederick Douglass, the runaway slave–turned-abolitionist, who read his first antislavery tract in that city and found a wife there. "Going to live at Baltimore," he would later say, "laid the foundation, and opened the gateway, to all my subsequent prosperity." Between 1880 and 1900, the city's black population surged by 47 percent to 79,258, accounting for about 14 percent of the population.

By the time Carrie arrived around 1907, the city was proudly touting its status as the sixth-largest city in the country, with a population of more than half a million people. The town pulsed with life. Striving, impoverished blacks crammed into tenements while African Americans who had made it—lawyers, doctors, teachers, and undertakers—entertained in their elegant Victorian homes and stately three-story town houses on Druid Hill Avenue on Baltimore's west side. "So far as I know there is no city in the United States where the coloured population own so many comfortable and attractive homes in proportion to the population, as in the city of Baltimore," Booker

T. Washington declared after taking in a fifteen-block stretch of Druid Hill Avenue.

For the first time in her life, Carrie was walking the streets of a city where African Americans had significant economic and political clout. A black-owned newspaper—the *Afro-American*—chronicled the community's triumphs and struggles. And on Election Day, African Americans lined up at the city's polling places to flex their considerable political muscles. Blacks in Baltimore had the right to vote, and they used their significant numbers to elect black men to the city council. (Two black councilmen, who served at different times, were so prominent in Republican circles that President Theodore Roosevelt invited them for a visit at the White House.) Of course, the city also had its pockets of poverty, squalor, and despair. Many blacks crowded into the filthy Biddle Alley neighborhood in West Baltimore, where garbage and animal feces littered the streets and untreated sewage spilled into alleys, basements, and communal living spaces. "There is not one house on Biddle Alley in which there has not been at least one case of tuberculosis," one health official said. Carrie and her husband, John, were not wealthy enough to live among the well-heeled black middle class on Druid Hill Avenue, but they managed to steer clear of the Biddle Alley slum. They settled on the east side of town, renting a narrow, two-story brick row house in a predominantly white working-class ward, on a block populated mostly by African American transplants from Virginia. By 1910, Carrie was washing clothes for a living and John was working in a stone quarry. But even as they and other newcomers settled into their new lives in the big city, racial tensions were beginning to boil.

"Negroes Encroaching" warned a headline in the *Baltimore Sun,* the city's biggest newspaper, as the influx of African Americans touched off a furor among whites. Most restaurants, which once allowed blacks and whites to eat side by side, had begun denying seats to African Americans. In 1910, a leading department store announced that blacks would have to go to its basement to try on hats and other clothing. In July of that year, riots broke out across the country, including in Baltimore, after the black boxer Jack Johnson knocked out his white challenger in a heavyweight match in Reno, Nevada. "One negro was badly cut by another and two other negroes were assaulted and seriously injured by whites in arguments over the big fight," a newspaper recounted. Seventy black people—half of them women—were jailed. White citizens had already been up in arms that summer because word had spread that a black lawyer had purchased a redbrick row house on the fringes of one of the city's best—and whitest—neighborhoods. Angry whites poured tar on the lawyer's front steps and hurled stones and bricks through his windows and skylights, and the white-dominated city council decided enough was enough. That December the council became the first in the country to pass a law barring blacks from moving into all-white neighborhoods. (Violators could be fined up to one hundred dollars or be sentenced to a year in prison.) More than a dozen cities across the nation, including Richmond, Atlanta, St. Louis, and Indianapolis, would follow Baltimore's lead. Edgar Allan Poe, the city's solicitor and a grandnephew of the famous poet, hailed the bill's passage as "a great public moment." Someone had to take a stand, he said, explaining that "wherever negroes exist in large numbers in a white community, [it] invariably leads to irritation, friction, disorder and strife."

Over the next seven years, the city's prominent African Americans battled the city's residential segregation ordinances in the courts. Carrie and John watched from the sidelines as the debate raged in black and white newspapers, in black and white churches, and at kitchen tables across the city. Only a tiny fraction of blacks—less than 1 percent—owned property in Baltimore, and most could not afford to rent in the city's gilded neighborhoods either. But the battle directly affected the aspirations of African Americans like Carrie and John, who had moved north to find opportunities that were denied them in the South. The U.S. Supreme Court would ultimately deem the ordinances unconstitutional, but the decision would not halt the steady, relentless creep of segregation. That harsh reality became clear even as Carrie and John dealt with their own pressing matters at home. On their block of Aisquith Street, which overflowed with boisterous young children, their row house was conspicuously quiet. At a time when married couples often had as many as ten children, Carrie and John remained childless, even after their fourteenth wedding anniversary. Carrie had given birth to a baby when she was a teenager, before she got married, but that child does not appear to have survived. By 1916, when she was thirty-two, she may have given up hope that she would ever have a son or daughter of her own. For better or worse, Carrie didn't have young children to consider as the racial climate deteriorated around her. That must have made their decision easier. After about a decade in Baltimore, Carrie and John decided to move on. There was nothing holding them back.

They had decided on a more hospitable city in the Midwest when terrible news trickled in from back home: an unmerciful plague had descended on North Carolina. It started spreading in September 1918, and the sick soon began pouring into the state's hospitals. The ailing men and women burned with fever. Their skin turned dark blue as fluid filled their lungs and their bodies were slowly starved of oxygen. Within three days, many were dead. It was the flu, but unlike any that doctors had ever seen. Previous influenza epidemics struck down the weak and the elderly. This one ravaged the young and healthy, and it raged across the country. As thousands died and people lost faith in their doctors and home remedies, panic spread throughout North Carolina. "Some of them locked themselves in their house, and refused to open the door for anyone," said Selena W. Saunders, who accompanied a trained nurse on her rounds. "Merchants nailed bars across their doors, and served the customers one-at-a-time at the doorway. We found whole families stricken, with none able to help the others. In one family the mother died without knowing that her son, who lay in the adjoining room, had died a few hours earlier." By October 16, Winston-Salem, which was only about an hour's drive from where Carrie's family lived, closed down its churches. Farmers stopped farming. Merchants shuttered their stores. "I was afraid to go out, to play with my playmates, my classmates, my neighbors; I was almost afraid to breathe," said Dan Tonkel, who was a child when the epidemic swept through the state. "People were afraid to talk to each other. It was like—don't breathe in my face, don't even look at me, because you might give me germs that will kill me. So many people were dying, we could hardly count them. We never knew from one day to another who was going to be next on the death list."

African Americans in North Carolina were hardest hit. They were barred from white-only hospitals. Acute shortages of black doctors and nurses meant that many patients were unable to receive any medical care at all. Between October 1918 and March 1919, more than thirteen thousand people died from the pandemic in North Carolina. Carrie's older sister, Eliza Jumper, a washerwoman and the mother of at least seven children, may have been among them. Precisely what happened to Eliza remains a mystery. It is an inevitable truth in the telling of old family stories. Some questions may never be answered; some mysteries remain unsolved. But it appears that some catastrophe struck Carrie's family, wiping out her sister, Eliza, and Eliza's husband, Jim. Some of their children were dispersed to far-flung corners of the country after their deaths. Carrie and John, who may have longed for a child of their own, decided to take in one of the orphans.

Rebecca, the First Lady's maternal grandmother, was only about eight years old when Carrie and John scooped her up and set off to begin their new life in the grand city of Chicago, leaving Baltimore behind. Perhaps John's brother, who was working as a coal miner in West Virginia, had told the Colemans the amazing stories he was hearing about that big city in the northern plains. Perhaps they were drawn by the songs and slogans of the time, like "Bound for the Promised Land" and "Farewell, We're Good and Gone," which celebrated African Americans moving north. Or maybe they heard the call of the *Chicago Defender,* the black newspaper that circulated across the country and received hundreds of letters from black men and women eager to find jobs and new lives up north. "Would like Chicago or Philadelphia," wrote a freight handler from Houston, Texas, who hoped to better the life of his young family. "But I dont Care where so long as I Go where a man is a man."

With more than two million people, Chicago was the second-largest city in the country, the place where the first skyscraper was born, the home of the Republican National Convention between 1904 and 1920, the city where Frank Lloyd Wright had begun his work of rewriting modern architecture. Carrie and John knew big city life, but this place would be like nothing they had ever seen. Whether young Rebecca eagerly embraced her new adventure or wept inconsolably for her mother and father and siblings, traumatized by her losses, remains unknown. But the little girl would clearly adapt. She became so close to her adventurous guardians that she even took their name, just as she would adopt the city they would carry her to. She gave up the surname she was born with, casting aside one of the last links to her lost parents, the Jumpers. For as long as she was a single woman, Rebecca would describe herself as a Coleman.

FOUR

A Family Grows in Chicago

THE HOUSE AT 5037 SOUTH DEARBORN STREET ON THE South Side, near the corner of West Fifty-First and the railroad tracks, was a far cry from Chicago's steel and stone glories. Dilapidated tenements and bungalows could barely contain the stream of newcomers pouring into the neighborhood, like a dam about to buckle under swelling waters. The stockyards and meatpacking industry butchered, processed, and shipped more meat than in any other place in the country. And the railroad was a constant presence. Its span of black tracks seemed to run on forever, and its passengers, crammed into those crowded carriages, seemed like the living-and-breathing reminders of the multitudes of journeys that are always beginning and ending. For Phoebe and James Johnson, the first of Mrs. Obama's relatives to set foot in Chicago, the journey was just beginning. The house on Dearborn Street was now home. It was cramped and hugged the path of the rumbling railroad. But that didn't matter. Life on the South Side offered something far more intangible, an opportunity for African American strivers to hitch their hopes to the urban experience and maybe, with a lot of hard work and a bit of luck, to the American dream.

When the family arrived in 1908, the South Side was years away from becoming Chicago's most storied African American community. The apartment buildings, grocers, and churches bustled with European immigrants and their children, and German and Swedish chatter filled the streets. African Americans accounted for only 2 percent of the city's population. They were just beginning to make their presence felt. The building that Phoebe and her family settled into no longer exists today. It might have been a two-family house or one that was partitioned for several families. They shared it with another couple and their daughter, possibly to help cover the rent. Their block was occupied by African Americans who, like them, had traveled from the Deep South and other parts of Illinois. They took up jobs as waiters, railroad porters, housekeepers, janitors, cooks, and washerwomen. The couple had landed among like-minded people, a new generation of literate black men and women who were poised to climb. They would become part of one of the earliest waves of migrants that would transform the city in the coming decades. Between 1900 and 1910, the number of blacks in Chicago rose from 30,150 to 44,103. Progress and opportunity, though, would come in small steps, and the grandeur of the family's newly adopted city could not shield them or their neighbors from the hardships of day-to-day living. Newcomers quickly discovered that they were relegated to the city's most menial, low-paying jobs, though there was consolation in the fact that those jobs still paid much more than what they could find in the South or in smaller cities.

Phoebe celebrated her twenty-ninth birthday in Chicago that December of 1908, and welcomed a new baby into the family, her fifth child, a boy she named Clifford. But life in the nation's second-largest city would offer no insulation from the heartbreak experienced by so many women in the early twentieth century. In the summer of 1909, Clifford contracted whooping cough. On August 16, after midnight, he died at the family's home. He was eight months old. Phoebe's daughter, Mary, who was born in Chicago six months later, suffered a similar fate. She was sixteen months old when she died on July 15, 1911. (Phoebe was pregnant at the time. On August 18, she gave birth to her seventh child, Astor.) Phoebe had buried three of her children in quick succession, one in St. Louis, two in Chicago, in what had become an agonizingly familiar ritual. One child was old enough to totter to Phoebe and call her name. The others were old enough to smile and crawl and babble. Of the three, none lived to celebrate a second birthday. At the time, growing numbers of women were calling for more government attention to the scourge of infant mortality. Thousands of mothers, some wealthy and some working class, fired off letters to the federal Children's Bureau demanding that the authorities investigate why so many young children were dying. "Is it the corsets we wear? Is it the food we eat? Is it the strain we live under? What is it?" one woman from Mississippi asked. "Something's got to be done—and done quickly."

Phoebe, herself, fell back on her familiar habits and swallowed her sorrows. She still had to tend to her husband, her newborn, and her boys, who were eight, seven, and five. There were meals to prepare, clothes to wash, a home to clean, children to shuttle back and forth to school. She may have been working, too, cleaning houses or taking in laundry to help cover costs. It may be telling that Phoebe's early years in Chicago corresponded with an intense period of religious exploration. There were only two black churches in her hometown of Villa Ridge when Phoebe was growing up; one was Baptist and the other Methodist. But in Chicago, she was exposed to the new churches sprouting up on the South Side. She was drawn not to the staid style of worship in the stone edifices of the black elite, but to the storefront churches where the congregants spoke in tongues, where the Holy Spirit moved among the people and faith healers cured those sick in body and heart. Like her husband, James, an itinerant preacher without a fixed church or flock, Phoebe became something of a spiritual wanderer, too. Her descendants do not know if she settled on one place of worship at the time. But they are certain that her faith became the bedrock of her life, her constant consolation during difficult days. It helped her keep going at a time when almost everyone around her was focused on moving forward, not on looking back.

By 1910, James had found employment as a laborer in the asphalt business, and the couple's sons were attending integrated schools. Racial tensions simmered in some schools, but in most classrooms, particularly at the elementary level, black and white children recited their lessons and raced gleefully through the playgrounds. "When one treats these dear little children, both black and white, with tenderness and makes no difference between them . . . they both lose their prejudice," explained the white principal of a local elementary school, describing his faith in the possibility of racial harmony. That her children were receiving the same education as their white counterparts must have been exhilarating for Phoebe, who had only known segregated schools in southern Illinois and St. Louis. Many African Americans described being awestruck when they saw blacks and whites mixing and mingling in ways that were unimaginable in the South. "When I got here and got on the street cars and saw colored people sitting by white people all over the car, I just held my breath, for I thought any minute they would start something," said one black woman who arrived in Chicago years after Phoebe. "Then I saw nobody noticed it, and I just thought this was a real place for Negroes."

The forays across the color line also extended into politics. That year, the South Side was abuzz over the possibility that a black man might be elected to the all-white city council. For the black residents of Dearborn Street, these were heady times. An unexpected snowfall that June—which caught the entire city by surprise—might also have convinced Phoebe and James that Chicago was a place where just about anything was possible. "Pull off your coat and roll up your sleeves and buckle down to a good live hustle; leave no stone unturned, root out every voter in the ward and tell them to go to the polls and vote for the colored candidate," the *Chicago Defender* proclaimed on its front page, so that the city "will be ablaze with a victory unprecedented in Chicago's history." As it happened, it would take five more years for the first black man to take his seat on the council. But the thrilling campaign left many convinced that this was a city where African Americans could make their mark. Black newspapers, led by the *Defender,* jubilantly chronicled the growing community's progress, the activities of the new local branches of the NAACP and Urban League, and the society weddings and European travels of the educated well-to-do.

The South Side was still about 90 percent white, but it had become the heart of the emerging black community. And Phoebe's stretch of Dearborn Street offered a snapshot of the sweeping changes to come. She had only one white neighbor: a salesman and his family of German immigrants. The rest were African Americans who had migrated from Kentucky, Missouri, Mississippi, Georgia, South Carolina, and other parts of Illinois. Like Phoebe, they had stepped into a city and a community that was deeply conscious of class and color. In the early 1900s, that color line could be blurry. People didn't always live neatly on one side or the other. Many occupied the space in between, not entirely white, not entirely black. In 1910, when a census enumerator visited Phoebe in her Dearborn Street home, he was tasked with determining whether she and her family were "full-blooded Negroes" or something else. We don't know who in the family he met that day, but we know what he determined: Phoebe and her family were "mulatto," the term used at the time to describe people with mixed ancestry.

In the early 1900s, such people were inarguably among the most privileged of African Americans. In the eyes of many Chicagoans, Phoebe's and James's ancestry was certainly an asset. Some African Americans descended from slave owners who favored them with education, skills, financial support, and social status. That legacy conferred incalculable benefits to the generations that followed, who often emerged as the black community's elite. Others were the descendants of free blacks, some of whom thrived, unburdened as they were by the physical or emotional scars of slavery. Others carried the genetic inheritance passed down from their American Indian ancestors who had owned slaves or had assisted and married runaways. Their lighter skin; their straighter, longer hair; and their European features often set them apart. Employers—both black and white—openly professed their preference for lighter-skinned employees. "I have a policy of hiring only real light girls with good hair," said one black business-man who ran a popular South Side restaurant. "I do this because they make a good appearance . . . A dark girl has no drawing power." The *Chicago Defender* reinforced the bias and stigma by publishing adver-tisements for hair straighteners and skin whiteners, which described a light complexion as a symbol of beauty and success. "Why Be Dark and Swarthy?" was the question posed by French's Celebrated Face Bleach. "Do You Want to Be Beautiful?" asked an advertisement for another, Ivore Cream, which promised that it "positively lightens the complexion."

Such views were so widespread at that time and in the coming decade that some parents worried that their darker-skinned sons and daughters would have fewer opportunities than their lighter ones. "I have five children, you know—all grown now—four girls and one boy," said one mother. "Three of the girls have decent light brown skins, but the boy and the other girl are dark-brown-skinned. The Lord in Heaven knows that I love them all dearly, but He also knows that I wish the two dark ones were lighter." There were formal re-ceptions, social clubs, and churches that were the sole province of the city's light-skinned elite. And there were churches, lodges, and reli-gious revivals that catered to the darker-skinned masses. In the Afri-can American community on the South Side, the dividing line often separated those with chocolate-colored complexions and those with crème de caramel. In this color-conscious society, the darkest, poor-est people were always relegated to the bottom rungs of the hierarchy. Even on Phoebe's block on Dearborn Street, which included black and mixed-race families in nearly equal numbers, mixed-race fami-lies tended to live next to each other. (Phoebe and James shared their home with the family of Harry Trent, a waiter of mixed-race ori-gins.) Phoebe was brown skinned, but James, her husband, was much lighter, "high yellow," his descendants say, a phrase used to describe someone with a café au lait complexion. In her personal life, Phoebe certainly ended up choosing two husbands who had a similar ancestry to her own.

Some African Americans discussed their white ancestors with great detail and pride—describing this great-grandfather from Ireland and that great-aunt with blue eyes. On the busy streets of the South Side, mixed ancestry conjured up notions of privilege. But it also evoked painful legacies. In 1910, many black adults knew someone who had lived in slavery—or had been a slave themselves. Yet in many families, the subject was taboo, shrouded in shame, silence, and heartache. In other families, it was viewed as an unfortunate bit of history better left to the past. James never even shared the names of his parents. Phoebe carried her mother's black-and-white photograph with her as she journeyed from village to town and from town to city, a talisman of sorts from a faraway place and a forgotten time. But to her children she described her mother's long, straight hair and little else. It is almost as if Phoebe wanted them to imagine that she had sprouted, nearly fully formed, in that house on South Dearborn Street. That the first sounds she heard were of that thundering railroad, her German neighbors chattering, and her three little boys running and laughing and relishing languid summer afternoons in a bright, shiny new world. To many of the city's new migrants, Chicago meant a fresh start, a shot at reinvention. The past wasn't what mattered. What mattered was what came next.

After four years of living in Chicago, Phoebe could talk proudly about her own family's good fortune. On August 31, 1912, on a sweltering summer day when the mercury soared to ninety-five degrees, Phoebe gave birth to a baby girl—the couple's second daughter—in the house on Dearborn Street. Little Esther arrived just ten days after Booker T. Washington, the prominent African American educator and leader, and dozens of black businessmen from across the country converged on the city, rallying African American up-and-comers with talk of the black community's progress. By then, Phoebe could cite her own husband's success. James had found work as a Pullman porter, waiting on wealthy whites in the five-star luxury coaches of the railroad line. It was a plum position and one with considerable social prestige. Black men who worked as Pullman porters, tending to well-heeled customers who enjoyed the railroad's white linen table-cloths and crystal glasses, were considered influential members of the emerging black middle class. "Now that was a top-flight job for black men," said Johnny D. Johnson, the youngest son of James and Phoebe. "Way back, in the early days, blacks aspired to be Pullman porters and ministers."

James was both. He was a freelance minister and part of an elite group of black men who traveled the country on the railroad, becoming keen observers of the politics, race relations, music, and local affairs in big cities and tiny towns, north and south. Pullman porters shined shoes, mended clothes, and made beds, but they also familiarized themselves with their customers' habits and manners: the fine foods they ate, the soft leather of their shoes, the delicate stitching on their jackets. Porters became increasingly worldly as they read copies of the *New York Times,* the *Saturday Evening Post,* and the *New York Herald Tribune* that were left behind in the cars. While most black men at the time labored in rough clothing in dirty, unskilled jobs, the porters navigated an immaculate, glittering white world in carefully starched uniforms. When he donned his midnight-blue jacket and crisp visored cap and that train started rolling, James knew he was carrying the hopes and dreams of his wife and his rapidly expanding family. (Phoebe gave birth to another daughter, Cleo, on November 19, 1913.) "The railroad waiter and Pullman porter tried to live like our passengers," recalled Robert McGoings, a veteran porter. "We carried a suit or sports coat with us on the road; some even carried a briefcase."

The pay, on the other hand, left a lot to be desired. In 1914, porters earned about forty dollars a month, a salary that some considered stingy, given the grueling hours and minimal time allowed for sleep. (Porters often slept as little as three hours a night.) But tips could push that wage up considerably. It also helped that in the black community, porters, along with postal workers and servants employed by the city's wealthy families and fine hotels, commanded considerable respect. Porters were so prominent that for many years the *Chicago*

Defender ran a regular column, "Sparks from the Rails," about their comings and goings. James was something of an unusual candidate for the job. George Pullman, the owner of the Pullman Company, preferred to hire porters with jet-black skin so as to better underline the social divide between the wealthy white passengers and the men hired to serve them. "The blackest man with the whitest teeth," one porter recalled. But if James's light skin was viewed as a shortcoming, he met the other criteria: He was tall, which meant he could easily reach the upper berths on the sleeper cars. He had a medium build and was slim enough to navigate the narrow corridors. And he was literate. Grammar school graduation was a plus for porters hired before the 1920s. It helped, too, that he had a stable family. Pullman recruiters often made surprise home visits, interviewed neighbors, and checked police records to assess the character of job applicants. Someone from the Pullman Company may well have spoken to Phoebe about James and carefully inspected her home. "Emphasis was placed upon your family background and character—as exemplified by the applicant's attitude toward wife, mother and father, sons and daughters," said Carroll R. Harding, a president of the company, during a speech to a gathering of porters. "Those were chosen who had the background of good homes, faithful at church, and good recommendation from the minister," he said. (James was far from the only ancestor of Mrs. Obama's to use the railroad as a stepping-stone. Pullman porters—including her maternal great-grandfather and several uncles—are sprinkled across her family tree.)

The railroad life was not without its downsides. The constant, relentless travel—porters were often gone for weeks at a time—posed a considerable hardship on the families left behind. James was away for long stretches, leaving Phoebe on her own with their children. His sons and daughters would remember him as a stern and distant father, who was quick with the strap when he was at home, which wasn't often. And his family was still growing. On February 6, 1915, Phoebe gave birth to another child, a baby girl. LaVaughn Johnson opened her eyes for the first time on a cold winter day in Chicago. The temperature dipped to seventeen degrees as Phoebe tended her newborn. Phoebe, who was thirty-five by then, watched anxiously over this brown-eyed little girl. She knew the dangers of infancy too well, having already lost three children. Even as LaVaughn outgrew infancy and started chattering and playing, Phoebe kept a careful watch. La-Vaughn was often tired and sickly as a little girl; her descendants suspect that she was anemic. So Phoebe kept her indoors to protect her from the damp and the chill, and she scolded LaVaughn for overexerting herself. As it turned out, Phoebe's fourth daughter would ultimately thrive on the South Side. When Mrs. Obama—born Michelle LaVaughn Robinson—moved into the White House, she carried her grandmother's name with her.

In all respects, that pinnacle was an unimaginable distance from the world in which LaVaughn grew up, a time when African Americans still found their lives circumscribed by racism and discrimination, even as their social and economic status improved. LaVaughn and her brothers and sisters mingled with whites in school and on streetcars, but most private organizations and institutions continued to exclude blacks. State laws prohibiting racial discrimination were seldom enforced. The year before LaVaughn was born, the Hippodrome theater refused to allow three black women to take their seats on the first floor. The women, who had paid twenty cents for those seats, were directed to the less desirable balcony. Outraged, they left and reported the incident to a lawyer. The *Defender* newspaper urged others to do the same: "Afro Americans who stand for such insult are less than men." But discrimination was painfully commonplace. The big department stores on State Street refused to hire black clerks. The Chicago telephone company did not hire black telephone operators. Taxicab companies employed African Americans to repair cars, but would not hire them as drivers. Blacks were largely excluded from the civil service, factory jobs, and most unions. Industrialists in Chicago preferred to fill their factories with native-born white and European immigrant workers.

It was the way of the world, and Phoebe and James gave their sons and daughters no hint of whether they had heard epithets shouted by strangers or encountered discrimination when they tried to find work. Keeping quiet might have been Phoebe's way of shielding her children from the ugliness of the world. She might have believed that they would experience the harsher side of life for themselves soon enough. With bills to pay, children to educate and feed, there may have been little urgency to discuss what was evident to everyone. And the truth is that for all the ugliness that existed in Chicago, the city still felt like nirvana when compared to towns in the South, even when compared to small towns in southern Illinois. That held true even into the next decade. In interviews with 274 families, a city commission appointed to explore race relations in Chicago found that "almost without exception" the African Americans interviewed "declared that their economic situation had improved in Chicago." For Phoebe, there was never any question. Life in Chicago had its challenges. But there was no turning back. She firmly believed that life would only get better.

It would take the advent of World War I for doors to finally swing open for blacks in Chicago and other cities. But they swung open nonetheless. Suddenly, European immigration into the United States—a prime source of the city's labor—came to a virtual standstill and young white men found themselves drafted into the military. Desperate for industrial workers, the factories began hiring African Americans. One meatpacking plant alone increased its workforce from eight thousand to seventeen thousand during the war. The *Chicago Defender* issued the rallying cry, calling on blacks to abandon the South for well-paying jobs in Chicago and beyond where they would be treated with respect. The newspaper, which was widely circulated throughout the South, also published thrilling images of city life and help-wanted ads. "Anywhere in God's country is far better than the southland," the *Defender* trumpeted. Factories were hiring so quickly, the newspaper estimated, that there were "places for 1,500,000 working men in the cities of the North."

These events and others helped ignite the first big wave of the Great Migration. Between 1916 and 1920, the African American population surged by fifty thousand. Nearly all of the newcomers moved to the South Side. The community, which was about 11 percent black when Phoebe moved there in 1908, would be a quarter black by 1920.

The influx of thousands of newcomers left apartments and houses in short supply. Housing was so scarce that the Chicago Urban League, which canvassed real estate dealers, found 664 black applicants for houses on a single day when only fifty homes were available. "For neither love or money could you find a decent place to live," recalled Langston Hughes, the Harlem Renaissance writer who spent a summer working in Chicago when he was in high school in 1917. "South State Street was in its glory then, a teeming Negro street with crowded theaters, restaurants and cabarets," he said. "And excitement from noon to noon. Midnight was like day. The street was full of workers and gamblers, prostitutes and pimps, church folks and sinners. The tenements on either side were very congested." By the time these migrants began pouring into the city, Phoebe and her family had been living in Chicago for eight years. Compared to the newcomers who were dazzled by the towering buildings and casual mingling of blacks and whites, they were established. They were "Old Settlers," the term used to describe people who had lived in Chicago before the First World War. They were not members of the tiny professional elite, but they were literate and mixed race, important class attributes at the time for those aspiring to move up from the working class and into better neighborhoods in the increasingly overcrowded South Side. By 1918, Phoebe and her family were in the rare position to do just that. James had found a new job. Like him, many Pullman porters became weary of the grueling schedule, the weeks and months away from home, and the toll it took on wives like Phoebe, who now had her hands full with nine children. (Ruth was born on March 15, 1916, and Arthur was born on November 2, 1917.) Others hated the racial slurs and daily humiliations that porters routinely encountered from passengers who asked them to bark like dogs or to tell "nigger jokes."

James was now hauling coal for the Consumers Company, which provided coal and ice to factories and households across the city. In terms of social prestige, the position was certainly a step down from his job as a porter. But it may have paid more. The Chicago Urban League, which collected wage data from Consumers and thirty-five other companies, found that workers typically earned about $3.90 a day, or $109 a month, for a six-day week. It was backbreaking work, particularly during that winter of 1918, when a blinding snowstorm forced coal wagons to traverse the drifts to make their deliveries. James still spent a lot of time away from home, preaching at various churches in nearby cities. But by that year, he had earned enough money to move his growing family to a new, prestigious address, 5470 Kenwood Avenue in Hyde Park, a neighborhood that was still beyond the reach of most black families, with its green parks, elegant mansions, and reasonably priced cottages. The one-story wooden house that they rented had a basement and a garage and was just blocks from the mansion that the Obamas own today.

At thirty-eight years of age, Phoebe had transformed herself from a sharecropper's daughter who grew up working the fields into a city woman with the wherewithal to move her nine children from a house near the railroad tracks into what many blacks considered to be the finest neighborhood on the South Side, within easy walking distance of the grand stone towers of the University of Chicago. "That was a big jump, both psychically and socially," said Timuel Black, a historian who has lived on the South Side since he arrived as a baby in 1918 with parents who migrated from Birmingham, Alabama. "You could brag. You could say, 'I live in Hyde Park.'"

The neighborhood was a natural destination for blacks looking to move up. White families had started to leave for new apartment buildings in the northern and southern sections of the city. Many Hyde Park houses were now available for sale or rent at relatively low prices. Phoebe's home no longer stands today, but in the 1920s it sat between a three-story brick apartment building and a two-story brick house. Phoebe could have walked to the Hyde Park AME Baptist Church, which had steam heat and electric lights, only a few blocks away. The family lived on a block primarily filled with Swedish, Danish, German, and Norwegian immigrants and their children. The white parents, like the black parents, rented their homes and mostly worked in blue-collar jobs. James worked on Lake Park Avenue, a bustling retail strip that was walking distance from home. The couple's one-story modest cottage could barely contain their large brood—nine children by then. It was challenging at times, their descendants say, to keep everyone fed and clothed, though even in hard times Phoebe was known as a wonderful cook, who could improvise with very little. "She was the keeper of wonderful recipes," remembered Nomenee Robinson, Phoebe's grandson. "Rhubarb pie. I've never had it since. She made dandelion greens, dandelion soup. That I remember very well." Still, despite the hardships, Phoebe must have counted her blessings. Her children were studying in integrated classrooms. Her husband appeared to have steady work. And her new address certainly would have elevated the family's social standing in the eyes of friends, relatives, and neighbors. But the tranquillity they hoped to savor in their new home would only last for so long.

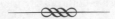

FIVE

Exploding Dreams

T HE EXPLOSIONS OFTEN CAME WITHOUT WARNING, IN THE darkness, while entire families slept peacefully, unaware of what was coming next. The bombs blew out front doors, shattered windows, wrecked stairways, and decimated entire front sections of homes, even those constructed of brick and stone. But more than anything else, they destroyed the peace of mind of black parents like Phoebe and James, who believed they had managed to find a better life. Loaded with dynamite, gravel, and bits of lead, the bombs targeted the members of Hyde Park's fledgling black community. The attackers, who hurled their lethal arsenal in the dead of night, made it clear that they intended to stop what many white residents were openly decrying as the black "invasion." Between July 1, 1917, and March 1, 1921, fifty-eight homes of black families and those of white men who sold houses to African Americans were bombed. Two blacks were killed. Phoebe and her family had moved into a neighborhood where whites were actively and unapologetically trying to oust them. In 1918, the Kenwood and Hyde Park Property Owners Association announced its determination "to make Hyde Park white." A year later, on May 5, 1919, the association held a meeting in which participants warned that the influx of black residents was "the worst calamity that had struck the city since the Great Fire." (The Great Fire of 1871 decimated three and a half square miles of the center city, destroying more than eighteen thousand buildings. At least three hundred people died, and a third of the city's residents lost their homes.) One prominent white real estate agent said, "Property owners should be notified to stand together block by block and prevent such invasion."

On June 4, 1919, at four in the morning, a bomb exploded about twelve blocks from Phoebe's home. Throughout the country, the killings were just beginning. During that summer and fall, more than two dozen racial clashes erupted across the nation, almost all of them instigated by whites, according to a federal report released that year. Racial violence gripped New York City; Knoxville, Tennessee; Philadelphia; Norfolk, Virginia; and Longview, Texas, and more than a dozen other cities in what became known as the Red Summer. Dozens of African Americans were killed and hundreds were injured as white mobs shot, stabbed, and attacked them with bricks, lead pipes, and chunks of wood. In addition to those killed in the riots, forty-three African American men were lynched between January 1 and September 14 of that year. Of those, sixteen were hung. One was cut to pieces. Others were shot. Eight were burned at the stake, including one man whose brutal murder was planned and extensively announced in local newspapers in Louisiana and Mississippi before it took place.

The violence was fueled in part by resentment at the pace and scale of the Great Migration and mounting concerns about the black soldiers who had returned from World War I. Emboldened by their experiences overseas, these soldiers had begun to demand equal rights at home, unsettling the accepted racial order. Rumors swirled in white communities that these African Americans, who had killed white men overseas and had been treated as equals by Europeans, including white women, no longer respected America's entrenched racial hierarchy. (Seven black World War I veterans were lynched in their army uniforms.) Meanwhile, white men coming home from the trenches in Belgium and France found high levels of unemployment in the industrial cities of the North. Some working-class white men turned their rage on the newcomers in their midst, the recently arrived black migrants from the South, who were believed to be stealing scarce jobs.

The riots that began that summer of 1919 even bloodied the nation's capital. Hundreds of white men went on a rampage after hearing rumors that a black man who was accused of sexually assaulting a white woman had been released by the police. The police stood by. So African Americans fought back. Nine people were killed in street battles, and some thirty more would die later from their injuries. More than one hundred and fifty people—men, women, and children—were wounded. The violence stunned the country. But the worst was yet to come. None of the riots that summer would prove to be as big or as deadly as the one in Chicago. It was touched off by a stone-throwing clash that began on a steamy hot day on July 27, when a group of black teenagers swam into the waters abutting the white side of the beach of Lake Michigan. White onlookers stoned the African Americans as they swam, which resulted in the drowning of a black seventeen-year-old. When a white policeman arrested an African American man instead of the white man accused of stoning the black teenager, the officer was mobbed by angry black onlookers and the riot was under way. Black passengers were dragged from streetcars and beaten to death. White mobs attacked and burned the houses of blacks living in mixed neighborhoods and stabbed, shot, and killed black men who ventured through hostile territory on their way to work. Crowds of white men rode trucks along Halsted Street, shouting that they were going to "get the niggers." Blacks fought back, opening fire, sometimes indiscriminately, on cars driven by whites and shot, stabbed, and killed several whites in retaliation. "That riot took all the religion out of me and all the patriotism as well because of what they did to blacks," said Robert Colin, a retired policeman and civil servant who was fourteen years old when the chaos started. "You know State Street was the main street for us back then, and they were out there pulling blacks down State Street with their cars and then shooting those blacks right out in the street!"

The violence spilled into Phoebe's neighborhood. Eight people were injured at the corner of Cottage Grove Avenue and Sixty-third Street, only blocks from her house and from James's workplace at Consumers. One black couple frantically called the police when their Hyde Park home was attacked by a white mob. When the police arrived, they decided to help the attackers, not the victims. The officers broke down the couple's front door at the request of the angry hordes and arrested the African American husband and wife. (The couple was acquitted, but their house was bombed three times afterward.) In the midst of the turmoil, and with the local police seemingly incapable of stopping the violence, the Urban League distributed thousands of circulars, urging blacks to stay off the streets. Black businessmen sent wagons rumbling through the South Side, warning people to stay home from work and not to congregate outdoors. Phoebe was thirty-nine years old then, alone in the little house in Hyde Park with nine children ranging in age from sixteen to one. Her descendants do not know whether James was out of town, preaching at a local church, or whether he actually witnessed the street battles as he ventured to work. Phoebe was unarmed and frantic as violence engulfed the city. "She talked about how terrible it was," recalled her daughter, Mary Lang, who was born after the riot. Mrs. Lang did not know whether Phoebe kept the children home from school, whether they huddled inside the house, whether they could hear or see any of the madness swirling around them. But she did know that Phoebe marshaled all her energies to find a way to protect her family from the rioters. With the violence lapping at her neighborhood, she made a decision. No one was going to break down her door without a fight. She was a devout woman, so first she must have prayed for divine intervention. Then she took matters into her own hands. She poured some water and lye into a kettle. She lit the fire in her wood-burning stove. Before long, the toxic brew was boiling. If any of those attackers were to come up her front steps, Phoebe was going to be ready. The boiling kettle of lye was her homemade weapon. She would thank God in later years that she never had to use it.

Four days after the riots began, the governor of Illinois called in thousands of troops from the state militia to restore the peace. By the end of it, on August 3, 1919, 38 people were dead, 537 injured, and about 1,000 left homeless. Of the dead, 15 were white and 23 were black. Of the injured, 178 were white and 342 were black. (The race of 17 injured people was not tallied.) For some African Americans, the riot and the bombings shattered the image of Chicago, and the industrialized north, as a haven for blacks on the rise. One black college student described his emotions after a harrowing escape from a white mob after the riots. He had fought for the country during World War I and he couldn't stop asking himself: "What had I done to deserve such treatment? The injustice of the whole thing overwhelmed me," he said. "Had the ten months I spent in France all been in vain? Were those little white crosses over the dead bodies of those dark-skinned boys lying in Flanders fields for naught? Was the risk of life in a country where such hatred existed worthwhile? Must a Negro always suffer merely because of the color of his skin? 'There's a Nigger; let's get him!' Those words rang in my ears—I shall never forget them."

Even as the rioting ended and tensions lowered, the racial hostility in Hyde Park only intensified. White property owners continued to blame their black neighbors for depressing the value of local real estate. "There is nothing in the make-up of a Negro, physically or mentally, which should induce anyone to welcome him as a neighbor," declared the *Property Owners' Journal* in February 1920. "The best of them are unsanitary . . . insurance companies class them as poor risks, ruin alone follows in their path . . . Either the Negro must vanish or decay sets in." The *Property Owners' Journal* made it clear that white property owners were not backing down. "Our neighborhood must continue white," the *Journal* said. The riots had ended, but the bombings only accelerated. The Hyde Park neighborhood witnessed as many bombings during the six-month period that ended on October 1, 1920, as it had seen during the previous three years. The bombs exploded west of Washington Park, within walking distance of Phoebe's house. Only two suspects were ever arrested. Outraged by the authorities' failure to act, prominent African Americans in the community carried their concerns to City Hall. "We have been to the mayor's office, we have been to the state attorney's office, we have sent representatives to both these offices, and nothing has been done," one member of the delegation said.

Phoebe was still living with her husband and nine children, including four-year-old LaVaughn, in the house on Kenwood Avenue that year. For James, whose family may have fled the racial violence of Mississippi in the 1880s, the experience may have given him an unsettling sense of déjà vu. Yet, like her mother before her, LaVaughn would not recount any stories from this difficult time to her children, who were astonished to learn that she had even lived in Hyde Park. LaVaughn's children suspect that Phoebe and James may have tried to shield their children from any knowledge of the bombs exploding less than a mile from their doorstep. They suspect that La-Vaughn may have done the same. Francesca Gray, LaVaughn's only daughter, said that she had always sensed that her mother was sheltering her, protecting her from a world she didn't want her daughter to know. "If you knew my mother, you would wonder: Did anything ever bother you?" Mrs. Gray said. "Did anything bad ever happen to you? I never saw my mother cry, never." They may have kept their reasons to themselves, given what we know about their tendency to shield their children, but sometime after 1920, in the wake of the racial hostility and violence, and in the face of high unemployment, Phoebe and James started to think about moving. After twelve years in the Windy City, Phoebe had decided to give up on Chicago. She was forty-one years old and venturing into middle age with a husband of nearly two decades and nine children. At least twenty years had passed since she first left her hometown of Villa Ridge as a teenager. Since then she had moved five times and buried three children. Some might have guessed that her wandering years were over. She might have thought so, too. Phoebe had always hitched her dreams to the notion that big city life would be better than the farms. But Chicago may have shaken her faith in that dream. The couple decided to move their family to the college town of Evanston, Illinois, where they had the chance at a peaceful, quieter life. It was the first time in her forty-one years that Phoebe decided to take a chance on somewhere smaller, somewhere greener, a place where her children could run barefoot and feel the grass under their feet. Maybe in a place like that she could grow some roots and finally stop moving.

Evanston, the home of Northwestern University, was only about twenty-one miles north of Hyde Park in Chicago, but it could not have been more different from the racially charged city Phoebe and her family had left behind. Evanston had a placid, small-town feel with dirt roads and wide open spaces. Phoebe's home—a wooden, one-story house with a shingle roof at 2455 Prairie Avenue—sat on a peaceful street where the fields and gardens outnumbered the buildings. For Phoebe's young children, it was a place of endless delights.

They jumped in mud puddles when it rained and delighted in the worms that squiggled in the muck. They loved the wide open spaces where they could run and run and run until their legs ached. It was as unlike Chicago as one could imagine. Still America's second-largest city in 1920, Chicago burgeoned with 2.7 million people. Evanston had 37,234 African Americans accounted for less than 7 percent of the population. It was the kind of town that Phoebe would have sailed right through, without looking twice, in the days of her youth. But her sons and daughters remember the city as something akin to paradise. "Oh, yes, I remember going to school barefoot and jumping over what I thought were worms when it was raining," said Johnny D. Johnson, Phoebe's youngest son, who was born on August 13, 1921, in the little wooden house on Prairie Avenue. He grinned at the memory of it. "They were still paving the streets in those days," he remembered. "And when an airplane would fly across, everyone would run out [of] the house and look up."

Phoebe, James, and their large brood weren't the only refugees from the South Side. Hundreds of other African Americans joined the trek to Evanston after World War I, fleeing the racial violence in Chicago and searching for steady jobs in a more tranquil setting. For years, the *Chicago Defender* had featured regular articles about Evanston, sometimes headlining entire pages of news from there. The town, which counted Methodist abolitionists among its early settlers, had a reputation for racial tolerance. After World War I, thousands of white families had moved in, and many started hiring servants and janitors. The local factory expanded its workforce, and blacks seized the growing opportunities. Between 1920 and 1930, the number of blacks living in Evanston nearly doubled to 4,938. James found work repairing shoes. Phoebe's occupation was described as "H.W.," in one record that dates to 1921. The acronym may have referred to "housewife" or "house work." Phoebe may well have done some domestic work for white families, which was a common occupation in Evanston for black married women. They could work part-time and typically earned around $15 a week. It was the kind of work she had started as a teenager, back in Villa Ridge, when she was still dreaming of leaving home. But Phoebe was forty-two now, at an age when many women were becoming keenly aware of their own mortality.

She was older, stockier, and at a point in life when many people began reflecting on their own mortality, pondering where they had been and where they were going. After her sixth move, Phoebe found herself at something of a crossroads. In Evanston, she would give birth to the last of her children, Johnny in 1921 and Mary in 1924. (She welcomed fourteen children into the world in a span of twenty years and buried three of them.) Around the same time, she would also watch as one of her older sons soared into America's professional class. Even as she continued to endure the ever-present racial discrimination that circumscribed her own promise and that of other African Americans around her, she could see in the lives of her children that it was possible to vault over those hurdles. Under Phoebe's watchful eye, the couple's second son, Howard, flourished in Chicago's integrated schools. After graduating, he headed east to enroll in college—an achievement that most Americans, black or white, could only dream about. He was a serious student, a dapper dresser, and an all-American basketball player. He graduated from Clark College in Atlanta, while his family was living back in Evanston. He went on to earn a master's degree from Atlanta University and to become the president of the Arkansas Baptist College, a small black college in Little Rock, as well as the owner of a small hotel. His siblings nicknamed him "the Dean." Howard's accomplishments were simply staggering at the time. In the 1920s, an estimated one in one thousand African Americans held bachelor's degrees. Far fewer still received advanced graduate degrees. He was the grandson of illiterate African slaves and the living, breathing proof of what a black man could achieve. In Phoebe's mind, his success must have validated her wanderings, her determination to leave her tiny, segregated hometown.

Howard's accomplishments, however, did not blind Phoebe to the inescapable realities that her generation, and that of her children, still faced, even in Evanston. The town was segregated. The local hospital often barred blacks as did the theaters and the white community's YMCA. Even the integrated movie house consigned blacks to the balcony. City officials strictly enforced "black codes" to limit the number of African Americans in the community and to confine them to black neighborhoods in the least desirable parts of town. "The hotels and the big places down at town weren't open to us except for the theaters," recalled Pauline Elizabeth Lewis Williams, who was fifteen when she moved to Evanston in the 1920s. "So we'd go to the theater from time to time. But most of the activity, most of the social activity, was in the homes."

Still, LaVaughn, who was about six years old when the family landed in Evanston, remembered those years as happy ones. She loved her school and was active in sports, including volleyball and softball, an indication that she most likely had outgrown the delicate health of her infancy, or at the very least didn't let it hold her back. With so many children to raise, Phoebe didn't have much time to spare, and LaVaughn treasured the moments spent with her mother, quietly absorbing Phoebe's lessons about how to make a house look and feel like a home. Phoebe's descendants believe that the placid life in Evanston must have felt like a balm after the racial hostility in Hyde Park. The color line may have sharply divided Evanston, but there was little racial strife. "It was a really good community, a peaceful community," said Francesca Gray, LaVaughn's daughter, who grew up hearing her mother's stories. "I think she loved it there."

The family moved several times during their time in Evanston. By 1925, they were living in a modest house at 2152 W. Railroad Avenue that James had built himself. James was something of a Renaissance man of his times: a preacher, a porter, a cobbler, a carpenter, a mason, and a craftsman who could build or fix just about anything. "He was very gifted with his hands," Johnny Johnson said of his father. The house sat next to New Hope CME Church, where Phoebe and her children might have worshipped and James might have preached. As the black community grew, so did the social outlets for African Americans. Evanston would never rival the thriving black social scene on Chicago's South Side, but it increasingly felt like home to Phoebe and her family.

There was the Emerson Street Y, which was created for the black community and served as a meeting place, offering dances, lectures, and theatrical performances. There was Foster Field, where children and teenagers played tennis and cheered on baseball games. American Steel and Tube Company was the largest single employer of blacks before 1930. By now, blacks also owned small businesses, from restaurants to a laundry to a taxi and trucking business. And in 1927, Phoebe could proudly point out that her husband had joined that list of black entrepreneurs, opening Johnson & Son, a shoe repair shop, right inside their house. James's dream of becoming a businessman had finally come true. Johnny Johnson, who grew up in the house that his father built, remembered him running the shoe repair business in the front. James partitioned the first floor with dividers made of corrugated materials, which served as movable walls. The family lived in the back. "We used to take a bath in those big huge tubs—they had big tubs back then—and we had an outdoor toilet in the back," recalled Mr. Johnson, who was six years old in 1927.

Phoebe cooked on a wood-burning stove. "When we ate, we would all sit at a long table with a long bench on each side," he said. "I think we might have had an upstairs, too, but I can't remember." Managing a big family, and one with so many rambunctious boys, filled nearly all of Phoebe's waking hours. She was so busy sewing, cleaning, and cooking that she rarely had time to herself. She kept her children busy with chores, too, when they weren't in school, boys and girls alike. Mr. Johnson said he still remembers scrubbing the outhouse and the hard wooden floors inside the house. "She was a meticulous housekeeper; she was meticulously clean; that was in her," he said of his mother. "She used to boil clothes to wash them in a big copper vat. You put lye in those things. She used to make me scrub the floor. I had to get down on my knees and scrub that outdoor toilet."

Meanwhile, James, who was trying to run the business in the front of his house while his wife kept order among the children in the back, made it clear that he wouldn't tolerate any nonsense. There was no smoking in James's house, no talking back, no questioning of his authority. He was a good man, but he could also be harsh. His children, who said he ruled with "an iron fist," sometimes shrank from his presence. "He was a serious disciplinarian," said Nomenee Robinson, LaVaughn's son. "Monday mornings was the day that the boys got whippings. I don't know if it was every Monday. But my mother talked about the Monday morning come-uppance." Mr. Johnson, James's youngest son, put it this way: "Even the dog got the message. When Jim Johnson came in the house, everybody was quiet. When he left, you took a sigh of relief."

There were warm times, too, filled with affection. Mr. Johnson still remembers sitting on his mother's knee while she sang to him. When he closes his eyes, he can still hear her voice rising and falling as she held him close. He can also remember her delight in the exploits of Jesse James, who was born in Missouri, just like her mother. Even as she got older, Phoebe still loved the stories about this man who challenged authority. "They looked at him like a hero," Mr. Johnson said. "She would sing songs about him." LaVaughn told her children that she was so happy in Evanston that she hoped her family would stay forever. She had been accepted to a new school—the Haven School, a business school—and she was giddy with excitement. Everyone was proud of her. "She didn't want to leave," said Mrs. Gray, LaVaughn's daughter.

Yet with the decade approaching its last years, sometime between 1927 and 1929, Phoebe and James started thinking about moving again. Mr. Johnson, who was a little boy then, doesn't remember why his parents wanted to leave. Phoebe, who had spent at least seven years in Evanston by then, was almost fifty. She had watched one son go off to college and several others join the workforce as barbers and cobblers alongside their father. Her brood of small children was shrinking. It is impossible to know whether she looked on the possibility of moving yet again with relish or weariness. But by 1929, the wooden house at 2152 W. Railroad Avenue, which James had built with his own hands, no longer carried the name of Johnson & Son. It was vacant. Phoebe and her family were gone.

SIX

A Child of the Jazz Age

FATS WALLER WAS POUNDING ON THE IVORIES AT THE METropolitan Theater on South Grand Boulevard. Cab Calloway and his older sister, Blanche, were swinging at the Grand Theater on South State Street. And that young Louis Armstrong, still fresh from New Orleans, was blowing his horn at Lincoln Gardens on East Thirty-first Street. "We cracked down on the first note and that band sounded so good to me after the first note that I just fell right in like old times," Mr. Armstrong recalled of one of his first gigs in Chicago with King Oliver's Creole Jazz Band. "The first number went down so well we had to take an encore." It was the 1920s and jazz, the hot, new American sound, was sizzling in sweaty speakeasies and packed dance halls across the South Side.

Purnell Shields, just eleven and already bruised by life's hard edges, landed on the streets of the South Side sometime around 1921 as the Jazz Age was starting to swing, just as Phoebe and her family were giving up on Chicago. He soaked up that intoxicating new music like it was a healing elixir, a soothing balm for a battered soul. He was still trying to find himself then, still feeling his way into adolescence, and he was navigating that unsettling journey in a new world, during rapidly changing times. The spasm of racial violence that had seared the city in 1919 seemed like old history as Purnell walked the crowded, unfamiliar sidewalks, absorbing the energy and the pulse of his newly adopted city. Between 1920 and 1930, the black population swelled by sixty-four thousand as African Americans migrants poured into the city. New skyscrapers soared. Factories boomed. Flush patrons, tipsy with drink, spilled out of brand-new theaters and restaurants. Purnell knew one thing as he soaked it all in: he was far, far from home.

Purnell, the First Lady's maternal grandfather, was born on December 19, 1910, in Birmingham, Alabama, where he was nurtured by a family that strived for success. His grandfather was a well-known businessman and property owner. His father, Robert Lee Shields, had a respectable job on the railroad, working as a Pullman porter, just like Phoebe's husband, James. And his mother, Annie, worked as a seamstress at home, helping to support the family, as she tended to Purnell and his older sister. Purnell didn't have a silver spoon in his mouth—his parents still couldn't afford to buy their own home—but everyone could see the path to better things. Purnell could have spent the rest of his life in Birmingham, followed his friends to high school, found a railroad job just like his dad's, and bought his very own house. But just like that, the fates intervened and things fell apart.

In those days, epidemics raged, diseases spread, and lives shifted course, exposing the fragility of even the most tightly knit families. Before Purnell turned ten, his father, who was still in his early thirties, died suddenly and his entire world unraveled. Purnell's mother, Annie, was forced to take on the role of the family's primary breadwinner. She struggled on her own. By 1920, she had become a boarder, sharing a house with her two children and nine other people. Sometime afterward, she decided to move her family out of Birmingham. She remarried and they all moved to Chicago, leaving behind a deeply segregated city in a deeply segregated state where blacks routinely found their political and job prospects circumscribed by the constant threat, and the regular practice, of racial violence. "There is nothing here for the colored man but a hard time (which) these southern crackers gives us," a stone mason in Mobile, Alabama, wrote in a letter, pleading for help finding a job somewhere, anywhere, in the North. They were the kind of words Purnell might have used himself, if someone had asked.

Around the time that he moved north, members of the Ku Klux Klan had begun donning their white robes and marching through the streets of several black neighborhoods in Birmingham. Tens of thousands of white citizens attended Klan rallies over the next few years as the group rallied its supporters with drum-and-bugle-led parades, fireworks, and barbecues. Klan members included some of the most powerful politicians in the state, including Hugo Black, the U.S. senator who would become a Supreme Court justice, and the governor. Their hooded compatriots soon began a campaign of flogging African Americans and others who dared to socialize across racial lines and committed what the Klan deemed to be public crimes. Many blacks felt helpless in the face of such intimidation. They certainly couldn't turn to the police. Birmingham's sheriff and commissioner for public safety were prominent members of the Klan. In 1926, when white police officers shot and killed a young black man, black insurance officials despaired of any proper investigation. "We know that these 'cracker officers' are likely to shoot any of us down for no cause in the world," one said. It is no surprise, then, given the experiences of his early years, that Purnell would view whites with great suspicion and anger for much of his life.

When Purnell finally ventured north, much of what he knew best in the world stayed behind in Birmingham: the school where he learned to read and write, his friends, his grandfather, and his uncle. But he also left behind the unanswered questions that would dog his family for generations: the unsolved mysteries of their origins. His grandfather, Dolphus Shields, the family patriarch, was so fair skinned that he looked nearly white. The blood in his veins carried a hidden inheritance that the old man rarely spoke of. Purnell may have learned to live comfortably with the blanks in his background. It was easy to do that in Chicago, where African Americans were clearly on the rise. Five black lawmakers from the city occupied seats in the state legislature. African Americans had $40 million on deposit in local banks.

Jesse Binga, a migrant who had become the city's preeminent black banker, boasted of "a new generation of (black) business and professional men, coming to the fore."

By 1928, Chicago voters had elected Oscar De Priest to Congress, sending the very first African American congressman from a northern city to Washington. Every day, Purnell and the other newcomers could watch black policemen, firemen, and city councilmen working and walking the bustling sidewalks, scenes utterly unthinkable in the Deep South. Purnell even ended up moving into an integrated neighborhood on the South Side, which must have been a foreign and eye-opening experience. His mother, Annie, who was living with her second husband, a tailor, likely smoothed Purnell's path, helping to ease the transition from the South to the North, caring for him and guiding him until he could support himself. Purnell found work as a carpenter—a trade that was passed down from father to son in his family—and factory work, too. By the time he was nineteen, he had earned enough at a syrup factory to move out on his own into a house where he lived as a boarder.

Purnell's true passion was the percussive and syncopated rhythms that had become the soundtrack of the burgeoning South Side. He was handy with the drums himself and for a jazz lover, there was no better place to be in the 1920s than Chicago, the epicenter of the nation's blues and jazz recording industry. Aficionados of "race music," as the sound was commonly called, could stumble across Count Basie, Ethel Waters, and Bessie Smith, among others. To newcomers like Purnell, those South Side jazz musicians epitomized style and sophistication, posing in tuxedos and bowler hats, butterfly bow ties, and patent leather shoes. Jazz so permeated the atmosphere of every South Side club, cabaret, and gambling den that one jazz personality claimed that a trumpet held aloft at night would actually play itself. In 1927, the Savoy Ballroom opened on the South Side. With more than a half acre of dancing space, it was the first large, commercial dance hall to cater to the city's African Americans. The ballroom could accommodate four thousand patrons, six thousand hats and coats, and, in later years, one thousand cars in its parking lot. "Never before have Chicagoans seen anything quite as lavish," the *Chicago Defender* raved when the ballroom opened. "Famous artists have transformed the building into a veritable paradise, each section more beautiful than the other." The place became a must-stop for stars like Duke Ellington, Cab Calloway, and Benny Moten.

Purnell worked a day job to make ends meet, but it was this music that inspired him. He was "by profession a carpenter and handy-man but by calling a chef, drummer and jazz aficionado, an impresario and all around magnet who made everyone in the family gravitate to his side," recalled Craig Robinson, Michelle Obama's brother. Years later, the First Lady would remember Purnell as the outgoing grandfather who blasted Miles Davis, Charlie Parker, and Ella Fitzgerald on his record player and kept speakers in every room of the house, including the bathroom. "He would play jazz 24 hours a day," Mrs. Obama said. In his household, she said, you learned to eat, drink, and sleep jazz. He listened to his music so often and at such volume that "I think he lost some hearing in one ear as a result," the First Lady's brother said. Maybe it was the healing powers of the music or the uplifting feeling that came from living in a city where black men could vote, make good money, and revel in a newfound sense of self-respect. Whatever it was, in Chicago, Purnell put aside the pain of his childhood and became confident, charismatic, and gregarious, the kind of man who always had people around him, drawn, as they were, to his keen insights, his joie de vivre, and his considerable talents on the barbecue grill. He was also an eligible bachelor. Somewhere along the way, he would stumble across a young woman from North Carolina with a tragic story of her own. Their lives would intertwine toward the end of the Roaring Twenties' economic boom. In the black press, some would hail the period between 1924 and 1929 in Chicago as "the Fat Years." Purnell didn't know it. No one knew it. But that gilded age was coming to a close.

SEVEN

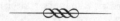

A Man of Promise

EVEN IN THE SMALLEST OF PLACES, THERE ARE PEOPLE WHO seem destined for greatness. Their feet seem poised to carry them on grand adventures; their minds seem drawn to greater intellectual pursuits. In the 1920s, in the tiny town of Georgetown, South Carolina, most white citizens would have scoffed at the notion that a black person of this caliber could be living and walking among them. After all, how many African Americans had college degrees? How many had run big businesses or plantations or had become powerful political leaders? Black men could climb only so far in society. African Americans, who worked in the sawmills or sharecropped on the farms, would have nodded knowingly. Whites had systematically blocked all the traditional avenues to success, but that did not mean there wasn't a man who could carry the hopes of his family and community, even if he had to leave home to do so. Georgetown had such a man. He had sawdust on his hands, but something akin to angel dust glittered whenever he spoke. Once they met him, people rarely forgot him. There was just something about Fraser Robinson Jr.

His parents welcomed him into the world on a summer day in 1912, the year that Theodore Roosevelt announced he was running for president again. Fraser was their first child, born on August 24.

He was named after his father, who would become a well-known entrepreneur and property owner in town and would harbor high expectations for his oldest boy. Fraser, the grandson of slaves, did not disappoint. He recited poetry, joined the debating team at school, and sang his Sunday praises to Jesus with a fine, reverberating tenor. He learned to love the spare newspapers that his father brought home, developing a passion for those broadsheets with inky type that would stay with him for the rest of his life. But he also excelled in mathematics and prided himself on understanding how machines worked. He could fix anything electrical: an iron that shorted out; a radio that had lost its signal; the tangled wiring inside the plaster walls of a house. And he quickly attracted the attention of his elders in school and church, who viewed him as a gifted thinker and a potential leader.

In Georgetown, there were few outlets for promising young black men like Fraser, who would become the First Lady's paternal grandfather. It was a town run by white men who expected blacks to respect the entrenched racial hierarchy, to serve as the unskilled, poorly paid workforce that kept the timber mills humming and the old rice plantations thriving, nothing more. But Fraser's church, Bethel AME, which was established by former slaves, did its best to challenge and nurture its youth. The Boy Scouts refused to accept African Americans at that time so the national AME church created its own troop, the Allen Life Guard, to focus on the physical, intellectual, and spiritual development of black boys. By 1927, when Fraser was about fifteen, the group had three thousand members across the country. He embraced its philosophy and its program, donning the military-style uniforms, complete with rimmed caps, button-down jackets, and high boots. He participated in study groups with the other young men in the troop who discussed the racial climate and their place in the world. It provided the kind of intellectual stimulation that made a young black man believe that almost anything was possible. An old, undated black-and-white photo shows Fraser and his counterparts in the troop standing side by side in front of the church steps. They are smartly dressed, serious young men with sober expressions on their faces and the dreams and weighty expectations of their families on their shoulders. From an early age, Fraser Jr. knew he was going somewhere. He knew he was destined for better things.

But there were also powerful undercurrents in his life, hints of pain and hardship that were often obscured from view as he grew from boyhood to adolescence. His father, Fraser Sr., was a powerful role model and an inspiration, but his descendants believe that Fraser Sr. was also a hard man who drove his son to succeed while offering little in the way of warmth and affection. He may have also passed on a reluctance to delve too deeply into the past and an unwillingness to talk too openly about family, history, and difficult times. Fraser Jr.'s family had deep connections to slavery and the old ways that Africans had brought to these shores. He and his relatives spoke Gullah, the Creole mix of African and English languages that emerged on the seacoast of South Carolina during slavery, and he lived in close proximity to the old rice plantations where his grandparents and great-grandparents were slaves. Yet Fraser Jr. would tell his children virtually nothing about their family history or about his own, nothing about his grandparents or their roots in slavery. And he would carry with him an ingrained wariness, a deep suspicion toward whites that hinted at some raw, unspoken family pain. But all that internal turbulence lurked far below the surface, hidden beneath the smooth, confident demeanor that Fraser Jr. projected to nearly everyone who knew him.

By the time he entered Howard High School in Georgetown, the only secondary school for blacks in the county, Fraser Jr. was known as a first-class student, an active debater whose way with words impressed those who heard him. He could have stayed in his hometown, where he and his family were respected in the black community. But he had fewer and fewer prospects. In 1930, Fraser was attending school and working in a sawmill factory. He graduated from Howard High School with a diploma, which in many cities was a ticket to the black middle class. But in Georgetown County, population 21,738, it seemed more like a ticket to nowhere. Good jobs were getting harder to find, and whites had rolled back most of the rights that blacks had gained after the Civil War. When a friend of his family moved to Chicago, Fraser announced that he was going to follow him. It was as simple as that. He was seventeen years old and aspired to more than a job at the sawmill or on the farm. He wanted to live in a city that would let him soar, a place without the imposed boundaries of his small, rice-growing hometown. His children say he dreamed of going to college and becoming an electrical engineer. "He wanted a different kind of life," said Francesca Gray, his daughter. "He had high hopes."

Fraser arrived in Chicago in 1931 and moved in with his family friends. Before long, he was attending services at the Full Gospel Mission, a lively black church on the South Side and one of the few ministries that was run by a woman. The story goes that the minister, Mother Ella Allensworth, found her calling one day when she looked into the sky and saw the words *Full Gospel Mission*. She had been leading a small congregation, an offshoot of the Quinn Chapel AME Church, a prominent black church in Chicago. But when Mother Allensworth saw those words in the sky, she knew she had to open her own house of worship for the city's lost and weary souls. She opened it up in a storefront, the kind of church that many of the city's black aristocrats viewed as low class, one that was frequented mostly by unsophisticated, newly arrived migrants from the South.

Fraser's friends had been attending Mother Allensworth's services. He had grown up in a churchgoing family and it might have just felt right to kneel before the altar on Sunday mornings. Maybe he was intrigued by the female pastor. His children said there was another possibility as well. "People used to joke that he came up here and went to church looking for a wife," his son, Nomenee Robinson, said.

EIGHT

Stumbling Backward

WHEN PHOEBE AND JAMES JOHNSON LEFT EVANSTON, Illinois, they had been married for about twenty-eight years. They had eleven living children and traveled across two states and four cities. They had mourned the deaths of their babies who did not survive infancy. They held on tight despite James's long absences on the railroad and his frequent travels on the itinerant preaching circuit. But in the end, that was not enough.

After leaving Evanston, they moved their family twice between 1927 and 1930. First, they stopped in Batavia, a town some forty-two miles west of downtown Chicago where James preached and opened a shoe repair shop. But the family was soon on the move again, edging back ever closer to Chicago, this time settling in Maywood, only about twelve miles from the big city, where James opened another shoe store. The couple's youngest son, Johnny D. Johnson, who was about eight years old at the time, said he couldn't remember why his parents moved from one tiny town to the other, dancing around the peripheries of the big city. But the news from Chicago was grim. "Something is happening in Chicago and it should no longer go unnoticed," warned the *Chicago Defender* in 1929. "During the past three weeks hardly a day has ended that there has not been a report of another firm discharging its employees, many of whom have been faithful workers at these places for years."

By April 9, 1930, Phoebe was learning the hard way about hard times. She was back in Chicago, back on the South Side. But this time, she was on her own. The Depression was already beginning to upend the lives of thousands of people. In Phoebe's house, the economic hardships were compounded by the enormous upheaval in her personal life. James, her husband and partner for nearly three decades, was gone.

How does a marriage come undone? Sometimes it starts with a slow unraveling, with the fraying of the countless tiny threads that bind two people together. Or with wounds, as tiny as pinpricks, that fester instead of healing. There are biting words hurled like daggers and unbearable silences that gnaw at the heart. Somehow, over time, the small intimacies that once enmeshed husband and wife—touch, laughter, conversation—seem to vanish. And the distance between lovers, whether across a kitchen table or a marital bed, grows so achingly wide that it seems impossible to bridge. Precisely what happened between James and Phoebe is hard to decipher, partly because the historical records for Phoebe and her family that year are somewhat contradictory, and partly because Phoebe, who was proud and private, appears to have clung to her old habit of keeping quiet about her troubles.

Their two youngest children, Mr. Johnson and Mary Lang, said they had no memory of a formal separation. But Mr. Johnson said that his father was away so often, for such long stretches of time, that he could easily have moved out without anyone taking much notice. He was working long hours at the shoe store, James often told his children to explain his absences. Or he was ministering to an out-of-town church for a month or two. Precisely how he spent his time, his children didn't know. "He was not much of a family man," Mr. Johnson said diplomatically. A census taker in 1930 found James living on his own in a home that he rented for $45 a month on East Fifty-fourth Street, just around the corner from Phoebe's place. He was close enough to stop by to see his children and for his children to stop by to see him. He had opened another shoe repair shop, his first in Chicago. His transition back to the Windy City seems to have gone relatively smoothly. Phoebe, on the other hand, was struggling. She had moved with seven of her children, ranging in age from five to twenty-seven, into a house at 2321 South Calumet Avenue. After years of careful climbing, she seemed to be stumbling backward. Timuel Black, the Chicago historian who grew up on the South Side, said that a move to Phoebe's new neighborhood might have been considered a step up if the family was buying its first home instead of renting. But even then, to many working-class blacks with middle-class aspirations, this move would still have seemed like a step in the wrong direction. "For my snobbish mama, it would have been a step back," Mr. Black said. "It would have been considered by many folks a step backward."

Phoebe was fifty years old. She had moved nine times in those years, each time hoping to inch a bit forward, to carry her own dreams and those of her family a bit further along. This time, however, the painful truth was impossible to ignore. Her husband was gone and so was her steady rise toward the middle class. Phoebe still had young children to feed and educate and $48 a month in rent to pay. She had managed to get one son, Howard, into college. She couldn't give up on the rest. Good jobs, though, were increasingly hard to find as Chicago's boom years gave way to the Depression. Jesse Binga, the black banker who proudly boasted in the 1920s of a new black, professional generation, saw his bank shuttered while angry crowds filled the streets, demanding their savings. Unable to pay their rent, hundreds of blacks were evicted from their homes. The police opened fire on a crowd of several thousand people who had gathered to protest the mounting evictions. Three black men were killed, and scores wounded, and they quickly became a symbol of Chicago's destitute masses.

Phoebe must have taken a deep breath before she took the plunge, before she got on a streetcar one day and started asking for work. Soon Phoebe was cleaning houses again. This time, she was scrubbing floors in Hyde Park, her old neighborhood where she now could no longer afford to live, the most heartbreaking sign of her sinking fortunes. Her older children contributed, too, when they could. Her two oldest daughters worked as maids for private families. Her oldest son worked with his father, repairing shoes.

LaVaughn worked alongside her mother, caring for children and washing clothes for white families in Hyde Park when she wasn't in the classroom. She was in high school then, one of a small group of black students attending Englewood High School, where ambitious young black women dreamed of finding office work, not domestic work. But LaVaughn took great pride in her job and she grew so fond of one of the children she cared for, a little girl named Caritas, that she vowed to name her daughter after her someday. (It was a pledge that her husband would categorically reject decades later.) "My mother would brag about how she was such a great laundress," Francesca Gray said of her mother, LaVaughn, who scrubbed clothes on a washboard even after she owned a washing machine. "If we wore something white, you had to wear sunglasses."

It was around that time that Phoebe began traveling back to southern Illinois, visiting the countryside where she grew up. As a girl, she had been eager to flee those rural communities. In her fifties, she found comfort there in the company of relatives who lived much simpler lives, growing vegetables and raising chickens and horses. Her visits were brief—usually several weeks during the summer months— but they offered an escape from the relentless pressures of city life. Phoebe's domestic work, and the wages brought in by her older children, was not enough to keep the family afloat during the Depression. So like thousands of families across the country, Phoebe turned to government charity to survive. "They would go around to neighborhoods and they would bring the food; they would bring food to you," said Mr. Johnson, Phoebe's youngest son, who recalled that the trucks would sometimes leave the goods on the doorstep. "Canned beef, dried prunes, dried peas and apricots. It was very nutritious food." Mr. Johnson vividly remembered those hard times and talked about them with his own family years later. But LaVaughn kept quiet about the difficulties and adversities that she and her family encountered. She had inherited her mother's penchant for keeping quiet. "She never talked about the hardships," said Mrs. Gray, who was stunned to learn that her mother had actually lived in the very neighborhood where she later cleaned houses. LaVaughn may not have remembered the years in her family's most prestigious address in Hyde Park. She was only a little girl when she lived there, somewhere between the ages of three and six. Or perhaps the family's downward slide was just too hard to talk about. Some things, LaVaughn might have reasoned, are better left unsaid.

During those days in the 1930s, Phoebe's sons and daughters viewed their mother as a quiet, simple woman who never complained. She never talked about racism or discrimination, even though her children were old enough to see it for themselves. She never challenged whites and never encouraged her children to do so either. To the best of their recollections, she never voted, either. "She knew her place," Mr. Johnson said. He had no idea that for much of her life, Phoebe, in her own way, had quietly (and sometimes not so quietly) pushed and prodded at the boundaries that defined a black woman's place. And that didn't change, even as Phoebe approached her sixties with her black hair going gray and her shoulders burdened by the heavy weight of poverty. Phoebe was a woman of faith, who had long ago dedicated her life to God. She couldn't move again; she was older now and had too many children depending on her. But when she finally settled on a church and a minister, Phoebe knew exactly who could best understand her life and guide her on her spiritual journey. She picked the Full Gospel Mission, the church that was run by a woman, Mother Ella Allensworth. Phoebe found solace there. It was the kind of place where the Holy Spirit lifted its congregants out of their seats and filled their mouths with the indecipherable cries of the divine. It offered assistance to the poor. (One of the church's assistant ministers worked at a slaughterhouse and brought back meat to distribute to hungry families.) And it was led by a strong, black woman, a rarity at the time, who dismissed those who insisted that churches needed men to lead them. "They learned to relieve their burdens with spiritual songs," Mr. Johnson said of his mother and the other women at Full Gospel. Phoebe went to Bible study during the week and church services on Sunday. She sang her heart out in the choir. She brought her daughters to church, too, so often that her youngest, Mary, complained: "'When I get grown,' I used to say, 'I'm never going to church.'"

Something about that church also struck a deep chord within La-Vaughn. At fifteen, she was baptized there. She embraced religious life and God with so much fervor that her sisters feared she would never, ever find a suitor. She was a serious young woman who sang in the choir and stuck determinedly to the church rules: no lipstick, no earrings, no sleeveless shirts or dresses, no dancing, and, most certainly, no unsupervised dating. She didn't attend her prom or her homecoming dance. "I think she used to get teased by her sisters, 'Little Miss Holy,' you know?" Francesca Gray said of her mother. "She was not with it back in the '20s and '30s. Her sisters were beautiful. They were just something. She was not one for adorning herself. Everybody figured she'd be the last one to get married."

NINE

Love in Hard Times

ROMANCE BLOOMED IN COUNTLESS CORNERS OF THE BIG city, even during hard times. Sweet smiles and giggles intermingled with the hallelujahs on Sunday church mornings and penciled pledges of love slipped from one hand to another in high school. There were playful whispers during backyard barbecues and first kisses stolen on front stoops. There were connections and intersections among the city's black newcomers, some fleeting and some seemingly destined to be. By 1931, all four of Mrs. Obama's grandparents had finally made their way to Chicago. Rebecca Jumper Coleman, the little orphaned girl from North Carolina who settled with her aunt and uncle, had arrived sometime between 1918 and 1920. Purnell Shields blew into town next from Birmingham, Alabama, in 1921. LaVaughn Johnson, Phoebe and James's daughter, who was born in Chicago, returned to the South Side from her family's travels to Evanston and beyond sometime around 1930. Then came Fraser Robinson Jr., from South Carolina, who took his place on the scene a year later. Tragedy pushed some out of the South; ambition and happenstance drove others.

Rebecca and Purnell, Mrs. Obama's maternal grandparents, stumbled across each other first. Purnell was a gregarious charmer and a passionate jazz enthusiast. Rebecca was much quieter, and Purnell might have divined a hint of sadness in her eyes. They were both young southerners trying to find their way in the big city and trying to cope with the personal heartbreak they had each experienced back home.

Rebecca had been living with her aunt and uncle, John and Carrie Coleman, in an apartment building in a predominantly white neighborhood on the South Side. Her aunt was a seamstress; her uncle found work in a meatpacking plant, then in the building trades as a plasterer. For most African Americans, migrating north meant moving forward, seizing opportunities, reclaiming dignity, delighting in new freedoms. But from the moment Rebecca set foot in Chicago, around the age of ten, she was confronted with the enormity of her losses. Both of her parents had died, leaving her orphaned, and she had no choice but to leave home in North Carolina to join her aunt and uncle up north. Purnell knew something about that kind of loss, too. His father had died before his tenth birthday. With each other, it seems, Rebecca and Purnell found not only companionship, but some sense of comfort.

He was nineteen and she was about twenty when they got married, around 1930. They couldn't afford a place of their own so they lived as boarders in a two-story brick apartment building, sharing an apartment with a steel mill worker from Mississippi, his wife, and his unemployed nephew. (Purnell's mother, Annie, and his stepfather, Frank Coleman, lived only a few blocks away.) The newlyweds lived in the Woodlawn neighborhood, just south of Hyde Park, which by now was somewhat run-down, only a shadow of its glory days. Rebecca and her new husband were among Woodlawn's earliest black residents, just like Phoebe and James were in their South Side neighborhood. In the early 1900s, Woodlawn's commercial strip on Sixty-third Street was heralded as the "foremost business street outside the loop," the city's historic commercial center downtown. By the 1930s, however, Woodlawn's Victorian elegance had faded. Only 13 percent of the population owned their homes; the rest were renters who shopped, danced, bowled, and watched movies in the small businesses that dotted Sixty-third Street. The neighborhood was populated largely by German and Irish immigrants and their children. African Americans accounted for about 13 percent of the population, but their numbers were growing. Purnell was working in a syrup factory, and before long Rebecca was busy tending to a growing brood of children.

Fraser, the First Lady's paternal grandfather, first noticed his bride-to-be during the cacophonous calls to Jesus at Full Gospel Mission, Phoebe's evangelical church. He and his cousins had found a welcoming community of faith there and Fraser was soon taken with Phoebe's pretty, stylish daughters. They were all Chicago born, with a big-city sophistication that might have seemed irresistible to a small-town southern boy. Singing in the choir was LaVaughn, still in high school and still intently focused on her spiritual life, not her social life. Her sisters liked to joke that she would never find a man, but La-Vaughn was smart and athletic and clearly going places. In those days, a young black woman with a high school diploma might dream of turning her back on domestic work and finding a job as a secretary or a receptionist. After considering his options, Fraser decided he would set his sights on LaVaughn.

Wooing her, though, turned out to be no easy task. Outside of school, LaVaughn was completely immersed in her church and had thoroughly embraced its tenets of modesty, humility, and keeping one's distance from amorous young men. But something about the striking young man from South Carolina appealed to her. Maybe it was Fraser's ambition or his manner, his smooth brown skin and razor-thin mustache, or his eloquent way with words. Whatever the reason, LaVaughn decided to throw caution to the wind: she decided to date Fraser, and to date him without a chaperone. Decades later, LaVaughn would laugh out loud as she described the day that Fraser borrowed a car to take her out. The couple was cruising across the South Side when Fraser unexpectedly drove past their church. In a panic, LaVaughn threw herself to the floor of the car to avoid the disapproving eyes of her fellow church members. As a little girl, her daughter, Francesca, loved that story. The image of her staid, unflappable mother flinging herself to the floor was simply irresistible. "You really did that, Mommy?" she asked over and over again.

It wasn't long before LaVaughn formally presented Fraser as her boyfriend to her church community. Everything seemed to be coming together. In February 1934, she graduated from Englewood High School. And soon the girl who everyone thought would never get married was planning her wedding day.

Sadly, LaVaughn's father, James, would not live to see it. A month after LaVaughn graduated from high school, James came down with stomach pains so severe that he had to be hospitalized. Phoebe kept up a faithful vigil, visiting the hospital daily with her youngest daughter, Mary, in tow. Phoebe and her husband may have reconciled by then. Or maybe she was just doing her duty, fulfilling her obligations to the man with whom she had shared so much of her life. James died at the hospital on April 12, 1934. He was fifty-four years old. The cause of death was pneumonia, but the doctors suspected that he also had stomach cancer. Phoebe's son, Johnny D. Johnson, who was twelve years old at the time, remembered coming home from school that April day and hearing one of his older sisters whisper, "Papa is dead."

James, the paternal great-grandfather of Mrs. Obama, was buried four days later at Lincoln Cemetery in Chicago after a full life that carried him to cities in Louisiana, Mississippi, Missouri, and Illinois. The son of a former slave, he was a minister and an entrepreneur who owned two shoe repair shops in Chicago. Phoebe, who was fifty-four when James died, stood somberly at his funeral. She did not weep in public. Any emotions she had, she kept hidden inside. "I never saw her cry or look sad, never in my life," said Mary Lang, Phoebe's youngest daughter. She said she had no idea how her mother felt as she watched James being lowered into his grave. "She wasn't a person to talk about those things," Mrs. Lang said.

Five weeks later, Rebecca was in mourning, too. On May 21, 1934, her aunt, Carrie Coleman, the woman who had raised her since she was a child, died around the age of forty-nine. Carrie, Mrs. Obama's great-aunt, the adventurous young woman who had journeyed from North Carolina to Baltimore before heading to Chicago, was like a mother to Rebecca. She took her in when the little girl had no one else. She fed her, bathed her, and made sure that Rebecca went to school and learned how to read and write. The doctors diagnosed cancer and conducted an operation at Cook County Hospital to try to save her, but Carrie didn't make it. It must have been a staggering blow. Carrie's husband, John, was about fifty-one. After more than three decades of marriage, he might have reasonably hoped to grow old with Carrie. Instead, he found himself burying her at Mount Glenwood Cemetery. Rebecca, who was twenty-five, had little time to lose herself in her grief. She had young children by then, a growing family to care for. She had to move on.

Phoebe, too, wanted life to go on. On October 18, 1934, six months after James's funeral, she opened up the apartment where she was living as a boarder to friends and relatives to celebrate a family milestone. On that day, LaVaughn, nineteen, became the first of her daughters to marry. She and Fraser, twenty-two, exchanged vows in a small, modest ceremony. Robert McDowell, a minister who served under Mother Allensworth at Full Gospel Mission, stood before them, stitching the two lives together before God. The newlyweds didn't have enough money to rent a place of their own. So they moved in with some of Fraser's South Carolina relatives, who lived in a bustling two-story frame house in a black section of the South Side. People who knew them say they were inseparable. "Everything they did, they did it together," said Mary Lang, LaVaughn's sister. Nearly ten months after the wedding, on August 1, 1935, the couple celebrated the birth of their first child, Fraser Robinson III, Mrs. Obama's father, who entered the world nearly three hours after midnight and who everyone would know as Diddley. It was a joyous occasion, but the gloom lurking outside of that warm, loving home would soon creep in. Mrs. Obama's grandparents—Rebecca and Purnell, LaVaughn and Fraser—were beginning their married lives and their lives as parents in the most difficult of times.

LaVaughn filled her home with the sounds of religious radio

broadcasts, as she hovered over her newborn, buoying the family spirits with prayer and song. But unlike earlier migrants, who found good fortune in Chicago and a seemingly endless array of well-paying jobs, her new husband, Fraser, found only adversity and poverty during those first years in his new city. Over and over again, wherever he went, the golden boy from Georgetown was told there was no work to be had. His ambition, his brimming intellect, and his silver tongue were no match for the worst economic times in the country. "Imagine now, my father moved from South Carolina at about eighteen, moved to the promised land and walked right smack-dab into the middle of the Depression," said Nomenee Robinson, Fraser's second son. "He couldn't get a job. Here's a man who was admired for his articulation and his mathematical prowess and he couldn't get a job."

Richard Wright, the noted writer, captured the desperation of those days in Chicago in his autobiography, *Black Boy*. He described the hardships faced by African Americans and his own personal struggles when he lost a temporary job at the post office and started haunting the city, desperately, for work. "But when I went into the streets in the morning I saw sights that killed my hope for the rest of the day," Mr. Wright wrote. "Unemployed men loitered in doorways with blank looks in their eyes, sat dejectedly on front steps in shabby clothing, congregated in sullen groups on street corners, and filled all the empty benches in the parks of Chicago's South Side," said Mr. Wright, who ended up taking a job selling burial insurance policies to make ends meet. He was lucky to have that. Fraser, who had dreamed of earning enough money to go to college, simply couldn't find steady, well-paying work at all.

He washed dishes and worked in a laundry. He worked as a bowling alley attendant, where he set up the pins, and as a handyman, anything to feed and house his family. But even that wasn't enough. The jobs were usually temporary—day labor jobs—and Fraser would quickly find himself back on the street again, searching for another way to make a living. He had hoped to become an electrical engineer, or, at the very least, an electrician. But those were union jobs and the white unions, which dominated the building trades, still barred ambitious blacks like Fraser from joining. "You didn't even have to worry about trying to find jobs because there weren't no jobs to be found," said Thomas Ellis, a retired aircraft mechanic and printer, describing the sharp economic downturn that he witnessed in Chicago during the Depression. "The best thing you could do was go down there to the post office and get those applications, fill them out, and that was it."

LaVaughn coped with the hard times the way she had been taught by her mother: silently, stoically. The family was struggling to make ends meet, and her husband was deeply unhappy. Yet she never discussed her troubles, not even with her younger sister. "She never mentioned it or showed it," Mary Lang said. LaVaughn devoted herself to raising her little boy and trying to hold the family together. But the family's hardships seemed to multiply wherever she looked.

In South Carolina, Fraser's father was out of work, too, and his younger siblings were struggling to help the family get by. Some dropped out before finishing high school so they could provide support. One of Fraser's brothers found work at a sawmill, peeling the bark from branches by hand. One of his sisters found work as a maid. Janie was in the eighth grade—about thirteen or fourteen years old—when she was forced to leave school for good. "She told me once that the hardest thing to find during that time was rice," said Harolyn Siau, Janie's daughter. "Everything was scarce, but the most scarce was rice. They had to really conserve what they had and make it stretch."

In Chicago, Fraser finally started earning a bit of steady money on a Workers Progress Administration job, described in the jargon of the time as "city relief," a job that paid anywhere from $65 to $100 a month. But it still wasn't enough. Soon LaVaughn, with a new baby and a high school degree, was back to cleaning houses again, this time on the North Side of Chicago. She would clean the houses of wealthy women during the day and then come home, exhausted, to clean her own. As he watched his dreams deflate, Fraser began to realize that he had pinned his life's ambitions on a city that might not deliver. His children wonder whether he encountered racial discrimination during this period of time, or whether he or members of his family had witnessed any racial violence in South Carolina. If so, he kept his boiling frustrations to himself. Fraser rarely commented on the strictly enforced housing segregation that left him stuck on the overcrowded South Side, but he would always reassure his wife that he would be sure not to stop if he had to drive through a white neighborhood. He was also so painfully deferential around whites that in later years his children would wonder whether he was scarred by some experience he could not bring himself to discuss.

There was one place, though, where African Americans could feel something akin to equality to whites, where they could prove that they had power and clout: that was in the city's polling places. That may be one reason why Fraser was so zealous about voting, no matter how bad the weather, no matter how uninspiring the candidates, no matter how tired he might have been from working late into the night or how discouraged he might have been from not working at all. (LaVaughn was equally passionate about exercising her civic rights.) When Fraser was growing up in South Carolina, he witnessed how blacks were routinely denied the right to vote. In Chicago, the city's polling stations were one of the few places where Fraser could feel like a man.

Chicago was certainly no promised land during the Depression, however. Migration north, which had boomed between 1910 and 1930, sputtered during the 1930s as economic opportunity waned. Some migrants who moved to Chicago around that time turned around and went back home. Those who stayed watched their dreams turn into disappointment. In their corner of the South Side, Rebecca and Purnell were confronting their own set of difficulties. In later years, Rebecca would find work as a nurse and her husband, Purnell, would earn a living as a painter, a handyman, and a carpenter. But during the Depression, the young couple struggled like everyone else. Purnell may have found some solace in his insatiable love for music. But he was also embittered by his experiences. "I had a father who

could be very angry about race," Marian Robinson, Purnell's daughter, said years after his death. "My father was a very angry man."

His anger may have stemmed from his time in Birmingham,
where his aspirations and those of his relatives were choked by the
heavy hand of racism and segregation. Or maybe he found that the
promised land of Chicago was far less promising than he had hoped.
Many blacks from the South imagined that they would escape segregation once they arrived in Chicago. But Purnell soon learned that
segregation was pervasive there as well. While blacks often studied
in integrated schools and traveled on integrated streetcars, they were
routinely barred from "white beaches" on Lake Michigan—where
a fence was erected to separate blacks from whites—as well as from
certain hotels, bars, restaurants, dance halls, roller-skating rinks, and
bowling alleys. Accidentally stumbling across the invisible dividing
lines that separated white neighborhoods from black ones could mean
a beating. "There were boundaries," recalled Dorsey Day, a retired
union leader and community organizer, who grew up on the South
Side in the 1930s. He sold newspapers as a boy and quickly learned
that "you were in dangerous territory" if you crossed the line. "There
were gangs," Mr. Day said. "They would take your newspapers and
take your money. And you were certainly a 'nigger' at all times."

During times of great prosperity, these slights might have
seemed easier for men like Purnell and Fraser to dismiss, particularly given the vibrant religious and social scene of the South Side.
But during the Depression, when the very basics of life were hard
to come by, some southern migrants might have wondered why
they had left and what, really, they had gained. Fraser's siblings in
South Carolina began asking those kinds of questions, too. What
good was Fraser doing for his family back home while he was living in Chicago, they wondered. Those questions took on a height-
ened urgency after November 3, 1936, when Fraser's father died of
tuberculosis at the age of fifty-two in Georgetown. His death left
Fraser's mother, Rosella, suddenly responsible for clothing, feed-
ing, and raising Fraser's younger brothers and sisters on her own. It

also left Fraser's siblings increasingly bitter. Many wondered openly why Fraser—the oldest, most accomplished child—had left them to struggle on their own. "Some of his brothers and sisters resented it," Nomenee Robinson, Fraser's son, said of his father's move to Chicago. "He was the oldest. They thought he needed to be there to help with all of those kids."

Fraser decided to mourn his father in Chicago. His children are still at a loss as to why he did not go back for the funeral. It is possible that Fraser was afraid that his family in South Carolina would finally realize how badly he was struggling in Chicago. Maybe he had hoped to send money to his parents and siblings and had been overwhelmed with guilt that he had been unable to do so. The gulf between Georgetown, where Fraser was viewed as a rising star, and Chicago, where he was just another jobless black man struggling to feed his family, must have been enormous and, at times, unbearable. "Maybe he was ashamed; maybe he couldn't afford it," Nomenee Robinson said of the trip to South Carolina. "That's something my dad didn't talk about . . . All of those things, he had too much pride to talk about. The best I can conjure up is that he had hoped to create a better life and come back a hero," said Mr. Robinson, who was born in 1937, eight months after Fraser's father died. "That better life never came. When it did come, it was too late to benefit his mother and father."

That same year, Rebecca gave birth to a baby girl, who opened her eyes for the first time on July 29. Rebecca and Purnell named her Marian Lois Shields. Born in the midst of the Depression, Marian Shields, with her smooth brown skin, her big brown eyes and pretty smile, would grow up to become a striking young woman and the First Lady's mother. Her parents would ultimately have seven children together. For much of their married life, though, there were far too many troubles weighing on their minds. Rebecca's uncle, John Coleman, who had raised her, had fallen while working on a WPA worksite and had ended up crippled and unemployable. Meanwhile, Rebecca and Purnell were slowly growing apart. Cracks began fracturing the foundation of their relationship. Over the years, Rebecca, who was a religious woman, found comfort in her church.

For Fraser, who grew up in the shadow of a proud and striving father who owned his own land, everything seemed to be falling apart. The hardships that he and LaVaughn encountered, the struggles he faced finding steady work, the grief that overwhelmed them when their third child, a baby boy, died just twenty-four days after his birth, all of it took its toll on their marriage. LaVaughn kept quiet about their marital troubles, so much so that her family was astonished when she and Fraser went their own ways. Her sisters often stopped by to visit the couple for dinner, and none were the wiser. "They were like peas in a pod," remarked Mary Lang, LaVaughn's sister, who said she was stunned when Fraser moved out.

On March 26, 1941, after ten hard years in Chicago, Fraser enlisted in the army, which would ultimately ship him out of the city, out of the country, right to the battles raging in Europe. He was twenty-eight years old, had two young boys, and had been married for nearly seven years. When the recruiter asked him about his marital status, Fraser made it clear that he intended to leave that life behind. His enlistment papers describe him as "separated, without dependants."

TEN

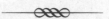

Struggling and Striving

I N THE TWILIGHT OF HER LIFE, PHOEBE STILL WATCHED OVER her daughter. LaVaughn was no longer the sickly baby that she had once nursed with so much care. She was grown now, with a quick smile that masked the hurts and aches in her own heart. The two women, mother and daughter, comforted each other once Fraser was gone. They prayed together at church and sang together in the choir. Phoebe even moved in with LaVaughn and her boys for a time. It is hard to imagine that they spoke frankly about their own heart-breaks or that they wept in each other's arms. That was not their way. But they spent time together, talking about the Bible, their children, and the ordinary rhythms of the day. There must have been something healing in that. "The house was packed to the brim," said Nomenee Robinson, LaVaughn's son. "There was my mom, two elderly aunts, and one of the aunts had four children." There were two boarders and the occasional sibling, too. When one of the women in the house got married, it made all the sense in the world for her husband to move right in.

"We were blessed in a way," Mr. Robinson said. "All children need their dad and they need their mom, but we never felt deserted.

All of those ladies in the family that lived with us, and those men, were our role models, our guides."

With that kind of support at home, LaVaughn started looking for work at a time when the doors that were previously closed to women had begun to swing open. During World War II, as the economy roared back, LaVaughn found her very first office job, at the United States Department of Agriculture, a coveted full-time position for a black woman. LaVaughn was about twenty-six years old, and her high school diploma was finally paying some dividends. She spent about seven or eight years there, and even became a supervisor. "She enjoyed that, she really did," Francesca Gray said of her mother's first office job. Phoebe, who had always cleaned white women's houses to make ends meet, must have glowed with pride: LaVaughn had finally washed her hands of domestic work for good.

Phoebe had given up on domestic work, too. She was older now, in her early sixties, and tired easily. She had heart trouble, too, though in her typical fashion she rarely let on. "She never complained. Never, never, never," said Mary Lang, Phoebe's daughter. "She never let on or let you know if she was sick. Her attitude, her manner never changed. She was like that until she died." In those last years of her life, Phoebe savored her religious magazines, listened to her religious radio broadcasts, and spent time sewing, often transforming old flour sacks into shirts or trousers. And she tended to her grandsons, soothing them if they got in trouble, scraped a knee, or hurt their feelings, and urging them to remember the Lord in their day-to-day lives. "You know grandmothers in those days, when your mother was there, they were a kind of a refuge from chastisement," said Nomenee Robinson. "And that's how I found her to be. She was deeply religious. I called her Grandma. Grandma was the lady who reminded you daily about your obligations to God." Phoebe later moved in with her older daughter, Esther, but she never lost that deep connection to LaVaughn. "My mother used to talk to her a lot," Mary Lang said of Phoebe and La-Vaughn, her older sister.

Even so, these were hard times for LaVaughn. She earned a salary, her very first, but she still struggled to make ends meet. She even wrote to Fraser overseas, pointedly asking him to send some money home so that she could feed his sons. Nomenee Robinson, LaVaughn's second-born son, still remembers the markers of the government charity, the worn clothes—the jackets, the trousers—and the free food. "You knew who was getting charity by what they wore at our elementary school," he said. "I remember us going to a warehouse environment to get free cheese, free margarine. You'd get white-looking blocks of shortening and they'd give you a little packet of coloring to make it the color of butter. So that was a tinge of post-depression."

And it was surely not an easy time to be separated from her husband. Being married meant being respectable, and being respectable meant everything to LaVaughn, who was still a devout, churchgoing woman. She felt ashamed that she had let her marriage fall apart, so ashamed that she hid the breakup for as long as she could. But unlike her husband, who never quite felt at home in Chicago, LaVaughn felt utterly at ease in the city of her birth and that may have provided some solace. While Fraser had to build a social life virtually from scratch, LaVaughn had her church, where she sang soprano in the choir every Sunday. She had her mother, Phoebe, and dozens of friends and relatives, all within a few blocks of her home on the South Side. And she had her two boys. She encouraged them to explore their own musical and artistic talents. (Fraser Robinson III, Mrs. Obama's father, would become a gifted sculptor and painter; Nomenee Robinson would learn to play the violin.) LaVaughn encouraged them to learn how to ice-skate and expected them to study hard in school. "She was there for those children all the time," said her sister, Mary Lang. "She took them everywhere. Everything educational, they got it." Being a single mother was not something LaVaughn had envisioned for herself. Phoebe had emphasized the importance of a woman's role in the home, and their church had emphasized the sanctity of marriage. But in her first office job, at the U.S. Department of Agriculture, where she was respected for her efficiency, LaVaughn began to enjoy a different kind of fulfillment, a sense of independence that she had never experienced.

It was a time of war and a time of fear and uncertainty. The Japanese bombed Pearl Harbor, shaking the nation, and as the war spread across the continents tens of thousands of military wives became widows. But for the separated couple, it was also a time of growth. Fraser, who had struggled to find success at home, was stretching in ways that he had never imagined overseas. He fought in Italy, serving as a master sergeant, and traveled across Europe. He and other black soldiers were forced to serve in segregated units and endured racial epithets and indignities. But the experience overseas broadened him. For the first time, his daughter believes, he really felt like a man, really felt like an American. Other black men who served during the war offered similar accounts. "I think the only man ever to call me an American, and say it like I was as good as any American he was likely to find, was a little Jewish man," recalled Staff Sergeant Bill Moore, who served in Europe during World War II. "We took our trucks to get them out of the concentration camps," Mr. Moore said. "I had just got out of the truck, and a Jewish man, who looked like a dead man walking, came right up to me. He called me 'American' and he fell into my arms. . . . [H]e hugged me like nobody ever hugged me in my life."

Fraser, a handyman with a knack for fixing electronic devices, handled radio operations overseas. And he found that Europeans sometimes treated black Americans with more respect and courtesy than their white counterparts at home. He told his children about a kindly Italian woman, named Francesca, who brought milk and eggs to him and the other black soldiers who were camped near her farm. (The woman left such an impression on him that he would name his only daughter Francesca years later.) He returned to Chicago with a love for classical music—Verdi and Beethoven, in particular—a taste for fine wine, and a proud military bearing. "I think he finally had the opportunity to use his skills and gifts in the army," his daughter said. "He had a sense of autonomy in some respects." In his discharge papers, his superiors described Fraser as a skilled electrician and radio operator. They suggested that he attend a trade or technical school after he returned to the United States. It never happened. Maybe, with two young sons to support, he simply couldn't afford it. Whatever the reason, his lifelong dream of parlaying his skills into a career soon evaporated. Instead, Fraser got a night job sorting mail at the post office, his first steady job in Chicago. It was a coveted civil service job, reserved for returning veterans. It wasn't the kind of career he had imagined for himself when he was leaving South Carolina as an idealistic teenager, but it finally gave him a stable financial footing. The military "rescued his life," Nomenee Robinson said of his father. Now, somewhat established, he began to inch his way back into his family's life.

He was still living on his own, apart from LaVaughn, but he started visiting his two sons regularly and taking them to the circus and to the movies. And, for the first time that his children could remember, he returned to South Carolina to visit his mother, brothers, and sisters and other relatives, taking his boys with him. Yet Fraser remained a gruff, often inscrutable presence, and his sons would spend much of their lives struggling to make sense of this father who so often kept them at arm's length, even when he was standing in the same room. He told them almost nothing about his childhood, his parents, and his grandparents and shared even less in the way of physical affection. He was a no-nonsense disciplinarian who expected excellence from his children in all things, but left his boys hungry for his touch. (It meant the world to Nomenee Robinson when, after so many years of absence, his father casually put his hand on his neck one afternoon at the movies. To this day, it is a moment that he still vividly remembers.) Fraser filled his home with dictionaries and drilled his children over and over again on the proper way of speaking. There would be no slang, no urban lingo in his house. "You're going to speak correctly" was his mantra. None of Fraser's children would be held back by the white world because they "sounded black." (Years later, his children would wonder whether his preoccupation with language stemmed from concerns that urban and southern cadences had set some African Americans back, maybe even some members of his own family, preventing whites from taking them seriously.) But while he was dubbed "an Einstein" by his in-laws, who admired his intellect, his love of newspapers and of poetry, Fraser rarely expressed pride in his own boys' scholarly accomplishments, leaving them bewildered and hurt. He did not attend any parent-teacher conferences, swim meets, or graduation ceremonies until they were older, according to Mr. Robinson. It was almost as if he could not bear to watch his sons flourish while his own dreams withered.

After the war, as Fraser coped with the collapse of his dreams, La-Vaughn was coming to terms with her mother's slow decline. Phoebe had been living with her daughter, Esther, for about six months. Everyone knew the end was near. "You just saw her going down," said Mary Lang, who was there by her bedside on that last day. "She slipped away. There was no pain. She went to sleep and she didn't wake up." Phoebe died on June 19, 1946, on a blustery spring morning, just a few hours after midnight. She was sixty-six. The cause of death was myocarditis, an inflammation of the heart, which stopped it from beating. Ever the pioneer, she died in Englewood, a predominantly white neighborhood on the South Side. Phoebe was the last in her line to bridge the nineteenth and twentieth centuries, the last to have heard firsthand the stories about her ancestors' origins and their journey from slave states to free states. When she died, many of those stories died with her. The woman who had journeyed from Villa Ridge to Carbondale, Edwardsville, St. Louis, Chicago, Evanston, Batavia, and Maywood was buried at Lincoln Cemetery on the South Side. It is a vast, serene expanse of green, the final resting place for many of the earliest African Americans in Chicago, prominent and ordinary. Her children honored her with a stone marker that bears her name and the single word *Mother*.

But Phoebe was much more than that. She was a pioneer who traveled more than any other woman in Mrs. Obama's family tree, in search of a better life. Phoebe's wanderlust must have been in her blood. It was an inheritance that was passed from mother to son. She did not live to see it, but her youngest son, Johnny, became a minister and a missionary, who ogled the pyramids in Egypt, the skyscrapers in Hong Kong, and Michelangelo's paintings in Rome and built schools for the poor in Nigeria, Ghana, and Liberia. One can imagine that had she still been alive, Phoebe would have fallen to her knees to thank God for guiding her son's footsteps. Then she would have tried to get on one of those newfangled airplanes to see the rest of the world herself.

LaVaughn and Fraser reconciled after Phoebe died, nearly a decade after he decided to go his own way. His son, Nomenee Robinson, still remembers the day that he moved back in. It was sometime around 1950; he walked through the front door, settled into a chair, and opened his newspaper as if he had never left. He and LaVaughn had three children in rapid succession after that, first Andrew in 1951, then Carleton in 1952, then Francesca, who was born in 1953. Fraser never discussed with his children his prolonged absence from the family. Their daughter was an adult before she learned that her parents had ever separated. Her mother and father had concealed it, as they did many of the difficult experiences they encountered. Though Fraser never talked in detail about the barriers that constrained him during his own childhood, he repeatedly urged his two oldest sons to tread carefully when dealing with white people—life lessons, perhaps, from a man who had been burned by racism and discrimination. Don't get too close, he warned them. Don't get too friendly. If you get into an argument with a white person, know that your chances of winning that argument are limited. Don't drink with white people because they might act up, Fraser told his boys. If you're around the wives of white men and they start drinking, find a polite way to excuse yourself. If she comes on to you, they might accuse you of rape. And finally: the best way to beat the white man is through education. But never, never tell them how much you know.

Fraser's sons listened and nodded. But it wasn't until his children were adults that they thought hard about what their father had said and tried to figure out what his lessons suggested about his own life. In later years, Nomenee Robinson and Francesca Gray learned to read between the lines, to look back and to glean clues from their memories, to carefully sift through what their father did, what he said, and what he kept to himself. Mrs. Gray still recalls the day when a white man kicked her as she was stepping off the bus with her father. She was a little girl, not yet in elementary school. To this day, she is not sure whether the kick was an accident or deliberate. But she spoke up, sure that her father would take some action, speak sharply to the man, interrogate him about what had happened. "That man kicked me," she told her father and waited for the explosion. "He was always so short fused," she explained. Instead, Fraser looked at the man and didn't say a word. Stunned, Francesca looked up at her father, the baffled questions bubbling up in her throat. "My father turned around and just gave the man a look," she recalled. "I wonder now if he thought he couldn't say anything." Not to a white man, not with his little girl standing right there. They never spoke of it after that.

"He was very cautious about our relations with white people," Mr. Robinson said. "If I remember well, I can't ever remember my dad having a white friend." In Fraser's world, the risks clearly outweighed the benefits of these relationships. Mr. Robinson believes now that those lessons were the survival mechanisms of his father and grandfather. "Something must have happened, something to him or to his father," Mr. Robinson said. But his efforts to find answers were repeatedly stymied. Growing up, Mrs. Gray heard only tidbits about South Carolina, the place where her father was raised. "I don't know that he had great memories about the South," she said.

Sometime around 1952, Fraser saved up enough money to put a down payment on a three-bedroom co-op, and he proudly moved his family in, a personal milestone. He and LaVaughn had reunited at a time when blacks seemed poised to make many breakthroughs. A year after their daughter was born, the United States Supreme Court barred school segregation in *Brown v. Board of Education*. Over the next decade, black students sat in at white-only lunch counters and black protesters took to the streets across the country, demanding the right to vote and to be treated as equals. LaVaughn found work at a religious bookstore where she tended to customers across the color line and melded her religious devotion with her quiet, capable efficiency. She became a first in her own right: the first African American woman to manage a Moody Bible bookstore. As the years passed and Fraser grew older, he watched his children and grandchildren climb and climb— attending college, entering the professional class, and buying their own houses, accomplishments that had eluded him. In a decision that remains difficult for his sons to understand, Fraser refused to help his four boys pay for their higher education. It is a subject that remains the source of some family tension even today, more than a decade after his death. Each of his four surviving children attended college. In fact, his son Nomenee Robinson earned two master's degrees: one in city and regional planning and the other an MBA. His daughter, Francesca Gray, got a graduate degree, too, and pursued a career as a graphic artist and a teacher. (Fraser, who doted on his little girl, did decide to pay for her college career. He may have concluded that his only daughter needed the education the most to ensure that she would never have to rely on a man to make her way in the world.)

Fraser's artistic firstborn child, who bore his name but was known as Diddley, also managed to attend some college at the University of Illinois, Navy Pier, before his funds dried up. He worked as a lifeguard during the summers and it was there, his brother Nomenee says, that he bumped into Marian Shields, the statuesque, self-possessed daughter of Rebecca and Purnell Shields. Handsome and athletic, Diddley was something of a man about town, "a cool cat," who favored dark sunglasses and jazz clubs. He wasn't looking to settle down. But he fell hard for Marian, who had two years of teaching college under her belt and was working as a secretary for the Spiegel Catalog. On October 27, 1960, about a year after they first met, the couple got married in Marian's aunt's home on the South Side. Three years and a few months later—on January 17, 1964—Diddley and Marian celebrated the birth of their second child, a baby girl they named Michelle La-Vaughn Robinson.

Fraser retired from the post office sometime around 1976, and several years later, he gave up on Chicago and moved back to the South for good with LaVaughn. Some fifty years after he first set foot in Chicago, he returned to his birthplace, the small, rural town of Georgetown, South Carolina. His long journey had come full circle. Fraser rejoined Bethel AME Church, the church where his parents and grandparents had prayed in the late 1800s. He reconnected with cousins and relatives and graying classmates from Howard High School, his alma mater. "I think he was happy being there," Mrs. Gray said. When he died on November 9, 1996, there was no question about where he wanted to be buried. His final resting place was in that church cemetery in South Carolina, alongside his ancestors. During the funeral, mourners sang the hymn "It Is Well with My Soul." "He was a very proud man. He was proud of his lineage," Mrs. Obama, his granddaughter, recalled. But, she added, "there was a discontent about him."

LaVaughn, a city girl who never took to the rhythms of rural life in South Carolina, made a different choice. She moved back to Chicago, to her siblings, to her children, and to her church. The city that Phoebe had finally settled in so many decades earlier was the one where LaVaughn felt most at home. Yet she, like her husband, offered her children few insights about herself or her family history. When she died of a heart attack at the age of eighty-seven on September 17, 2002, she left many questions unanswered. In her long life, LaVaughn had never talked about her own personal experiences in segregated Chicago, nor had she shared any details of her grandmother Mary's life during slavery or the origins of her family's multiracial lineage. Nearly a decade after her death, her only daughter still wonders from where exactly had her family emerged? "I don't know, but I felt like there was a sort of unspoken or unwritten shame in the whole thing," Francesca Gray said. "For so many years or decades, your ancestry was squashed, squelched. Maybe at some point along the line, people said we shouldn't talk about it. I always wonder if the reason they didn't talk about it back then was because it was too painful," she said. The unspoken message, Mrs. Gray said, the one that she got from her parents was: "We want you to get what you can. We want you to look forward. We don't want you to look back."

That reluctance to probe the past, to look back over one's shoulder, to examine the half-healed sores that festered in grandparents and great-grandparents, reappears over and over again in Mrs. Obama's family tree. It has made the search for the truth that much harder. But it is also understandable. People often turn away from what is too painful to witness. They almost always want their children to see the world as a better place, to be free of their pain.

Purnell Shields never shook the bitterness and anger that he felt after a life shaped by the Jim Crow South and the segregated North. But he taught his children to view life differently, to accept people, regardless of race. His children absorbed his message of racial tolerance. "He did not let it carry over," said Marian Robinson, Purnell's daughter and Michelle Obama's mother. "We couldn't be racially divisive. That wasn't allowed." He may have been inspired by the progress he saw within his own family. His sister, who married a Pullman porter, became a teacher and owned her own house. His mother, Annie, who Mrs. Obama and her brother knew as Mamaw, lived long enough to attend family barbecues where she could admire her children, grandchildren, and great-grandchildren. (Annie, who was known as Annie Lawson or Annie Laws before she got married, died in 1975 at the age of eighty-seven.) But Purnell couldn't salvage his own marriage to Rebecca, who had become a nurse at Grant Hospital. Several decades after their wedding, Rebecca and Purnell split up. They didn't divorce. In fact, they lived only blocks away from each other. But they took pains to remove themselves from each other's lives.

"After having seven children together—Carolyn Ann, Robbie Joyce, Adrienne, Marian (Mom), Gracie, and then David and Steve—my grandparents had separated, for reasons never discussed,"

Craig Robinson, Mrs. Obama's brother, said of their maternal grandparents, Rebecca and Purnell, who was known in the family as Southside. "Possibly they just weren't compatible. Where Southside was gregarious and loved to blast Charlie Parker and Miles Davis on his record player so loud that I think he lost some hearing in one ear as a result, Grandma Rebecca was a former nurse and a very reserved, though kindly, woman who preferred reading the paper quietly from cover to cover rather than entertaining the masses . . . After they separated, even though Grandma Rebecca lived around the corner from Southside with her youngest daughter—my aunt Gracie—and Gracie's husband, my mother's parents almost never saw each other again."

Purnell and Rebecca, who bonded over their childhood losses and separated when living together became harder than living apart, died within three years of each other. He died of cardiac arrest on July 30, 1983, at the age of seventy-two. She died similarly, at the age of seventy-eight, on January 24, 1988. Purnell passed on many things to his grandchildren: his love for music, his magnetic personality, his wide-open spirit, his love for barbecue. (When Purnell fired up the grill that he had fashioned from an old garbage can, neighbors could smell his savory chicken, ribs, and sausage from blocks away.) He gave his granddaughter, Michelle Obama, her first Stevie Wonder album, starting a musical love affair that she would share with her husband in Washington, D.C.

One thing that didn't get passed down, though, was the story of his white ancestry. Perhaps there was too much pain or shame in the story of his father, who died young, and his grandparents, who were born into slavery. Perhaps the stories seemed so commonplace to a man of his generation that they didn't seem worth telling. Or perhaps he simply didn't know the truth himself. It would take a black-and-white photograph of a man from Purnell's past, a sober, distinguished-looking man with wavy hair and pale skin, to help reveal something of his family's story. I stumbled across the photo decades later, long after Purnell's death, and a colleague of mine passed it along to aides of Mrs. Obama who was living, by then, in the White House. The mystery man in the photograph occupied a prominent place in the First Lady's family tree, and his descendants held the keys to some of the locked doors of her past. But Mrs. Obama had never laid eyes on his face before. She didn't even know his name.

ELEVEN

The Search for the Truth: Cleveland

J EWELL BARCLAY, THE LONG-LOST COUSIN OF MICHELLE
Obama, sits at her tiny kitchen table in Cleveland, poring over
the photographs of the stern, silver-haired man she has kept for
decades in a plain manila envelope. "I called him Grandpapa," she
says, smiling at the memory of her great-grandfather as she fingers
the black-and-white images. "He was kind of short, not real tall, had
a little weight on him. But he was real light. He's another one that
could pass for white, just like my daddy." And there he is, the First
Lady's mystery man, her great-great-grandfather whose photograph
surfaced so unexpectedly in the White House all those years after
Purnell's death. The old man is frozen in time, as he holds tight to
his cane on her couch on her wedding day in Cleveland in 1947. In
another photograph, a decade or so earlier, he sits on the front steps
of his own house in Birmingham, so much the proud patriarch, as
his children, grandchildren, and great-grandchildren gathered around
him. Jewell laughs when she thinks about that day. Her whole family
had piled into the gleaming chrome Hudson to drive down to Alabama. She still remembers blushing over the adolescent pimples that
dotted her cheeks, so sure, so absolutely sure, that everyone would see
them and snicker. That was almost seventy years ago, and those im-

ages in her mind are as clear as day. But she still cannot remember her great-grandfather's first name.

Jewell is eighty-five now. Her curly hair is white, and faint lines creep across her forehead. They hover around her mouth, too, when she laughs, which is often, because she loves funny jokes and telling a good story. But ask her about her family history and Jewell shakes her head. She still has as many questions as answers. "People didn't talk much about that," she says. "I don't know why they kept it so quiet." We were sitting side by side in her kitchen on a warm spring afternoon, poring over the pile of census records, death certificates, and marriage licenses that I had brought from my office in Washington. I had flown in that morning to walk her through them all, to show her exactly how she was related to the First Lady of the United States, Michelle Obama. That was when Jewell pulled out her old photos. Until I reached out to her, Jewell had no idea that so many of her relatives had ended up in Chicago, or that one of her cousins was living in the White House. One of the first things I told her was the name of her great-grandfather, the man she knew as Grandpapa. His name was Dolphus Shields.

Bit by bit, generation by generation, we pieced together the complicated family saga. Dolphus had a daughter named Pearl and a son named Robert Lee. Pearl was Jewell's grandmother. Robert Lee was Purnell's father. That made Jewell and Purnell first cousins once removed. Their family lines bloomed from the same root. But they never knew each other. The Great Migration swept their ancestors apart, scattering them from Birmingham to cities across the Midwest. Cousins lost touch with cousins during those northward journeys. Sisters lost touch with sisters-in-law. The first flurries of letters dwindled to a handful. And then there were none at all. The branches of many African American family trees were dislocated and transplanted in different cities.

In Jewell's family, the break came when Dolphus's descendants left Birmingham and moved north. The children of his son, Robert Lee, moved to Chicago between 1920 and 1930. His daughter, Pearl, moved to Cleveland, perhaps by way of Detroit, sometime after 1910. She found work as a seamstress there and her services were in such demand that she opened her own shop near the corner of Seventy-ninth Street and Quincy Avenue across from Emmanuel Baptist Church, where she prayed on Sundays. She specialized in children's clothing and bedecked her store window with frilly organdy dresses. She organized style shows at church, too, where little girls dazzled in her creations. When her son, James, had his first child, a daughter, Pearl named the child herself. She called her Jewell. "She said I was a jewel to her," her granddaughter remembers all these decades later. "She said I was her heart." Pearl had light-brown skin and wavy hair that didn't need straightening. James had even lighter skin and green-gray eyes. "People would say, 'You got a white father,' and I'd say, 'I don't have no white father!'" Jewell says. "But my daddy had them funny cat eyes and people actually thought that my daddy was white." Jewell knows that her father, who was a painter, was born in Birmingham, where Dolphus lived. When she was a little girl, she and her grandmother would head down south to visit Dolphus during the summer months, when school was out. They'd start out in Cleveland and end up in another world. It was the 1930s, and Birmingham was a place where whites and blacks had separate bathrooms and water fountains, where black women washed clothes on scrub boards, not in washing machines, and southern grandmothers like Pearl watched carefully to make sure northern granddaughters like Jewell didn't accidentally step out of line. (Jewell had her first taste of southern-style segregation when she was warned to steer clear of the whites-only water fountain.)

Some older black women even balanced big straw baskets on top of their heads, harkening back to a time that few people seemed to want to talk about. "Cleveland didn't have nothing like that," Jewell says, remembering how she was struck by the novelties of southern living. Jewell and her grandmother stayed with Dolphus in his white frame house with the swing on the porch. She still remembers the savory, homemade biscuits and grits that Dolphus's wife cooked up for breakfast and the treats he sent to her house in Cleveland. During the school year, when she was back home in Cleveland with her parents, Jewell would see her father opening the paper-covered packages that Dolphus would send in the mail. Inside were spiky stalks of sugarcane and nutty brown pecans. The sharp sweet crunch of sugarcane still brings Dolphus and the taste of Alabama to mind. "It's good to have old memories," Jewell says, nodding. But when she looks at a photo of Dolphus as a young man, so handsome in his dark suit and tie, she wonders about his early life. No one in her family spoke about slavery and no one said much about the family's white heritage, though it was plain to see. It was clear, too, in the very first photograph of Dolphus as an older man that I had uncovered when I was reporting for the *New York Times*. The photographs, historical records, and interviews with people who knew him made it clear to me that Dolphus's father was at least one of the white ancestors in the First Lady's family tree. Jewell nodded when I asked her about it. As a teenager, she had heard talk that Dolphus was half white, but nothing more. "Slave time, you know how the white men used to fool with them black women, that's what I heard," Jewell says. "Being young like that I never asked no questions."

Now, there is no one to ask. Her father and grandmother are dead. The old dress shop is gone, the building torn down. A green sea of scrub grass and dandelions sways in its place. The redbrick church in Cleveland still carries the names of the old founders carved in its cornerstone, migrants like Jewell's grandmother, who moved north and carried their southern ways with them, creating a new urban landscape in the North. Jewell is an old woman herself now, alone in a house that is comfortably worn with so much living. She raised three children there, worked as a hospital dietician's aide and then spent more than two decades working as a part-time crossing guard at a local elementary school. She survived the death of her husband and the shattering grief that came with the unexpected passing of her youngest daughter, who collapsed from a heart attack at the age of forty-three. At this stage of her life, Jewell would like some answers to the questions that she kept to herself when she was a little girl. Who was Dolphus's white father? What is her family's story?

So she agrees to take a DNA test. I've brought along a DNA collection kit that includes two cotton swabs that look a little like toothbrushes, and two small vials for storing those swabs after the test is complete. I explain that I have tracked down several descendants of the white man who owned Dolphus when he was a young slave boy. I hope to persuade some of them to take DNA tests, too. If we compare the results, we just might be able to determine whether that white slave owner or someone in his family was Dolphus's father. That would make him one of Jewell's ancestors and one of the First Lady's, too. Jewell nods, fascinated by the prospect of the shared relations. "Wouldn't that be something," she says. She washes her hands in the kitchen sink and sits down, back at the table, ready to get started. I hand her a white swab and she carefully swipes it up and down, up and down, on the inside of her cheek, amazed that the tiny cells inside her mouth might hold the clues to her family's past. "It's my history," Jewell says. "After all these years, I'd like to know the truth."

DNA testing, she believes, may be the only way to know for sure. When her great-grandfather died, his world and his story largely vanished, fading slowly from the memories of his closest descendants, who have gone now, too. Jewell never went back to Birmingham after she got married in 1947. And when her grandpapa died, those packages of sugarcane, that sweet, last connection to that old world, stopped coming.

PART II

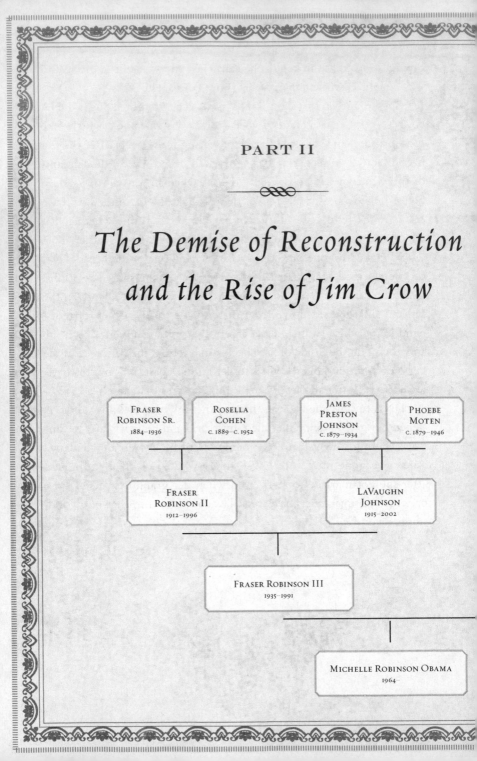

The Demise of Reconstruction and the Rise of Jim Crow

| FRASER ROBINSON SR. 1884–1936 | ROSELLA COHEN c. 1889–c. 1952 | JAMES PRESTON JOHNSON c. 1879–1934 | PHOEBE MOTEN c. 1879–1946 |

FRASER ROBINSON II 1912–1996

LAVAUGHN JOHNSON 1915–2002

FRASER ROBINSON III 1935–1991

MICHELLE ROBINSON OBAMA 1964–

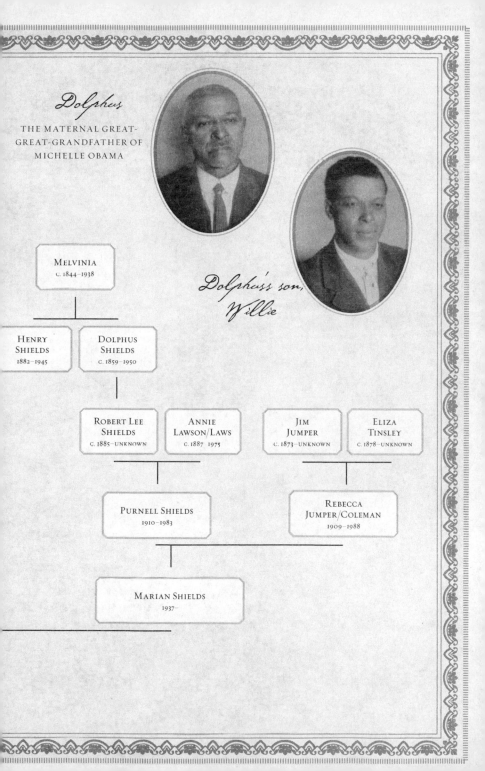

Dolphus

THE MATERNAL GREAT-
GREAT-GRANDFATHER OF
MICHELLE OBAMA

Dolphus's son,
Willie

MELVINIA
c. 1844–1938

HENRY
SHIELDS
1882–1945

DOLPHUS
SHIELDS
c. 1859–1950

ROBERT LEE
SHIELDS
c. 1885–UNKNOWN

ANNIE
LAWSON/LAWS
c. 1887 1975

JIM
JUMPER
c. 1873–UNKNOWN

ELIZA
TINSLEY
c. 1878–UNKNOWN

PURNELL SHIELDS
1910–1983

REBECCA
JUMPER/COLEMAN
1909–1988

MARIAN SHIELDS
1937–

TWELVE

A Man on the Rise

HIS FULL NAME WAS ADOLPHUS THEODORE SHIELDS AND he was something of a ladies' man. He was strikingly handsome, with piercing brown eyes, an aquiline nose, olive skin, and an irrepressible sense of confidence. In the rustic hamlets of rural Georgia, he must have been hard to miss. In another time, he might have been a college-educated minister or a commanding politician, an influential man who could sway legions of supporters and congregants with his rumbling voice and easy charisma. But Dolphus came of age in the South in the last decades of the nineteenth century, when the powers that be were methodically and violently repressing black men and women. For him, and for the members of his generation, the doors of opportunity were slamming shut. In 1880, just fifteen years after Emancipation, Dolphus was living in the rough farm country of northern Georgia near the town of Cartersville. He was about nineteen or twenty years old and hungry for a different life. Most of his family and friends were sharecroppers, former slaves who scrabbled in the sandy, red-clay fields. They had rejoiced when slavery ended, but the promise of freedom had withered like spring grass seared by the summer sun. During those relentless summer days, Dolphus could close his eyes and think back to his own time in bondage, back when he was a little boy, clinging to his young mother. He might have even remembered the chatter about his white father, a man who had given him fair skin and razor-thin lips, but kept him at a careful distance, never claiming him publicly or cloaking him with legitimacy. Dolphus had been born a slave, to an enslaved teenage girl and a man whose identity he may have never known. He was about five years old in 1865 when African Americans across the South cried out to the heavens to celebrate freedom's arrival. He was old enough to be awestruck by the sight of black men lining up to cast their first ballots, and to rejoice when his mother, Melvinia, finally earned some money of her own—maybe only a handful of coins and wrinkled bills—for her labor.

But he also lived to witness the hard, bitter years that followed. He grew into adulthood at a time when Klansmen rode freely across Georgia, shooting down black men and women who dared to vote, without fear of arrest or imprisonment. His generation watched African Americans vanish from Congress and the state legislature as men who had won the right to the ballot box lost it, bit by bit, terrorized by vigilantes and disenfranchised by a white-dominated legislature intent on turning back the clock. The first black man to represent Georgia in the U.S. House of Representatives, Jefferson Long, served for less than three months, stepping down in 1871. It would be just over a century before another African American from the state returned to Congress. Instead, blacks found themselves at the mercy of white officials like Governor James M. Smith, who energized his supporters by vowing that he and his allies would pass laws to ensure that Georgia would "retain our old plantation system." The terrible tidings left many prominent black men in despair, leading some to declare that their precious freedom had become "only another and worse form of slavery."

Many of Dolphus's descendants—his daughter, his grandchildren, and the great-grandchildren who would call him Grandpapa—would know a very different world: up north, they would relish the right to vote, elect black men to political office, and send their children to integrated schools. Dolphus, on the other hand, lived in a world of narrowing opportunities and endemic racial violence. Like most members of his generation, he would spend his entire life in the South. He was Mrs. Obama's maternal great-great-grandfather, though she would grow up without ever hearing his name. None of us has the power to choose when and where we will take our place in history. Dolphus grew into adulthood as the walls of segregation were rising and hardening around him. The white establishment made it brutally clear that African Americans would never be considered equals, never be considered men. Yet a powerful sense of drive and ambition grew within Dolphus. Something inside him, and maybe the people around him, told him he could be more than just a sharecropper.

In that summer of 1880, Dolphus had an epiphany—a conversion experience was how he described it years later—at Pleasant Grove Baptist Church. Founded by former slaves in a barrel shop in 1872, the rough-hewn church had no ceiling or roof. The impoverished men, women, and children who gathered there to praise the Lord could find little protection from swarms of mosquitoes, biting winds, or sudden drenching rains. But they could lift their heads on warm Sunday mornings and send their hallelujahs straight into the clear blue skies. In that makeshift temple, Dolphus felt a calling, a divine mission. That summer, he made up his mind. He accepted the Lord as his savior and decided to help lead his flock.

In August 1880, Dolphus was ordained a deacon at Pleasant Grove and became superintendent of its Sunday school. He was young, certainly no older than twenty-one, but in the eyes of the black men and women in his community he was clearly an up-and-comer, a man of promise. With few of the avenues open to white men available to him, he took a leadership role in what had become the most powerful African American institution to emerge after the Civil War: the black church. It would become an incubator of ministers, community leaders, and politicians for generations.

During slavery, when Dolphus was a little boy, most slaves worshipped in their masters' churches, where they were relegated to separate pews, excluded from Sunday schools, and barred from decision making. In rural communities, whites often appointed or accepted a particular slave as the plantation's pastor and carefully monitored his sermons. Many slave owners viewed religion as a tool to bolster their dominance. They made sure that religious services, whether led by white or black preachers, emphasized Ephesians, the New Testament verses that urged slaves and servants to obey their "earthly masters with respect and fear, and with sincerity of heart, just as you would obey Christ." (Unsurprisingly, African Americans emerged from slavery with a deep antipathy for that particular verse.) "The black people of this country hate that passage," one black minister said after the war, "and I cannot get my people to like it, even now." Still, slaves overwhelmingly embraced Christianity, finding great solace, hope, and inspiration in its teachings. Even before the Civil War, African Americans sought to wrest control of their spirituality from their owners, worshipping in prayer circles in slave cabins or in the woods, away from the presence of whites.

After the war, freed slaves left predominantly white churches in droves, rejecting the insistence of white pastors that blacks maintain their subservient roles, and created their own centers of worship wherever they could. In Atlanta, former slaves called out to Jesus in a railroad boxcar. In Memphis, they gathered under an arbor. In Mississippi, they prayed in a half-built structure that had so many cracks that congregants could see the stars shining through the roof. All the while, they scrimped and saved enough money to build their own churches of timber and stone. The emptying of the pews remade the religious map in the South. Before the Civil War, forty-two thousand black Methodists worshipped with whites in churches in South Carolina. By the 1870s, that figure had shrunk to six hundred. That pattern repeated itself across the South. By 1877, the vast majority of southern blacks were praying in their own places of worship. These fledgling black parishes opened schools, assisted the needy, and became vital social centers for millions of newly freed slaves.

Dolphus, who was still illiterate when he was about nine years old, may have learned to read and write at the school that was run by Pleasant Grove Baptist Church in Cartersville. As an adult, he would be among the many men in the church who embraced leadership opportunities that white society had denied them. With few other options available, the ministry inevitably attracted the most capable and ambitious men. Ministers and deacons, who were often among the few literate black men around, were some of the most respected members in a community still struggling to find its footing. "You know those who are the real leaders in every community of freedmen," wrote a white North Carolinian after the war, "are religious exhorters." At Pleasant Grove, Dolphus found a place where his worth was measured by more than how much cotton he could pick or how carefully he could mask his ambition by bowing and scraping before his white bosses. He could stride through that modest church brimming with confidence as he led the singing, clapping congregants in prayer or taught the community's wide-eyed children about Moses, the man of God who led his enslaved people to glory.

In August 1880, the very month that he became a deacon, Dolphus took another step that would solidify his standing as a responsible and respectable citizen. He got married. He vowed before God and family that he would spend the rest of his life with Alice Easley. His bride was only about fourteen when she stood by his side and agreed to become his wife. She was born in South Carolina sometime around 1865, when freedom came. She worked as a laborer, probably for one of the many white farmers who grew cotton, corn, and wheat in and around Cartersville. But she could also read and write, skills that could carry her to a life beyond the fields. She might have dreamed that her new husband would be the ticket to that kind of life. Dolphus was fair skinned enough that he could move easily back and forth across the color line. At a time when many blacks were still illiterate, he could read and write and sign his name with a flourish, unlike many black sharecroppers who used a painstakingly penned letter "X" as their signature. He grew up on a farm and knew hard work in the fields, but he also had a skill. He was a carpenter, a man who could earn a living without getting soil under his fingernails.

It is unclear how Dolphus picked up his craft. His younger brother, Henry, who was about twenty-two years his junior and grew up in his shadow, never learned carpentry. Unlucky in love and in life, Henry struggled to make his mark. (But then, the two brothers, who may have had different fathers, would ultimately take very different paths in life.) Some of Dolphus's descendants speculate that his white father might have taught him his trade, but that is just a guess. Dolphus's surviving relatives say that he never talked about his father. His mother didn't either. People looked at mother and son—Melvinia with her dark brown skin and full features and Dolphus with his near-white complexion and slash of a mouth—and surmised the truth about his origins without asking painful questions. Everyone knew what often happened between white men and enslaved women during the decades before Emancipation. But many wondered privately: Who is his father? Where is his father? Does he know his father? Alice might have wondered, too. Dolphus might have viewed her as a soul mate and told her things that he would keep from his children and their children. We can only imagine what Dolphus saw in Alice, since the details about her life, her looks, her personality, and her dreams are so scarce. She was described as black, so Alice, it seems, was not biracial like her new husband. Later in life, Dolphus would refer to her as sensible and energetic, a "good homemaker" with "a splendid" Christian character. Her religious devotion may certainly have appealed to Dolphus, who had promised before God to make his faith the bedrock of his life. But to onlookers, it might have seemed as if the wedding was predestined, as if the angels had brought the couple together so that their love might soothe the raw wounds of slavery. Their marriage, almost inconceivably, formally united two families that had been ripped apart.

There are losses in life that are so wrenching, so unbearable, that words can scarcely convey the enormity of their raging power. The mothers of Dolphus and Alice—Melvinia and Mariah—experienced this deep emotional trauma when they were little girls living on an estate in Spartanburg, South Carolina. In another time, they might have been schoolgirls, immersed in storybooks and dolls and make-believe. But they were slave girls, and what they learned was that the people we hold most dear can suddenly be snatched away, and that feelings of unquenchable grief and loneliness can become as normal, as commonplace, as breathing itself. The two girls, who lived and worked and played together as children, were separated when their master died. One by one, his slaves were parceled off among his heirs. Melvinia, who was about eight, was sent off to Georgia sometime around 1852. Mariah, who was about twelve, was left behind. Anyone who knew anything about slavery knew that the two girls, who may have been sisters or cousins, would probably never see each other again. These separations were so devastatingly common that when freedom came, thousands of former slaves embarked on frantic quests to find their lost sons and daughters, sisters and brothers, husband and wives. "In their eyes," wrote one federal official, "the work of emancipation was incomplete until the families which had been dispersed by slavery were reunited." One former slave walked six hundred miles, from Georgia to North Carolina, seeking his wife and children who had been sold. Even into the late nineteenth century, families kept searching. One couple, unwilling to give up hope nearly half a century after losing their children, placed an advertisement in the *Nashville Colored Tennessean,* begging readers for help. "During the year 1849, Thomas Sample carried away from this city, as his slaves, our daughter, Polly, and son," the parents wrote. "We will give $100 each for them to any person who will assist them . . . to get to Nashville, or get word to us of their whereabouts."

Many families torn apart during slavery never reunited. But Mariah, the mother of Dolphus's bride, somehow found her way to Georgia. The Civil War was three years gone when she and her husband had their first child in Georgia. At some point, they settled on Cartersville. Between 1874 and 1880, Melvinia moved with Dolphus and her other children from the Jonesboro area of Georgia to Cartersville, too, joining hundreds of black newcomers who were drawn by the promise of open land and an expanding railroad that offered jobs beyond sharecropping. Was it fate or chance or sheer dint of will that brought the childhood companions back together? No one knows. But more than two decades after they last cast eyes on each other, Melvinia and Mariah once again stood face-to-face. No records or diaries have survived to document the moment. They were slave girls when they were separated. They were free, grown women with children of their own when they reunited. Mariah had married a slave from the old Spartanburg estate and together they had Alice. They had all survived the harsh days of servitude, the war, the demise of slavery, and then found this unexpected gift, this miracle of a reunion. "I wish you could see this . . .," a Union officer wrote to his wife after witnessing the joyous reunions that followed Emancipation. "Men are taking their wives and children, families which had been for a long time broken up are united and oh! such happiness. I am glad I am here."

Dolphus and Alice's wedding was the sweet fruit of that unexpected and joyful reunion. On New Year's Eve in 1882, the couple cemented the bonds between the two families. Over the years, they would have many children and grandchildren and great-great-grandchildren, including one who would make history as First Lady. But on that day, they celebrated the birth of a son, a boy named Willie. It was the kind of moment that might make a man take stock of his life, to think about his place in the world and his future. Some men might have decided to deepen their roots in the town where their babies were born. Not Dolphus. Sometime after his son's birth, he began thinking seriously about leaving Cartersville for good. As he weighed his options, Dolphus had to acknowledge that there were plenty of reasons to stay put. His family was increasingly rooted in and around Cartersville, which was the government seat of Bartow County. And by 1885, Dolphus and Alice had already added two more children to their own family: first Pearl, then Robert Lee. In some ways, Cartersville was becoming a hub for aspiring African

Americans, with a number of its black entrepreneurs already beginning to thrive. Dolphus could repair his carpentry tools and pass the
time at a blacksmith shop on Main Street owned by African Americans. His wife could repair her Sunday-best shoes at a black-owned
shoemaker or gossip with neighbors at a black-owned eatery. Their
friends and relatives could pray at any one of four black churches,
two Methodist and two Baptist, including Pleasant Grove Baptist,
where Dolphus served as a deacon. There were some instances, too,
of interracial cooperation. Poor tenant farmers—black and white—
joined forces in 1880, for instance, and went to the polls to resound-
ingly defeat a measure that would have required all livestock to be
fenced in on private property. Sharecroppers on both sides of the
color line viewed the plan as a scheme to dispossess them of their
livelihoods, since many of them did not own any land. Blacks in
the county—many of whom could vividly remember their time in
slavery—took their rights seriously, and those who could lined up
to vote.

These partnerships were rare, however, and Cartersville was also
becoming infected with discriminatory legislation and other tactics
of intimidation. The goal was to prevent blacks from advancing, and
men like Dolphus already saw that opportunities were clearly shrinking, not expanding. Dolphus may or may not have gotten a chance to
cast a ballot; voting records from the time are scarce. But given the
mushrooming legal obstacles intended to prevent blacks from voting,
that right could easily have been out of Dolphus's reach. In 1880, only
39 percent of blacks in Georgia voted in the presidential election. In
the 1888 presidential balloting, that figure plummeted to 19 percent.
The poll tax, devised by white legislators, was principally to blame.
It required voters to pay about $1 to $2 a year, which was simply out
of reach for many black sharecroppers. The per capita income of all
southern residents was about $86; the vast majority of people earned
significantly less. Voters had to pay all their poll taxes, even those for
previous years, before they could cast a ballot. The effect was staggering: once a poor man fell behind on his taxes, he could be disen-

franchised for life. One observer at the time called the Georgia poll tax "the most effective bar to Negro suffrage ever devised." But the Georgia legislature did not stop there. It required African Americans to get permission from their landlords before allowing them to sell agricultural products at certain times; it sharply restricted hunting and fishing rights and made it a crime to hire a laborer who was already under contract with another employer.

White men across the state were picking up their shotguns to make sure that blacks remained on the bottom rung of the social and economic ladder. Between 1880 and 1889, fifty-one African Americans were lynched in Georgia. Many were accused of raping white women, like a man named Reuben Hudson, who was hanged from a tree in nearby DeKalb County before a mob of several hundred people who shouted, "Hang him, kill him, burn him!" Steering clear of white women did not guarantee a black man's safety, however. Other black men were killed for engaging in so-called wild talk, which meant demanding higher wages, arguing with a white employer, or leaving a job before the end of a contract. Atticus G. Haygood, a white Methodist bishop, lamented that the killing of blacks in Georgia had "become so common that it no longer surprises."

Meanwhile, parents like Dolphus and Alice were struggling to find decent schools for their children. During Reconstruction, only two schools in Cartersville were open to black students. One school, which was run by the African Methodist Church, did not have a furnace and had to shut its doors during the cold winter months. Its teacher could barely read or write. The second, the Union School, operated in the small log cabin of a black man who worked during the day. Students went without textbooks, and African Americans at the time complained that "all educational associations have failed because people were too poor . . . and [they] never received aid." The situation had not improved much by the time Dolphus moved into the county, sometime between 1870 and 1882. Even during the early 1900s, public education for blacks there was "minimal at best," characterized by small, scattered rural schools that routinely lacked adequate facilities and supplies. Fifteen years after Emancipation, the nation's 6.6 million blacks were overwhelmingly impoverished, southern and rural. While most whites owned a home or farm, nearly 90 percent of blacks owned no property at all. People of multiracial ancestry like Dolphus, mostly the products of illicit liaisons before the Civil War, accounted for about 15 percent of the African American population as the country neared the twentith century, straddling the line between black and white. But white southerners made it clear that the only way for a black man to survive in the South—whether light skinned or not—was to scale back his aspirations and pick up a hoe.

Sometime around 1888, Dolphus decided he had to pursue his dreams elsewhere. It was a challenging time to be embarking on this kind of a journey. He was about twenty-eight years old then with three young children, and his wife, Alice, was pregnant again. He was leaving the place where he had become a deacon, a husband, a father, a man of standing and respect. He was leaving his mother, Melvinia, who had raised and protected him during their days in slavery, and his baby brother, Henry, who would grow up to adore and resent him in equal measure. It could not have been easy saying good-bye to Cartersville. Decades later, Melvinia would speak with pride of her son's decision to build a new life in a new city. No one knows what Dolphus's father made of his decision, or whether he even knew of it. But by 1888, Dolphus had packed up his family and his belongings and was gone. He was on his way, with or without his father's blessing.

THIRTEEN

Left Behind

T HE ROUGH SETTLEMENT SPRANG UP FROM THE RUINS OF
an old cornfield, at a railroad crossing in the shadow of the
looming Red Mountain. From the beginning, it beckoned
the ragtag and the gilded, hard-up immigrants and wealthy industrialists, freed slaves and former Confederate soldiers. Most came seeking
the treasures of the earth, the iron ore secreted in the innards of the
mountain and the rich deposits of limestone and coal nearby. But the
settlement offered something more ephemeral, too: the intoxicating
promise of reinvention and transformation. The city's creators called
the place Birmingham when they founded it in 1871 in Alabama, six
years after the Civil War, and it would become the industrial capital of
the New South. But for the poor people who flocked there, nothing
captured the feel of Birmingham better than its nickname. For them,
it was always the Magic City.

Dolphus had chosen a place where a man could become someone
new, where a sharecropper could shed the dirt from the cotton fields
in the sweltering heat of the roaring foundries, steel mills, and coke
ovens. He picked a city where the rigid lines of segregation had yet
to be drawn and a fair-skinned man could almost lose himself in the
cacophonous mix of people. The newcomers who crowded into the

city dreamed of easy riches or, at the very least, steady wages in jobs far from the fields.

But the burgeoning city had rough edges, too, a hardness that could wear on gentle sensibilities and gnaw at the fragile bonds that held families together. The city that Dolphus chose for himself and his family had, in some places, the smell and feel of the Wild West. It had muddy streets, shootouts, and a county jail that was often packed to the brim. Flies and mosquitoes swarmed. The stench of human waste, commonly discarded in backyards, was inescapable. There was no properly functioning sewage or sanitation system and little uncontaminated water. (The carcasses of dead rats polluted one of the most heavily used water wells.) Typhoid and scarlet fever raged and spread. In 1885, the city's *Weekly Iron Age* reported that "everything that ever got loose that was in the least wild flocked to Birmingham." Yet the people kept coming. In 1880, there were 3,086 residents. By 1890, the population had grown to 26,178. African Americans, who viewed the industrial town as a refuge from the peonage of tenant farming, accounted for 43 percent of Birmingham's population. It was easily four times as big as Cartersville, the town that Dolphus left behind.

Dolphus found work as a carpenter and settled his family in an integrated residential neighborhood, away from any riotous living. He joined Tabernacle Baptist Church, founded only a year or two before, on the north side of the city. He prayed in that small, white wooden church alongside other black migrants as he found his bearings and his family continued to grow. In March 1888, he and his wife, Alice, had their fourth child, Fannie. Dolphus welcomed his new daughter and embraced his newly adopted city, where he would never have to pick cotton again. Birmingham had its rough patches, but it offered him the freedom to advance in his chosen profession. It was also a place where blacks still treasured their voting rights, though that would soon change. In the 1880s, about 45 percent of the city's registered voters were African American. (That figure would begin to plummet the year that Fannie was born, when white officials began moving to eliminate the influence of African Americans at the polls.) Dolphus would go home to Georgia, at times, to visit his mother and siblings. He would journey to other cities during his lifetime. But the people who knew him say that once he stepped onto the streets of Birmingham, he never considered living anywhere else. He had found the place where he wanted to be.

His wife, Alice, had a harder time. She arrived in Birmingham pregnant and with three young children who ranged in age from three to six. When her baby was born, she found herself tending to a wailing infant in a rowdy city full of strangers. The couple had been married for about eight years and the relationship was starting to fray from the strain. Dolphus was handsome and hardworking and his eyes began to wander, even as he settled into his career of building cabinets, minister's pulpits, and the like. Dolphus was a man of God, but he was a man first. It may be that he married Alice out of a sense of obligation to his mother and to hers. Maybe the stress of adapting to city life, after spending their formative years in the countryside, ate away at their connection, too. Maybe he and Alice simply fell out of love, or were never in love in the first place. Whatever it was, they just couldn't hang on. Sometime around 1893—about thirteen years after they were married and about five years after they arrived in Birmingham—Dolphus and Alice split up. He was about thirty-three years old and she was about twenty-seven when they went their separate ways. He found a one-story wooden house with a shingled roof in a predominantly white neighborhood where he lived as a boarder, across the street from the city's first synagogue. She found work as a cook and a place to live not far away. By October of that year, Alice was forced to accept that she had given up everything—her life in Georgia with her parents, her brothers, and her sisters—for a man who had moved on.

Dolphus, never one to be on his own for long, found another female companion. She was Alabama-born and about thirteen years his junior. They wed on October 31, 1893. Dolphus never forgot the children from his first marriage; he remained a presence in their lives for as long as he lived. But the children continued to live with Alice, who moved from place to place as she sought work and struggled to raise them. Alice and Dolphus had arrived in Birmingham together, convinced that they could build a better life as a couple. Once separated, however, it became clear that they were headed in vastly different directions. As Alice battled to stay afloat, Dolphus prospered and continued his steady climb into the working class. His hard work paid off. By 1900, Dolphus had managed to buy his own home in an integrated, middle-class neighborhood. It was a singular achievement. While nearly half of all whites in the nation owned property that year, only about 20 percent of blacks did. Dolphus had become the first person in his family to own the four walls around him. He and his second wife had white neighbors on both sides: one worked as a salesman, the other as a landlord. It wasn't unusual at the time to find blacks and whites, middle class and working class, living side by side in Birmingham. "The city tax collector lived on the same block with a railroad flagman, a black gardener, a civil engineer, and a carpenter," wrote Paul Worthman, who has studied class mobility during this period. Yet Dolphus managed to stand apart from his black neighbors. He would never be a member of Birmingham's college-educated black elite, but he had achieved a standard of living that remained painfully out of reach for most African Americans and many white Americans, too, for that matter.

Alice, on the other hand, was still having a tough time of it, living on her own as a single mother. None of the families on her street could afford to buy their own homes and neither could she. She moved at least three times in the seven years after she and Dolphus divorced, trying her hand at various jobs. One year, she worked as a cook. Another, she washed clothes. In 1900, she was making dresses as a seamstress. The children she had with Dolphus also helped out. Willie, seventeen, was a carpenter like his dad. Pearl, sixteen, cleaned houses. Robert Lee, fifteen, worked as a day laborer. Fannie, thirteen, was the only one in school that year. Thankfully, Alice could turn to her mother, Mariah, for some support. Mariah, who was so close to Dolphus's mother, Melvinia, had moved to Birmingham from

Cartersville, Georgia. She helped care for Alice's children, which was a consolation. But it didn't change the bitter reality: at thirty-five, Alice was alone. She would never remarry. She must have envisioned a more magical existence when she and Dolphus first moved to big-city Birmingham, the life of a proud, married woman who could sing alongside her husband in church, who could laugh and gossip with him over supper, who could count on him to instill discipline in their children, and who would never have to worry about making ends meet. It is impossible to know how Alice coped with her estrangement from Dolphus or how she felt as she watched him move up and on without her. But there are hints that she did all she could to erase him out of existence. In 1900, when the census enumerator asked if she was married, the answer he got spoke volumes: he was told that she was a widow.

Dreams and ambition drove dogged African American men like Dolphus to cities like Birmingham where they embraced urban rhythms. But life didn't stop in the countryside. People slowly reshaped their lives, adjusting to the absences. Some sobbed or cursed. Others cheered their brothers, sons, and daughters who had moved. But they all carried on. Dolphus's family certainly did. There were no roaring steel mills, no bustling downtowns, no streetcars clattering along Main Street in the tiny towns that dotted the Georgia up-country. There, residents savored the spring rains that blanketed the earth in lush green tendrils, endured the blazing summers that left sharecroppers wilting in the merciless heat, and suffered through the winters that chilled the bones and hardened the soil. The local economy was still driven by cotton, as it was during slavery, with planting time in April, after the final freeze, weeding after that, and then picking time in September. Melvinia, Dolphus's mother, certainly picked cotton as a young woman, and she may well have picked cotton as a middle-aged woman, too, as she strained to care for her extended family without her oldest son. But somewhere along the way she shifted, too, turning her focus from the agricultural seasons of the earth to the ebb and flow of human life.

Melvinia moved with her remaining children to Kingston, Georgia, a speck of a railroad town about thirty miles from Cartersville, sometime after Dolphus headed to Birmingham in 1888. It was there that she started working as a midwife, bringing newborn babies into the world and tending to their exhausted mothers. Only about five hundred people lived in Kingston, and Melvinia rented a house that was surrounded by farms owned by white families. White women came knocking at her door, too. When a woman's birthing time came, everyone knew where to find Melvinia. She was sitting on her porch or in her backyard, chewing tobacco and praying to Jesus as she rocked in her chair. She had sure, careful hands that could coax reluctant infants out of the womb. And when the call came, Melvinia would leave home for two or three days and move in with the expectant mother. She would tend to the pregnant woman, deliver the wailing baby, and get both mother and child settled. Then she would return to her porch and her Bible until the next call came. "There wasn't no hospitals," explained Harold Wise Sr., who grew up in Kingston and lived down the street from Melvinia during her later years. His parents reached out to her when he was about to be born. Melvinia "midwifed me," he said. "Back then, when I knowed her, she was about the only one that was doing that." Melvinia had a sweet way with newborns, but she also had a sharp tongue—and a switch—that could send rambunctious neighborhood children scrambling on their heels. "She kept a switch all the time," said Mr. Wise, recalling how Melvinia would stand at the ready for any rowdy children who ventured into her yard. "You can't go out there fighting and cussing. You go in there hollering and crying and you're gonna get one."

In 1900, when Melvinia was in her fifties, delivering babies was one way she could keep food on the table in a house packed with children and grandchildren. She was a single mother without a man to lean on, though historical records suggest that she might not have always been on her own. She had long been known as Melvinia Shields, a surname she took from her white owner after slavery. (Her friends called her Mattie.) But by the time she arrived in Kingston, she had a new surname, McGruder. A census taker was told that year that she was a widow. But Mr. Wise and Ruth Wheeler Applin, who also knew Melvinia, said they never heard any talk of her having had a husband.

Mr. Wise and Mrs. Applin knew her sons, Henry and Dolphus, who came to visit sometimes from Birmingham. But they never knew the identity of their father. (They didn't even know if the two brothers had the same father.) What they knew was what was clear to everyone: Melvinia was very dark in color and her sons were very light. "Henry was light and Dolphus was light," Mr. Wise said. "Their mother wasn't light; she was dark skinned. She wasn't no black woman, but she was dark skinned." Mrs. Applin, who later married Melvinia's grandson and lived with her for a time, suspected that Melvinia, a former slave, might have been raped by her white owner during slavery days. "The master," Mrs. Applin said, "that's what I believe." But that wouldn't explain how Henry was conceived; he was born nearly two decades after slavery ended. Was Melvinia still involved with a white man she knew before the Civil War? Or had she met someone new? "Didn't nobody come to see her," Mrs. Applin said. Some thought that Henry, who had straight black hair, might have had some Indian blood in him, Mrs. Applin said. Harold Wise suspected that the two brothers had a father who was white or very light skinned. Mr. Wise was young at the time, though, and steered clear of sensitive questions. But Henry and his brother certainly stood out, he said. There simply weren't many other people in the black community who were as light skinned as they were. "You could tell he wasn't white," Mr. Wise said of Henry, the brother he knew best, "but he looked close to white."

White ancestry often conferred benefits on lighter-skinned African Americans, and Dolphus's path in life certainly might have been smoother because of it. But Henry, who was about eighteen in 1900, had few of his older brother's advantages. Dolphus could read and write, had a trade, and owned his own home. Henry was an illiterate tenant farmer who rented his land, probably from a white neighbor. (Some of Dolphus's descendants suspect that his white father taught him carpentry, the skill that would help him climb.) But those were not the only differences between the two brothers. Henry felt bound by the powerful pull of family obligations in a way that Dolphus clearly did not. While other family members moved to bigger cities in the South and, later on, in the North, Henry stayed put. He was devoted to Melvinia and never strayed far from her side. But he learned quickly that he had to tread carefully to survive in rural Georgia.

As Melvinia delivered babies and Henry worked the land, efforts to marginalize blacks picked up steam across Georgia. In 1900, the state's Democratic Party restricted its primaries to whites. Blacks could still participate in general elections, but their votes were virtually meaningless in the one-party, Democratic-controlled state. In 1908, Henry and other blacks were effectively barred from the ballot box altogether when whites amended the state constitution to require voters to pass a literacy test and own property. (Melvinia and other women, of course, did not have the right to vote under any circumstances.) Under the amendment, voters had to be able to read the federal or state constitutions and to explain any paragraph in either document. They also had to own forty acres of land or property valued at $500. It meant, for all practical purposes, the demise of the franchise for blacks for decades. Meanwhile, closer to home for Henry and Melvinia, the Ku Klux Klan had become increasingly active, and prominent white citizens promoted racial violence. Cartersville, where Henry was born and Melvinia lived for several years, was home to two of the region's most passionate supporters of lynching: Rebecca Felton, the first woman to serve in the United States Senate; and Charles Henry Smith, a local newspaper columnist. Mrs. Felton defended lynching as the only sure way to protect a white woman's virtue. "If it takes lynching to protect women's dearest possession from drunken, ravening beasts, then I say lynch a thousand a week," Mrs. Felton said. Mr. Smith, the newspaper columnist, didn't mince words either. "Lynch 'em! Hang 'em! Shoot 'em! Burn 'em!" he wrote in 1899.

Five years later, a mob in Cartersville, which sits about nine miles from Kingston, lynched a black man accused of attacking a young white woman. His name was John Jones and, like many black men in the community, he worked on the railroad. The woman, Mrs. Oscar Banister, said a black man broke into her home on the evening of July 1, 1904, and choked her until she fainted. She said her attacker fled the scene, and white men across the region mounted a manhunt. Georgia's governor offered a reward to anyone who could catch the man. Mr. Jones was arrested in a nearby county and driven to the jail in Cartersville, where a mob of more than a hundred white men awaited his arrival. The men seized Mr. Jones and took him to a nearby hill where they debated whether to burn him, hang him, or shoot him. Most agreed on burning, so they tied him to a tree, piled some wood around him, poured oil on him, and set the wood ablaze. The men quickly extinguished the fire, though, apparently hoping to trick Mr. Jones into giving a confession. Newspaper accounts in the local white-owned newspaper at the time described his answers as evasive. Then the young Mrs. Banister, mother of three, who was apparently present to witness the killing, asked the men to shoot Mr. Jones. He was hung in chains from an oak tree before the men raised their rifles. The *Cartersville News and Courant* vividly described what happened next. "With coolness and care, the men ranged themselves on one side in line, and at a given signal fires in to the negro's body, which was finally pierced by over five hundred bullets from Winchesters, pistols, and shotguns," the newspaper reported. "The shooting began at 6 o'clock. The crowd was extremely orderly, no oaths being sworn or indications of whiskey drinking being visible in the talk or actions of the men."

Melvinia and other members of her family and social circle may have known Mr. Jones because the black population in surrounding Bartow County was so small. In any case, news of the public killing would have spread like wildfire through both the black and white communities in the area. Did Melvinia warn Henry to keep his head down and avoid confrontations with the white families who lived around them? Did she urge her son to avoid white women at all costs? Mr. Wise and Mrs. Applin suggested that the family hunkered down and focused on day-to-day survival and quiet advancement, casting off any hopes of actually participating in the electoral system that had closed its doors to them. As Melvinia approached her seventies, responsibility for the extended family shifted from mother to son. In 1910, Henry celebrated his twenty-eighth birthday. By then, he was a married man who had learned to read and write and had become the principal breadwinner of a household that included his wife, Ida; his mother; and a fourteen-year-old nephew. The family still lived in a rural stretch of Kingston, but its complexion had changed: the neighborhood, composed almost entirely of sharecroppers, was nearly all black. In that community, Henry became known as something of a jack-of-all-trades: he farmed on rented land, and he found work as a porter on the railroad, a solid, stable job in those days.

But bad luck seemed to trail Henry, who never came close to matching the success of his big brother, Dolphus, either in love or in work. Henry's first wife, Ida, died young. His second wife ran off with another man. He would never have children of his own. In 1918, when Henry registered for the draft, he described his mother, Melvinia, not his wife, as his nearest relative. Nearly five months later, one of his sisters, who had been working as a washerwoman, died in the influenza epidemic of 1919, leaving her children in the care of Henry and Melvinia. Suddenly, there were more mouths to feed. Tragedy struck again on April 13, 1925, when one of Henry's nephews was shot to death in Atlanta in a fight over a woman. Henry had been close to the young man and traveled to Atlanta to sign the death certificate and make funeral arrangements. It must have been an agonizing ordeal. Henry had dedicated himself to supporting and nurturing his young nieces and nephews.

In death, however, his nephew repaid that debt. The young man had life insurance and the proceeds went to Henry. Henry could have spent that money on women, on fine clothes. He could have used it as a down payment for one of those newfangled automobiles or for a ticket to a new life in the big city. But that was not his way. Three months after the killing, Henry took the cash and bought a house on Shaw Street in Kingston for $125 and moved his extended family into it. It was a simple place without running water or electricity, but it was a home of their own. The property remains in the family today.

Henry cared for his extended family in every way that he could. He was Melvinia's loyal companion and a loving and protective guardian for his niece and nephew. But when his big brother, Dolphus, came to town—with food and gifts for everyone—none of that seemed to matter. Dolphus was wealthier and more established. He was a man of God with a formal position in the church. He was a charmer who captivated women and the proud patriarch of a large family. He lived in faraway Birmingham, but his intangible bigger-than-life presence still filled the little house on Shaw Street. Henry couldn't measure up and he couldn't escape his brother's shadow. Over time, a wedge grew between the two men. "They didn't speak," Mr. Wise said of the two brothers. "I don't know what they fell out about, but they fell out and stayed out."

FOURTEEN

Neither Black nor White

I N THE SOUTH, IN THE LATE NINETEENTH CENTURY, THERE
was little room for swashbuckling black men, for adventurers
who brashly challenged the system and won. Klansmen and
vigilante mobs made sure of that. African Americans with fiery incli-
nations often ended up broken, imprisoned, or dead. Yet these men
existed, though many had to move north to stay alive. Phoebe, who
loved the stories of the daring frontiersmen of the Wild West, knew
such a man when she was growing up in Villa Ridge, Illinois. The
shackles of slavery couldn't hold him. He knew how to fire a rifle and,
when it counted, he fought the white southerners who threatened his
liberty. He was a wanderer, who traveled to at least five states in his
lifetime. And even at the age of forty-nine, with his most vigorous
years behind him, he still had the shimmering aura of the hero about
him. On December 26, 1887, when Phoebe's family was teetering on
the brink of calamity, he swooped in and saved them. He took them
in and became the man Phoebe knew best as a father. It is hard to
imagine that anyone was surprised.

His name was Jerry Suter, though he was better known as Sergeant during his fighting days. He had dark eyes, dark hair, and skin
the color of yellow corn. He was a wiry man who stood about five

foot nine, and in his later years he was as lean as a post. Phoebe's children knew him as Peg-Leg Suter because he had lost one of his legs in battle, or so the story goes. In fact, there is no truth to that tale. Medical records show that Mr. Suter lived to a fine old age—with both legs intact. But he was the kind of man who inspired fanciful imaginings. A mythology bloomed about him, and outlandish yarns about his exploits passed from one person to the next. He didn't actually need the fancy embellishments. His life story was remarkable enough in its own right. Born in Alabama, he had escaped from slavery, had fought against the Confederacy during the Civil War in a unit that was recognized for its bravery by some of the most powerful men in the Union Army. He had soaked up a world far beyond the farm where he had been held as a slave, traveling from Tennessee to Mississippi to Louisiana, before he settled in Villa Ridge, Illinois.

Phoebe would chose to flee the green hills and black soil of Villa Ridge for the opportunities and adventures of urban living. But many former slaves like Jerry and Phoebe's mother, Mary Moten, cherished the slow-paced, rural community in Pulaski County, Illinois. It was a place, they believed, where African Americans could prosper. By 1870, Jerry was already making his mark. He could not read or write, but he was one of only two black landowners in Villa Ridge, with a farm valued at $400. (Jerry was even more prosperous than some white men in the community, including his neighbor, who was a landless, white sharecropper.) By 1880, about a third of the county's residents were black migrants from former slave states, and nearly half of them had managed to save enough money to buy their own plots of land. Some enterprising African Americans were opening small grocery stores and barbershops. "The people are thrifty, energetic and intelligent, and are rapidly growing wealthy," one writer observed of the settlers in Villa Ridge in the early 1880s.

It was in Villa Ridge that Jerry caught his first glimpse of Mary Moten, who was Mrs. Obama's great-great-grandmother. He was married by then, with seven children, and Mary was married, too.

But something about Mary intrigued him. Photographs that have survived from the late nineteenth century suggest that she had a complex racial lineage. She had light eyes, a hooked nose, and a thin line of a mouth. Her raven-black hair spilled over her shoulders and down her back and she often twisted it up in a bun when her daughter Phoebe wasn't brushing it. In one photograph, Mary wears a high-necked bodice that laces up in the front and a hoop skirt that flares at her waist. Her long hair is swept up in a knot on top of her head. In a close-up photograph, Mary stares, unsmilingly, straight into the camera with heavy-lidded eyes, her hair pulled back. There is little hint of any African ancestry in these old photographs. Mary was born in Missouri, sometime around 1835, and her descendants believe that she had Native American bloodlines, that she was Cherokee or part Cherokee. It is also possible that she had European ancestry.

Jerry had multiracial roots, too; he was classified as mulatto in the census and in military records. In 1880, he lived only a few doors away from Mary, who was living with her husband, Nelson Moten, and their children. Jerry was close enough to wave whenever he passed by on his way to town and to stop and linger on warm, spring afternoons. He knew that, despite their best efforts, Mary and Nelson were struggling. Nelson, who was born in Kentucky, never managed to buy any land, or escape the sharecropping life, and his family and their troubles multiplied as he and his wife approached middle age. Mary had four children living at home in 1879 when she became pregnant again around the age of forty-five. Phoebe was born in December of that year. Mary, who was illiterate, did the best she could: She sent her oldest children to segregated schools where they learned to read. She sent Phoebe, too, once she was old enough. And she and her husband eked out a living on the land in a county where most black tenant farmers and sharecroppers grew corn and wheat and raised pigs, chickens, and at least one milk cow.

Hope, however, was not strong enough to sustain them. Nelson, Mary's companion for more than twenty years, was in his fifties when he died sometime between 1880 and 1887, leaving Mary adrift, a single mother with five children. Jerry was a widower by then, too, and a man of some standing in the black community in Villa Ridge. Sometime after her husband was buried, her neighbor came calling. When he proposed to Mary, he had been a landowner for nearly two decades. No one knows whether Mary fell in love with his adventurous spirit or whether she was simply trying to find a way to provide for her children. Undeniably, Jerry could offer her a degree of financial security she had never known. By the winter of 1887, Mary had made up her mind. On the day after Christmas of that year, she and Jerry stood before a minister and exchanged wedding vows. Mary was about fifty-two and he was about forty-nine when their two sprawling families became one. Jerry's children, who ranged in age from eighteen to seven, became as close as siblings to Mary's children. And Jerry became the father figure that Phoebe would remember best. He could be a demanding patriarch, and as soon as his stepchildren were old enough, he put them to work on his farm, alongside his own children, insisting that they all rise each morning before the sun crept up from the horizon. Phoebe hated that farm work. But as an adult, she reminisced much more about Jerry than about Nelson, her biological father who died when she was about seven. That should come as no surprise. Jerry, a prosperous and storied Civil War veteran, had rescued the family from hardship. Maybe Phoebe viewed him with starry eyes, too.

But her fondness for Jerry wasn't enough to keep Phoebe in Villa Ridge. When her mother, Mary, died sometime between 1887 and 1900, Phoebe set out to see the world. In the end, nearly all of the children went: Phoebe to Chicago, her sisters to points north in Illinois; and Jerry's children to Chicago, St. Louis, and Detroit. Jerry, a widower once again, stayed put, and he didn't remain single for long. He was about sixty-five when he married for a third time in 1903 to a woman who was fifteen years his junior. He was no longer the daring young man who fought the Confederates so many decades earlier. His eyes were weak and watery. His knees and joints ached. He could no longer work, and his rich store of memories was beginning to fade. In

1906, a doctor who examined him ticked off a laundry list of ailments, including "rheumatism, disease of the heart, neuralgia and general and senile debility."

Soon afterward, the federal government awarded Jerry a monthly pension in recognition of his military service. Over the next fourteen years, his health would continue its slow and steady decline. By the time he died, on May 28, 1920, around the age of eighty-two, many of his exploits and adventures had been forgotten. (He might not have been able to remember them himself. His cause of death was listed as "senile debility.") Jerry's will, though, offered a hint of how he had prospered over the years—by dint of hard work and sheer force of will. At the time of his death, Jerry owned seventy acres of land. Known as a man with full pockets, he had provided loans to several people in the community, in amounts ranging from $13.50 to $300. He was buried at Henderson Cemetery with a fine headstone, befitting his station. (One suspects, however, that Jerry would have raged against the wording on that headstone. He is described there with his former slave owner's surname, Sutton, which he had discarded more than fifty years earlier, linking him in perpetuity to the white man who once held him in bondage.)

BY THE TIME that Jerry died, the government was only a decade away from abandoning its efforts to track people of mixed race. Jerry, who was often described as mulatto in the 1800s, was simply described as black in the last census in which he appeared. Like Mary, Mrs. Obama's great-great-grandmother, Jerry seemed deeply integrated in the African American community in Villa Ridge. There is no indication that the couple tried to distance themselves from their darker neighbors. There are signs, however, that their heritage did hold some meaning to them. Mary made sure that her daughter, Phoebe, never forgot about her multiracial background; and Phoebe, who married two men who had mixed bloodlines, carried the fragments of that knowledge with her to Chicago. As for Jerry, all three of his wives had multiracial ancestry just like he did, suggesting that it counted for something with him.

IN THE LATTER PART of the nineteenth century, many former slaves and their children did not fit neatly into the racial categories of black or white. "Mulatto" forebears pop up all across Mrs. Obama's family tree, on her mother's side and her father's side, in Illinois and Louisiana, Virginia and North Carolina. Some seem to have regarded their multiracial ancestry with a sense of shame, seeing it as proof of an agonizing history, even though their light skin and straight hair sometimes opened doors. Others viewed their white or Native American heritage as little more than a family footnote, a passing curiosity. (None of the First Lady's ancestors were wealthy or very educated. Most struggled to make ends meet and to provide the basics—food, shelter, and education—for their children, leaving little time for abstract, existential musings about identity and race.) And then there were those who appear to have embraced a multiracial identity; it defined who they were, who they married, who they chose as neighbors, and how they viewed themselves. While Mary and her family were struggling to make their way in Illinois, Mrs. Obama's maternal great-grandfather in Virginia was wrestling with the quandaries that often confronted people at a time when white officials accepted a vision of race that encompassed much more than black and white.

On June 10, 1880, in Henry County, Virginia, a rural community of rushing creeks and lush tobacco farms nestled in the fertile foothills of the Blue Ridge Mountains, a census taker arrived at the home of an illiterate black sharecropper and his family. He sized up one of the children, James Jumper, who was about seven, and then jotted down the boy's racial classification: mulatto. It was immediately apparent that young Jim was a member of the nation's sizable mixed-race population, a group of 1.1 million people that was formally recognized at the time by government statisticians. Some whites called them tawny or yellow or red and took note of their wavy or woolly hair, their full lips, or their fine features. For decades, the Census Bureau took pains to identify and quantify them and sent out enumerators to determine who was who. By 1890, the bureau had developed mathematical formulations to more precisely measure the drops of black blood. There were the octoroons: people who were one-eighth black or who had "any trace of black blood." There were the quadroons: people who were one-quarter black. And then there was the broadest category, the mulattoes, who had "from three-eighths to five-eighths black blood."

Decades later, Jim's daughter, Rebecca, who moved from this rural corner of the South to Chicago, was described by enumerators as Negro or black, a racial designation that has followed her descendants ever since. In Virginia, her father occupied a different racial space, one that was more ambiguous, complicated. Jim probably paid very little attention to the label. He was just a little boy in the countryside where children spent their time running barefoot through green fields, not pondering their multiracial roots. The racial designation of mulatto was nothing new to the Jumpers, who had lived and worked in the tobacco fields of southern Virginia for nearly a century. But as an adult, everyone knew, Jim would not be able to escape the question that had long confronted his clan: Which community will you choose? Will you align yourself with blacks? Or will you stick with your own kind?

In Henry County, everyone was intimately aware of the agonizing choices being made. Some African Americans, who were fair skinned and fine featured, had decided to live as whites. Others kept to themselves, socializing and intermarrying with other members of their community. Jim came from a long line of Jumpers who had done just that. His parents, Peter and Eliza Jumper, were both classified as mulatto, as were his paternal grandparents years before. For at least two generations, the Jumpers had chosen their mates from within that tightly knit circle. But there were hints early on that Jim might decide on a different path.

To this day, no one knows exactly how Jim's family acquired its multiracial ancestry. The Jumpers tread lightly through the 1800s. Almost completely illiterate until the early twentieth century, they left no letters or diaries. There are no written records that describe their origins or indicate how they viewed themselves through the shifting prism of race. But if identity is largely an internal construct determined, in part, by genetics, family traditions, and community customs, it is also shaped by personal circumstances. Jim was still a child when his mother died, a tragedy that would alter the course of his life. His mother, Eliza, had married into the Jumper clan in 1870 when she was about twenty years old. She and her husband, Peter, had four children, one after another. Peter worked in the fields to keep food on the table. Eliza, who cared for their two boys and two girls, was the glue that held everything together. But the young woman did not live long enough to celebrate her fortieth birthday. The family splintered after she was gone. By 1880, Peter had parceled off his two oldest children—Jim and Alice—to the middle-aged couple who had raised Eliza. Their names were Esau and Amy Wade and they were black. They would care for Jim, immersing him in southern Virginia's black community.

In some southern cities—like Charleston, New Orleans, Savannah—black people with visibly identifiable white roots took pains to separate themselves from darker African Americans. (Phoebe witnessed this decades later in early-twentieth-century Chicago, but the practice had its origins in the South.) They formed their own clubs, attended their own churches, and intermarried to maintain their bloodlines and to prevent their progeny's complexions from getting too dark. It was no surprise, then, that tensions between light and dark, wealthy and poor, sometimes sizzled. After Emancipation, Rev. Henry M. Turner lamented that in his church "the blacks were arrayed against the brown or mulattoes, and the mulattoes in turn against the blacks." Descended from wealthy white planters, who sometimes provided them with schooling, training, and other privileges, people with mixed ancestry often had more education and more skills than blacks. Whites often treated mulattoes better than blacks, too, offering them better jobs and better pay. Fair skin and straight or wavy hair were idealized in urban communities, both as powerful symbols of beauty and refinement as well as predictors of success and achievement. Uniquely positioned among African Americans to ascend to public office after the Civil War, mixed-race officeholders outnumbered their darker counterparts during Reconstruction. Among them was P. B. S. Pinchback, the son of a black slave and her white owner, who became the nation's first African American governor, albeit for thirty-five days. (He ran the state of Louisiana.) His father, like the Jumpers, was born in Virginia. Fair skinned and bearded, Mr. Pinchback carried himself with such an aristocratic bearing that whites sometimes stopped twice when they saw him. In the streets of New Orleans, one white policeman demanded, "Are you a white man, or what are you?"

The Jumpers and other families like them in Henry County, Virginia, often intermarried, so they may well have placed a premium on their lighter complexions, too. But they differed considerably from their urban counterparts. They were poor and illiterate, not members of the prosperous, educated mulatto elite. They were sharecroppers who tilled borrowed land, not skilled city craftsmen who owned their own homes or farms. The class gap between darker and lighter blacks was much narrower in the rural countryside of the upper South than it was in the big cities of Georgia, Alabama, and Louisiana. In his new home, under the guidance of his black guardians, Jim became intimately acquainted with the African American community in a way that he might not have otherwise. Esau Wade, a former slave who was like a grandfather to Jim, worked for white families after Emancipation and never managed to buy his own land. But slowly, steadily, he acquired the accoutrements of modest success. Over the years, Esau managed to buy a cow, a gun, and assorted household and kitchen furniture. In the fields, he grew bushels and bushels of the county's cash crop, tobacco, until he acquired a stash worth $2,100, a veritable fortune at the time. Esau appears to have lost his fortune somehow, but he and his wife, Amy, still opened their home to Jim and his sister, Alice, and cared for the siblings.

Somewhere along the way, Jim met a young black woman named Eliza Tinsley, who lived on a farm in another corner of the county. She was the daughter of an illiterate sharecropper, an ambitious former slave, who would buy his own property one day. They started thinking about spending their lives together. The potential match, however, would have inevitably attracted dubious glances from the more conservative families of Henry County. There was no mistaking Eliza for one of the community's fair-skinned girls: she was dark enough in complexion that she was never described as mulatto in the census. In some families, her dark skin alone would have been reason enough to try to snuff out her blossoming relationship with Jim. But there is no calculus to love, no formula for romance, no way to precisely measure the influence that Jim's middle-aged guardians may have had on his heart. He saw something special in Eliza and he set out to win her. When he was around the age of twenty-one, he broke with tradition and became the first man in his father's family to choose a black bride. On August 5, 1896, Jim stood alongside his eighteen-year-old betrothed and pledged his love to her. With their marriage, Jim decisively cast his lot with the African American families in Henry County.

By 1900, Jim and Eliza had three children and were living in a farming community inhabited by blacks and whites. Jim, twenty-five and illiterate, was renting a house and working as a farm laborer. But all around him, friends and relatives were packing up and trying their luck in Rockingham County, North Carolina, just across the border with Virginia. Tobacco factories, sawmills, and cotton mills had sprouted there, offering jobs and steady wages to hardworking men eager to leave the fields. A clattering railroad carried the hopeful migrants to the new land of opportunity. Eliza's grandfather moved first. Then Jim's father. Then Eliza's father. Finally, sometime between 1900 and 1909, Jim and Eliza decided to join them. They moved to the town of Leaksville, North Carolina, where the population of 1,000 had nearly doubled since 1900. The couple had a brood of six children—five daughters and one son—by 1909, with another on the way. Eliza gave birth in the spring of that year to a baby girl. They named her Rebecca and, in many ways, she represented the new life that Jim and Eliza had chosen for their family. Rebecca was born on April 5 in a small North Carolina city, not on a farm in Virginia like the rest of her siblings. She grew up on a bustling street filled mostly with laundresses and workers at the local cotton mill; there were only a handful of sharecroppers. Both of her parents had finally learned how to read, and her mother could even write a little. Life in town was far from easy: Jim and Eliza had seven children to feed. Jim found employment as a laborer, and his wife worked as a washer-woman at home; their oldest children, barely in their teens, had to get jobs, too. But despite the hardships, it was clear that success could be had in Rockingham County. Black entrepreneurs were thriving. G. W. McCain and G. M. Miller had opened a grocery store and stocked its shelves with spices, teas, smoked meats, cigars, and canned merchandise. A. Broadnax clipped hair in his barbershop, which he dubbed the "Big Six Shaving Parlor," where he offered, according to a local newspaper, "the most approved sanitary methods in the service." E. M. Townes founded a mutual insurance company and blacks could buy policies to help cover costs in the event of deaths or illnesses.

It wasn't long before the up-and-coming community attracted the attention of one of the nation's most prominent black men. In 1910, Booker T. Washington, the president of Tuskegee Institute, decided to visit Rockingham County during a train tour of North Carolina towns. Like Jim, Mr. Washington was a man of mixed race who iden-tified with ordinary African Americans, regardless of skin tone. (Mr. Washington joined forces with his rival, W. E. B. DuBois, the promi-nent black intellectual who also had mixed ancestry, to help persuade the Census Bureau to drop the mulatto category, in part because it threatened racial solidarity. By 1930, the category had been officially abandoned.) When Mr. Washington arrived in the county on Oc-tober 31, 1910, he was met "by practically the entire colored pop-ulation," a local newspaper reported. Schoolchildren tossed flowers along his path. So many people poured into a local warehouse to hear

Mr. Washington speak—prominent white citizens included—that the crowd "taxed the capacity" of the space. Mr. Washington urged blacks in the county to work hard, to save money, and to build their own homes. He also urged them to stay in the South, as opposed to moving north. "The South is the best place for the Negro," Mr. Washington said, according to the Reidsville newspaper.

His message of self-sufficiency and economic uplift might well have resonated with Jim, who was thirty-five at the time and still straining to push his family up the economic ladder. Many African Americans, though, were already dismissing Mr. Washington's call to stay in the South. Jim's half brother, Julius, was one of the first in the Jumper clan to leave North Carolina. Julius headed to West Virginia—often a first stop on the journey north—and decided to try his hand in the coal mines there. Jim and his wife, Eliza, never got the chance to venture northward. Within a few years, the two were dead, perhaps from the devastating influenza epidemic that tore through the region. Jim and Eliza's surviving children scattered to the winds, and the Jumper clan, who had lived in the Virginia countryside for generations, faded from memory.

FIFTEEN

The Reckoning

D EATHS, SEPARATIONS, AND HARD TIMES SHATTERED
many families into fragments that could not be stitched
back whole. Some women took their troubles to the government during those first decades of freedom, filing hundreds of pleas
for help with wayward husbands who ran off with lovers or refused
to support their children. Other families disintegrated more quietly.
Fraser Jr., the First Lady's grandfather, remembered his father as a big
man, a powerful patriarch who painstakingly climbed the segregated
ladder of success in South Carolina and carried his family up with
him. But in the 1880s and 1890s, his father was just a scared little boy
who watched helplessly as his family splintered right before his eyes.

Born on March 24, 1884, Fraser Robinson Sr. grew up in the lush
land of sea and swamp on South Carolina's Atlantic coast. He spoke
his first words in rural Georgetown County, where the salty ocean
breeze blended with the sweet scent of honeysuckle and magnolia and
the dark, placid rivers teemed with trout and carp. In the summer-
time, in the sweltering, malarial heat, emerald green rice fields swayed
for thousands of acres, as far as the eye could see. Cotton was king in
Georgia, where Dolphus and Henry were born. In South Carolina,
the cash crop was rice.

Fraser's parents, Jim and Louiser Robinson, were former slaves who labored on Georgetown's vast rice plantations during slavery and who probably worked as sharecroppers in the rice fields afterward. Louiser, who lived long enough to taste freedom, died before she turned forty, before her son turned ten. Soon, the young, motherless boy was struggling to find his way during turbulent times in a tumultuous family. His father remarried after Louiser's death, and he and his siblings were trying to adjust to life with a new, harsh stepmother. One fateful day, the young boy ventured into the woods to collect firewood and a small tree fell on him, breaking his left arm and leaving a gaping wound. He ran home to tell his family, but his stepmother dismissed the injury and he did not receive proper care. Her negligence came with a terrible cost. The wound got infected and Fraser's arm had to be amputated. Just ten years old, he was marked for the rest of his life.

Everyone around him knew that the boy was having a difficult time at home, but there was no bevy of aunts, cousins, or grandparents nearby to intervene. Instead, a helping hand came from the most unexpected corner. A white man who had grown fond of the one-armed boy took Fraser under his wing. The man, Frances "Frank" Nesmith, who had known Fraser's father, Jim Robinson, moved the boy out of his troubled home in the countryside and into the city. It was an act of kindness that Fraser's relatives would never forget. At a time when the Klan was terrorizing black communities across the South and racial animosity was on the rise, that act of charity might have seemed particularly singular. But blacks and whites had developed a history of working together in Georgetown, a sort of partnership that set the county apart from others in South Carolina. In northern parts of the state, where blacks were in the minority, white men cloaked in sheets were riding in the night, lynching, beating, and shooting African Americans, determined to strip them of their newfound rights. But Fraser was growing up in an overwhelmingly black community where African Americans were determined to hold on to the rights they had gained during Reconstruction.

After the Civil War, newly freed slaves in Georgetown had flexed their political muscles and elected the nation's first African American to serve in Congress, Joseph Hayne Rainey, a barber who was born and raised in Georgetown. Mr. Rainey sat in the House of Representatives for four and a half terms, from 1870 to 1879, becoming a passionate advocate for the men and women who had emerged from bondage. And his hometown remained something of a political oasis, even as whites began methodically rolling back advances by blacks in other parts of South Carolina.

Georgetown, where blacks accounted for 82 percent of the population, settled on a political compromise in 1879, just five years before Fraser Sr.'s birth. The strategy, known as fusion, allowed the Republicans (who were almost entirely black) and Democrats (who were all white) to share offices in local elections. Each party nominated their slate of candidates and the other party agreed not to oppose them. The Democrats picked the sheriff, clerk of court, two county commissioners, and one state representative, and the Republicans selected the state senator, one representative, the probate judge, the school commissioner, and one county commissioner. All the Republican positions were held by African Americans, save for one, and the fusion plan worked successfully for nearly two decades. Growing up, Fraser would have known that black men from Georgetown sat in the state legislature. He would have seen black men in town serving as postmaster and probate judge. As an adult, Fraser would raise a son who would become deeply suspicious, even fearful, of whites, both in the South and in his adopted city of Chicago. Descendants suspect that these traits in the son were instilled by the father. But during Fraser's early years, many African Americans in Georgetown felt cautiously optimistic about race relations.

Fraser's white benefactor, Frank Nesmith, taught him firsthand about kindness across the color line. Nesmith was not a rich man by any stretch of the imagination, nor was he known as an advocate for equal rights for African Americans. In 1900, he was working as a train conductor to support his family. Fraser had to work for his keep, serving as a "house boy." Frank Nesmith had been out of work for two months and couldn't afford to buy any property of his own. He rented the house that he shared with his wife and two daughters. But he still made room for Fraser, making sure that he was clothed and fed and treated him well. "He said he would take good care of him and he did," according to Fraser's niece, Carrie Nelson. "Uncle Fraser and that man's children grew up together."

The Nesmiths were not wealthy, but they were literate and that left a strong impression on Fraser. While he worked in the house, he watched the family's oldest daughter attend school and tend to her lessons. "They pushed their kids hard into education and one day Uncle Fraser would, too, because that's what he learned from them," said Mrs. Nelson, Fraser Sr.'s niece. But over time, Fraser learned some painful lessons about the limitations imposed on a young black man in navigating the white world. The Nesmiths' benevolence only went so far. The illiteracy rate among blacks was declining as growing numbers managed to get educated. Yet it does not appear that the Nesmiths sent Fraser Sr. to school. They might not have been able to afford it. Perhaps they thought it unsuitable or unnecessary for a black teenager who would probably make a living as an unskilled laborer. Whatever the reason, the effect was plain. At sixteen, Fraser could not read or write. And while he worked tirelessly to improve his condition—he would ultimately learn to read and may well have been taught by the Nesmith children—powerful whites in South Carolina were equally determined to prevent blacks from advancing, politically or economically. By 1900, South Carolina's white-controlled legislature had disenfranchised tens of thousands of black voters across the state. One hundred thousand African Americans who would have been allowed to vote under South Carolina's 1868 state constitution were now effectively barred from doing so.

Georgetown, with its black majority and political cooperation across the color line, was one of the few remaining islands of opportunity in the state where blacks could still use the power of the ballot box to press for change. In 1900, more than half the registered voters in the city were black. But the political consensus that kept the peace between blacks and whites in Georgetown was about to abruptly, and violently, collapse.

The gunshots rang out at Washington's barbershop on Front Street on Saturday, September 29, 1900. When the blasts stopped, John Brownfield, a black barber, had a gun in his hands. A white deputy sheriff who had stormed into Mr. Brownfield's shop to arrest him for failing to pay his poll tax, was fatally wounded, shot in the scuffle with his own gun. He would die several hours later. Mr. Brownfield, twenty-two, who could read and write and was registered to vote, dashed out the back door of his shop. A black policeman quickly caught him and placed him in the three-story brick building that served as the local jail. Mr. Brownfield was too well known by blacks and whites in the small community to escape. The next day, several armed whites decided to lynch the black barber. Word spread through the African American community—George Herriott, a black school commissioner who happened to be one of Fraser's neighbors, was one of the many informed—and African Americans quickly took to the streets.

By that evening, hundreds of black demonstrators—as many as a thousand or more, according to local newspaper accounts—had gathered in front of the county jail, shouting, "Save John!" and "Free John!" Some carried pitchforks and rakes. Others carried firearms. Women marched, too, with hoes and rice hooks. The demonstrators threatened "to burn down the town" if the barber were hurt. Only about four thousand people lived in the city at the time so the protesters probably accounted for most of Georgetown's black adults. It was an astonishing scene—many whites viewed it as a menacing one—in a town where there had been little racial violence and few racial confrontations since Reconstruction. But the number of lynchings and murders had been soaring across the rest of the state. In 1880, a black man was lynched in nearby Clarendon County. In 1882, six more were lynched. In 1889, a mob stormed a county jail in Barnwell County, near the Georgia line, and murdered eight black prisoners. By 1890, South Carolina had three times as many murders as did all the New England states combined. Whites were responsible for the largest share of the killings. Many African Americans in Georgetown feared that their barber would be next.

Fraser was young and impressionable at the time. When he heard the news, did he rush outside to watch the protesters, stunned by the sight? Did he join the demonstrators, marching and chanting, as he walked through the streets? Did he know the barber? Had he sat in his chair? Fraser may well have felt torn by his strong sympathy for the barber and his anxiety about the precariousness of his own personal situation. The Nesmiths, like many whites at the time, may have felt threatened by the unexpected protest. It is possible that Fraser felt safest staying quietly at home, keeping his opinions to himself. He could hardly have been unaware of the protest and its aftermath, which dominated the local newspapers and galvanized the entire community. His own church, Bethel AME, took up a collection and hired two black lawyers to represent the barber. No one knows for sure what Fraser made of the tumult; he didn't live long enough to describe that day to his great-grandchildren. If he talked about it with his children, they kept it to themselves, choosing not to pass it on to their own sons and daughters. Fraser's family had no idea that he had lived through such an epochal, turbulent moment in their city's history. In fact, even though many of Fraser's great-grandchildren were born and raised in Georgetown, they never knew that the episode had even taken place. And yet his descendants have long suspected that he experienced something that scarred him, like the sapling that broke his arm, a trauma that he would bequeath to his own children. That would account for his son's, Fraser Jr.'s, warnings about white people, for his fierce passion for voting, and for the way he tried to steer clear of confrontations or even social interactions with whites. "He never spoke of things like that, but something must have happened," said Nomenee Robinson of his father and grandfather. "Something to him or his dad."

The history books tell the story: Officials, both black and white, tried to calm the black protesters and urged them to go home. But the next day, the protest resumed and the white mayor decided to take action, calling the governor and asking him to send four companies of soldiers to put down the unrest. The governor agreed and the soldiers headed to Georgetown. On Tuesday, October 2, nearly three hundred armed troops marched through the streets to show "that the white man was in the saddle." With the black protests suppressed, white officials charged and tried six black women and three black men—including the barber—who were described as ringleaders. They were convicted and ordered to pay fines or serve on the chain gangs. Mr. Brownfield, the barber, was indicted by an all-white jury on the charge of capital murder and was ultimately sentenced to death. His legal appeals went all the way up to the state Supreme Court, but they were denied. He escaped the hangman's noose only because he committed suicide in jail.

The shooting, demonstration, and its aftermath fundamentally changed life for Fraser and other African Americans in Georgetown. One year later, some of the town's most prominent residents formed a "White Supremacy Club" in an effort to crush the electoral power of the county's black majority and to prevent any similar showing of force again. "There is a general feeling in our community that the time has come for a change in our political condition, and that the interests of all our people will be best looked after by installing white men of known respectability and intelligence in all public offices," wrote Josiah Doar, the editor of the *Times*. Mr. Doar, who also served as secretary of the White Supremacy Club, dismissed the power-sharing agreement between blacks and whites that had governed political life in Georgetown for more than two decades, deeming it outdated. "A 'compromise' was good in its day and time, when it was necessary to divide the offices, but we have outgrown this method—'expanded,' as it were, from infancy to full grown manhood—and this method of settling our political disputes will no longer obtain," Mr. Doar continued. "No harm is meant to the colored man, and no harm shall come to him; but times change, and men change with them, and Georgetown is no exception to this rule."

Employing intimidation, literacy tests, and strict enforcement of the poll tax requirements, whites in Georgetown succeeded in forcing most blacks off the voter rolls. On January 1, 1902, the *Times* reported that of 523 registered voters in the city, only 110 were black. For the first time since Reconstruction, more whites than blacks were registered to vote in Georgetown. That year, whites won every seat in the municipal elections. The white minority continued to control local politics, and to prevent blacks from participating, for decades. The United States Supreme Court had legitimized the marginalization of African Americans in its *Plessy v. Ferguson* decision, which affirmed "separate but equal" as the law of the land in 1896. Bolstered by the ruling, states like South Carolina began to enact measures at the turn of the century that would disenfranchise African Americans for generations. After 1902, only voters could serve on juries, which meant that blacks standing trial almost never faced a jury of their peers. In 1904, the state's trolleys were segregated by law. In 1915, the state's textile mills were segregated by law. If you were a black man "you could walk through a town like that in the early 1900s and get angry every 15 minutes, especially if you were an achiever," said Nomenee Robinson, Fraser Sr.'s grandson, who has tried to imagine what effect this kind of life might have had on his grandfather and father. "All the doors were basically closed to you."

The whites in power made it clear that there was no future for ambitious black men in Georgetown. Whether he marched or not in that protest, Fraser Sr. probably learned a powerful lesson in that first year of the new century. There was no room in his hometown for black men and women who openly challenged white authority or demanded the right to vote or participate in the political system. Fraser had to find another way if he wanted to survive and advance. W. E. B. DuBois, the African American scholar, might have been speaking about Georgetown and the men of Fraser Sr.'s generation when he reflected on the disillusionment that followed Emancipation and the collapse of Reconstruction: "The slave went free; stood a brief moment in the sun; then moved back again toward slavery."

SIXTEEN

Birmingham, the Magic City

THE STOMPING, CLAPPING, PRAISE-SINGING CONGREGA-
tions poured into the wooden pews on Sunday church mornings. They shouted to Jesus and called to the heavens with
sweet spirituals and jubilee songs that spilled like drenching, healing waters on the overburdened shoulders of Birmingham's new black
settlers. In fledgling churches around the city, deacons like Dolphus
Shields helped lead the newcomers in prayer, shepherding their cries
to the Lord. The crowds parted respectfully before the dark-suited,
dignified men. Yet even as Dolphus led his congregation in cherished
hymns—songs like "I Love the Lord and He Heard My Cry"—he
began to feel a restlessness he could not shake. He wanted something
more than his church, Tabernacle Baptist, could offer. Fourteen years
after he moved to Birmingham from Georgia, Dolphus was a proud
homeowner, a skilled carpenter, a respected man of God, and the father of a growing family. But he was no longer satisfied serving in
someone else's church. He wanted to help create his own.

Somehow, Dolphus became acquainted with the Reverend F. R.
Kennedy, a bespectacled minister who was born a slave in Alabama
and painstakingly taught himself to read and write after Emancipation. The two men were kindred spirits. Mr. Kennedy had a vision:

he could see a brand-new church rising from the green, open land in northern Birmingham, and he had the financial means to make it happen. Mr. Kennedy bought a house near the railroad tracks and gathered together a group of four like-minded men, including Dolphus. Together, in 1902, they created Trinity Baptist Church. So many people flocked in when they opened the doors to their small wooden church that the founders soon decided that the modest structure wouldn't do. They rebuilt it, brick by brick, stone by stone, until the new church climbed from its foundations. It was one of the first brick buildings in the neighborhood, and over the years, worshippers there took such pains to beautify the structure that even outsiders stopped to stare. "The people of Smithfield are proud to see the progress of work on Trinity Baptist Church," the *Birmingham Voice of the People* newspaper reported.

Dolphus became one of Trinity's first elected officers, and it would not be the only church he would help nurture. Over his long life he helped found another congregation in Birmingham. Both of those churches still exist, leaving his indelible fingerprints on the city's religious landscape. Dolphus was inextricably linked to the feverish explosion of church building within the African American community in the early twentieth century. The flowering black religious movement would create a powerful incubator for leadership, an engine that would launch the civil rights movement, and, after that, the careers of countless black politicians. Dolphus would not live to witness that, but he could see the expanding role of the church in Birmingham. Between 1900 and 1920, the number of black churches listed in Birmingham's city directories soared from 28 to 115, as migrants poured into the city, seeking comfort, solace, and guidance in an increasingly hostile racial climate.

Dolphus himself turned to his spiritual adviser, Rev. Kennedy, when his second wife died, sometime between 1900 and 1902. Before long, the minister was officiating at Dolphus's third wedding, on June 11, 1902. Dolphus was in his early forties then, and Rev. Kennedy might have believed that with fervent prayer, and the grace of a forgiving God, this latest marriage might hold. Dolphus was a proud, devout man, but in his personal life, his faith and his earthy nature often seemed to wage war over his soul. His intense focus on religious principles seemed to drift when it came to the raw, heated questions of love and marriage. Dolphus left his first wife, Alice, for his second wife, consigning Alice to a life of poverty with their children. Even after his third marriage, Dolphus was still a good-looking man who could draw admiring glances from the women around him. He could charm the ladies on the streets of Birmingham and the gray-haired elders at Trinity with equal ease. But if Dolphus found it difficult to stick to one woman, he certainly resolved to remain loyal to the Baptist church. It was the one institution in Birmingham where a motivated black man was allowed to lead. In churches like Trinity and Tabernacle, Dolphus and other African Americans created sanctuaries where they could worship, socialize, and take on supervisory roles that were becoming impossible to find in a city where racial dividing lines were hardening and, in the process, marginalizing the swelling black population.

Dolphus was fair skinned and literate, a skilled craftsman who owned his own home. In African American circles at the turn of the century, he stood apart from the masses of miners and factory workers as an early member of the emerging middle class, which also included other small businessmen and ministers, as well as teachers and lawyers. Many of those up-and-coming African Americans were drawn to churches like Trinity, which had literate ministers and more educated congregations. "These were churches that were conscious of color, conscious of education, conscious of home-ownership versus non ownership," said Wilson Fallin Jr., a history professor at the University of Montevallo, who has studied the black church in Birmingham. Members of these churches also included poor and working-class families, but the men who led them in prayer were "strivers for social status," Mr. Fallin said. Strivers like Dolphus found a measure of dignity and respect in the black church. He wore his carpenter's apron at work, but always donned his finest suit on Sundays. Whites in Birmingham might refer to Dolphus as "boy" or "uncle," but inside those church doors at Trinity he was always "Brother Dolphus" or "Deacon Shields."

In the fall of 1901, white Democrats campaigned for a new state constitution with a slogan that made their intentions crystal clear: "White Supremacy, Honest Elections and the New Constitution, One and Inseparable." The constitution, which was approved by voters that year, stripped civic power from a third of the city's black population. It instituted residency restrictions, literacy requirements, the poll tax, and property qualifications and barred citizens from voting if they had been convicted of one of a long list of crimes, many of which (like vagrancy) were frequently charged against blacks. Meanwhile, white officials had also begun to take steps to eliminate integrated neighborhoods, like the one where Dolphus lived, and to wipe out the few spaces in the city where blacks and whites intermingled.

In 1902, while Dolphus was helping to form Trinity Baptist Church, city officials were barring whites and blacks from mixing in waiting rooms at railroad stations. (Separate rooms were provided for each group.) That same year the city jail was segregated. Some whites were so determined to separate themselves from blacks that a white prisoner protested when he was scheduled to be hanged on the gallows alongside a black man. He demanded a new time and a different set of gallows. The city accommodated him. In 1903, the city began to restrict blacks' access to public parks. Within a few years, the only African Americans who were allowed into the parks were servants accompanied by their white employers. Anyone else had to petition the white-controlled city commission for permission to stroll within Birmingham's urban greeneries.

As the web of segregation widened, some African Americans began to protest. In 1905, the *Birmingham Wide-Awake* newspaper urged blacks to challenge segregation on the city's streetcars. "We advise Afro-Americans in every section of the south where an attempt is made to separate the races on the street cars to boycott the street railways," the newspaper editorialized. "We advise the people never to get on a street car where the color line is drawn." But African Americans in Birmingham, including Dolphus, relied on the streetcars to get to and from work. They had few other options, so the boycott didn't materialize.

The period also marked a tumultuous time in Dolphus's life. By 1906, he was standing with a new bride before yet another minister. His third marriage had come to an end; his wife had either died or moved on. Now he was looking for divine blessings for a fourth wedding. On April 1, 1906, Dolphus pledged his love and loyalty to wife number four: Mrs. Lucy Ellis, a thirty-six-year-old widow. People who knew Dolphus, who was about forty-six at the time, might have looked with some pity on his new bride, particularly given the groom's marital history. But something was different this time. Maybe it was Dolphus's age. This time, the marriage held. Maybe he needed someone to help raise the young children he had with his second wife, who had died. Or maybe it was something about Lucy, a brown-skinned woman with long hair from South Carolina with a well-deserved reputation for being a master in the kitchen. Her specialties were mouthwatering, homemade biscuits, ham, and fried chicken, dishes that the guests at her table still remember today.

Lucy didn't have any children of her own. So she looked after Dolphus's brood, at least the three children he had with his second wife. In 1910, they were all living under one roof in a little house that Dolphus had bought at 854 Lomb Avenue. It sat in a stable, working-class black neighborhood where most families owned their own homes. It had two stories, a tin roof, and a porch with a swing. There were three bedrooms upstairs, simple pinewood floors throughout, and an outhouse out back. In the kitchen, Lucy cooked and heated her irons on an old wood-burning stove that Dolphus kept fiery hot with the wood he chopped outside. Lucy washed her clothes out back, too, with a scrub board and a big black barrel full of soapy water.

At the end of the day or on sleepy Sunday afternoons, the couple would while away the time out front. Lucy tended the beautiful flowers that bloomed in pots along the steps leading up to the porch. And Dolphus would rock in his rocking chair, greeting his neighbors and watching the world go by. Over the years, Dolphus made improvements to his home. He installed a toilet and got rid of the outhouse. He bought a bathtub, too, so that he could soak in comfort instead of washing with a bucket. By the time his great-grandchildren from up north started visiting, the house had electricity and running water.

Some things, however, Dolphus was powerless to fix. In 1900, he had lived in an integrated neighborhood on a predominantly white block. By 1910, those neighborhoods had been mostly wiped out of existence by white officials anxious about the city's surging black population. Dolphus would never live side by side with whites again. Indeed, by 1919, any African American who dared to move into a white neighborhood could be arrested and charged with a crime. A city ordinance declared it to be "a misdemeanor for a member of the colored area to move into . . . or having moved into, to continue to reside in, an area in the city of Birmingham generally and historically recognized at the time as an area for occupancy by members of the white race."

Dolphus did not stop striving, though. By 1911, he had opened his own business, a carpentry shop at 302 N. Fifteenth where he worked with one of his sons, in a downtown area that catered to both blacks and whites. He hung up a sign, D.T. SHIELDS & SON. From inside, he could watch his world closing in around him. It was a harsh period, a time when Dolphus might have turned inward, finding comfort in his new business, his religious life, and his family. He could certainly look with pride at his twenty-four-year-old son, Robert Lee, who was thriving. Robert Lee, one of at least four children Dolphus had with his first wife, Alice, had found work as a Pullman porter, a stable, middle-class perch for many of Mrs. Obama's ancestors. Robert Lee's wife, Annie, was working at home as a dressmaker. Both could read and write and seemed poised for progress. He must have dreamed of watching his children climb even higher than he could. But he would never have the chance.

Between 1911 and 1920, Dolphus would witness the deaths of four of his children. All across the country, the deaths of young children from illnesses like pneumonia, polio, flu, and other diseases were agonizingly common. But Dolphus's children were older. He might have breathed easy, believing they had escaped that fate. But in Birmingham, African Americans young and old suffered from high mortality rates caused in part by unsanitary conditions and a tainted water supply. Tuberculosis alone killed blacks at a rate that was five times higher than that of whites. One study conducted in Birmingham in 1912 described the housing that most blacks lived in as "nests of infection." Even a businessman and homeowner on the rise like Dolphus was not immune. In 1911, two of his sons from his second marriage died within two months of each other. Influenza killed Sylvester, age eighteen, Dolphus's partner in the carpentry business. Pneumonia and consumption struck down Charlie, who was about thirteen.

Two years later, in 1913, Dolphus would grieve the death of a daughter, Fannie, whom he had with his first wife, Alice. It was a devastating blow for Dolphus, who was about fifty-three at the time. But it may have been even harder on Fannie's mother. Alice was a hopeful young bride when she left Georgia with Dolphus, ready for a new, more prosperous life in Birmingham. But after Dolphus left her, she seemed to lose her footing, moving from place to place with her children, finding work here and there, as a seamstress, a washerwoman, and a maid. She was in her forties and clearly struggling to find much work. Someone in the family told a census taker that she had been unemployed for the previous twelve months. Alice, who had never remarried, only had her children, and having to watch her daughter, Fannie, die must have been unbearable. Alice had moved once again and was living at a new address on Sixteenth Street South when she fell ill with tuberculosis herself. She died on April 26, 1915, just a few weeks after the second anniversary of the death of her daughter. Alice's death certificate, which described her in stark, simple terms as "a Negro domestic," gave little hint of the heartbreak and hardship that had characterized her journey to the big city. It is less distressing to think that she may have been surrounded by her surviving children in the end. Robert Lee might have stood at her bedside, giving her comfort in the knowledge that he was climbing steadily into a stable, promising world that had remained out of her reach. But Alice was afflicted with a highly infectious disease, and doctors could have insisted that she remain isolated as much as possible. She may well have died alone.

Within a span of two years, Robert Lee had lost his mother and his little sister. But he couldn't let his grief consume him. He still had a wife and six-year-old daughter, and the couple had also welcomed a son, Purnell, to their family, who was now four. Robert Lee had to think about the future, and about moving on. And increasingly for black people, that often meant saying good-bye to Birmingham. A black man could find a living wage up north, it was said. Blacks could vote and send their children to better schools. As a Pullman porter on the railroad, Robert Lee could have already seen those northern cities up close. He might have even walked the streets of Chicago and talked to his wife, Annie, about moving there someday. But he never made it. Sometime between 1917 and 1920, Robert Lee died. How and when remains a mystery. His older sister, Pearl, told her descendants about his death, but never described the circumstances. "Mama did tell me that she had a brother and her brother died," recalled Jewell, who was Pearl's granddaughter.

Dolphus, who was in his late fifties at the time, might have wondered how much more he would have to endure. He had lost four of his children within the span of a decade. Some men might have raged and wept, shaking their fists at God. But in the end, Dolphus clung tighter to his faith, to his religion. He did not embrace the notion of a warm, forgiving God who would turn a blind eye to the shortcomings of man. The man with the wandering eye, who had abandoned his first wife for another woman, increasingly espoused a harsh view toward those who bucked God's will. In Dolphus's view, the world was full of sin and willful sinners. Punishment for those who turned from God could be severe. "You don't do right, you're going to hell," said Bobbie Holt, describing his thinking on the subject. (Bobbie was about two years old when Dolphus and Lucy took her in. She was sickly and her mother could not afford to care for her.) To steer clear of temptation, Dolphus embraced a life of austerity: There was no dancing, no listening to jazz or blues on the radio, which was strictly reserved for hymns. There was no smoking, no drinking, no gum chewing, no cursing, no whistling, no comic book reading, and no moviegoing. "That was the devil's work," Mrs. Holt remembered him saying. She learned to expect a spanking if she failed to follow the rules. But Lucy was the one who usually set Bobbie straight. Despite his tough talk, Dolphus couldn't bear to witness any spankings. He always had a soft spot for the little girl. (Jewell, Dolphus's great-granddaughter, also fell afoul of those strict rules when she was young, during one of her summer visits to Birmingham. "I turned the radio on one time and I was dancing," she recalled. "And he said, 'Turn that radio off. You don't dance in my house.' I was so used to dancing with my mother and father, my brother and sister, jitterbug, you know." But she quickly learned that was a no-no in her great-grandfather's house.)

Dolphus had long been religious. He became a deacon as a young man. He was a founder of Trinity Baptist. It is tempting, though, to speculate that he adopted a more stern and austere religious vision after the deaths of his children. Perhaps he wanted to get right with God to stop the relentless hammering from the heavens. Unfortunately, the death of Robert Lee did not end the heartache. In the 1920s, as Dolphus entered his sixties, he watched his family splinter as the younger generation abandoned Birmingham. Pearl, his daughter, moved to Cleveland. Annie, his daughter-in-law and Robert Lee's widow, and his grandson, Purnell, were destined for Chicago. Over time, the Birmingham, Chicago, and Cleveland branches of the family fell out of touch. The distance between them spanned hundreds of miles. Purnell became an old man without ever talking much, if at all, about Dolphus. The only tangible bit of evidence of that forgotten life in Birmingham was the old black-and-white photo of Purnell's grandfather. The two men were long gone by the time it would resurface.

SEVENTEEN

Two Brothers, Two Destinies

T HERE WAS NO EASY WAY TO BE A MAN IN KINGSTON, Georgia, in the 1920s and 1930s if you were black. The writer Claude McKay had called on African Americans to stand up and confront their white attackers in the riots that exploded across the country after World War I. "Like men we'll face the murderous, cowardly pack; pressed to the wall, dying, but fighting back!" he thundered in his famous poem, "If We Must Die." But Mr. McKay lived much of his life up north. In the South, so many black men were hung from trees that Billie Holiday sang of it in her haunting number "Strange Fruit": "Black bodies swinging in the Southern breeze, strange fruit hanging from the poplar trees." For Henry Shields, Dolphus's younger brother, surviving in the South meant forgoing the traditional notions of self-respect. It meant stepping down into the street whenever a white man approached on the sidewalk. It meant never looking a white man in the eye and never questioning his authority. It meant being called boy and accepting it, no matter how much the bile boiled in your throat, no matter how much the blood burned in your cheeks. Henry was his family's principal breadwinner, a loving son and uncle, a protective guardian. He longed to be respected and revered in his community, but he lived in a part of the country where manhood was hard to come by. Even in his own home, where he yearned to play the role of family patriarch, he never measured up to his big brother. Henry's wife ran off with another man. He struggled to find work. And as he approached middle age, it seemed that the blows came hard and steady, one after another, especially when the Depression settled in. "You know, of course, there wasn't no jobs then," said Ruth Wheeler Applin, who married Henry's nephew, Emory, and moved into the family's home on Shaw Street. "We didn't have much to go on."

The house that Henry had bought had only three rooms, she recalled, two bedrooms and the kitchen. There was no running water, no electricity. They walked to get water from a well, about half a mile away, and chopped firewood for the stove and to warm the house in the chilly winter months. They still had white neighbors in 1930, including the family next door whose father worked at a grocery store. They were friendly, on the whole, Mrs. Applin recalled. But the pleasant smiles and polite waves sometimes felt like a brittle, shiny veneer that barely concealed the racial discord boiling below the surface. These were still tense times between blacks and whites. That year, another black man was lynched in nearby Cartersville. His name was John William Clark and he was accused of fatally shooting the city's police chief when the officer tried to intervene in a fight between Mr. Clark and Mr. Clark's brother. On September 1, 1930, shortly after midnight, a mob of about fifty white men showed up at the jail where Mr. Clark was being held. Ten men walked into the jail, overpowered the three sheriff's deputies on duty, and put Mr. Clark in the backseat of one of their cars. They hanged him from a telephone pole. The authorities discovered his body around dawn, but they left it there for most of the morning. Hundreds of people came to see the corpse and to photograph themselves alongside the dangling black man. At least one of those photos was made into a postcard that was sold door-to-door in nearby Cartersville. Local authorities defended the mob, saying it was the only way to guarantee justice. They pointed out that Mr. Clark's trial had been delayed by his lawyer's appeal for a change of venue. County Commissioner Arthur Neal said in a statement that the appeal "so incensed our people that I believe I am safe in saying the action of the men who took the negro from the jail is not only condoned, but has met with practically unanimous approval."

In this racially charged environment, the little house on Shaw Street might have felt something like a precious refuge, but it was a crowded one. The house was valued at $450 in 1930, but there was barely enough room for the extended family to breathe. They all squeezed in somehow: Henry and his mother, Melvinia; Henry's niece, Lola; his nephew, Emory; and Emory's wife, Ruth Applin, and their newborn baby boy. Some of Melvinia's other grandchildren also lived with them at times. "Me and Lola and Grandmom slept in one room and the others slept in the other," said Mrs. Applin, who called Melvinia Grandmom. "It was a pretty tough time," she said. Emory didn't have a job and neither did his sister, Lola, who picked cotton in the fields when there was work, which wasn't often. Mrs. Applin had her hands full with her baby. And by the time Mrs. Applin moved in, Melvinia was in her nineties; her days as a midwife were long past. So Henry did his best to carry the load. He was employed as a porter on the railroad, but it was irregular work. He would get laid off for a time and then pick some cotton or corn to bring in food and money. Government relief supplemented what Henry brought home, and his extended family also grew their own food. Emory planted cabbage and corn in the garden and tended the family's hogs and chickens. He would later follow in his uncle Henry's footsteps and get a job on the railroad, but that was after the Depression, when times got better. In the meantime, Henry tried to keep the family afloat, but he had no savings and more bills than he could afford to pay. He was barely keeping above water. "Uncle Henry didn't have nothing," Mrs. Applin said matter-of-factly.

Everyone looked forward to Dolphus's visits from Birmingham. Dolphus was the son who had left home and made it, the one with the trade, the one who owned his own business and a two-story house. Mrs. Applin doesn't remember how he got to Kingston, but he didn't drive so he may well have taken the train. "I'd say about every three months" he would visit, usually with his wife, Lucy, recalled Mrs. Applin. "I don't know what he did, but when he would come he would bring all kinds of food," she said. "He'd load up on food, he'd send them money or clothes or whatever. He was good." Most people in the community knew about Henry's prosperous brother in Birmingham, even if they didn't know him well. "I think he must have been doing pretty good down there," Harold Wise Sr., the family's neighbor, said admiringly.

Melvinia was particularly pleased with her oldest son's success, Mrs. Applin said. "Real proud," she recalled. "Real proud." Henry, though, felt differently. Neither Mr. Wise nor Mrs. Applin can remember now why the two brothers fell out, but it is easy to see why they might have rubbed each other the wrong way. Henry liked to play cards, Mr. Wise recalled, a pastime that Dolphus certainly would have frowned upon as sinful. Henry also wasn't the kind of man you'd run across praying in the pews every Sunday morning. "He'd go, but not regular," said Mr. Wise. The brothers feuded while their mother, Melvinia, grew frail. When Mrs. Applin first moved into the house on Shaw Street in 1935, Melvinia was clear of mind and could easily get around. "She helped us around the house," Mrs. Applin recalled. "She would wash and help cook and tend to the babies. I had my first baby when I was sixteen. She helped with my baby. She'd help wash and then she'd make soap and patch clothes, sew a button on a shirt, or she'd iron."

Mrs. Applin still remembers Melvinia in her glasses hovering over a big, old steaming pot atop a wood-burning fire in the backyard as she boiled old meat, grease, and lye to make handmade soap for the family. Inside, Melvinia shucked corn on the cob to make hominy. And then she would relax with her Bible and one of Mrs. Applin's babies. "She'd get out on that porch, and we had an old porch, she'd get on that porch and just have a Bible in her rocking chair and she'd sit on that porch and she'd rock and hold that baby," Mrs. Applin said. "She was a good babysitter." But within a few years, Melvinia grew weak and her mind began to wander. "She got kind of feeble," Mrs. Applin said. Melvinia started thinking about her own mortality and began planning for her funeral. She talked to her son Dolphus about the coffin she wanted to be buried in. She had a white blouse and a green skirt that she wanted to wear in the grave. She kept the outfit in an old trunk. She wanted to be ready. Soon Melvinia began confusing the people around her with people from her past, relatives she knew. Sometimes, Mrs. Applin said, it was hard to understand what she was saying. Her speech became garbled, unintelligible. "She would be talking that gibberish talk," Mrs. Applin said. "I don't know what she was saying. When you get that old, you're like a little baby."

Melvinia started having fainting spells, too, what Mrs. Applin called "old age spells." On June 4, 1938, Melvinia had another one of those fainting spells in the little house on Shaw Street. It was a Saturday afternoon when Melvinia closed her eyes. The usually crowded house was pretty much empty except for Mrs. Applin. This time, Melvinia didn't wake up. "She was in my arms," Mrs. Applin said. "She died in my arms." The doctor established the time of death at 5:00 P.M. that day. Her death certificate described her as Mattie McGruder, a black domestic who had lived for nearly a century. (To this day, no one knows where she came by that surname.) As for the cause of death, the doctor simply wrote: "Senility." Melvinia's son Henry, who rushed back to the house when he heard the news, gave the medical authorities the bits and pieces of biographic information that he had about his mother. He didn't know much. He said that she was born in Henry County, Georgia, which wasn't true. He said she was "approximately 100 years old," when she was probably closer to ninety-four. And he seems to have had no idea who her parents were or where they came from. In the space available on the death certificate for mother's name and father's name, someone simply wrote "Don't Know." Mrs. Applin says that she knew Melvinia had probably been a slave. At that time, there were still many old people around who had been born into servitude. But Melvinia, who witnessed countless births—some of the most intimate experiences of life—rarely talked about the birth and origins of her own family. Mrs. Applin, who was a teenager when she first met Melvinia, said she was too young to think much about those things. Then again, in those times, very few were willing to discuss it. When asked why Melvinia might have kept so quiet about this formative period in her life, Mrs. Applin shook her head. Maybe she had a reason for staying silent about the father of her sons. Maybe what happened was just too difficult to talk about. "You know," Mrs. Applin said, "she might not have wanted nobody to know."

Dolphus, who was about seventy-eight years old by then, sent the coffin down from Alabama on the train. It arrived at Kingston station on Sunday, June 5, the day after Melvinia died. But Dolphus wasn't aboard the train. Melvinia's oldest son had not shown up for his mother's funeral. The resentment and bitterness that simmered between the two brothers—Dolphus and Henry—finally burst into public view on the very day the family laid Melvinia to rest. "Him and his brother, they hadn't spoke in a good while," Mrs. Applin said of Dolphus and Henry. "I was young then. I didn't understand why." Mrs. Applin said she learned later that the brothers had battled over the arrangements for their mother's funeral. Henry wanted Melvinia's coffin to be carried from the church on a wagon pulled by a horse. Dolphus thought their mother deserved something nicer, a hearse, a gleaming black car that would carry Melvinia to her final resting place. Henry probably couldn't have afforded that kind of luxury in the midst of the Depression, tasked as he was with the support of so many members of his family who were out of work. Mrs. Applin didn't hear the conversation between the two brothers, but one can easily imagine Henry seething with anger at Dolphus's suggestion. There was Dolphus, yet again lording his prosperity over him, trying to micromanage the extended family that he only managed to visit a few times a year, trying to overrule Henry who was the one who had supported Melvinia day after day, year after year, during hard times. Dolphus—on the other hand—might well have argued that his little brother was stubborn and selfish and putting his pride before what was best for their mother.

Mrs. Applin doesn't know what words went between them. What she knows is what happened. Dolphus stayed home in Birmingham, but he paid for the funeral. The service was held at Queen Chapel, the historic black church where Melvinia had prayed. And though he didn't see his mother lowered into the ground, Dolphus surely felt some satisfaction knowing how she got to the cemetery: in a hearse. Mr. Wise can still remember Melvinia's funeral, the prayers at the green, grassy cemetery that flanks Queen Chapel, and her coffin descending into the earth. No one put a marker on the spot. Dolphus was more successful than his little brother, but he was still a working-class man whose dollars could only stretch so far. He couldn't afford to buy a headstone to mark his mother's grave. But his family believes he may have tried to honor his mother in another way. The coffin that Melvinia was buried in was made of wood. It's nice to think that Dolphus, the carpenter, built that casket, carefully, lovingly, with his own hands.

As for Henry, no one remembers him crying over his mother. No one remembers him mourning. Whatever he felt—the public humiliation at the hands of his brother, the overwhelming grief at his mother's death—he absorbed it quietly. He was in this fifties when he stood beside Melvinia's coffin, a lonely man who never remarried. That might have been around when he started drinking. He was discreet, of course. He had too much respect for his family to shame them in any way. But once Henry started drinking, he found it hard to stop. Even in a brutally unfair and circumscribed world, people make their own choices. They pick one path or another and live with the consequences. There are opportunities missed and mistakes made. There are those who seem destined to achieve and those whose failures seem preordained. In the 1940s, while Dolphus was celebrated for his successes, Henry was viewed by the people who knew him, even those who loved him most, as a man who never achieved much of anything. Henry chose to stay put. He chose to support his extended family, to be the broad shoulder his mother could lean on. It must have been unbearable for Henry to watch his brother—the man who left Georgia to follow his own dreams—become the man in the family who was most revered.

In 1943, Henry carefully typed up a one-page will and testament. He had no children and owned no property, but he was determined to leave what little he had to the niece and nephew he had raised as his own. He bequeathed to them "all the money I have if any, my Barber chair and tool" and he asked to be buried "in a Christian like manner." Henry died two years later, on November 10, 1945, around the age of sixty-three. The medical authorities described him as a widower and railroad porter, the son of Mattie McGruder; father, unknown. He was buried at Kingston Cemetery, near his beloved mother. No one today can speak to Henry's private torments and anguishes. But the spare prose on his death certificate hinted at a life of struggle and disappointment. Under cause of death, the doctor in his slanting script wrote simply: "Cirrhosis of the liver, possible alcoholism." His big brother, whom he had not spoken to for years, did not attend his funeral.

A shoe repair shop in Chicago run by James Preston Johnson. *Courtesy of Johnny D. Johnson*

James Preston Johnson, the paternal great-grandfather of Michelle Obama. He was among the first of Mrs. Obama's ancestors to move to Chicago, arriving sometime around 1908. *Courtesy of Francesca Gray*

Francesca Gray, the paternal aunt of Mrs. Obama, holding a photograph of the First Lady's paternal great-grandparents, Phoebe and James Preston Johnson. *Courtesy of Rachel L. Swarns*

LEFT: Johnny D. Johnson, Mrs. Obama's paternal great-uncle, traveled the world as a missionary for the Seventh-Day Adventist Church. *Courtesy of Rachel L. Swarns*

RIGHT: Fraser Robinson Jr., Mrs. Obama's paternal grandfather, fought in Europe during World War II. *Courtesy of Francesca Gray*

Fraser Robinson Sr. and his wife, Rosella Cohen Robinson (*inset*), the paternal great-grandparents of Mrs. Obama. They lived in Georgetown, South Carolina. Washington Post/*Getty Images*

Dolphus Shields, Mrs. Obama's maternal great-great-grandfather, was born into slavery in Georgia—the son of a white father and an African American mother. He became a carpenter and well-known deacon in Birmingham, Alabama.
Courtesy of Bobbie Holt

Bobbie Holt holding a photograph of Dolphus Shields, who raised her in Birmingham, Alabama.
Damon Winter/New York Times

The Birmingham, Alabama, house of Dolphus Shields.
Birmingham, Alabama, Public Library Archives, File 29-4-1-24-18

Dolphus Shields sitting in front of his house in Birmingham
with members of his extended family. *Courtesy of Jewell Barclay*

Moses Shields, the brother of the man who owned Melvinia Shields. He grew up in Spartanburg, South Carolina
Courtesy of Greg Shields

McClellan Charles "Mack" Shields, the grandson of the man who owned Melvinia Shields, Mrs. Obama's maternal great-great-great-grandmother. He lived in Birmingham, Alabama.
Courtesy of Greg Shields

LEFT: The tombstone of Henry Wells Shields, who owned Melvinia Shields.
Courtesy of Rachel L. Swarns

RIGHT: The tombstone of Charles Marion Shields, the slave owner's son who grew up with Melvinia Shields.
Courtesy of Rachel L. Swarns

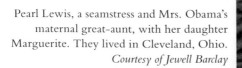

A List of Free Negros over 12 years [1856]

		Age	
1	James Jumper	40	
2	James Davis	15	
3	Joseph Davis	13	
4	John Jumper	16	
5	Raney Jumper	21	
6	~~Leathy Jumper~~	24	
7	Dolly Jumper	45	
8	Jefferson Artis	56	Blacksmith
9	Martha Artis	50	Hous Keeper
10	Benjamin Mans	65	Farmer
11	Aggy Mans	35	Hous Keeper
12	James Jumper	24	Weleving Band
13	Mary Jane Mans	13	
14	John Goin	46	Waggoner
15	Manda Goin	22	Hous Keeper
16	Peter Goin	24	Workin in Factory
17	Leticia Goin	26	Hous Keeper
18	Margret Goin	19	Sec
19	Thomas Barker	23	Farmer
20	Sargan Barker	18	
21	Nancy Jane Barker	15	
22	Elizabeth Barker	18	
23	Washington Barker	13	
24	Lucy Mans	21	
25	Mahlda Mans	43	
26	Lotty Damron	60	

Dolly Jumper, Mrs. Obama's maternal great-great-great-grandmother, appeared on a list of free blacks in Henry County, Virginia, in 1856. *Henry County, Virginia, List of Free Negroes: 1842–1860, Reel 104, Library of Virginia, Richmond, Virginia*

Pearl Lewis, a seamstress and Mrs. Obama's maternal great-aunt, with her daughter Marguerite. They lived in Cleveland, Ohio.
Courtesy of Jewell Barclay

First Lady Michelle Obama unveiling the bust of Sojourner Truth in the U.S. Capitol in 2009. *Chip Somodevilla/Getty Images News/Getty Images*

The first family in 2009 touring the Cape Coast Castle in Cape Coast, Ghana, a West African site where traders once shipped slaves to the New World. *AP Photo/Haraz N. Ghanbari*

LEFT: Jewell Barclay, the great-great-granddaughter of Melvinia Shields and Mrs. Obama's long-lost cousin, at her home in Cleveland, Ohio. *Courtesy of Rachel L. Swarns*

RIGHT: Joan Tribble, the great-great-granddaughter of the man who owned Melvinia Shields, standing outside of the Georgia Archives in Morrow, Georgia. © *Damon Wood*

Fraser Robinson and Marian Shields Robinson, Mrs. Obama's parents, with baby Michelle and her brother, Craig Robinson. *Barack Obama Campaign*

EIGHTEEN

The One-Armed Patriarch

I N THE ONLY SURVIVING PHOTO OF FRASER ROBINSON SR.,
he looks to be in the prime of his life, a prosperous man. He
lounges in a convertible with red leather seats, one hand on
the steering wheel. He wears a dark, full-length topcoat, a tie, and a
fedora, and his head is tilted back oh-so-slightly as he looks directly
at the photographer. The boy who had watched African Americans
lose most of their rights and all their political power had found a way
to maneuver in the limited space afforded to ambitious black men in
his hometown of Georgetown, South Carolina. As an illiterate teenager, Fraser had lived with the Nesmiths, the white family that had
plucked him out of his tumultuous home after his mother died. But
sometime after 1900, he set out on his own. The state's discriminatory
laws probably prevented him from voting, but he taught himself to
read and managed to save his pennies. He sold newspapers. He made
and repaired shoes. He delivered lunches in a wagon to the laborers in
the lumber mills that sprouted up in Georgetown, and he found work
there himself. He became known as a self-made man, a charismatic
force of nature who could charm anyone who heard him speak, someone who could summon his own luck and create his own possibilities,
even during hard times. But as he approached his thirties, something

was missing in his life. Luckily, somewhere along the way, he came across the young Rosella Cohen.

Rosella had high cheekbones and smooth brown skin the color of pecans. She carried the name of a prominent Jewish family, though there was no hint of white ancestry in her features or her complexion. Her precise date of birth remains unknown, but she was between five and ten years younger than Fraser, just a teenager, perhaps, when he came courting. The age difference didn't seem to matter. Neither did his disability. In many ways, the two had led parallel lives. Rosella's parents, like Fraser's, had worked as slaves on Georgetown's vast rice plantations. Like Fraser, she had moved out of her parents' home at a young age. By the time she was about ten, she was living with her older sister and her sister's family. Sometime around 1910, when Rosella was about eighteen and Fraser was about twenty-eight, the couple were married. They pledged a lifetime of devotion, and it was a promise they would keep. They had their first child on August 24, 1912, a baby boy who would bear his father's name and would ultimately migrate to Chicago as an adult and become Mrs. Obama's grandfather. But even up north, far from the rice fields of South Carolina, the son would struggle to measure up to his father. Fraser Sr. was a hard act to follow.

By the time he registered for the draft in 1918, with World War I raging in Europe, Fraser Sr. was thirty-four years old and the proud father of three children. The childhood amputation of his left arm disqualified him from serving as a soldier in the war, but it hardly kept him from moving forward. At the time, Fraser worked with the fiery kilns at Atlantic Coast Lumber Company, the huge ovens used to dry the freshly cut timber that had become the town's chief export. Some workers shoveled sawdust into the furnace to produce the hot steam that dried the wood boards. Wartime orders of shipbuilding products and other maritime materials kept those ovens burning and hundreds of people working. By the early 1920s, the company employed as many as five thousand workers. Fraser was still counting on those wages from the lumber company to support his growing family. They were living in a house on an integrated block. He counted among his neighbors a white foreman at the lumber company, a white salesman, and a white undertaker. Most whites at the time abhorred any social encounters that suggested blacks were in any way equal. It was unlikely, for instance, that Fraser was ever invited for tea in the family parlor of his white colleague from the timber mill. But Fraser had an easy way with people on both sides of the color line, and his descendants say that he got along well with whites, as well as he could during those times, and that he earned their respect.

Fraser Sr. had learned to carefully negotiate the treacherous waters of race relations in his small southern town. In public, he accepted his place and never challenged the town's whites-on-top hierarchy. (To have done otherwise, of course, would have put his family and his dreams in great peril.) The Nesmiths could have helped to smooth his path by vouching for him among their white friends and colleagues. He certainly made a name for himself with his work ethic and genial personality. His children were struck by the way he could warm up anyone with a joke, a kind word, or a compliment. "He was a charmer, very loquacious," said Francesca Gray, Fraser Sr.'s granddaughter. "He was really respected." But Fraser Sr. came of age at a time when many African Americans believed that in order to survive, they had to present one face to the white world and another at home. His amiable personality masked a much more complicated interior. Fraser Sr. inspired affection from customers, friends, and neighbors, but at home he was a demanding disciplinarian whose own children never described him as warm or loving. Many black parents at the time offered sunny smiles to their white employees while warning their children never to trust, never to let down their guard. They wanted to prepare their sons and daughters for the harshness in life, and some believed that too much affection would spoil their children, leaving them dangerously unprepared for what was yet to come.

Fraser's personal life may have only reinforced that kind of thinking. He lost his mother before he was ten years old and had a tumultuous relationship with his stepmother. After that, he was taken in by the

Nesmiths, who supported him, but probably not with the same kind of affection they shared with their own children. Fraser may never have known what it was like as a child to be hugged and kissed and comforted. Ms. Siau never met her grandfather, who died before she was born. But she grew up hearing stories about him from her mother, aunts and uncles, and people in the community. She said Fraser Sr. had a lot in common with his oldest son, Fraser Jr., who was Mrs. Obama's grandfather and Ms. Siau's uncle. "I heard that he was somewhat like Uncle Fraser, stern in his demeanor," Ms. Siau said. "He was kind of gruff. He talked with authority, commanded respect." Fraser Sr.'s descendants believe he gave his namesake his work ethic as well as his passion for the written word and for the right to vote and participate in the political system, a right that he himself was denied. But they wonder whether he also passed on some of that hardness, that habit of keeping one's children at something of a distance.

Fraser Jr. rarely hugged and kissed his sons or praised them, even when they were little boys running home to show off their good grades. Like father like son? wonders Nomenee Robinson, the son of Fraser Jr. "There's no doubt that my dad admired his father, but I often wonder, did his father represent too much of the disciplinarian, too severe a life?"

Fraser Sr.'s grandchildren know nothing about his complicated relationship with his parents and his children, his experiences with discrimination, or his family's time in bondage. But they know he found great comfort and community in his church, Bethel AME Church. Freed slaves had established the church in 1865, two years after Abraham Lincoln issued his Emancipation Proclamation. Even during the harsh years of the early twentieth century, when African Americans were systematically stripped of their rights, the church found a way to thrive. Its brick building was the first owned by blacks in the county. Its worshippers raised enough money to buy a pipe organ—the first installed in any black church there—and to hang chandeliers from the ceilings. Bethel AME served as an inspiration, a model for what was possible at a time when blacks were repeatedly told that their aspirations were out of reach. Fraser became that kind of model, too. He sold newspapers—the *Post and Courier*—on a downtown street corner and saved spare copies to bring home at night for his children to read. He read those newspapers from cover to cover, a habit that he passed on to his sons. He drummed the message into his children—faith in God and education was the key. "It was the belief that education was our salvation—education and religion," said Dorothy Taylor, who lives in Georgetown and used to watch Fraser Sr. sell his newspapers. "You've got to trust in God and learn all you can."

By 1930, Fraser Sr., forty-six, and his wife, Rosella, in her late thirties or early forties, had bought a wooden frame house on the lower end of Prince Street in a predominantly black neighborhood where they lived with their children. The house—valued at $500—abutted the railroad tracks and would remain a vital presence in the lives of their sons and daughters, who grew up there, and their grandchildren who came to visit. Those grandchildren still remember the big bathtub on the porch and the outhouse in the back. A fig tree and lemon tree stretched their branches, bedecked with fruit, toward the sun. Vines heavily laden with grapes twisted over an arbor. The Robinsons raised chickens, too, that chased and pecked unsuspecting city children in from Chicago for the summer.

"My grandmother had a garden," Ms. Siau recalled. "Collard greens, you can count on that. Okra, squash, tomatoes . . . There was lots of land. Everybody had a good little parcel of land and they (Rosella and Fraser) had more than most. I remember everything about that house. I can see it now. We would approach the house from the back. The front of the house faced the railroad, which is still in place today. There were four bedrooms in that house, a breakfast room, a kitchen, a living room, two porches, fruit trees everywhere.

"When I grew up, I realized that for the time, that was a pretty nice house," said Ms. Siau, who still treasures one of Rosella's glass pitchers. "That was a pretty big house, bigger than the one that I live in today. I think my grandfather had a lot to do with that. I don't know if he did it by hand, but it was done under his reign."

Inside the house was Rosella's domain. Her grandchildren say she was short and stocky. She could not read or write. But she cuddled Mrs. Siau on her knee, scolded those big-city grandchildren who were foolish enough to mess with her chickens, and cooked up amazing meals on an old-fashioned stove in the kitchen. "It was a wood-burning stove," recalled Nomenee Robinson, Rosella's grandson, who watched those chickens chase his older brother, Diddley. "She could make rice on that stove, grits and oatmeal, and it would come out so smooth. Everything she cooked was so wonderful." Rosella herself, however, remained somewhat inscrutable. Her grandchildren grew into adulthood without ever knowing the names of her mother or father. Rosella inevitably stood in the shadow of her charismatic husband. But even Fraser Sr. had trouble weathering the Great Depression, which hit Georgetown particularly hard. By 1931, the man who prided himself on finding work no matter how difficult the circumstance, was struggling. His firstborn, Fraser Jr., decided to move to Chicago, hoping to find steady work and to help out, but the Depression shattered those dreams. All these things took their toll on Fraser Sr., the family patriarch, who had built the family's reputation through decades of careful and diligent work. He was the rock of the family, a seeming immovable and eternal presence. But time was gradually wearing away at him.

In the spring of 1935, Fraser Sr. contracted tuberculosis and just couldn't shake it. By the time the cold winds of winter hit a year later, he was gravely ill. His doctor saw him on November 1, 1936, but nothing could be done. Two days later, Fraser took his last breath. He was buried in the cemetery of his beloved church, Bethel AME, on November 4, 1936. Rosella was left to pick up the pieces, to raise her children on her own, in the midst of the Depression. Several of her children dropped out of school and went to work. The girls worked as domestic servants. The boys picked up whatever work they could. Rice, the staple food, was scarce, but she and her children got by somehow. Rosella kept the family together. She outlived Fraser Sr. by nearly two decades, but her grandchildren ended up knowing more about him and his past than about her.

They've shared the tiny snippets of information with one another in hopes of finding more. Ms. Siau remembered that Rosella had family in Charleston and that her maiden name was Cohen (She still can hear her mother, Janie, at the doctor's office telling the nurses her mother's maiden name as she filled out the forms.) Another cousin remembered that Rosella lived apart from her parents for a time when she was a child. As for the name Cohen, everyone shakes their heads. There was no sign of white ancestry on that side of the family, no hint of Jewish ancestry. They have no idea where the name came from. "She was brown; she wasn't yellow. She was light brown, like a pecan," said Ms. Siau, who called her grandmother Rosella "Mama." There were hints of white ancestry on Fraser Sr.'s side, Ms. Siau said, though no one has ever been able to pin that down either. "In that family, there were four different shades of them," said Ms. Siau, referring to the complexions of Fraser Sr.'s children. Ms. Siau said that her mother, Janie, looked Asian in one photo. "They ranged from really dark to really light; and they're all full brothers and sisters," she said. "There's a great mixture. It's all mixed up."

Rosella never left that house on Prince Street, even as the decades passed, her children moved on, and she grew older and frail. She passed away about forty years after she met and married her one-armed man. It was sometime around 1952 and Rosella was about fifty-nine years old when she apparently suffered a stroke and died. Ms. Siau was just a little girl then, but she has never forgotten that day. "I went to school and I came back and she wasn't there," she said of her grandmother Rosella. "I remember my mother sitting on a woodpile and she looked like she had been crying. Something told me to ask, 'Where's Mama?' She told me, 'She's gone.'"

Fraser Jr., who had missed his father's funeral, traveled to South Carolina from Chicago for his mother's wake and funeral and he brought his two oldest sons, who were teenagers, with him. One of them, Nomenee Robinson, still remembers it: how they carried her body into the old house on Prince Street, how countless relatives and friends prayed, wept, reminisced, and mourned. "I remember her body being in the living room," Mr. Robinson said. He and his brother slept in a bedroom that opened into the living room and they were scared, at first, by the presence of their grandmother's body. But they got up the nerve to touch her. They knew then that she was gone.

The next day, the mourners carried Rosella to the cemetery at Bethel AME Church and lowered her coffin into the ground. When she died, the story of her own ancestry and that of her husband's died with her. It was only when Mr. Robinson and Ms. Siau were adults that they realized how complete that loss was. There was no one alive to answer the questions they had about their family's time in slavery, the white ancestry that appeared to lurk in the family tree, the origins of the Cohen name and how Rosella came about it.

Mrs. Obama didn't know much more. She started visiting the house on Prince Street regularly in the 1970s when she was about ten years old. The First Lady can still remember the crickets that kept her awake at night and the fresh deer meat that made her sick. But she said her family never talked about the old plantations in the community or about her enslaved ancestors who might have lived on them. Nomenee Robinson, Mrs. Obama's uncle, said it wasn't "until this presidency" that he learned anything about his enslaved ancestors. Campaign aides for then senator Barack Obama decided to dig into Mrs. Obama's family tree. They hired genealogists from Lowcountry Africana, a research center at the University of South Florida in Tampa, to find out more about Mrs. Obama's roots. That's how Mrs. Obama and her aunts and uncles learned the name of Fraser Sr.'s father, Jim Robinson, who was born into slavery.

It was amazing to finally have the name of the ancestor who bridged slavery and Emancipation. But the details about Jim Robinson's life were scant, raising more questions and leaving relatives frustrated and puzzled about why their parents and grandparents hadn't been more forthcoming. "A lot of times these stories get buried, because sometimes the pain of them makes it hard to want to remember," Mrs. Obama said. Nomenee Robinson said the family was tight-lipped when confronted with such questions, even when its elders were alive. "I was always asking people about slavery time," he said. "But none of my relatives, none of my grandmothers discussed that, discussed their racial heritage. It was just not the subject of conversation. . . . They may have been told something, but it wasn't like folklore that you wanted to pass down to your progeny. Maybe they weren't proud of it."

NINETEEN

Twilight

IN THE LAST DECADES OF HIS LIFE, DOLPHUS SHIELDS STRAD-
dled two worlds. The integrated neighborhoods that he had
once inhabited were gone, erased by white flight and city officials who decreed that people of different colors could no longer live
side by side. But the old man, stooped and silver haired, still served
as a rare bridge between blacks and whites, even in Birmingham,
one of the nation's most segregated cities. By the 1940s, Dolphus was
a familiar figure on the streets and in the churches of his adopted
city. He was in his eighties and he walked slowly, carefully, with
a cane. But wherever he went, people—white and black—stopped
to greet him. Friends called him "D.T." Everyone else called him
Mr. Shields. Neighborhood children swarmed him with delight,
shouting—"Mr. Shields! Mr. Shields!"—whenever he alighted from
his streetcar after work. They knew that his pockets were always
brimming with sweet peppermints that he loved to share. Even the
young men who hung out on the street corners, joking and talking
loud, took pains to treat him with respect whenever he walked by.
"Be quiet! Here comes Mr. Shields," they would call to each other
as they threw down their cigarettes. (Smoking was yet another of
those habits that Dolphus simply couldn't abide.) "Everybody knew

him," said Bobbie Holt, who was taken in by Dolphus and his wife when she was a child. "Everybody in Birmingham, even the white people."

He was a fixture in Birmingham's black religious circles. As a young man, he helped found Trinity Baptist Church. As an old man, he went on to establish First Ebenezer Baptist Church. He built the wooden pulpit there by hand, and his name is still etched on the church's cornerstone. In the last years of his life, he joined Regular Missionary Baptist Church. He was a well-known deacon, who supervised Sunday schools and traveled around the country to meetings of the National Baptist Convention, riding in segregated railroad cars with his wife, Lucy, and Mrs. Holt, who can still remember the motion sickness the hurtling train would bring on. Dolphus embraced the notion of charity and good neighborliness in his everyday life, taking in an impoverished two-year-old who was covered in sores—the young Bobbie Holt—when he was already an elderly man and raising her as his own. He was so well regarded that one church even printed up flyers, calling on the city to celebrate a special "D. T. Shields Day" on April 10, 1949. Members of Regular Missionary Baptist Church invited Birmingham's church leaders and churchgoers to attend a special service honoring Dolphus, who they described as "the only man living as we know of in the United States of America who has served the office of Superintendent of a church school for 71 years."

That same year, Dolphus was included in a book about the city's most prominent black religious men: *History of Colored Baptists in Alabama.* The book, which described Dolphus as "sound in judgment," said that "his integrity, his conscientiousness in the performance of duty are highly valued by his companions in Christian work." It included a sober photo of the stern-looking, bespectacled man in a dark jacket and tie and ticked off a string of the assorted titles he carried over the years: district treasurer of the Mount Pilgrim Sunday School Convention, president of the Deacons' Union, and chairman of District Number One. "He was the dean of the deacons in Birmingham, he had been around so long," said Helen Heath, a retired schoolteacher who attended church with him in the 1940s. "He was a serious man. He was about business."

Dolphus had certainly lived long enough to see the city churn and change around him. The old world of integrated Birmingham, the one he lived in when he first arrived in the 1880s, had vanished. The white neighbors he had in 1900 had died or moved on to all-white enclaves. By 1926, the city had adopted zoning rules that rigidly enforced residential segregation. And the Ku Klux Klan did its part to keep African Americans in line. The Klan, which claimed nearly half of the city's thirty-two thousand registered voters as members, marched through black neighborhoods in white robes. They prevented Oscar De Priest, the black congressman from Chicago, from speaking at the city's auditorium, burning him in effigy to show what would become of black politicians who visited. By 1930, the city had barred blacks and whites from playing dice, dominoes, or checkers together and prohibited any race mixing in restaurants, pool halls, streetcars, and toilets. That same year, the city adopted an ordinance that made its stance absolutely unambiguous. Black and whites had to be separate in "any room, hall, theatre, picture house, auditorium, yard, court, ball park, public park, or other indoor or outdoor place."

Yet at a time when blacks despaired at the intransigence and violence of whites who hemmed them in at every turn, Dolphus stood out as someone who could dictate his own terms, at least when it came to his livelihood. His carpentry shop stood on Third Avenue between Fifteenth Street and Sixteenth Street in a predominantly white block. There was a fire station on one side and a welding shop on the other. He mixed easily and often with whites, displaying a comfort level that was highly unusual. "He had white and black customers," Mrs. Holt said. "His shop was in the middle of white people and he could walk in and out of those buildings and he was received real well. Even the white people, they would come to his shop and sit and talk." Birmingham's zoning code allowed blacks and whites to occupy businesses next to each other in commercial areas, although in practice it rarely happened. Today, as an adult, Mrs. Holt still cannot fathom how Dolphus managed to run a business on that street. Mrs. Heath, who also remembers his carpentry shop, wonders at it, too. "There were certain areas where blacks weren't allowed to go," Mrs. Heath said. "You didn't have black businesses downtown."

The dividing lines were plain, she said: Blacks lived on the east side of Center Street; whites lived on the west. Black businesses were located on Fourth Avenue, roughly between Sixteenth and Seventeenth Streets. Dolphus's shop was on Third Avenue, "about the only one that we knew of" in the shopping district, said Mrs. Heath, who was an adult at the time. Angry whites hurled rocks through the windows of a house that had been purchased by a black woman in a commercial district in the 1940s. Yet Dolphus built his tables and cabinets unmolested, passing the time comfortably with his white clients and neighbors. His light skin may have made him less objectionable to the white business owners around him. Mrs. Heath said Dolphus's skin color and hair texture "told you he had to be near white," though she said she didn't believe that he actively passed for white. He lived in a black neighborhood, attended black churches, and had a wife who was clearly recognizable as African American. "Black people could immediately identify him" as a man of color, she said, though some of his white customers may not have known. As for his origins in slavery, Mrs. Heath said she never heard Dolphus speak of it, which was no surprise. Many black people tried to distance themselves from that painful period, feeling deeply ashamed of their time in forced servitude. "We got to the place where we didn't want anybody to know we knew slaves," Mrs. Heath said. "People didn't want to talk about that. We had to learn later that that history was important."

Dolphus's fair skin might have helped him to stay in business. It could not, however, always shield him from the day-to-day indignities that African Americans endured. His wife, Lucy, who worked as a laundress, was always called Aunt or Aunty by her white customers, never Mrs. Shields, a practice that she resented. And one evening, a rowdy bunch of young white men hurled a liquor bottle at Dolphus's house as they shouted, "Nigger!" The bottle shattered on the porch, narrowly missing Bobbie Holt, who was no more than ten or eleven at the time. The attack so terrified her that she avoided the porch swing after that. And then there were the bombings. Between August 18, 1947, and April 22, 1950, whites threw seven bombs into the homes of middle-class African Americans who had moved into a white neighborhood known as North Smithfield. The neighborhood was close to downtown, where Dolphus worked, and the blasts shattered windows, blew down walls, and demolished porches and flooring. No one was injured, but it was a terrifying time. Mrs. Holt remembers hearing Dolphus and Lucy talking about the Klan, the attacks on blacks, and the racist police officers who refused to investigate or arrest any perpetrators. The searing experiences that Mrs. Holt had with racism and discrimination left her frightened, angry, and bitter. "Why white people so mean?" Mrs. Holt would ask. Dolphus would shrug. "It's always been that way," he would say matter-of-factly.

While others used harsh language in talking about whites, Dolphus never did. "I never heard him speak negative about any of it, say anything about the white people this, the white people that," Mrs. Holt said. "He would always say that with prayer it's going to come together one day."

Even during these tumultuous times, Dolphus mixed so easily with whites that one white man became a regular visitor to his home. Social interactions between blacks and whites were very unusual in his predominantly black neighborhood. When white people came calling, it was typically for business, not to socialize. "If they came, it was usually something like, 'Can you clean my house? Can you iron my clothes?'" Mrs. Holt said. But it was different for the man who came to sit a spell with Dolphus on his front porch. "They would laugh and talk," Mrs. Holt said. "He felt at home."

She was a child at the time and does not remember the man's full name. At first, Dolphus described him as a real estate man, who collected rent in the neighborhood. But later, he took her aside and told her that the white man was his brother and sternly admonished her never, ever to speak of him. "He said, 'Don't ever say anything to your little friends about it because it will be big trouble,'" Mrs. Holt recalled. He spoke with such urgency and such intensity that she was frightened. "He scared me," she said.

Dolphus's descendants have never heard any stories about a white half brother. But there was a white man in Birmingham who shared Dolphus's last name. His name was McClellan Charles Shields, known as Mack to his friends, and he was born in Stockbridge, Georgia, only about nine miles from the Jonesboro area where Dolphus lived as a boy. Mack, who had blue eyes, light brown hair, and narrow lips, left Georgia for many of the same reasons that Dolphus did. Mack did not come from a wealthy family—his parents worked as teachers in one-room schoolhouses—and he had to make his own way. "I think he had to look for work," said Sherry George, Mack's granddaughter, who called him Pop.

By 1923 in Birmingham, Mack lived only about eight blocks from Dolphus's carpentry shop, which at the time was located at 410 Sixteenth Street North in the downtown area. Shoppers routinely strolled by the shop with its sign, D.T. SHIELDS & CO. Mack might have dropped in one day to meet the man who shared his surname. They could have wondered, as they exchanged pleasantries, whether they had more than just a name in common. Dolphus would have been about sixty-three then. Mack was thirty-two with a wife, a toddler, and a new job working at a dairy company. The two men were both members of Baptist churches—one white and one black—and they both struggled at times to make ends meet. Mack moved frequently, from one home to another and from one dairy to another, as he tried to find his bearings. He moved at least ten times between 1923 and 1940, as his family grew and he sought some stability.

Dolphus struggled, too. He still owned the three-bedroom house on Lomb Avenue that he had shared with his fourth wife, Lucy, for at least three decades. He owned the carpentry business, where he sharpened tools and built cabinets. ("I loved to go to work with him," Mrs. Holt said. "I called myself making something, hammering nails, making a little chair or whatever, watching him file saws.") But despite his hard-fought journey into the urban working class, Dolphus scraped by in his later years. He rented the upstairs bedrooms in his house to boarders, and his wife, Lucy, took in laundry from white families to help make ends meet. "They washed clothes outside then," recalled Jewell Barclay, who spent two summers as a young girl with Dolphus, her great-grandfather, and Lucy. "She had a big black pot, you know, boiling water, fire under it and a washboard. She washed with that washboard." Lucy also raised chickens and grew greens and other vegetables in the backyard and canned apples, pears, and figs from the fruit trees to help conserve on cash. Some neighbors even raised cows and sold the milk. "You had greens, a little rice and some bread," recalled Mrs. Holt of the meals that constituted much of their daily diet. "The cabinets were not stocked with a whole lot of stuff." Mrs. Holt remembers pestering her elderly guardians—unsuccessfully—for new shoes. "They didn't have a lot of money," she said. "When she fried a chicken, you were really living."

In class-conscious Birmingham, Dolphus would have been keenly aware that his accomplishments only counted for so much in some circles. He was well known and well regarded, but he was never a member of Birmingham's college-educated black elite. He certainly shared many of the characteristics of that elite group: He was a businessman and a property owner; he was literate and fair skinned. He mingled in church with black college-educated professionals, and his working-class neighborhood was quite close to the neighborhood where the city's prominent black ministers, educators, newspaper owners, and doctors lived. But Dolphus was a carpenter who lacked much in the way of formal education. His wife, who was in her sixties, could not read or write. ("I had to write her letters," Mrs. Holt recalled. "She would make an X and I would sign her name.") And members of the African American elite who were college educated in the 1920s and 1930s were acutely aware of who traveled in their social circles and who did not. Dolphus's last pastor, Rev. C. H. George, who picked him up every Sunday to take him to church, drove a Cadillac. Dolphus, who never owned an automobile, rode the city's public street-cars. "Oh no," said Helen Heath, who like her father, Rev. George at Regular Missionary Baptist Church, was college educated. "He was not an educated man. He hadn't been to college." Mrs. Heath, who was a young teacher when she knew Dolphus, said she didn't know precisely how much education he had, but she suspected it was of a vocational nature. "He had an industrial education," she said. "He was very, very capable with tools."

Dolphus could take pride in his son, Willie, who showed promise as an amateur inventor, and his daughter, Pearl, the seamstress who had moved to Cleveland and opened a shop there. In the sunset of his life, Dolphus could also look back on his personal journey from the farms of Georgia to the big city of Birmingham with a sense of satisfaction. Mack, the white man who also carried the Shields name, could also take pride in his own progress. He would work his way up from entry-level positions to managerial roles at the dairies and would ultimately retire as an insurance salesman. He would build a stable home for his family. He had two sons who served in the army, including one who fought in World War II and was killed on D-Day in France. Dolphus and Mack lived and worked in Birmingham, at one time within blocks of each other. They were born in neighboring counties in northern Georgia and shared the same surname. If the two men did meet and discover their kinship, they clearly decided not to spread the word. The secret, they may have decided, would die with them.

Dolphus suffered a stroke in April 1950, a few weeks after his ninetieth birthday. He was paralyzed on one side and bedridden for weeks. He could barely walk. On June 3, 1950, at 9:20 P.M., on a day when the mercury climbed to nearly eighty degrees, Dolphus Shields died of pneumonia at home. He was about ninety years old. His death certificate reflected the lingering questions about his origins that had always dogged him, even at the very end of his life. It listed his moth-er's name as Melvinia McGruder. In the box for his father's name, someone put a question mark. Dolphus did not leave behind any letters or diaries. There is nothing in writing that would provide his descendants with any semblance of the truth, nothing that would tell them whether his father's name was a mystery to him or an unspoken truth he chose not to share.

Mrs. Holt still remembers the waves of grief that coursed through that little house on Lomb Avenue when Dolphus died. Somehow Lucy pulled herself together to make the funeral arrangements. She went to Shadow Lawn Memorial Park, where most blacks were buried at the time. In the 1950s, even the dead were segregated in Birmingham. Lucy paid $50 for a funeral plot, cemetery records show. In what seems now like a flash of foresight, she paid an additional $30 for a place alongside him. Maybe it was a premonition. Or maybe the salesmen at the graveyard simply offered her a good deal. In any case, Lucy would die within two years of her husband. By Christmastime in 1951, the couple would be together again, side by side, at Shadow Lawn Memorial Park.

At Dolphus's funeral, the mourners streamed into Regular Missionary Baptist Church at 2:00 P.M. on Sunday, June 11. Members of the two churches that Dolphus had helped found—Trinity Baptist and First Ebenezer Baptist—served as honorary pallbearers. One by one, the people who knew him stood up to testify: there was a woman who taught Sunday school, a fellow deacon, a neighbor, a friend. There were prayers and soaring solos, amens and hallelujahs, as his children, Willie and Pearl, and his widow, Lucy, grieved in the pews. Born into slavery, Dolphus managed to move up steadily, enduring his own personal tragedies and hardships. He was a complicated man who defied easy categorization: a deacon who devoted himself to God yet abandoned at least one wife for another and nursed such grudges that he refused to attend the funerals of his own mother and brother. He was a biracial man who kept one foot in the white world and the other in the black world. He was a onetime sharecropper who transformed himself into a businessman who helped found churches that still exist today, a man so well known in the black community that his obituary would appear on the front page of the *Birmingham World*. He advanced even as he and his children chafed at the laws and restrictions that forced African Americans into second-class citizenship. But even as Dolphus's family wept at his funeral, times were changing.

On the day his obituary appeared in the *Birmingham World*, the black newspaper also ran a banner headline that read, "U.S. Court Bans Segregation in Diners and Higher Education." The Supreme Court had outlawed separate but equal accommodations on railway cars and in universities in Texas and Oklahoma. The sturdy walls of segregation were starting to crumble. Amid the sea of black mourners attending that Sunday-afternoon funeral, one white man stepped in to pay his respects. It was the genial man who Bobbie Holt knew as Dolphus's brother.

TWENTY

The Search for the Truth: Atlanta

JOAN TRIBBLE STILL REMEMBERS THE MOMENT WHEN SHE first laid eyes on the old black-and-white photograph of Dolphus Shields. She was sitting at the kitchen table in her house in the Atlanta suburbs when she saw him staring out of the pages of the *New York Times*: this stern, bespectacled African American man who happened to share her mother's last name. Joan is a sixty-nine-year-old descendant of the white Shields clan that traces its roots back to the red-clay farmland near Jonesboro in Clayton County, Georgia. Her great-great-grandfather was Henry Shields, the man who owned Dolphus and Melvinia. Joan grew up in Clayton County, as did her mother, her grandmother, and her great-grandfather before her. She grew up hearing stories about those ancestors and their children, tales of struggling white farmers of Irish ancestry who were dirt poor and had little more than elementary-school educations. Her own mother never got past the seventh grade. Black people never figured into any of the family stories, but then, why would they? Joan never had any doubts about her family's ethnic background. Her light eyes and fair skin made her genetic inheritance clear to anyone who looked at her. Yet as she stared at that photograph of Dolphus that day, Joan felt something unexpected: a strong stirring of recognition. "I just thought, 'Well, he looks like somebody who could be in my family,'" she says.

Joan prides herself on her openness, on her acceptance of others. She is a silver-haired retiree who gets by on Social Security these days, a woman who exudes a warm, no-nonsense manner from behind her wire-rimmed glasses. Arthritis has gnarled the fingers of one hand, but she is always reaching out, shaking someone's hand, patting someone's shoulder. She was inclined to delve into the story about Dolphus, to try to sort out the truth, to openly consider the painful possibility that her family tree might include some black relatives who had been owned and exploited by some of her white relatives. Other members of her extended family wanted to keep it all quiet, concerned about the implications of the possible revelations about the family. Joan saw things differently.

And so, finally, on a steamy summer afternoon, she decides to take the plunge: she decides to find out whether she is actually related to Dolphus and to talk about what she knows about her family. She asks me to bring the historical records that I've been collecting on the family and we meet in the snack room in the gleaming, state-of-the-art Georgia Archives Building, sitting at a small table not far from a beeping microwave and a Coca-Cola vending machine.

Even before she saw the photo of Dolphus Shields, Joan had spent many days here over the past few years, digging into her family tree, poring through census records and property records, marriage licenses and faded wills, deciphering spidery, nineteenth-century script as she tracked her ancestors through the decades. That was how she finally discovered that her great-great-grandfather was a slave owner. But on this afternoon, those old Shields men feel real in a way they had not before. They are no longer just handwritten names scrolling down the screen on the archives' microfilm machines. They are human beings, flesh and blood, with desires and heartbreaks. They are frontiersmen and churchgoers, fathers and husbands, the ultimate symbols of moral authority in their large sprawling families. They also owned human property.

One of the Shields men owned Dolphus and his mother, Melvinia. And one of them may have forced himself on the young slave girl. As she pages through my records, Joan talks openly about slavery and race and wrestling with century-old wrongs. It is the kind of discussion—under fluorescent lights in a public space—that most of her relatives have been reluctant to hold outside of the closed doors of their homes. "They don't want to think that things like this happened in the family, that a young girl might have been raped against her own will," Joan says of her relatives, who still prefer to remain anonymous. "It's horrible and shameful to think that relatives of mine would treat people that way, raping or taking advantage of a young woman just because they could. That part I don't even like to think of. But I know enough history to know that that kind of thing did happen."

For a family that prided itself on knowing something of its history, the news has been staggering, almost unspeakable: someone in the family owned Dolphus, the great-great-grandfather of Michelle Obama, the First Lady of the United States. And someone in the family may have been Dolphus's father, and not just his father, but a man who might have brutalized Dolphus's mother, Melvinia, when she was just a young girl emerging from adolescence in the fields of Clayton County more than a hundred years ago. The horrible possibility—jarring, unsettling, disturbing—is still reverberating through the far-flung Shields family, whose members in Georgia, Alabama, Texas, and elsewhere have been examining their family records, questioning their elders, and sifting through their memories.

For some members of the family, the revelations have forced something of a personal reckoning with the intimate details and painful legacy of slavery, an institution that most had consigned to the history books. They have found themselves asking uncomfortable questions that they would have otherwise preferred to leave unanswered. Sherry George, whose great-grandfather and great-great-grandfather were white Shields men who lived in Clayton County prior to and after the Civil War, still struggles to find the right words to describe her reaction the revelations. "I'm appalled at slavery," says Ms. George, who is one of Joan's distant cousins and a hospital respiratory therapy manager. "I don't know how that could have even gone on in a Christian nation. I know that times were different then. But the idea that one of our ancestors raped a slave . . ." She trailed off for a moment, considering the awful possibility. "I would like to know the answer, but I would not like to know that my great-grandfather was a rapist," Ms. George continues. "I would like to know in my brain that they were nice to her and her children. It would be easier to live with that." She points out that at least two of Mrs. Obama's relatives—her mother, Marian Robinson, and her great-great-uncle, Henry Shields—ended up with first names that were also carried by members of the white Shields family that owned Melvinia. It suggests that affection between the two families may have carried across the generations. Ms. George finds some comfort in that.

Some members of the extended Shields family know each other. Others have never met. Many cling to the hope that someone else— not a Shields man—might have fathered Dolphus. Surely the Shieldses had white male friends, visitors, workers who might have been drawn to the young woman, they say. One member of the Shields family provided me with a handwritten list of the names of several great-great-uncles who might have fathered Dolphus, in the hopes that an additional investigation might prove that her direct line was in the clear. Others pray that the liaison might have been a romance or, at the very least, that the sexual relationship might have been consensual. Aliene Shields, a descendant of the white Shields family who lives in South Carolina, firmly believes that Dolphus's father was a member of her family. But she believes that her ancestor treated Dolphus and Melvinia with love and tenderness, even if he had to hide his relationship with them during slavery times. Mrs. Shields has no proof, of course, but she has extensively researched the men in her family and says she knows they were good people. "To me it's an obvious love story that was hard for the South to accept back then," says Mrs. Shields, who points out that such relationships were viewed as unacceptable all across the country at the time. "I genuinely think he took care of them. They were his family; there was genuine affection. They were loved." Others are less certain. Melvinia was a young girl—somewhere between the ages of fourteen and sixteen—when she got pregnant. She was a slave at a time when enslaved black women had no rights or legal recourse. How much power did she really have in those days to tell a white man no? "I would hope that there was no force, no fear," said one Shields descendant, whose eyes filled with tears at the prospect and who spoke only on condition of anonymity. But that descendant remains unconvinced that Melvinia could have refused the attentions of her suitor, whoever he was, given the power dynamics between white men and black women in Georgia at the time.

Many Shields descendants worry there could be repercussions from the revelations. They fear that they and their children could be labeled as racists, vilified, and forced to publicly atone somehow for the sins of long-gone ancestors, and that the Shields name could become fodder for tabloids. Such ugly stories from the past, they believe, are better left unspoken. Joan worries less about the possible stigma, despite the concerns raised by some of her relatives. But she admits that learning that her ancestors had owned human property came as something of a shock. The children and grandchildren of the white Shields men who farmed the soil in Clayton County before the Civil War mostly led modest, working-class lives as homemakers, machinists, insurance salesmen, railroad conductors, and salesmen at local dairies. There was no grand plantation in the family, no sprawling estate. Joan's mother, Lottie Bell Shields, was an orphan, who picked cotton as a girl and was passed from relative to relative in a family that could ill afford an extra mouth to feed. How in the world, many Shields descendants wondered, did such a family end up owning slaves? "I know what happened in those days; I know how the blacks were treated as property," Joan says. "But my family, well, they were just your most basic people who never had a lot. I never imagined that they owned slaves."

Many members of the white Shields clan have kept it from friends and extended family. But Joan fully accepts this new reality. She has shared the unlikely story with her friends and relatives and marvels at how her very ordinary family has suddenly become something of a fascinating footnote in history, with their unsettling link to the family of the country's first black president. "I told everybody," Joan says. "Some people laughed; some of them said they didn't know if they would claim the connection."

"I think it's great," Joan says of the possibility that she and Mrs. Obama might be distantly related. "But I'm probably the only one of my relatives who thinks so." Few members of her generation have embraced the idea, she explains, though her children and grandchildren are delighted by the possibility that they might have a relative in the White House. The widely divergent views reflect the diversity within the white Shields family, who are scattered all across the country. A handful voted for Barack Obama in the 2008 presidential election and felt a strong sense of pride at having helped elect the nation's first African American president. But most voted against him and strongly believe that he is taking the country in the wrong direction. Some are college-educated professionals; others are blue-collar workers, who find it somewhat ironic that some of Dolphus's descendants have done better for themselves than the descendants of the white Shields family who owned him.

Many, like Joan, have done some research into the family tree. They are on a first-name basis with their great-grandparents and great-great-grandparents and treasure the few surviving black-and-white photographs of these men and women. Several have trekked to see the old Shields family cemetery near Jonesboro, where overgrown grass obscures some of the white tombstones. One Shields descendant even visited the old house where a great-grandfather and great-grandmother had lived and recalled a two-story farmhouse that once had a front porch. They grew up listening to the stories that their parents and grandparents told about the upright, hardworking, churchgoing men who struggled to make a living and cared deeply for their families. Those stories helped shape their sense of their roots and their identity.

So the discovery that these ancestors were slave owners and that one may have fathered a biracial child brings on more than just fears of negative publicity. It threatens to shake what was once an unshakable sense of self, the comfort of knowing who their people were, where they came from. One descendant confronted her mother—hoping to find out that this was all just a lie, that this talk of slave-owning Shieldses was just an ugly untruth—and was shaken to hear that it was true. It was something that the descendant's mother had kept to herself for many years. "She was a good person, I know that," the descendant says with confidence, speaking of a great-grandmother, who never owned slaves. But the descendant hesitates now when asked about the men, the great-grandfather and great-great-grandfather, who lived on the farm where Melvinia and Dolphus were held as slaves. The question reverberates, unanswered. What kind of people were they?

Several members of the Shields family have declined to undergo DNA testing. They don't want to know whether the black Shieldses and the white Shieldses are related; they don't want to know whether they share bloodlines with Mrs. Obama. They are worried about what the results might show, fearful that the world will impose twenty-first-century judgments on them and their ancestors who lived in a radically different time and place. A handful of others are willing. They want to know the truth. There have been phone calls and face-to-face meetings among the members of the Shields clan. There have been fierce debates over how much to share, how much to keep hidden. Some have tried to unravel the family history with their naked eyes, poring over the photographs of Dolphus and their white ancestors, holding them side by side and asking each other: Do you recognize something in the narrow line of his lips, the thrust of his jaw, the shape of his head? One descendant, who was anxious about how much the elderly Dolphus resembled a great-grandfather, was relieved to see another photo of Dolphus as a younger man. The two men looked decidedly less similar, the onlooker pronounced. "We'll never know what happened," one descendant said over and over again.

But then that family member and two others decide to take the DNA test, to clear the mists of the centuries, to look back. Joan struggles for the words to explain what compels her to move forward. She may not be a huge fan of President Obama's, but she admires his wife. "Michelle, I like her," she says. "She's a very strong woman." (Later on, she jokes, "She's a very attractive woman so I'm going to say she looks just like me.") She thinks a lot about her young grandchildren and the world that they will live in. She would like for them to know the truth someday, even if it is a difficult truth. Joan has traveled extensively around the country. She lived for a time in California, where she and her ex-husband worked for a trucking company that brought crops harvested by Hispanic migrant workers to American markets. She is proud that her children grew up having friends from across the rainbow. "It didn't matter if they were Asian, Hispanic, black, or white," she says. "They were all welcome in my house. I'd like to think they're raising their children the same way."

She says that "thinking about the history and knowing what happened" during slavery to people like Dolphus and Melvinia has persuaded her to move forward. She would like to meet their progeny, their great-grandchildren and their great-greats, not just Mrs. Obama, but their ordinary descendants who live everyday lives far from the spotlight. "I can't really change anything, but I can be open-minded to people and accept them for whatever and hope they'll accept me," Joan says. She takes the swab and carefully rubs the inside of her cheek as we sit in the Georgia Archives. I carefully place the swabs into tiny vials and close them tight. We may have an answer, I warn Joan, but we may simply end up with uncertainty. In the meantime, I tell her, I'll continue my research into her ancestors. Joan nods and turns to the stack of records that I have placed on the table before her.

Her family's story and Melvinia's story intersected in South Carolina, where her forebears lived in the 1840s. Joan looks at the census records, at the list of white men whose lives would soon be upended by the Civil War and Emancipation. The name of her great-great-grandfather is there, handwritten in neat, careful script. She taps the pages with her finger. Spartanburg. This is where it all began.

PART III

Slavery and Emancipation

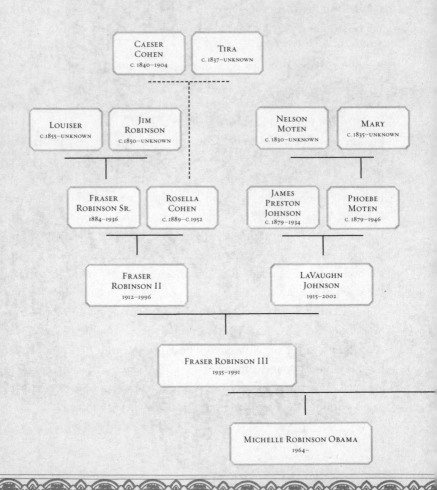

CAESER COHEN
c. 1840–1904

TIRA
c. 1837–UNKNOWN

LOUISER
c.1855–UNKNOWN

JIM ROBINSON
c.1850–UNKNOWN

NELSON MOTEN
c. 1830–UNKNOWN

MARY
c. 1835–UNKNOWN

FRASER ROBINSON SR.
1884–1936

ROSELLA COHEN
c. 1889–c.1952

JAMES PRESTON JOHNSON
c. 1879–1934

PHOEBE MOTEN
c. 1879–1946

FRASER ROBINSON II
1912–1996

LAVAUGHN JOHNSON
1915–2002

FRASER ROBINSON III
1935–1991

MICHELLE ROBINSON OBAMA
1964–

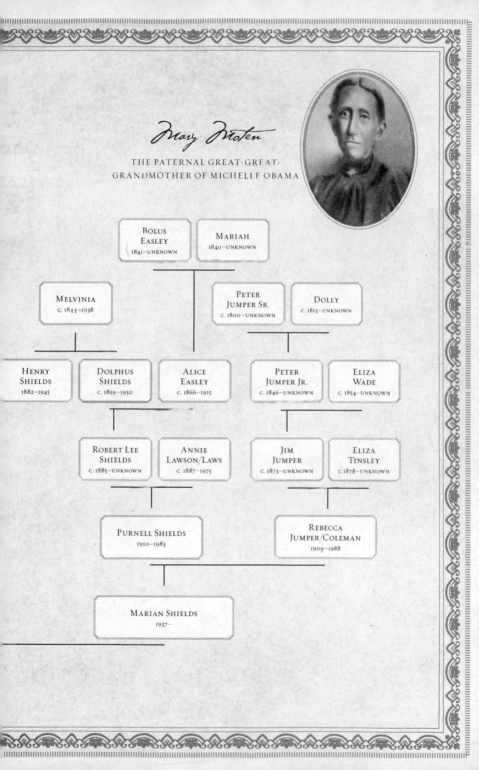

Mary Moten

THE PATERNAL GREAT-GREAT-
GRANDMOTHER OF MICHELLE OBAMA

BOLUS
EASLEY
1841–UNKNOWN

MARIAH
1840–UNKNOWN

MELVINIA
C. 1844–1938

PETER
JUMPER SR.
C. 1800–UNKNOWN

DOLLY
C. 1813–UNKNOWN

HENRY
SHIELDS
1882–1945

DOLPHUS
SHIELDS
C. 1859–1950

ALICE
EASLEY
C. 1866–1915

PETER
JUMPER JR.
C. 1846–UNKNOWN

ELIZA
WADE
C. 1854–UNKNOWN

ROBERT LEE
SHIELDS
C. 1885–UNKNOWN

ANNIE
LAWSON/LAWS
C. 1887–1975

JIM
JUMPER
C. 1873–UNKNOWN

ELIZA
TINSLEY
C. 1878–UNKNOWN

PURNELL SHIELDS
1910–1983

REBECCA
JUMPER/COLEMAN
1909–1988

MARIAN SHIELDS
1937–

TWENTY-ONE

A Slave Girl Named Melvinia

I N THE BEGINNING, THE CHEROKEE ROAMED THE BLUE RIDGE
Mountains, the oak and chestnut-covered heights adorned with
waterfalls and wildflowers. Then came the white men, first in
a trickle, then in a flood. There were British, Scots, Irish, and first-
generation Americans. Soldiers fresh from the Revolutionary War
poured into Spartanburg, South Carolina, nestled in the foothills of
those mountains, drawn by the promise of up to two hundred acres of
land for their wartime service. Patrician landowners from the state's
sweltering Atlantic coast estates joined the throngs decades later,
drawn by Spartanburg's temperate climes and its cool mineral springs,
which were believed to heal those afflicted with rheumatism, ulcers,
and malaria. Melvinia grew up in this place of rolling hills and val-
leys, near the rushing rivers full of shad, trout, and catfish, amid the
peach, quince, and cherry trees. She lived near the banks of Peters
Creek, where the trilling mockingbirds, whippoorwills, and red-
headed woodpeckers soared in springtime. As a little girl, she did not
know that the woods also whispered another story, that the earth had
tasted the blood of Native Americans decimated by disease and battle,
that the patriots who fought so valiantly for American freedom had
so eagerly embraced the enslavement of other human beings. But in-

nocence could only be savored for so long. Melvinia, after all, was a slave, and soon enough she would learn what her elders knew, and what the Cherokee knew before them, that this land of beauty was also a place of countless sorrows.

Her life would encompass nearly one hundred years of American history, from the days of slavery through the soul-crushing decades of Jim Crow segregation. She would take the first steps in an epic, northward trek and become the matriarch of a family that would journey from slavery to the White House in five generations. For the women searching for their origins, here, at long last, was their human link: Melvinia was the great-great-great-grandmother of Mrs. Obama; the great-great-grandmother of Jewell Barclay; and the young slave girl owned by Joan Tribble's great-great-grandfather. Melvinia's descendants would end up scattered across the country, in Georgia, Alabama, Michigan, Ohio, Illinois, and the nation's capital. Even if she had tried to conjure up a vision of what was to come, she could have never imagined the summits her progeny would climb.

Melvinia was born around 1844, at a time when African Americans were considered little more than chattel. By 1850, her home state of South Carolina had 384,984 slaves, more than any other in the country, save for Virginia. It is likely that she had never even seen a free person of color back then. She was dark-eyed, with dark skin and wavy hair, and her entire life revolved around her master's five-hundred-acre estate in Spartanburg. Her owner, David Patterson, was one of the district's wealthiest men, and she was one of his family's favorite slaves. In his house, Melvinia might have run her small fingers gently over his books, wrinkled her nose at the sharp smell of freshly ground coffee, peered through the windows draped with calico curtains. On the grounds, bees swarmed around sweet-smelling hives and a bevy of enslaved men tended to the livestock and plowed and sowed the fields of cotton, corn, wheat, and oats. Local visitors would have been impressed by Mr. Patterson's wealth. He owned twenty-one slaves at a time when only 2 percent of households in Spartanburg owned twenty or more. Most residents—nearly 70 percent in 1820 and 1860—did not own slaves at all. The vast majority of white farmers in the county worked the land with their own hands.

His family was keenly aware of the precariousness of it all. Mr. Patterson was eighty-six years old in 1850 and had already begun preparing for the end. His farm was valued at $1,500, a substantial amount in those days, and his slaves were worth far more. On August 1, he took pen in hand and updated his will, which he had written several years earlier. In it, he mentioned the slave girl Melvinia, promising her to his wife, Ruth, along with some kitchen furniture, cows, and two other slaves. "I give and lend to her during her natural life one other negro, a girl about six years old, named Melvina," he wrote. "My will is that my wife Ruth have the use and services of the said negro girl & her issue & increase if any free from the control or interference of my executors or any other person." Of the twenty-one slaves working on Mr. Patterson's estate, he mentioned only three by name, a hint that he and his wife must have been attached to Melvinia. He didn't describe her duties, but enslaved children often began doing chores for their owners at a young age, carrying water from wells or springs, sweeping and cleaning in the master's house, and helping to serve tea or meals. The elderly Pattersons may also have delighted in Melvinia's childish laughter and play. She was born in South Carolina, possibly on their farm, so they may have known her since she was a tiny baby. She had chocolate-colored skin, but her thick wavy hair suggested some racial mixing in her family line. If the Pattersons knew anything about Melvinia's parents or her origins, though, they left no record of it.

Someone must have held Melvinia as a baby and cuddled her. Someone must have fed her and sang to her and soothed her when she cried. Someone must have had dreams for her, too, though those dreams would certainly have been tempered by the knowledge of the harsh life ahead. As an adult, Melvinia would tell census takers that her mother was born in Virginia. Her owner, Mr. Patterson, was born in Virginia, too, and he lived there into his late twenties. He moved to North Carolina, where he owned at least one slave, before finally settling in Spartanburg, South Carolina, by the 1820s. Did he buy or inherit Melvinia's mother or father in Virginia and bring one or both of them with him? There is no way to know. The genealogical trail goes cold. Melvinia busied herself with chores for her owners. She played with her friends in the fields and slave quarters. But her imprint on the historical record was fleeting. By the time Joan and Jewell looked back, nearly all the details of Melvinia's early years had been lost, save for the blurriest hints of the young girl's time in bondage. If Mr. Patterson had not mentioned her in his will, she would have been an ephemeral being who occupied a plane somewhere beyond human existence. In this way, Melvinia was something of an everywoman. The day-to-day lives of American slaves were rarely recorded or chronicled. Some owners wrote down in business ledgers or family Bibles the dates of their slaves' births and deaths, and the purchases and profits they made at auctions. But this kind of note-taking was the exception. As a result, it is nearly impossible to re-create in detail the lives of enslaved African Americans. Descriptions of their baptisms, marriages, and funerals almost never appeared in local newspapers, which were run by white men who generally considered the lives of their human property about as newsworthy as the lives of their cattle and hogs. Even in the federal census—which aimed to track every American and remains an invaluable resource for historians—slaves were rendered anonymous and faceless. Census takers listed the gender and ages of the black men, women, and children held in captivity, but nothing else. Not their names or birthplaces, not the languages they spoke or the families they loved. Millions of African Americans lived and died, celebrated and struggled without leaving a trace. That Mr. Patterson mentioned Melvinia at all in his will speaks to the special place she occupied in his household and family.

We may never know whether Melvinia had any relatives on that farm, but there is no doubt that she formed strong attachments to the other African Americans in her community there. No description of the slaves, their housing, or their specific labors has survived, and Mr. Patterson, of course, had not specifically included them in his will. The scattered fragments of information are often contradictory, with the census suggesting that nearly all the slaves—aside from two—were male, whereas other property records indicate that several more women worked on the Patterson estate.

Several young children lived there, too. Mr. Patterson owned a young girl named Mandrew, a boy named Dillard, and another boy named Simpson. Melvinia kept a special place in her heart for two other playmates, Mariah and Bolus, who were both about ten years old when Mr. Patterson amended his will in 1850. Mr. Patterson did not mention them by name, so Mariah and Bolus may have labored in his fields instead of in his house, where Melvinia most likely worked. But those differences between the children, between the spaces they occupied in the hierarchical rungs of slavery and in the minds of their owners, didn't seem to matter. The simple affections of companionship could be a balm for young boys and girls in a system that was otherwise inherently dehumanizing. In up-country South Carolina, children entertained themselves by shooting marbles, tossing balls back and forth over houses, and playing clapping games like "Molly Bright," in which the children sang: "Can I get to Molly's bright? Three course and ten. Can I get there by candlelight? Yes, if your legs are long and light." Like Melvinia, Mariah was born in South Carolina and her mother was born in Virginia, too. The two women may have been sisters or cousins or best friends. Whatever their connection, their bond would prove to be strong enough to survive slavery and decades of separation.

As children on Mr. Patterson's farm, there was little time to indulge in sentimental musings. Work came first, and there was lots of it. There were four cows to be milked and a range of livestock to feed and tend to, including two horses, ten head of cattle, three sheep, and twenty pigs. The slaves cultivated Indian corn, wheat, oats, beans, and Irish potatoes. The slaves picked cotton, too, which was Mr. Patterson's most lucrative crop, generating four bales of ginned cotton in 1850. All the while, they kept a careful, anxious eye on Mr. Patterson and his health. In the day-to-day lives of slaves, few happenings were as traumatic as the death of an owner. Farms were typically divided among heirs, and enslaved families were often pulled apart as husbands and wives, parents and children, brothers and sisters were separated and handed off to relatives of the master or sold at the auction block. If Melvinia overheard conversations about Mr. Patterson's will or his health, she may not have known what to make of such talk. She was only a little girl. But the older slaves on the estate surely understood. They must have watched that old man with eagle eyes and taken, as best they could, as frequently as they could, a constant measure of his well-being. Mr. Patterson was already in his mid-eighties; they knew that his time on earth was short. His every cough, his every stumble, his every sneeze counted. The slaves knew that their very lives depended on it.

Mr. Patterson seemed to have a sense of the anxiety sweeping through his enslaved community. Some masters dismissed their human property as savages incapable of deep emotions and true feelings. But other slave owners thought otherwise. Mr. Patterson was a religious man, a trustee in the local Methodist Episcopal church, and he knew that there were devoted families living on his property. In his will, he asked his executors to respect and preserve those family bonds after his death. "My will and desire is that in the partition and division of my negroes, that the family be kept together as far as possible and no separation of husband & wife if it can be prevented," Mr. Patterson wrote in 1850. That sentiment might have reassured some of his slaves, at least for a time. Whites in the community must have watched with considerable interest and concern, too, as the health of Mr. Patterson, one of their wealthiest citizens, deteriorated. In 1850, whites outnumbered blacks in the district of Spartanburg. African Americans accounted for more than 50 percent of the population in the state, but they were a distinct minority in up-country South Carolina. Whites in Spartanburg, for instance, accounted for about 70 percent of the district's 26,400 people, and Mr. Patterson's white neighbors would have admired him for his wealth, his longevity, and his considerable land holdings. How the rest of the population viewed him—the 30 percent that was black and in bondage—remains unclear. Mr. Patterson obviously felt close to some of his slaves, particularly Melvinia and the two others he mentioned by name in his will, and he wanted to protect their families from being split apart. But no records have survived that describe his day-to-day treatment of his human possessions, or indicate whether he meted out or supervised the whippings and beatings that were so commonplace.

Corporal punishment was widely used in the 1800s, even within free white families, and children and wives often suffered at the hands of their parents and husbands. But that paled in comparison to the violence employed by masters against their slaves. In his survey of American slavery, Peter Kolchin notes that it was "rare the slave that escaped the lash." David Harris, a Spartanburg slave owner and one of Mr. Patterson's contemporaries, included periodic, casual references in his journal to the punishments he meted out. He whipped one teenage boy for leaving his property without first asking permission. He thrashed an elderly man, probably for stealing eggs. A female slave who was six months pregnant earned "a little floging" for briefly running off "to the wood." And he warned that another slave, who complained of shoulder pains and couldn't work, would "have a pain in his back . . . unless he gets well soon." The comforts of family life helped slaves endure the rigors and hardships of servitude and the rules and orders of their masters, which governed their day-to-day existences. But those family comforts were often momentary. Slave owners, sometimes systematically and sometimes haphazardly, determined when their slaves would wake, when they would work, what they would eat, what they would wear, when they would sleep. Most important, they determined who would marry and which families would remain intact. Mr. Harris viewed his slaves not as people to be protected, but as livestock to be bought and sold, noting one day that he had "exchanged negroes and horses" with another man.

Mr. Patterson obviously viewed his slaves somewhat differently. But as the months and years passed, it became clear that his kindliness extended only so far. At the end of the day, Melvinia and the other black men and women who worked for him were still valuable property. In the early 1850s, a ten-year-old slave girl went for about $400. This was no small sum. It would take most white farmers four or five years to earn that much money. Able-bodied men and women went for much higher. And so despite his pledge to keep families together, what his slaves feared most finally came to pass. In the last year of his life, Mr. Patterson began parceling out "his negroes" to his sons and daughters. On February 6, 1851, Mr. Patterson amended his will once again, noting that he had given a young slave girl to his daughter, Christian Shields, who had moved to Georgia with her husband, Henry Wells Shields. Mr. Patterson gave one of his sons a young slave boy. Over the next year, the African American community that he had acquired over the course of several decades was divided and scattered.

Mr. Patterson died in 1852 around the age of eighty-eight. His wife, Ruth, who was meant to inherit Melvinia, died that year, too, leaving the executors of Mr. Patterson's will to begin the painstaking process of inventorying his possessions. There were cows and steers, at least five head of sheep, and one gray horse. There were three spinning wheels, two plows, one wagon, one set of blacksmith tools, and two beds. There was a dresser, one chest, and one side saddle. There were two scythes, two tablecloths, one grindstone, and one loom. There was a coffee mill, one lot of cotton, one lot of books, one lot of crockery, and a clock. There was bacon, cheese, some honey and butter, and countless other food items. And then there was the human property. We don't know how Melvinia and the other slaves learned of their fates, whether they kept a vigil over their ailing master or whether some thought he was better off dead.

We don't know if they wailed at his passing or welcomed it, whether he was beloved or hated or simply tolerated by the people he owned. What we do know is that each of his human beings, just like the cows, the sheep, and the barrels of corn, was assigned a price. Melvinia's dear friend, Mariah, who was valued at $550, ended up with Mr. Patterson's daughter, Nancy. Bolus, valued at $300, landed in the home of another daughter, Sarah. Christian Shields, the Patterson daughter who lived in Georgia, ended up with three slaves: the young girl, Mandrew, who was valued at $340; Tom, a grown man, who was worth $500; and Melvinia, the family favorite, who was valued at $475.

Historian Michael Tadman estimates that in parts of the South "about one first marriage in three was broken up by forced separation and close to half of all children were separated from at least one parent." One of the most common causes of separation was the death of a slave master. Laura Clark, a former slave from North Carolina, remembered vividly the moment when she was taken from her mother and shipped to Alabama in a wagon with nine other children. She was just a girl then, and her owner gave her some candy to keep her quiet. At the time, she struggled to understand her mother's grief. "I knows now," she said sadly. "I never seed her no mo' in dis life."

Melvinia was a little girl, too, about eight years old, when she learned one of the harshest realities of slave life: that she had no control of her own life, her own body, her own choices. She was being forced to leave the place she knew as home, the people she knew as family. Did she weep? Did she long for freedom? Or did that seem like an impossible notion for a black girl in the 1850s, especially in the midst of an economic boom in the South that cemented those states' reliance on slavery? Sometime around 1852, Melvinia began the journey that would take her from the home she knew in South Carolina to a new state and a new owner in northern Georgia. The mountains and rushing rivers of Spartanburg, that ever-present backdrop of her early years, would soon fade from her view.

TWENTY-TWO

Journey to Georgia

T HE SOUTHERN PLANTATION IS A FIXTURE OF THE AMERIcan imagination. Close your eyes and you can almost see it: the grand white manor with its ornate columns, the sweeping expanse of green clover, the stately magnolias filling the warm spring breezes with their sweet perfume. Some conjure up visions of Thomas Jefferson's Monticello, his five-thousand-acre mountain estate in Virginia with its forty-three rooms, eight fireplaces, and two hundred slaves. Others invoke Scarlett O'Hara's mythical mansion in *Gone with the Wind,* which bustled with the clink of fine china and silver and the comings and goings of the housemaids and more than a hundred enslaved laborers. That fabled mansion stood near Jonesboro, Georgia, only about five miles from the farm where Melvinia ended up sometime around 1852. But Melvinia's new home, situated in the state's rough up-country, was nothing like those vast plantations that often come to mind. She never knew that kind of life. In truth, most slaves didn't. They lived on farms that were dramatically more modest than the plantations popularized by film and literature. Only a tiny fraction of American slave owners—less than 1 percent—had two hundred or more slaves. Only one-quarter of blacks even lived on properties with more than forty-nine slaves. The overwhelming majority of African Americans—about 75 percent—lived on farms that owned fewer than fifty enslaved laborers. Even in South Carolina, where Melvinia had lived on the estate of one of the wealthiest men in Spartanburg, her master owned only twenty-one African Americans.

Wealthy slave owners in Spartanburg, though, still enjoyed some of the finer pleasures in life, occupying spacious, two-story homes with wood paneling, elegant moldings, bookcases, glass mirrors, and four-poster beds. In Georgia, Melvinia's new home was far smaller and humbler than the one she had known. She was still only about eight years old when she journeyed to the hills of Henry County, a sleepy town carved out of the Creek Indian territory of hickory forests and gurgling brooks. The settlement, founded in 1821, became a relay station on the stagecoach line that ran from New York to New Orleans, a place where drivers traded in their weary horses for fresh ones. Many travelers kept on going once those horses were ready, their hearts and hopes set on more prosperous places. When Melvinia arrived in 1852, she stepped into a place of dirt roads and neglected bridges, a community of "plain and unassuming" people, according to observers, who raised their families in log cabins or rough-hewn cottages. The fields were filled with white men, many of them illiterate or nearly so, who handled the backbreaking labor of planting, plowing, and harvesting corn, wheat, and cotton on their own. It was the kind of place that many wealthy southerners dismissed as backward and provincial.

Archibald T. Burke, a slave owner who settled in the region around the same time that Melvinia did, worried that his wealthy fiancée would be unhappy with his choice of a new home. "I am sometimes fearful that you will not be pleased with the Society in the up Country," he wrote his bride-to-be. "You will think it strange . . . to see white people living in Log Cabins . . . [and] you will find all sorts of Society here except Aristocracy." It is unlikely that anyone asked Melvinia her thoughts on the matter, but the little girl might have been startled, too, when she laid eyes on her new home and her new master, Henry Wells Shields. He was a man in his prime: a property owner in his mid-thirties and the married patriarch of a growing clan that already included eight children. Yet he, like the other white yeoman farmers in the county, worked the land with his own hands. He had never owned a slave in his life.

There is no record of this first encounter between Melvinia and Henry, between the dark-eyed slave girl and her new white master. There is no way to know whether Henry felt at a loss at that moment, uncertain of his bearings as he looked at this young child suddenly thrust into his care, or whether he had been eagerly waiting, praying for this day to come. Born in South Carolina, Henry had been trying for at least four years to carve out a future for himself in the rocky, middling soil in up-country Georgia. Melvinia's arrival—and that of her enslaved companions, Tom and Mandrew—completely transformed his prospects. He was now, suddenly, a member of the county elite, the tiny, privileged class of men who owned human property. As for Melvinia, she was forced to adjust to a completely new existence. She had been a little girl nurtured in a bustling community of African Americans; now she would be one of only three black slaves in a sea of white faces. Once the favorite slave of a wealthy family, she was now the prized possession of a farmer still struggling to make a name for himself. No matter how much or how little she knew about Henry that day she stood before him in Georgia, she certainly understood that her fate and her future, and her very survival, rested in the hands of a man who was learning how to be a master.

Melvinia's and Henry's lives intersected at a time when more than 3.2 million enslaved African Americans lived in the United States. Slaves accounted for about 40 percent of the people in the South and about 14 percent of the nation's population. Human bondage was already deeply embedded in the nation's fabric by the time Melvinia set foot in Georgia. The first recorded arrival of twenty African captives took place in 1619 when twenty blacks stepped off a ship and into the British colony of Virginia. The institution flourished in an untamed land hungry for unpaid labor, despite the American Revolution and its clarion call for freedom and equality among men. In 1830, when a small group of abolitionists declared that slavery was a sin and an abomination, most Americans—in the North and in the South—viewed them as dangerous radicals. What could be more American than slavery, the vital underpinning of the southern economy? After all, eight of the first twelve American presidents, who ran the country during its first forty-nine years, owned slaves. But that's the meta story. The human story unfolded day in and day out, not in the White House or on grand plantations, but on modest farms across the South, where white men and women worked alongside and lived alongside their human property, old men, babies, children, grandmothers, newlyweds. On small farms like Henry's, the relationships between the master, his family, and his slaves were not mediated by overseers. They were more intimate, more personal.

Henry's descendants like to think that he welcomed Melvinia, that he clothed and fed her and treated her as a member of his family. He certainly did not come from a wealthy background himself; he knew what it was like to struggle. But Henry also lived in a slave society and was well aware of the tangible benefits that African Americans conveyed to their owners. While he had never owned a slave before 1852, his father, and possibly his grandfather, had personally benefited from the peculiar institution. Henry was the descendant of Irishmen who had emigrated to the country and discovered that some of the most prominent men in the new world were slave owners. It was only through several strokes of luck that the Shields family joined their ranks. Henry's grandfather, Andrew Shields, embodied many of the contradictions of American slave society. According to family lore, Andrew moved to the American colonies sometime in the 1700s. He embraced the revolutionary cause and fought the British in Georgia during the Revolutionary War. In return, his descendants say, the new American government awarded him some land. Like many newly minted citizens, Andrew seemed to have no problem embracing the American ideals of democracy and freedom on the one hand while benefiting from slavery and subjugation on the other. Georgia state records from 1782 indicate that an Andrew Shields was given more than two hundred acres of land in Georgia's plantation belt that had been confiscated from the British in exchange for his war service. He was also allowed to "take into his possession any negroes belonging to the confiscated estates," the records show. Andrew, the Irish immigrant, may have become the first of his line to own human beings.

What happened to that land and those slaves remains unclear, but they definitely did not end up in the possession of Andrew's son, Moses, who was Henry's father. Moses was landless and slaveless when he lived in Spartanburg, South Carolina, in 1810. He had six children then—Henry was born a year later, on September 22, 1811—and he probably rented land or worked as a farm laborer to make ends meet. His chances of speedy economic and social advancement might have seemed fairly remote, save for one thing: he had married well. His wife, Jane, was the daughter of a wealthy farmer, and over the years Moses would reap the benefits of his father-in-law's largesse. He received 212 acres of land from him in 1823. And when the older man died, sometime around 1838, Moses inherited his very first slave, a man by the name of Stephen. His son, Henry, was about twenty-six then. Henry had also benefited from a good match, to Christian Patterson, the daughter of the prosperous farmer, David Patterson. Henry was living with his wife and their three children around the time his father, Moses, became a slave owner. Henry did not own any land at the time so he probably rented farmland or worked as a hired laborer, cultivating and tilling the earth with his own hands. But he lived near his father and father-in-law and could see firsthand what the experience of slave ownership was like. He could certainly witness up close the enormous benefits that slavery bestowed upon its white beneficiaries.

In up-country South Carolina, even farmers who owned just one or two slaves typically produced 50 percent more corn and cultivated twice the arable farmland than their non-slave-owning peers. The median wealth of these farmers was typically more than two times higher than those who did not own slaves. Yeoman farmers had to hire extra help or rely on their unmarried sons to boost their agricultural output; slave owners, on the other hand, did not have to worry about salaries or complicated family dynamics. David Golightly Harris, a Spartanburg farmer who owned several slaves, described the sense of satisfaction he felt when he sent a four-year-old slave girl to fetch some water for the first time. In that small gesture, he could envision a lifetime of unpaid labor, all for his benefit. "Our little negro brought her first bucket of water from the spring," Harris wrote in his journal. "That was the first of many trips if she lives long."

Henry, who had a wife and at least five children to feed in 1840, might have hoped to inherit a portion of his father's farm as well as his slave. It was not to be. Moses died in debt, virtually insolvent. In 1842, the sheriff of Spartanburg seized all the land where "Moses Sheals lived at the time of his death" to cover those debts. His land was sold at public auction. The fate of his slave, Stephen, is unknown. Moses could have sold him before he died, in a desperate attempt to get his financial house in order. No matter the reason, Henry did not inherit any land or slaves from his father. Seeing little hope of climbing the social and economic ladder in Spartanburg, he decided to move to the new frontier, the wilderness opening up across the Deep South. Thousands of South Carolinians were moving around that time, drawn by the availability of cheap, fertile land. So many left, in fact, that the state's *Camden Journal* reported that "the old and the young are preparing to emigrate, and the inquiry is not whether you are going, but when do you go."

Moses Shields's children scattered after his death. One of Henry's sisters packed up and moved to Alabama with her husband and children. One of his brothers headed to Tennessee. His sister-in-law migrated to Henry County, Georgia, with her family and Henry ended up there, too, right next door, sometime around 1848. In Georgia, Henry was able to buy a farm, his first piece of property, which was worth approximately $500 in 1850. He was starting small. His neighbors, by contrast, owned farms valued between $1,000 and $2,000. But Melvinia's arrival—along with the two other slaves, Tom and Mandrew, from his father-in-law's estate—boosted Henry's prospects significantly. He was no longer an ordinary yeoman farmer forced to scrape by solely on the strength of his own labor. Suddenly, he was a slave owner, a man of means, in a rough-and-tumble community that seemed poised to prosper.

A recently established railroad rumbled through Jonesboro, the nearest town. The Macon and Western Branch Telegraph Company had connected the small communities in the region—via Morse code— with nearby Atlanta. A new post office had flung open its doors, along with a Methodist church, an Episcopal mission, and three schools. George White, a noted historian at the time, described the town as "a thriving place." (In the 1840s, Mr. White's assessment of local society was less kind; he noted then that the population was "improving.") But it was still tough living. In that part of Georgia, droughts, floods, and windstorms battered crops and livelihoods; and sicknesses ravaged families. The soil wasn't fertile enough to grow much cotton, the state's cash crop, and the biggest settlements were still nothing to speak of. Jonesboro, with a population of 200, was a speck on the map compared to Spartanburg.

It was in this strange new world that young Melvinia was forced to find her bearings. The familiar faces that she had grown up with were long gone. The bustle and comforts of life in South Carolina amid the sizable enslaved community she knew so well was little more than a memory. Melvinia shared a single house that Henry had designated for his three new human possessions. And when she left it, to walk or to work in the green fields, she no longer toiled alongside dozens of African Americans. Instead, the little girl inevitably spent much of her time with Henry and his family. Her owner, after all, had more children than slaves. In such close quarters, local historians say, it was impossible for blacks and whites "not to know each other on a personal, human level."

In northern Georgia, where white men and women worked side by side with their slaves, social interactions across the color line were typically more relaxed and intimate than on larger estates. Masters and slaves often attended church together—though blacks were usually segregated inside—and white men often adopted a more lenient attitude toward discipline. This kind of casual relationship between whites and their slaves raised eyebrows in some quarters, particularly among wealthy planters, who complained that some blacks even referred to their owners by their first names. Daniel Robinson Hundley grumbled that yeoman farmers like Henry made "so little distinction between master and man, that their negroes invariably become spoiled . . . and in all things [are] treated more like equals than slaves . . ."

Mr. Hundley was certainly overstating the matter; whites almost never treated their slaves as equals. But there's little doubt that Melvinia got to know her owners in a way that would have been nearly impossible on a vast plantation with hundreds or even dozens of slaves. Her new life in Georgia revolved around Henry, his wife, and their children, and the day-to-day happenings on the farm as she went about the chores common for young slaves: fetching water, cleaning house, helping to serve meals, milking cows, and tending livestock. Some historians have argued that life was better for slaves in a small, intimate environment. Melvinia had a face-to-face, personal relationship with her owner and his family. She had been the favored slave of Mr. Patterson, the father of Henry's wife, Christian, and she may have held some sentimental value to her new owners as well. She might have been somewhat privileged, as a result, receiving extra food, better clothing, less onerous duties, and more free time to play with Henry's children. But more modern scholarship has cast some doubt on the assumption that smaller farms were always better. "For a long time, historians assumed that slavery would be less brutal and exploitative on small farms than on large plantations," said Steven Hahn, the author of the Pulitzer Prize–winning book *A Nation Under Our Feet: Black Political Struggles in the Rural South from Slavery to the Great Migration.* "The idea was that slaves and owners would be in close quarters, work out in the fields together, and have a more cooperative experience. But from the slaves' point of view, this environment was far more problematic. Because small farmers had fewer resources, the slaves likely received even poorer quality food and housing, and were more vulnerable to sale. And slaves generally regarded proximity to their owners—and to their owners' demands—as a real liabilty. Most preferred to be among other slaves than among white folk."

Slaves like Melvinia, who lived in close quarters with their owners, were often forced to give up what small measure of independence they enjoyed. It was much easier for their owners to monitor and dictate the course of their daily lives, to decide, for instance, whether Melvinia could tend to a small garden or Tom could hunt small animals on the farm to supplement their meals; whether they could meet privately with other slaves to pray, sing, and worship; whether they could secretly learn to read or write. And with so few other slaves close by, it was harder to find social outlets, friends, counselors, and potential mates. Melvinia, at least, knew Mandrew and Tom from their time together in South Carolina. They may have comforted her, and each other, as they coped with the agonizing separation from the world they knew and made their peace with the world they didn't. Melvinia's new owners may have favored her to a certain degree, but she was still treated as a servant, not as a member of the family. Henry and his wife believed in educating girls and sent their daughters to school, but Melvinia was not taught to read or write. Henry and Christian may have thought that education was best reserved for white people, not blacks relegated to servitude. They may have also feared the authorities: Georgia was one of four states—along with Virginia, North Carolina, and South Carolina—that banned teaching slaves to read and write during the last thirty years of slavery. (In Georgia, teaching a slave to read or write was a misdemeanor punishable by fine and imprisonment, though some white owners chose to defy that law.) Whatever the reason, a clear dividing line separated the Shieldses' daughters from the young slave girl in their care. Melvinia would be in her forties before she learned to read.

But there is no doubt that she knew the family intimately. Henry certainly knew her by name, as did his sons and daughters. When Melvinia arrived, Henry had eight children, a veritable slew of potential playmates. There were four boys and four girls, ranging in age from five to eighteen. Blacks and whites often played together as children, and Melvinia may have found some solace in the silly games and childish diversions. She could have closed her eyes and, for a moment, felt just like any other little girl, lost in the joy of play. That would soon change. In the 1850s, while Henry was establishing his reputation as an up-and-coming farmer, Melvinia was maturing, blossoming from a child into a young woman. The white men on and around that farm would soon start to see her in a different light.

TWENTY-THREE

South Carolina Gold

I N THE VAST, SWELTERING PLANTATIONS THAT HUGGED THE
South Carolina coastline, white men spoke of rice with something akin to reverence. It was the cash crop, the maker of
princely fortunes, the delicate morsel that powered the state's economy. No wonder they called it South Carolina gold. It sprouted forth
in stalks, row upon row, from the carved-out tidal basins of the winding rivers that flowed to the Atlantic, nature's gift of bounty from
what had once been branch and muck. Here, a world away from the
small, rough slaveholdings of northern Georgia, thousands of enslaved
African Americans dedicated their working lives to the tiny, precious grain. They chopped and dug with axes and hoes and carved
rice fields out of swampy thickets of sweet gum, cypress, and tupelo
trees. They harnessed the rushing tides to irrigate the fledgling, tender
sprouts. They hitched their lives to rice-growing rhythms as familiar
and predictable as the drenching torrents of springtime and the malarial swelter of summer. There was plowing in March and planting in
April, followed by the flooding and draining and hoeing of the fields.
Over the next months, the cycle repeated with flooding and draining,
flooding and draining until September, when those lush fields were
finally ready for harvest. Rice cultivation originated in Africa, and

many black men and women were keenly aware that the state's booming rice production would be impossible without them. "All dem rice field been nothing but swamp," said Gabe Lance, a former slave who worked those fields in Georgetown, South Carolina. "Slavery people cut kennel (canal) and cut down woods—and dig ditch through raw woods. All been clear up for plant by slavery people."

American slavery is often viewed as uniform and static, but it varied enormously, from place to place, from owner to owner, from city to countryside, from North to South. In South Carolina alone, there were small holdings and grand plantations, yeoman cotton farmers and rice-planting Brahmins. That breadth and depth unfolded in the ancestral lines of Mrs. Obama's family tree as well. It would be in coastal Georgetown County, among those green rice fields, that the First Lady's paternal forebears would come of age in that rarest of slaveholdings, the sprawling southern plantation. Georgetown was about 220 miles away from Spartanburg, where Melvinia grew up as a child, but it might as well have been worlds away. In Spartanburg, which was predominantly white, a man was considered wealthy if he owned twenty slaves, and most struggling farmers owned no human property at all. In Georgetown, wealthy white aristocrats owned hundreds of slaves, so many, in fact, that they often hired white overseers to manage their vast supply of black laborers. There, the enslaved African American population so exceeded that of whites that white visitors to Georgetown were often astonished by the endless sea of black faces. One startled Northern visitor noted, upon his arrival in town, that "not a white face was to be seen."

The steamy, sultry climate—so different from Spartanburg's temperate climes—was ideal for the cultivation of rice, but it took its toll on the people who lived and worked there. In the summer, the sun blistered and the thick humid air settled over the town like a damp, sticky blanket that was impossible to escape. Snakes, malarial mosquitoes, and alligators lurked in the winding rivers. And for much of the growing season, the standing water in the rice fields emitted a stench that assaulted the senses. One local historian described the climate in plain terms, calling it "moist, hot, and unhealthy." Another southern planter warned one of his cousins in Scotland of the "marsh miasma, which engenders fevers of a dangerous nature; fatal, indeed, to white men in most cases; and even negroes in some seasons, suffer greatly from it." Wealthy planters frequently fled Georgetown altogether during the searing summer months for Charleston, Spartanburg, and other locales. Mrs. Obama's ancestors didn't have that option. Slaves labored there year in and year out, sometimes up to their knees in the swampy muck, plagued by biting mosquitoes and reptiles. The harsh working conditions meant high mortality rates, and many slaves died young, struck down in droves by disease. Three of Mrs. Obama's paternal great-great-grandparents were among the survivors.

They were full-blooded human beings, real people with hopes and joys and agonies. But they left behind little evidence of their presence, as if they had flitted for a time through those South Carolina rice fields and then dissipated into nothingness. They were some of the countless, faceless slaves who toiled for owners who barely knew their names and rarely bothered to record them. The three ancestors left their imprints here and there, enough to reveal the sketchy outlines of their lives, but never their fullness. The hungry swampland, the twisting vines, and the thick grasses seemed to have swallowed their footsteps, one by one, as soon as they passed by. We may never know for sure, but historical records suggest that a teenage girl named Tira and a young man named Caeser were two of those enslaved great-great-grandparents. A young boy named Jim was the third. Tira and Caeser worked on one plantation while Jim lived on another. He may never have met the other two. But their stories, and their histories, would intertwine years later through the bond between their children, inheritors of the familial fortitude that took root here in South Carolina's low country.

Tira was born sometime around 1837; her precise date of birth remains unknown. She lived and worked on Weymouth plantation, a sprawling estate that stretched for more than a thousand acres along the winding Pee Dee River. More than two hundred enslaved African

Americans worked there, forming a deeply interconnected community that supported and comforted its people and, at times, eased some of life's harshness. They also helped to make their owner—Ralph Stead Izard Jr.—one of the richest men in Georgetown. (Before the Civil War, his slaves produced 1.2 million pounds of rice and 2,500 bushels of corn in one year alone.) Educated in Europe, Mr. Izard was accustomed to life's finer pleasures. He was the worldly, patrician scion of one of South Carolina's oldest rice-planting families. His second cousin, who shared the same surname, served in the United States Senate. And as president of the local Planters Club, he convened social gatherings for some of the wealthiest men in South Carolina who dined, at least on one occasion, on venison and shrimp, champagne and brandy. Mr. Izard, who spent the hot summer months in Newport, Rhode Island, may not have known Tira at all and probably gave little thought to her hopes and dreams. As he mixed and mingled with Georgetown's most powerful men, Tira was trying to fashion a life for herself within the confines of bondage, to seize and savor those moments that make life worth living. It was no easy task.

Slaves like Tira often found themselves upended by forces beyond their control, their existences buffeted like green leaves torn from their branches during the raging storms that swept the Atlantic coast. The slave experience varied from farm to plantation, plantation to city, but there were some harsh, universal truths: epidemics and illnesses snatched newborns away from wailing mothers; slave owners often separated husbands from wives, brothers from sisters, parents from children. Yet even as they endured agonizing moments during their years in captivity, Mrs. Obama's ancestors found ways to bring beauty into lives so often bereft of it: they cherished their families; they found glimmers of humanity in some of their white masters and overseers. And when Tira found love, she held on tight.

She met the man she would spend her life with on the plantation where they both worked. His name was Caeser Cohen. Born in South Carolina, he had dark skin and a surname that suggested an intriguing connection to one of Georgetown's oldest and most distinguished Jewish families. Moses Cohen, who emigrated from London to South Carolina around 1750, was the first chief rabbi of Charleston's Congregation of Beth Elohim, the birthplace of Reform Judaism in the United States. His two sons, Abraham and Solomon, moved to Georgetown and became deeply involved in its civic and political life. Abraham, who fought in the Revolutionary War and served as the town's postmaster, met with George Washington when the American president visited Georgetown in 1791. Solomon was a director of the Bank of the State of South Carolina and his son, Solomon Jr., was elected to the South Carolina State Senate in 1830. The family was so prominent that its weddings, funerals, and family happenings were often chronicled in the local newspapers. As members of Georgetown's high society, it should come as little surprise that the Cohens also owned plantations and slaves. Solomon Sr. had nine slaves in 1790 and twenty-four slaves in 1810. His son, Jacob Cohen, owned 302 slaves in 1830. (Even the family's patriarch, Rabbi Moses Cohen, appeared to have relied on indentured labor—though in his case, his servant was white. On August 15, 1753, the rabbi advertised in the *South Carolina Gazette* for "a runaway Dutch servant-girl about 10 years of age and 4 feet 6 inches high.") Most of the Cohens eventually left Georgetown for Charleston, but before they did, it is possible that one of the members of this prominent Jewish family owned Caeser or his parents.

By 1858, Caeser belonged to Mr. Izard at Weymouth, where Tira caught his attention. Men and women were often assigned different tasks on the rice plantations, but they could frequently steal glances of each other. One observer on a rice plantation recalled watching a crew of black men digging trenches for a group of enslaved women who were planting rice. The men started first. "Some little way behind them came the sowers, all women, with their skirts tied up, and carrying the seed-rice in handle baskets, open-mouthed bags, or even in their aprons. With the regularity of machines, their hands went into the receptacles and with a long, graceful, far-reaching and apparently careless swing of the arm, they sent the rich yellow grain flying through the air straight into the ditch." Maybe the courtship between Tira and Caeser started during the planting. Young people also courted at dances and corn shuckings in the slave quarters, where they flirted, sang songs, and played matchmaking games. Some young men would sing, "I'll give you a half dollar if you come out tonight." Others, who stumbled across a red ear of corn during the shucking, would have to "tell who his best gal was." Caeser may have also noticed Tira as she went in and out of the plantation's manor. She appears to have been close to her mistress, Rosetta Ella Izard. Many slaves have described their experiences with brutal masters and harsh mistresses, but Mrs. Izard appears to have been a kindly woman. She left a deep impression on Tira that would endure years after slavery ended.

Love on a plantation was a refuge from the hardships of slavery. But it could also be fleeting and heartrending. There were countless perils to consider for any enslaved woman considering marriage, first among them the prospect that she might be sold and separated from her beloved and any children they might have. Tira must have pondered that possibility. But in the end, she decided not to let fear stand in the way of her happiness. Tom Jones, a runaway slave who wrote about his time in bondage, could have been speaking for her when he described why he so desperately wanted to get married: "I wanted a friend to whom I could tell my story of sorrows, of unsatisfied longing, of new and fondly cherished plans." When Caeser, who was in his twenties and stood about five foot seven, finally proposed, Tira accepted.

As slaves, Tira and Caeser had no right to earn a wage for their labor and no right to demand a lifetime of living with their families. As a young couple in love, that didn't stop them from dreaming of a common-law wedding. They sought out the assistance of Tony Izard, the plantation's enslaved blacksmith and preacher. Mr. Izard married the living and buried the dead at Weymouth, and at least one of his weddings, held on a Monday night in the slave quarters, drew a crowd of whites and blacks alike. Slaves knew that these common-law weddings were not formally recognized under the law, but that did not stop them from making enduring commitments to each other. Tira and Caeser took their turn before that preacher and exchanged their vows with his blessings. There was no wedding license, no marriage certificate to mark the moment. There is no indication that their master deemed the ceremony worth mentioning in his private papers.

Tira and Caeser were just two of the millions of slaves who would never appear in a will or a master's records. But Tira never forgot that day. She would describe it herself, in her own words. "There is no record or certificate of my marriage as it was before the war and not in use then among colored people," Tira said several decades after the Civil War in one of the rarest surviving records from one of Mrs. Obama's enslaved ancestors. She described the year of her marriage, the place, and the name of the preacher. Tira and her new husband were as bound to each other as if they had been married in a white man's chapel. One of their fellow slaves would later describe Tira as "a lawful wife."

The wedding vows they exchanged that day held for more than four decades. Years after they were married, nearly a decade after Emancipation, Tira's thoughts would wander back to those days on Weymouth plantation, and to Rosetta Izard, her former mistress, who must have treated her with compassion. When Tira and Caeser welcomed their second-born daughter into the world, they named her Rose and called her Rosetta for much of her childhood. Rosetta, known as Rosella as an adult, would ultimately meet and marry the son of Jim Robinson, the last known forebear of the First Lady to grow up on Georgetown's rice plantations. That union drew those two paternal lines together and inched the family that much closer to its march northward.

JIM ROBINSON, Mrs. Obama's great-great-grandfather, was born in South Carolina sometime around 1850. He took his first steps there and spoke his first words under the careful watch of the enslaved women around him. Efforts to identify his parents have proven fruitless, given the scanty historical records that have survived from that time. Jim is where the story begins. Mrs. Obama's paternal line can be traced back no further. The names of his parents and grandparents—and the parents and grandparents of Tira and Caeser, for that matter—appear to be completely lost. But Jim did leave something behind, a gift to his descendants, a clue that offered a hint about his family's earliest origins. He left them his language, called Gullah, a Creole hybrid that blended African and English elements and was commonly spoken by the slaves on South Carolina's coastal rice plantations.

Gullah emerged from the clash of cultures, the collision between the tongues of Africa and America. It was created by Africans who were stolen from the rice-growing region of the continent, which stretched from Senegal to Sierra Leone, and then shipped to these English-speaking shores. White plantation owners in South Carolina prized slaves from that corner of the African continent because of their rice-growing expertise. As early as the late 1600s, planters in the American colonies knew that rice could grow in the semitropical Atlantic coast. But they did not know how to make the crop flourish. They learned to import Africans who knew how to plant, harvest, and process the grain. Slave traders who brought their human wares to Charleston promoted the rice-growing skills of their shackled merchandise, noting in auction posters and newspaper announcements that their slaves were "accustomed to the planting of rice." Those slaves and their descendants held on to their customs and to their language for generations, just as Mrs. Obama's ancestors did. We may never know the identities of Jim's parents, but we know that they were likely the children or grandchildren of West Africans who created an entirely new way of speaking on South Carolina's coastal plantations and then passed that language from one generation to the next. The First Lady's grandfather, Fraser Robinson Jr., knew how to speak Gullah. He was Jim Robinson's grandson. When Fraser Jr. died in 1986, the old language finally died with him. Today, none of his children or grandchildren can speak it.

Jim might have grown up with his parents, and if he did, they probably worked in the rice fields while he was young. "Nurses"—enslaved women who were too old or too young to work in the fields—usually watched over the children. Margaret Bryant, a former slave in Georgetown, recalled that her aunt did that kind of work. "My Pa sister, Ritta One, had that job. Nuss (nurse) the chillen . . . All size chillen." Jim would have played with the other boys and girls while his parents tended to the fields. The Georgetown region at the time was the leading rice producer in the country, supplying 33.3 percent of the nation's rice in 1850. White overseers—not patrician masters, who often spent months away from their plantations—typically supervised the work. Slaves in predominantly black Georgetown had little contact with their white owners, little contact with whites in general. Historians say that left slaves with some measure of autonomy, but only so much. Some slaves struggled to complete their work. Others rebelled or chafed at the arduous labor. And when they did, they paid the price. Hagar Brown, who was enslaved on one of the Georgetown plantations, said that the estate's overseer whipped her sister because she constantly fell behind in her work. "Beat me sister," Mrs. Brown said. "Me sister sickly. Never could clear task like he want." There was no escape, she said, from the backbreaking labor. Some slaves learned that the hard way. Mrs. Brown's mother told her about the time when some of her fellow slaves decided to run for freedom. "Ma say some dem plan to run way. Say, 'Less run! Less run!'" Mrs. Brown remembered. "Master ketch dem and fetch dem in. Lay 'em cross barrel. Beat dem till they wash in blood." Not all white owners and overseers treated their black laborers harshly, though. As young Jim grew up, he appears to have developed a deep, lifelong connection with the man who supervised him and the other slaves. It was a connection that would change the course of his son's life.

Precisely which plantation Jim lived on, though, has been something of a mystery. Jim's name does not appear in any documents kept by Georgetown's slave owners. Many records that described slaves in some detail were destroyed during the Civil War when some courthouses were burned in the South. "We never heard anything about slavery," said Ms. Siau, Jim's great-granddaughter, who said her parents and grandparents never spoke of it. During the 2008 presidential campaign, aides to the Obamas decided to try to find out the truth. They hired Toni Carrier, director of Lowcountry Africana, a research center at the University of South Florida, and told her that some members of the Robinson family believed that their ancestors had lived at Friendfield, which sat along the Sampit River. Friendfield was owned by Francis Withers, a Harvard-educated planter who lived in an elegant mansion on the property, with front steps and a porch made from flagstone, wrought-iron banisters and stair railings, and wallpaper from Paris. His slaves lived in three parallel rows of ten to thirteen cabins, along a road known as Slave Street. The cabins were just nineteen feet deep and housed several families. Mr. Withers also built a meetinghouse where slaves could pray, and he paid the salary of the preacher. In his will, he asked that his slaves at Friendfield be "treated with great kindness and be fed and clothed." He died in 1847, three years before Jim was born, and left the plantation to his stepdaughter. In 1860, 273 slaves lived on the Friendfield plantation, census records show, including six boys who were ten years old, the age Jim would have been then.

Several of the First Lady's cousins have toured the old Friendfield plantation in an effort to connect with the family's lost past. They have wept at the slave cemetery on the property, believing that their ancestors were buried there. But beyond the fragmentary record that mentions the nameless ten-year-old boys who were enslaved at Friendfield, there is virtually nothing that directly links young Jim to that plantation. In an interview, Ms. Carrier, the historian hired by the Obama campaign, said that the link between

Friendfield and Jim Robinson was tenuous. She said that she and her team had only twelve days on the ground in Georgetown to do their research, and they were limited to studying historical records because the Obama campaign did not give them permission to speak to members of Mrs. Obama's family. "This is what these documents suggest, but we didn't have an awful lot to start on," Ms. Carrier said. "There's no smoking gun at all. We don't have a document that ties him to Friendfield."

In fact, a closer look at historical records suggests that Jim actually lived elsewhere—on another rice plantation called Maryville, which sat between the mouth of the Sampit River and Winyah Bay. Maryville was owned in the 1800s by John Harleston Read Sr., a legislator in the state assembly. Mr. Read's son, John Harleston Read II, inherited Maryville shortly before the Civil War. The Reads spent the hot summer months in their Charleston mansion and sent at least one child to Switzerland for schooling. Slaves on the plantation, which spanned 4,250 acres and was valued at $185,000, produced 1.5 million pounds of rice in 1850. The white men who supervised Mr. Read's slaves at Maryville that year lived near the plantation. One of those overseers was a man whose family is well known to the elders in Mrs. Obama's family. His name was William Nesmith. He was the father of Francis Nesmith, the white man who would welcome Jim's son, Fraser, into his home decades later and transform the young boy's prospects.

The First Lady's relatives say that the Nesmith and Robinson families were close for years. In 1860, 564 slaves lived and worked at Maryville, including three boys who were ten years old, Jim's age. Census records also show that twenty years later, after Emancipation, Jim Robinson and William Nesmith both lived near Georgetown's Black River. It seems likely, then, that the friendship between the two families began in slavery and endured for decades afterward, extending from one generation to the next. The census records suggest that it all began at Maryville plantation, where Jim Robinson was a young slave and William Nesmith was an overseer. We don't know what might have drawn them together. But somehow, that young black boy appears to have left a deep impression on his white boss. Despite the inevitable tensions between slaves and overseers, blacks and whites, Jim Robinson and William Nesmith seem to have forged a rare bond that would last for decades.

TWENTY-FOUR

A Child Is Born

NO ONE ALIVE TODAY REMEMBERS HEARING STORIES OF what Melvinia was like as a teenager, whether she was willowy or shapely, shy and demure, or vivacious and spirited, the kind of girl who drew men to her without even trying. But sometime between 1858 and 1860, the coffee-colored slave with dark eyes and long, wavy hair began to attract the attention of a white man on or near the Shields farm, where slavery was helping her owner to flourish.

In 1860, Henry Shields was about forty-nine years old and in the prime of his life. He had ten children, including four grown sons who still lived at home. His green farmland extended as far as the eye could see, nearly two hundred acres in all. As he strode across his property, past the rows of white cotton, the fields of swaying wheat and Indian corn, past Melvinia and the two other slaves who helped him plant, plow, and clean, he might have thanked God for his good fortune. He would always have to work with his own hands. He would never be rich. But he was no longer the landless young man who had left South Carolina to find his way in the rough, untrampled wilds of northern Georgia. He was established: between 1850 and 1860, he acquired more land and watched the value of his property triple, from $500 to

$1,800. His personal estate was worth $3,475, more than that of any of his close neighbors. He owned three horses, five milk cows, eight head of cattle, twenty sheep, seventeen pigs, and other livestock. He grew rye and sweet potatoes as well as corn, wheat, and cotton. He tended bees, too, for the honey. He had sons who could help him work his farm and sell its bounty. But it was his ownership of two teenage girls and a fifty-year-old man that truly distinguished him from ordinary neighbors. Only 117 people—about a third of the white heads of household in the county—owned human property. Roughly half of those people—like Henry—owned fewer than five slaves. Like other small slaveholders, he and his sons would have worked side by side with their African American laborers. They would have known each of their slaves by name, and they would have watched as Melvinia grew from girlhood to womanhood.

Melvinia, who arrived on Henry's farm when she was about eight years old, was about sixteen in 1860. She shared a house with the other slaves, Tom and Mandrew. Melvinia's small universe also included her master and his wife, Christian, and their six sons and four daughters. Whether she was cooking meals in the house, tending the master's younger children, or picking cotton in the fields, Melvinia was rarely on her own. At the same time, she was forced to navigate the treacherous period of adolescence without her mother or her aunts or any black women to guide her. She may have listened to Henry's older daughters whisper about courtship and marriage when she helped them cook in the kitchen or tend to the crops in the fields. She may have dreamed of it herself. Maybe she noticed a young black man in town who was driving his owners' carriage or flirted with a young man owned by one of the Shieldses' neighbors. She may have tried on the castaway frocks of her masters' daughters and imagined her own wedding day. She may have envisioned living in her own house, with a husband and young children, creating the kind of family she had lost when she was forced to leave South Carolina. Melvinia was a slave, but she was still a young woman with a young woman's hopes and dreams. For the white girls on the Shields farm, those years before the

Civil War may well have been full of romantic musings and wedding plans. Melvinia may have longed for the same. What she may not have known, being so far from aunts or cousins or anyone who could have warned her, was that those years could be perilous for enslaved African American women.

Harriet Jacobs, who was a slave in North Carolina, described those teenage years as harrowing ones in a memoir that was published in Boston in 1860, around the time when a white man began pursuing Melvinia. "The slave girl is reared in an atmosphere of licentiousness and fear," said Miss Jacobs, who was relentlessly pursued by her fifty-five-year-old master once she turned fifteen. "When she is fourteen or fifteen, her owner, or his sons, or the overseer, or perhaps all of them, begin to bribe her with presents. If these fail to accomplish their purpose, she is whipped or starved into submission to their will. She may have had religious principles inculcated by some pious mother or grandmother, or some good mistress; she may have had a lover, whose good opinion and peace of mind are dear to her heart; or the profligate men who have power over her may be exceedingly odious to her. But resistance is hopeless."

Miss Jacobs's master followed her wherever she went. He offered her favors in exchange for sex. When she refused, he threatened to kill her if she did not submit. He "met me at every turn, reminding me that I belonged to him, and swearing by heaven and earth that he would compel me to submit to him," she wrote. "If I went out for a breath of fresh air, after a day of unwearied toil, his footsteps dogged me. If I knelt by my mother's grave, his dark shadow fell on me even there. The light heart which nature had given me became heavy with sad forebodings . . . O, what days and nights of fear and sorrow that man caused me!"

Miss Jacobs is a rare voice from that time. She escaped from her master, moved north, and wrote the memoir that described her plight. Melvinia was illiterate as a young woman, not that she would have written about what happened to her anyway. It is her silence that echoes across the centuries. She did not name the white man who pursued her, or describe whether he was tall or short, young or old, handsome or unattractive, well off or poor, married or single. She may have found her situation too shameful, or too commonplace.

Sex between white men and black women was a regular part of life on big plantations and small farms. Masters and their young sons, overseers, and others often preyed on their female slaves. Some white men wooed their enslaved women with small presents and promises of privilege. Others made no pretense of such pleasantries. In Hancock County, Georgia, David Dickson set his sights on a thirteen-year-old slave girl on his plantation and "just rode up and swung her up on his horse and that was the end of that." Worse still was what Mollie Kinsey remembered of her sister's experience as a young girl: "They'd make her go out and lay on a table and two or three white men would have in'ercourse with her befo' they'd let her git up." These women had no recourse. Their fathers, brothers, and husbands risked lashings or worse if they protested. The women themselves could not appeal to the police or to the courts. Georgia had instituted the death penalty for any man of color who dared to rape a white woman. But no penalty existed for white men who raped a black woman. Such assaults were not considered crimes under Georgia's criminal code.

The men on the Shields farm had known Melvinia since she was a little girl. She worked for them, cooked and cleaned for them, and probably played with them when they were all young children, innocent of what was to come. Some of Henry's descendants pray that Melvinia fell in love. Some slaves did grow fond of the white men who kept them as mistresses. In Melvinia's case, such feelings may well have depended on the identity of the man who was pursuing her. There were five grown men in the Shields family, including Henry, her owner. No images survive of Henry, but a photograph of his younger brother, Moses, has remained in the family for generations, offering an idea of what the white Shields men looked like. Moses was a strikingly handsome man with light eyes and dark hair, high cheekbones and a narrow nose. As Henry aged, his descendants imagine that he looked much like his sons and grandsons did when he approached fifty, with a full head of hair, soon to turn snow white, and a narrow sliver of a mouth. Henry was married, but that rarely deterred a determined slave owner from having his way with his female property. His four grown sons ranged in age from nineteen to twenty-four. David and Moses, the two oldest at twenty-three and twenty-four, were farmers in their own right, who had already earned their own money. They may have admired Melvinia as they worked in the fields. Charles Marion Shields, who was twenty-one, was partially paralyzed on his right side and walked with a limp, the result of a childhood bout with polio, his descendants believe. Maybe because of his physical limitations, he continued his schooling into adulthood. Elisha Shields, nineteen, had given up on school and must have worked on the family farm, though he had yet to put aside any money of his own.

These brothers had watched Melvinia grow from a little girl to a young woman on the farm. She watched them grow, too. There is no way to know whether she was fond of them; whether she admired the older Shields boys, David and Moses, who must have dreamed of owning their own farms and slaves someday; or whether she took to bookish Charles Marion, or his younger brother, Elisha. It is possible, too, that she tried to keep her distance from the men in the family as she grew up. She might have been warned by Tom, the fifty-year-old slave, to be careful, to keep to herself. Given how closely the slaves must have worked with the Shields family, his admonitions, though, would have been meaningless. Descendants of these Shields men point out that there may have been other white male visitors to the farm, too, relatives or friends of the family or merchants who purchased the farm's cotton and corn. Those men could have noticed Melvinia as well.

There is no doubt, however, that someone was drawn to her. One day, between 1858 and 1860, a white man had sex with Melvinia, who was between fourteen and sixteen years old at the time. Was she raped? It is certainly possible, given the circumstances of the times. Melvinia was a young, vulnerable teenage girl—separated from any close family—living in a society that viewed a white man's rape of his slave women as a right, not a crime. But whether that actually happened, whether she cowered from her attacker, whether she was beaten or wept in shame and anger at the outrage, we will never know for sure. For while rape was common, all too common, there are hints that Melvinia's dealings with the white man who pursued her were more complicated, more complex. The liaison that began on that farm in Georgia that year appears to have endured for at least a decade. Historians have tried to better understand such liaisons, which were often inscrutable because they were, by their nature, often kept hidden. Some enslaved women maintained long-term relationships with white men, who sheltered them, offered them financial stability, and cared for their children. In rare instances, those relationships appear to have involved real affection, on both sides, and sometimes even love. Some may have started with violence and evolved into something else over time. Others were consensual, though always framed by the fact that the white man held all the power in the relationship—he could beat his woman, maim his woman, or sell his woman—while the enslaved woman had no power at all. Some women looked at their circumstances and decided to enter into the relationship, whether out of love or out of more practical considerations. A white suitor might provide his slave mistress with better clothing, better food, and some protection from the harshness of slavery.

Harriet Jacobs, the enslaved woman who wrote her memoir, highlights the complexity and ambiguity that existed in some of the dealings between black women and white men during slavery. She hated her owner who pursued her so relentlessly. But she wrote with some affection about another white man, a prominent lawyer, who also wanted a sexual relationship with her. The attorney lived in Harriet's neighborhood and knew that her master was pursuing and persecuting her. "He expressed a great deal of sympathy, and a wish to aid me," she wrote. Miss/Mrs. Jacobs, who was fifteen at the time, was flattered, she said, by attention "from a superior person." But she also viewed this kindly white man as her best hope of thwarting her master's efforts to have sex with her. She thought her owner might be so furious that she had spurned his advances in favor of those of another man that he would sell her and that the lawyer would buy her. It was the only way she could envision escaping her master's ongoing pursuit. So her decision to enter into a sexual relationship with the lawyer wasn't entirely voluntary. Inexorably tied to her decision was the hope that this white lawyer would buy her and free her, along with any children they might have. She felt like this was the only way to save her life. It demonstrates how difficult it is to categorize these relationships more than a century later.

No one knows whether the man who impregnated Melvinia boasted of his exploits or tried to keep them quiet, but within months, the truth would have been apparent to everyone on the farm, whether they worked in the house or in the fields, whether they were Henry's young daughters or his wife or his sons. Her stomach swelled as the months passed. Melvinia was pregnant. There was no hiding that. Pregnancy often triggers a tumult of emotions. There are the surging hormones, the excitement about the prospect of one's first child, the morning sickness, the fatigue. All of that must have been coupled with anxiety about her circumstances. Henry might have seen Melvinia's swelling belly as a symbol of his expanding wealth and prestige. Soon he would have an additional slave to add to his assets. His wife, Christian, might have greeted the news with some unease, on the other hand, particularly if she worried that her husband or one of her sons was the father.

Such reckonings were typically hardest on the wives of the slave owner. Most kept their feelings private. In polite circles, interracial sex was condemned in public discourse and frowned upon in polite circles. Often it was blamed on black women themselves, who were said to engage in "lustful entrapments" of helpless white men. But in practice, it was commonplace and accepted with averted eyes. Wives suffered quietly or kept their complaints to whispers among close friends and family. On the Shields farm, Christian may have felt betrayed and humiliated if she believed that her husband impregnated Melvinia.

But if she suspected one of her sons, on the other hand, she may well have just shrugged, as was the custom. Either way, it was the way of the world. Men were men, after all. Many owners counted children they had with African American women among their enslaved population, as did their neighbors. Few would raise more than an eyebrow about that, even in the most genteel of families. "Which of us has not narrowly escaped petting one of the pretty little mulattoes . . . as one of the family?" asked Judge C. J. Lumpkin of Georgia in 1864.

Henry would certainly have been concerned about his reputation. He was a member of his community's prosperous class. He was literate—he could sign his own name at least—and his assets were increasing in value. In addition to the farmers, who made up the backbone of the community, Henry would have mingled with the county's merchants. He would have known the men who ran the steam-powered saw and the grist mill, and the hotel and livery stable, the blacksmiths, the carpenters, the doctors, the physicians, and the clergymen. In 1858, his small but bustling community became part of the newly established Clayton County. Jonesboro became the new county seat. The county, which spanned about 140 square miles in 1860, had 4,466 residents. Twenty-seven percent of those residents—1,216 of them—were enslaved. Georgia law attempted to govern the relationships between white men and enslaved black women by instituting fines and three months' imprisonment for those who lived together "in a state of adultery or fornication." The law, however, was rarely enforced.

And any concerns that Henry might have had would have been allayed by the appearance of mixed-race children on white-owned farms in his corner of Clayton County. Jesey Wade, a sixty-year-old married farmer with two teenage sons, lived next door to the Shields farm. He owned four slaves: two black women, a baby, and one three-year-old mulatto girl. W. Chambers, another farmer in the community, owned two slaves, a twenty-two-year-old black woman and a seven-year-old mulatto girl. Melvinia wouldn't have stood out much. She would have been just another slave with a white man's baby. "In them times, white men went with colored girls and women bold," one former slave from Georgia recalled. "Any time they saw one and wanted her, she had to go with him, and his wife didn't say nothin' 'bout it."

Newman Roane of Virginia allowed his slave mistress and their children to live in his house, along with his white wife. He gave his mistress a regular seat at the dinner table and barred his wife from scolding his children. James Norman, also of Virginia, told his wife that his enslaved lover "was as good and as worthy" as she was. He told his white wife that if she objected, she could "leave his house and take herself to some place she liked better." John C. Clark of Texas spared his biracial children from any plantation work and ordered his slaves to wait on his black mistress, who shared his house and his bed. She also carried his keys and managed the household's affairs. Fellow slaves said that Mr. Clark "regarded her as his wife & she was so considered."

Many more slave owners, of course, were happy to keep their black mistresses out in the fields, away from their homes. Many ignored their offspring, viewing them as little more than additional assets. Many treated their mistresses with disdain and brutality, as sexual objects unworthy of the kind of consideration merited by white women. But there was some middle ground, too. The vast majority of slave owners did not treat their enslaved sexual partners as de facto wives. But many owners did try to ease their burdens; the women could lose those privileges, however, if they fell out of favor. "Before my old marster died, he had a pretty gal he was goin' with and he wouldn't let her work nowhere but in the house, and his wife nor nobody else didn't say nothin' 'bout it; they knowed better," one former slave from Georgia recalled.

If she had still been living on the South Carolina estate where she grew up, Melvinia could have turned to the older women she knew for advice about her complicated situation, and about pregnancy and childbirth. Doctors were a rarity. Enslaved women typically relied on black midwives to guide their newborns into the world. On the Shields farm, there was no one who could easily play that role. She might have confided in Mandrew, the only other black woman on the farm. But Mandrew was an inexperienced teenager just like Melvinia. It is unlikely that Mandrew had much experience delivering babies. One of Henry's neighbors owned several slaves, including a forty-five-year-old woman. Melvinia might have turned to her for help when her labor pains started.

On the day Melvinia finally gave birth, any doubt among the Shields family about the race of the father would have been immediately put to rest when they saw the child, a boy. The wailing infant had fair skin and narrow lips. Something about the experience of childbirth inspired Melvinia. Maybe it was the kindness and efficiency of the woman who helped her, the comforting touch of those sure, steady hands. Maybe it was her own joy of holding that wiggling, slippery infant. Later in life, when she became a midwife, Melvinia's own steady hands would shepherd countless newborns into the world.

As a slave, Melvinia had no other option but to continue working for Henry and his family after the birth of her son. She might have also hoped that her child's father would offer some protection. If the father were a member of her owner's family, he might feel kindly enough toward the child to ensure that he would never be sold. She might have dreamed that her son's father would teach her son to read or give him a trade or even give him his freedom someday. Surely a father—regardless of his race—would care enough to want a better life for his son? "Neither color, caste nor law of slavery could resist altogether the corrosive influences of human feeling and sentiment generated in these lawless families," wrote E. Franklin Frazier, the preeminent black sociologist. Some white fathers made their affections clearly known, providing their African American children with education, skills, work privileges, and even freedom. Those affections sometimes extended to the enslaved mother of the children as well.

On the modest farm in Clayton County, the Shields family seemed to bestow no such distinctions when it came to Melvinia's son, a symbol of forbidden intimacies across the color line. Whatever the family believed, whomever they suspected or knew to be the boy's father, they made it clear that they did not want to accept the baby as a member of the Shields clan. The family did not keep journals or save letters. But they painstakingly recorded every birth, every marriage, and every death in the family. Melvinia's son never appeared in that official history of the Shieldses. The precise date when she gave birth to her little boy remains in dispute. In later years, her son would claim April 10, 1859, as his birth date. But a census taker who visited Melvinia's house in 1870 was told that her oldest child was born in 1861. And that she named him Dolphus.

TWENTY-FIVE

Born Free

THE LIST MAY HAVE BEEN NAILED TO THE COURTHOUSE door in Henry County, Virginia. A copy was certainly kept inside, available for routine inspection by the white men who mattered in the tobacco-farming community there. Getting on that list meant everything to the county's people of color. It guaranteed a measure of self-respect and some social standing. It meant a chance to actually get paid for one's labor. Most of all it meant freedom: possessing the power to choose when you worked, if you worked, and who you worked for. In 1856, this simple, handwritten record was entitled "A List of Free Negros Over 12 Years." Dolly Jumper had the extraordinary good fortune to have her name on it. She was in her forties, the wife of a farm laborer, and a free African American woman living in the heart of southern slave society. Dolly belonged to the tiny, black elite that managed to break the bonds of slavery and savor liberty in the years before the Civil War. She was a living-and-breathing symbol of the complexity of the nineteenth-century black experience, a sort of icon for the otherwise hidden lives of the men, women, and children in Mrs. Obama's family tree who struggled to hang on to a measure of freedom long before Emancipation. In 1860, only 11 percent of blacks in Virginia—58,042 people in all—were free from bondage. The figures dipped even lower across the South as a whole, where only about 6 percent of the region's four million African Americans were free. Most slaves, doomed to spend their entire existence in servitude, could only dream of a life like Dolly Jumper's.

She was born free around 1813 in Henry County, a rural hamlet of densely forested hills and rolling plains that sits on Virginia's border with North Carolina. The free people of her community were mostly illiterate farm laborers, but Dolly knew from her earliest days that she was a child of great privilege. All around her, enslaved children worked in the verdant tobacco plantations that blanketed the county. They carried water and swept the slave quarters, ran errands, and served meals to their owners. Dolly, Mrs. Obama's maternal great-great-great-grandmother, knew she was not like them. She would never have to endure whippings at the hands of a white master or mistress, or be sold away from her mother and father. As a little girl, she could dream bigger dreams: at a time when slaves were barred from marrying, Dolly could indulge in romantic reveries about having a proper wedding someday with a minister to bless the sacred union and a marriage license to enshrine it with the legitimacy of the law. She could become the respectable wife of a farmer and live in his home, safe from the lecherous men who often preyed on their female property. Or she could become a cook or a housekeeper or a laundress and earn her own money, her own living. Dolly was described as mulatto, which meant she could have been near white in coloring or caramel in complexion. She left few hints of her origins and no image of her has survived into modern times. As she grew older, Dolly discovered that she could never take her freedoms for granted.

Her hometown prided itself on being a cradle of liberty. Nestled in the foothills of the Blue Ridge Mountains and traversed by the Smith and Mayo Rivers, Henry County was named after its most famous citizen, Patrick Henry, the American patriot who famously declared, in his cry to take up arms against the British, "Give me liberty or give me death!" His call for liberty, though, extended to whites only, not to people like Dolly, who was Mrs. Obama's great-great-great-grandmother. Patrick Henry was a slave owner himself, the proprietor of some ten thousand acres of land in Henry County in 1779. He acknowledged, with some sense of shame, that his continued ownership of human beings contradicted his democratic ideals. "Would any one believe that I am the Master of Slaves of my own purchase!" Henry wrote in a letter in the 1770s. "I am drawn along by the general inconvenience of living without them, I will not, I cannot justify it." He spoke of the enslaved labor force—on his lands and in the newly independent country—with pained regret. But he was in the minority. Most white landowners celebrated the human chattel that powered the county to new levels of prosperity in the early 1800s. "No other combination ever brought such rewards, such prosperity, to the county as tobacco and slavery," wrote Judith Parks America Hill in her history of the county. Most whites viewed the terms "Negro" and "slave" as mutually interchangeable. Dolly was becoming a woman in a time of great peril, as well as a time of great privilege, and she would spend much of her life trying to ensure that she and the people she loved most would never be swept into servitude. Her prized liberty, she learned, was fragile, tenuous, and vulnerable.

During her lifetime, more than a dozen members of her free black community were forced into servitude for failing to pay taxes. Others were ordered to leave the county and their families for running afoul of the white authorities, who viewed free blacks with deep suspicion, fearing they would inspire or lead slaves to rebellion. Some free people tried to keep themselves distant from slaves and the taint of subjugation. But there was no way of escaping the sight of it. Slave traders routinely auctioned off their human wares in the public square outside the courthouse; some black men were even whipped in public view. When Dolly stepped inside that imposing brick building, with its grand white columns, to register with the authorities as a free person of color, she would have had to pass the horrifying spectacle of men, women, and children in shackles and chains, sold off to the highest bidders. It was impossible on those days not to be confronted with the bitter truth: in Henry County, Virginia, only a fine line separated the enslaved from the free.

White lawmakers worked tirelessly to restrict the rights held by free blacks, banning them from voting, from attending school, and from mingling with slaves. Dolly managed not to stray beyond the boundaries of those laws. She knew how quickly her freedom could be snatched away. In a color-conscious world, her ancestry gave her higher social status than most African Americans, but only so much higher. (Because so many free blacks had white or Native American forebears, they were disproportionately lighter in color than their enslaved brethren.) In the big cities of the South, free blacks often worked as artisans and craftsmen. Educated by white parents and white patrons, some amassed wealth and property and socialized in the exclusive circles of the mulatto well-to-do. But in the tobacco fields of southern Virginia, Dolly and her relatives and neighbors were mostly illiterate and impoverished, relegated to living on the very fringes of free society. "We had no more privileges than servants," recalled Benjamin Dabney, a farmer in rural Virginia who was free before the Civil War. "We couldn't vote; we couldn't carry arms. And if we were caught with a book in our hand we were liable to be whipped."

Many free blacks were forced to live furtive lives, hidden in the shadows, to avoid running afoul of the law. Some, who had light enough skin and straight enough hair, vaulted over the color line and vanished into white society altogether. The rest of the community, which was tiny and insular, stuck together. Only about 6 percent of the African American community in Henry County—some three hundred people in all—was free. They often lived side by side, socializing together, working together, and intermarrying each other. It was no surprise then that Dolly was drawn to a young, mixed-race man who was also born in Henry County. His name was Peter Jumper. Precisely how he came to be free remains a mystery, but his surname had echoed for decades among the green hills and rushing rivers. There had been free Jumpers living in southern Virginia, and across the border in North Carolina, for generations.

There were Jumpers among the Tuscarora Indians who claimed the wilds of North Carolina along the Neuse River as their birthright in the early 1700s. John Lawson, the surveyor general of North Carolina at the time, described the Tuscarora as a welcoming people, who were more generous than the white settlers who viewed them with scorn. "They always freely give us of their victuals at their quarters, while we let them walk by our doors hungry," Mr. Lawson wrote. That generosity of spirit faded as whites began enslaving their children and stealing their land. On October 14, 1707, a group of Tuscarora Indians, including one man by the name of Tom Jumper, killed a settler in New Kent, Virginia. The Tuscarora ultimately went to war against the whites of North Carolina in 1711, but they were defeated and the tribe scattered. Some migrated north to Virginia and New York; others were enslaved and intermingled with both Africans and whites.

One of the enslaved descendants of that racial mélange surfaced decades later in Dinwiddie County, Virginia, not far from the North Carolina border. Her name was Hagar Jumper. She stood about five foot two and had dark brown skin and thick, kinky hair. Local officials described her as a "dark brown Mulatto or Indian woman" and she belonged to a white man who had inherited 150 acres of land from his father. Born around 1750, Hagar came of age during the heady days of the American Revolution, when the talk of freedom and liberty inspired men and women, slave and free. One day she rallied her courage and made her way to the local courthouse. Hagar presented herself to the white officials there and announced that she was challenging the system of slavery that condemned her to servitude. On that day she filed a lawsuit against her owner, demanding her freedom on the basis of her Indian ancestry. The testimony from the case did not survive, but the decision endures: Hagar triumphed in court. She won her freedom—and that of her children and grandchildren—and soon appeared on lists of free blacks in the county.

Hagar was joining the nation's first large communities of free blacks, which emerged after the American Revolution when some slaveholders embraced democratic ideals. One Maryland woman said she freed her slaves because holding black people in bondage contradicted "the inalienable Rights of Mankind." That egalitarian spirit also inspired slaves, like Hagar, to take matters into their own hands and to fight for their liberty in the courts. "Whole families," recalled one abolitionist, "were often liberated by a single verdict, the fate of one relative deciding the fate of many." It is possible that Peter was descended from this line. He and Dolly may have also been the children of slaves who were freed by their masters, or the progeny of white indentured servants or poor white women who had relationships and children with African slaves. It was not uncommon for free blacks in Pittsylvania and Henry Counties, where the Jumpers lived, to report to the local courts that their mothers were white. The petitions—filed by men and women hoping to gain their freedom through the courts—suggested that these mothers were close to their children and willing to testify on their behalf.

However they won their freedom, Dolly and Peter clearly joined the free black community at a time when it was growing at an unprecedented clip. Between 1790 and 1810, the number of free blacks in the United States rose from 59,466—about 8 percent of all blacks—to 186,446—about 13.5 percent of all blacks. In Virginia, where the Jumpers lived, the free black population more than doubled during that time. By 1810, some 30,570 African Americans—or 7.2 percent of the population—were living free.

Most free blacks in Henry County worked as farm laborers, cultivating and harvesting tobacco, which locals boasted was the finest in the world, known for its "sweet chew." Few owned any land, but they hoped to advance. They had enormous advantages over their enslaved counterparts: they could buy property, if they could afford it; they could choose who they worked for; they could keep their families intact without having to worry about slave auctions and the whims of slave owners. But the idealism of the postrevolutionary period only lasted so long. The sight of growing numbers of free blacks living beyond the control of whites, earning their own wages, even if those wages were meager, outraged some prominent citizens who believed that blacks were born to be servants. White masters worried, too, that the existence of a free class of blacks would inspire envy and rebellion among the men and women living in slavery.

So by the time Dolly and Peter began courting, white officials in Virginia and across the South had already passed a series of laws that would increasingly marginalize them and their community. Bit by bit, the officials started stripping free African Americans of the rights and liberties they had begun to enjoy in the late eighteenth century. Under the law, free blacks could be sold into servitude if they fell behind on their taxes. They were forced to register with local town clerks, who collected their names, ages, occupations, and personal descriptions and compiled lists of each town's free Negroes. Those who failed to register were fined $5 and could be sold into servitude if they were unable—or refused—to pay the fine. (A North Carolina law took the registration process even further, requiring all free blacks to wear a shoulder patch inscribed with the word *Free*.) They were barred from attending white schools, from testifying in court, and from gathering with other members of her community in large groups. Some Virginia cities also barred free blacks from socializing with slaves, whipping those who violated the law. Free blacks were also prohibited from working as riverboat captains or pilots, doctors or lawyers, or merchants or tradesmen and, at times, from forming their own churches.

These restrictive laws ensured that Dolly and other members of her community would never enjoy any semblance of true equality with whites. Indeed, many free African Americans in Henry County—including some members of the extended Jumper clan—were so poor that they had to hand over their own children to white families as servants. Some did this by choice, others were pressured to do so by families eager for unpaid servants. It was heartbreaking, no matter how it happened. Parents bid their children good-bye, knowing they might not see them for years. Children were indentured or "bound out" for long stretches of time, separated from their loved ones until young adulthood, when they were supposed to be returned to their families and independent life. But some whites were reluctant to give up their unpaid labor, and some young adults were forced to go to the courts to try to regain their liberty. Faced with chronic economic hardships and occasional hostility from whites and enslaved blacks alike, many free blacks turned inward, taking comfort in the camaraderie of their friends and family, the soothing rhythms of ordinary family life.

Dolly and Peter turned to each other. In 1831, when Dolly was about eighteen years old and Peter was near thirty-one, they decided to spend their lives together. By the mid-1840s they had three children. Their youngest, Peter Jr., Mrs. Obama's great-great-grandfather, entered the world in 1846. (Peter Jr.'s granddaughter, Rebecca, would move to Chicago and become the First Lady's grandmother.) Dolly and Peter left Henry County soon after their son was born. They didn't go far. Everyone was talking about the opportunities in Danville, a thriving manufacturing town in neighboring Pittsylvania County that had seven tobacco factories. The town had already attracted some Jumpers, who may have been Peter's relatives.

It appears that Dolly and Peter never registered with the authorities there, choosing instead to join the elusive community of free blacks who managed to live below the radar. The family quietly blended into an agricultural community populated mostly by white farmers, laborers, and craftsmen. Peter found work as a laborer, probably in one of the factories that produced chewing tobacco, while Dolly cared for their growing family. In 1850, they lived next door to another free black family, the Valentines. One of the Valentine boys worked as a ditcher. One of the young Valentine women, twenty-one-year-old Nancy, had a yellow complexion and stood five feet two inches without shoes, according to the record of her court appearance. (Only one record describing a member of the Jumper family has come to light. Richard Jumper, who registered at the Pittsylvania courthouse in 1838, was described as a "free born man of color" who was "five feet ten and a half inches high and 20 years of age." He had several scars on his fingers and a striking anomaly: a sixth finger on each hand, the clerk of the court reported. There was no mention of his color.)

Despite their efforts, Dolly and Peter, who were both illiterate, never managed to earn enough money to buy any land of their own. Soon, the couple was right back where they started. In 1856, Dolly, who had about seven children by then, had returned to Henry County and found herself walking back into the brick courthouse there to register as a free person of color. She appeared on the "List of Free Negros" that year along with several farmers, blacksmiths, housekeepers, wagon drivers, and three women who were living "at the poor house." Her husband, Peter, was not on the list, suggesting that he remained in Pittsylvania or simply chose to evade the authorities in Henry County.

All across the South, free African Americans were testing the limits of their freedom. The advent of the 1850s ushered in a decade of economic prosperity across the South and some free blacks began demanding higher wages. Many slave owners had moved southward from states like Virginia and Maryland in the Upper South, taking their slaves with them, causing labor shortages. The result: in some places, wages nearly doubled as free blacks flexed their negotiating muscles. "Some farmers are paying as high as $120—the same hands a few years ago could have been hired for $75," one newspaper reported. In the cities, free people of color began to challenge the restrictions that governed their lives in the courts and in petitions to city councils.

Meanwhile, officials, businessmen, and newspaper writers began complaining about what they viewed as an increasing attitude of defiance toward white authority among free blacks. One white man in Petersburg, Virginia, south of Richmond, complained that free black men and women were even boldly asserting themselves on local sidewalks. When a white man happens to stroll down the street, he said, "they plant themselves square in the middle of the walk, and nine cases out of ten they are slow to give way." Local newspapers decried the impudence, reporting that free blacks were getting out of hand: "The insolence with which many of our city's negroes locomote about the city is positively unbearable."

The rising tensions between North and South over slavery increased the anxiety among white southerners over the free black presence in their midst. In 1857, the United States Supreme Court issued the *Dred Scott* decision, ruling that blacks—even free blacks—could never be citizens of the country. The decision breathed new life into efforts to wipe out or, at the very least, marginalize the free African American community. All across the South, emboldened officials began taking action. Legislators in Virginia debated whether free blacks should be enslaved. And Dolly and Peter soon found themselves in the midst of a crackdown in Henry County. More than a dozen African Americans there were summoned to court for technical violations of the law that required them to register as free persons of color. Several were ordered to leave the county for good. Just across the border, in neighboring North Carolina, the authorities hauled two members of the extended Jumper clan into court for marrying slaves.

Some free blacks, of course, did not need the authorities to tell them to keep their distance. Their light skin and free status already placed them above slaves in the social pecking order, and in many places tensions between free and enslaved people of color simmered at times. In Norfolk, Virginia, the free black congregants of a Methodist church stirred an uproar when they chose to sit separately from slaves. And one free African American who moved to Virginia from Kentucky grumbled that "he suffer[ed] more abuse from the slaves here than we ever did from white people where we came from." (When Peter was in his early twenties, a man who appeared to have been a distant relative was arrested on charges that he had murdered a slave in Henry County.)

But the Jumpers and other rural free blacks often found that their experiences tended to unite them—rather than divide them—from slaves. All African Americans, whether free or enslaved, lived with discrimination and poverty in the South in their day-to-day lives. They lacked land, education, and specialized skills. So while some free blacks kept their distance, others intermingled and even chose their husbands and wives from among the enslaved population. (Some free blacks had relatives among the black men and women in bondage, which made socializing a matter of course.) On a farm near Petersburg, Virginia, Elizabeth Wingfield, a black woman who was about twenty-five and born free, was building a life with an enslaved man and raising their young children. Mrs. Wingfield rented the hundred-acre farm from the white woman who owned her husband. He worked as a cobbler for his mistress, who hired him out to other whites and then pocketed his wages. "My husband hired his time and we all lived together," Mrs. Wingfield said. Her husband, Henry, said that because he was a slave, all their belongings had to remain in his wife's name. "The farm was rented in her name and she owned all the property," said Mr. Wingfield, who was most likely referring to their household goods. "I was a servant and could not own anything."

In Henry County, more than two dozen free African Americans had enslaved common-law spouses, suggesting that white officials there often turned a blind eye to these kinds of liaisons and that free blacks did not frown on them. In 1859, Peter took care to register with the authorities, suggesting that the crackdown on free blacks in the county continued unabated.

By then, the nation was marching headlong toward war. White southerners began ringing alarm bells after Abraham Lincoln won the presidency on November 6, 1860, warning that the new president and his Yankee allies intended to free their slaves, decimate their wealth, and destroy their society. South Carolina seceded first, just one month after Lincoln's election. Georgia followed in January. In Virginia, the debate over whether to secede or not raged furiously. Mrs. Obama's forebears, those enslaved and those free, who were scattered across Virginia, Georgia, South Carolina, and Illinois, knew that their lives would be determined by what came next. Then, on April 12, 1861, Confederate soldiers opened fire on Fort Sumter in South Carolina and the simmering hostilities between North and South erupted into war. One month later in Virginia, the die was cast: the state joined the Confederacy.

For the free black community, the onset of the war only increased the uncertainty they lived with and clouded their fate. A few allied themselves with the Confederacy, hoping to maintain their slim range of privileges and superior status to slaves. Most others supported the Yankees. William Henry Brisby, who worked as a blacksmith and sheep farmer, said that whites in his community vowed to enslave him if they won the war. These threats only reinforced his political sympathies. "I was always a Union man," Mr. Brisby explained. "I was born free, but I was badly treated in many ways, especially I could not get the education I wanted."

Free blacks probably kept such thoughts to themselves, particularly in the company of whites, who were increasingly calling on free people of color to support the Confederate cause. In 1861, Henry County officials began compiling a list of "able-bodied male free negroes" to aid the war effort. The list would certainly have included Dolly's oldest son, John, who was about twenty. Free blacks in the county, though, were reluctant to sign up, and local officials had to force them into service. In 1862, the medical director and surgeon of the General Hospital in Danville, Virginia, wrote to the Confederate War Department, pleading for the department to draft blacks to work as nurses in his hospital. "The want of nurses to perform the menial work of the hospitals is exceedingly urgent," the surgeon wrote. The medical director asked the War Department to force the county's tobacco farmers to send their slaves to the hospital, and his plan was approved in June of that year. Free blacks were ordered to report to the hospital as well. Officials were told "to impress free negroes for nurses and to pay them $20." A year later, the military ordered free blacks to feed and care for the horses used in battle. Others were assigned to Dublin Depot, the central supply depot and headquarters for the Confederate Army in southwestern Virginia.

One Confederate document—which noted that fifty-two meals were provided to free blacks from Henry County over the span of two days—suggested that dozens of men were "carried" to Dublin Depot for the "public defence." The archival records do not contain a complete list of the men who were ordered to serve the Confederate government in some capacity. But the voices of free blacks that have survived suggest that many of those men despised the cause they had no choice but to support. Dolly's son, John, may have been tasked with readying the Confederate horses for battle, but in his heart he may well have been praying that Lincoln's men would win. "We hoped to see slavery put an end to, to get the rights and privileges of other men," said Benjamin Dabney, the farmer in rural Virginia, describing his support for the Union Army.

As many of the men around them were compelled to fight for the Confederacy, Dolly and Peter found themselves coping with the ravages of war. People were forced to use thorns instead of pins, sorghum instead of sugar. "Times are very hard here; every thing is scarce and high," wrote a woman named Ann to her sister Nancy, describing sky high prices in Henry County for everything from corn to bacon to brandy. "Crops are looking very badly for the time of year." Dolly, now in her fifties, must have struggled to keep food on the table for her family. She had seven children, including several who were not yet teenagers. Everything she held most dear was at risk. Virginia's legislators never passed the law calling for the enslavement of free African Americans, but they had never seemed more disposed to support it. As the war raged around them, many free blacks like Dolly began to fear that their liberty, so precious yet so tenuous, might slip forever out of reach. The Civil War was imposing enormous hardships on Mrs. Obama's ancestors. They found themselves battered by food shortages and hunger, drought and disease, and the anxiety over what was yet to come. But in one corner of the country, the war between North and South brought something altogether different, something utterly unexpected. It brought opportunity.

TWENTY-SIX

Exodus

T HE RUNAWAYS FROM KENTUCKY SET OUT IN THE DEAD OF night. Some plunged into the waters of the Ohio River with their belongings bound to their backs. Others slipped away by foot, or in wagons stolen from their masters. Mary Moten was a young mother in her twenties when she and her common-law husband plotted their flight to freedom. Countless perils lurked along their path. Runaway slaves were often recaptured and whipped or maimed. Vengeful masters sometimes split up their families, too, selling off husbands from wives, infants from parents. Kentucky's newspapers carried advertisements from slave owners, who promised cash rewards for the return of their fugitives. No one could predict what dangers lay ahead, but Mary knew well what she was leaving behind. She knew the life of working on someone else's land and in a house you could never own. Her children, Mary decided, would never know that life. They would grow up free. And so Mary, her husband, Nelson, and their little girl, who was no more than a toddler, fled sometime between 1860 and 1863, as the volleys of war had begun to threaten the seemingly unshakable foundations of American slavery.

Escaping was a harrowing experience for slaves, and many ran off with their hearts pounding and their ears ringing, gasping for oxygen like drowning men flailing as they sank into the depths. James and Matilda Busey, slaves who also fled Kentucky with their children, ran into bloodhounds during their escape. Hence Chambliss took his chances swimming the Ohio River, which had swallowed unluckier men. Mary and Nelson could not know for certain whether they or their young daughter would survive the journey. But the state of Illinois sat just across that rushing Ohio River. That extraordinary place where African Americans could live as free people glimmered like a beacon.

Henry Bibb, a Kentucky slave who was tortured and stripped of his wife and children after his first failed flight from slavery, might have been speaking for all runaways when he described the North's irresistible siren. "Sometimes standing on the Ohio River bluff, looking over on a free State, and as far north as my eyes could see, I have eagerly gazed upon the blue sky of the free North, which at times constrained me to cry out from the depths of my soul. . . . Oh, that I had the wings of a dove, that I might soar away to where there is no slavery; no clanking of chains, no captives, no lacerating of backs, no parting of husbands and wives; and where man ceases to be the property of his fellow man." It was that kind of dream that kept Mary and her family going. "The great aspiration was the land of freedom, the north, then you're free," said Johnny Johnson, who was Mary's grandson and Mrs. Obama's great-uncle, who grew up hearing only the tiniest fragments of their story. He knew one thing for sure about his grandparents. "Their great ambition," he said, "was to go as far north as they could."

One month after the war began, runaway slaves began pouring into Union camps around the country. They trickled into Fort Sumter first, then across Union lines in Virginia, Mississippi, and Florida. Within a little more than a year, tens of thousands of slaves, maybe even hundreds of thousands, had escaped from their owners. They "flocked in vast numbers—an army in themselves—to the camps of the Yankees," a Union chaplain wrote. "The arrival among us of these hordes was like the oncoming of cities." Word of the widening exodus spread from cities to rural communities, encouraging enslaved African Americans across the country to take their chances. Mary, who was Mrs. Obama's paternal great-great-grandmother, may or may not have heard the news. Either way, she summoned up her courage as she and her family fled from Kentucky, where Nelson was born. Her owners may have believed that she was born to be a slave, but Mary must have had a feeling that her life had to hold more than that.

She was born around 1835 in Missouri where, according to family lore, she was the descendant of a Cherokee Indian and an African slave. Her maiden name has been lost, but her face—with her straight, prominent nose and narrow lips and her long black hair—certainly suggests mixed parentage. Later in life, Mary said that her father had been born in Tennessee, which was part of the Cherokee nation. (Between 1819 and the late 1830s, most Cherokee lived in northwestern Georgia, but their territory also extended into southeastern Tennessee, northeastern Alabama, and southwestern North Carolina.) Pressured by white settlers, some members of the tribe moved to Missouri, where Mary was born. The Cherokee tribe owned about sixteen hundred slaves in 1835 and four thousand by 1860. Mary's great-grandchildren have wondered whether Mary and her family ended up in Missouri as thousands of Cherokee marched through that state during the Trail of Tears, when the tribe was forcibly relocated from North Carolina, Georgia, and elsewhere to Oklahoma. Thousands of Cherokee Indians died from disease and starvation. "I can't help but wonder: What was life like for her?" said Francesca Gray, who is Mary's great-granddaughter. "Did she walk that Trail of Tears?"

It is impossible to know for sure, but it seems most likely that Mary was spared that devastating experience. The march lasted roughly from January 1837 to March 1839. Mary was born in Missouri at least two years earlier than its onset. But she was still a slave, and somehow she ended up moving from Missouri to neighboring Kentucky, where she met a black man by the name of Nelson Moten. Mary was about twenty-four years old and Nelson was about twenty-nine when they decided to unite. And sometime around 1859, Mary gave birth to their first child, a baby girl named Cora. (The identity of their owner remains unknown, but in 1860, a white woman by the name of Mary Moten owned thirteen slaves in Versailles, Kentucky, not far from Lexington, including two mulatto female slaves who were about the same age as Mary and Cora.) Mary and Nelson were both illiterate, and both had been born slaves, but that didn't stop them from dreaming of a better life.

Across the border, in the free state of Illinois, they could live that dream. At the time, Illinois was a destination for hundreds of runaway slaves and for abolitionists from the neighboring states of Kentucky, Missouri, and beyond. In 1819, former president James Madison's secretary, Edward Coles of Virginia, a wealthy abolitionist who had inherited more than a dozen slaves from his father, put the state on the map when he traveled there with his slaves and set them free along the way. He gave the head of each family 160 acres of land to start out their new lives as free people. "I proclaimed in the shortest and fullest manner possible," Mr. Coles recalled, "that they were no longer slaves, but free—free as I was." In 1822, Mr. Coles was elected governor of Illinois and successfully fought during his term to prevent Illinois from becoming a slave state. (He also tried to persuade the retired Thomas Jefferson to embark on a public campaign to abolish slavery, a request that Mr. Jefferson politely rejected.)

Yet the communities in southern Illinois, which were closest to Kentucky, were far from an oasis. Whites in the southern part of the state were deeply conservative, supportive of slavery and harsh codes that severely restricted the rights of free blacks. It was a battleground where proponents of slavery and segregation clashed fiercely— and sometimes violently—with abolitionists in the legislature and churches, and on the streets. The state's "Black Laws," enacted in 1853, prohibited blacks from settling in the state. Those who entered after that date were considered "illegals." Many conservative members of the clergy supported those laws. One Methodist minister told his congregation that "catching and returning runaways slaves to their masters is a Christian duty binding upon any church members."

A year later, a mob formed to drive a black family from a town in Randolph County. In 1861, whites in Pope County threatened two abolitionists who were forced to flee for their lives. Some dubbed this section of Illinois Egypt—both for the cotton that was grown there and for its sympathies toward slavery.

Abolitionists in southern Illinois, however, also made their presence felt. Some residents of Randolph County, for instance, welcomed fugitive slaves. And some slave owners, who developed an abhorrence for the institution, moved there for the specific purpose of freeing their slaves. By the time the Civil War got under way, Mary and Nelson were among thousands of runaway slaves to pour into the state, particularly into the city of Cairo in the southernmost tip of Illinois along the Ohio River. One reporter for *Frederick Douglass's Paper* described the incredible sight of hundreds of former slaves—known as "contrabands" in the military parlance of the time—streaming into Cairo's military camp in September 1862. So many newly freed blacks were arriving there that it felt like jubilee, the long-awaited day when slavery would finally end, he wrote. "Cairo now begins to look as though the jubilee, sure enough has come, in this country," the writer observed. "Besides what are here already, filling the old barracks, from one end to the other, still they come. Every evening, when I go down to the 'Ohio Levee,' I find it literally dotted over with new arrivals of contrabands. Old men and young men, old women and young women, and children are here."

The reporter spoke in a celebratory tone, but later observers described appalling conditions, violence, and severe shortages of food and medical care. In October 1862, the *New York Times* reported that the eight hundred to a thousand former slaves were "in a most miserable condition" in the Cairo camp. They lacked clothing and bedding and many were sick. Some were victimized by white soldiers and citizens who were described as "bitter negro haters." One observer noted that the attacks on women and their daughters "would shock the moral sensibilities of any well-regulated mind or community." Military officials relocated some of the newly freed men and women to points north. But in early 1863, about five thousand people remained in the camp. At the end of the war, two thousand were still there. For some, that first taste of liberty was unexpectedly bitter.

No one knows exactly how Mary and Nelson made their escape, nor the perils they may have encountered on their journey, nor whether they spent any time in the Cairo camp. They may well have passed through it. Mary's daughter, Phoebe Moten Johnson, told her children decades later that her parents came to Illinois looking for freedom. "She used to talk about the Mason-Dixon line that was between north and south; she said they would escape from over there," said Mr. Johnson, Phoebe's son.

What is clear is that by 1862 or 1863, in the midst of the tumult of war, Mary and Nelson and their little girl, Cora, found their way to Illinois. After a lifetime in servitude, Mary and her husband were finally free. They ultimately settled in Pulaski County, just a few miles north of the military camp in Cairo. For many former slaves, the tiny villages of verdant hills and fertile soil seemed like the perfect place to start over. As the Civil War raged, its population boomed. In 1860, only about 40 of Pulaski County's 3,943 residents were black, but hundreds poured in over the next few years. There was ample land to farm, along with dozens of small factories, including sawmills, a flour mill, a pork-packing plant, and shingle mills where former slaves could find work. A free black family could build a good life in a place like that. Mary gave birth to her second child there, a baby girl named Aby, sometime around 1862 or 1863. Aby, who was also known as Ibbe, was the first in the Moten family to be born into freedom. And as the Civil War raged, the exodus continued. Day by day, month by month, thousands of slaves abandoned their masters for a life of liberty in Pulaski County and other parts of southern Illinois. (Toward the end of the war, a black man named Nelson Morton joined the One Hundredth U.S. Colored Infantry in Lexington, Kentucky. Knowing that the spelling of the family's surname appears to have changed over the years, one wonders: Could Nelson have returned to his home state and taken up a rifle for the Union Army?) Mary was not a scholar or a wartime general. She was an illiterate runaway slave, who had no training in war strategy and no experience in national politics. But in her new home in Pulaski County, where she rocked her newborn baby girl, Mary could feel the winds of change. The institution of slavery, which had once dominated nearly every facet of her life, was crumbling before her eyes.

TWENTY-SEVEN

The Civil War

THRONGS OF FLAG-WAVING WHITE MEN AND WOMEN
poured into the streets of Savannah in celebration when
Georgia seceded from the Union on January 19, 1861. Alexander Stephens, the vice president of the Confederacy, who hailed
from the state, pronounced that the South was prepared to go to battle
to keep its African Americans in bondage. The signers of the Declara-
tion of Independence were wrong, he declared, if they had intended
to suggest that blacks were worthy of freedom and equality. "Our new
government is founded upon exactly the opposite idea," Mr. Stephens
said. "Its foundations are laid, its cornerstone rests, upon the great
truth that the negro is not equal to the white man. That slavery . . .
is his natural and normal condition. This, our new government, is
the first in the history of the world based upon this great physical and
moral truth."

In April of that year, after war had officially been declared, Georgia's governor called on the state's able-bodied white men to enlist
and fight for the South. All of a sudden, on the Clayton County farm
where Melvinia was raising her son, the men in the Shields family had
a decision to make. The call to battle inspired a prompt and passionate
response. So many white southern men rallied to support the Confed-

erate cause that their army leaders found themselves short of weapons. In up-country Georgia, though, some white men were reluctant to embrace the secessionist movement. Most didn't own slaves, and one of Clayton County's two delegates at the state convention on secession had voted against leaving the Union. Sending men off to war would create considerable hardships for families who worked their own land. Even slaveholders like Henry Shields, who owned Melvinia, her son, Dolphus, and two other African Americans, counted on the labor of their able-bodied children to help cultivate cash crops like cotton and corn. Still, historians say that it is very difficult to comprehensively assess white attitudes toward secession in northern Georgia. We may never know how Henry and his sons felt about the war, whether they rooted enthusiastically for the Confederacy or viewed the fighting with ambivalence or opposition. What we do know is that five months passed—allowing, perhaps, for the completion of the planting and harvesting seasons—before one of the Shields men decided to enlist.

The first to go was David T. M. Shields, Henry's oldest son, who traveled to Fairburn, in nearby Campbell County, to sign up with the Confederate Army. David was twenty-five years old on September 25, 1861, when he joined. The next year, two of his brothers, Moses and Elisha, also enlisted. But despite the early enthusiasm of the troops, morale began to plummet as the government started cutting back on food rations in 1862. Poor sanitary conditions transformed military camps into breeding grounds for disease, and many soldiers succumbed to pneumonia, dysentery, typhoid, scurvy, and tuberculosis. In the fall, only a year after he left home, David fell ill. In October of that year, he was hospitalized in Lake City, Florida, just thirty miles south of the Georgia border. Confederate officials reported that his short-lived military career ended on November 8, 1862. "Died of disease," the officials wrote in his personnel file. David would return home in a box, a private who never saw battle.

That year, unbearable grief and the mounting hardships of war came home to Clayton County and the Shields family. The Confederate government in Richmond, Virginia, had ordered the conscription of white men ages eighteen to thirty-five—the nation's first wartime draft—pulling more farmers from the fields. A severe drought battered the countryside, leaving family farms bereft of badly needed grains and vegetables. Food shortages led desperate women to loot stores and warehouses. Food, salt, cloth, and cash were in such short supply that the state legislature began appropriating funds to distribute goods to struggling white families, though not to their slaves. But the aid scarcely met the growing needs. Outside Jonesboro, Melvinia and her owners struggled to navigate the harsh new world, which seemed to grow worse by the day. A smallpox epidemic now raged, leading county officials to call for the quarantine of affected whites and slaves alike. Henry, who was about fifty-one, had a wife, as many as seven children, and four slaves to feed and no easy way to keep food on the table. Sugar, tea, and coffee quickly became unattainable luxuries. Drought had decimated the fields, and Henry had lost his firstborn son. Homes and farms in the county became increasingly shabby and ill-repaired. The food shortages hit slaves like Melvinia, who had a growing boy to feed, doubly hard. Ineligible for the state assistance their white counterparts received, African Americans were forced to rely on the generosity of their owners, which wasn't always forthcoming. Nancy Boudry remembered bitterly that her owner managed to find some chickens, which he shared with his family, but not with his slaves. "We done de bes' we could," Ms. Boudry said. "We et what we could get, sometimes didn have nothin' to eat but piece of cornbread but de white folks allus had chicken."

In September 1863, fighting erupted in the northwestern corner of Georgia as Confederates and Yankees clashed in the Battle of Chickamauga near the border with Tennessee. The Confederate Army repulsed the Union soldiers, but suffered staggering losses. Sixteen thousand Confederate soldiers lay wounded or killed. That year, amid the chaos and privation of war, Melvinia, who was about nineteen or twenty, fell pregnant. Once again, the man who impregnated her was white. By 1864, she had a second child, a newborn girl who was also biracial. Melvinia named her Jane. Her son, Dolphus, who was somewhere between the ages of three and five, was walking and chattering by then. There was a gap of at least three years, and perhaps as many as five, between the births of her first and second children. At the time, women who had husbands or regular sexual partners often had children every year or two, since there was no birth control. Melvinia may have lost a child to illness or disease, like smallpox, which would explain the gap. Or she may have learned to space out her childbearing as some women did.

David T. M. Shields, Henry's oldest son, was dead by then. So he could not have been the father of Melvinia's daughter. That left the other adult male members of the Shields family: Henry, her owner, and his son Charles, who were still working on the farm; Moses, who left the Confederate Army in July 1863; Elisha, who also could have been discharged by then, as well as any white male neighbors or visitors. Melvinia's descendants hope that she had developed some kind of meaningful bond with the man who fathered her children. Whether she was in an ongoing relationship or a sporadic one, sex between white men and enslaved women in the midst of the Civil War must have been particularly fraught. In the most intimate of moments, Melvinia could have wept and prayed that a Union victory would finally stop this white man from demanding a place in her bed. Or she could have dreamed that she and her lover might finally be able to live together, more openly. Many enslaved women hoped that the white men they were involved with would educate their children and free them someday.

But as the war raged on, slaves in Georgia increasingly pinned their hopes not on benevolent masters, but on the Union Army that was marching through the South. By then, the notion of freedom—once an elusive dream—was beginning to seem tangible, possible, if not entirely within reach. Melvinia was cradling her baby girl at a time when many enslaved young mothers were daring to envision their children savoring free, independent lives. There was no way to know what that freedom would feel like or look like in practice. All that Melvinia and most other African Americans knew was slavery. Of the 1,217 blacks who lived in Melvinia's community, only one was free, a man named Frank of whom little is known.

Still, word spread through slave quarters on small farms and sprawling plantations alike that Union soldiers were bringing liberty along with their muskets and military might. African Americans whispered jubilantly about Lincoln's Emancipation Proclamation, which went into effect on January 1, 1863, and ordered the release of every slave in rebel states. Many slaves pretended to be ignorant of the happenings of the war and its implications for them, particularly in their conversations with whites. But secretly, African Americans followed the history unfolding around them with intense interest, gleaning tidbits from left-behind newspapers and the overheard conversations between their masters and other visitors. Mariah Heywood held clandestine meetings with other African Americans where they prayed to God for their freedom. Other slaves rebelled in quiet ways, engaging in work slowdowns, disregarding rules, taking their time following orders. So many men had been called up to war that many slaveholdings were left under the management of white women, who struggled to keep their human possessions in line. "All de white folks was off a-fightin' 'cept dem what was too old to fight or what was too bad crippled and 'flicted," recalled Jasper Battle, a former slave from Georgia. "Dey stayed home and looked atter de 'omans and chillun."

Thousands of slaves ran off from their masters to join the Yankees in battle, including Jerry Suter, Phoebe's adventurous stepfather. Jerry was born into slavery in Jackson County, Alabama, though he was never certain of the precise date. When he was young, he was separated from his father and sold from one master to another, finally ending up in the possession of a man named Roland Sutton in Tennessee, near the Mississippi border. Few details about Jerry's earliest days have survived, but by the time the Civil War was rumbling across the South, he had decided that he could no longer endure life in captivity. He wanted to find his father. He wanted to live as a free man. He was about twenty-five years old when he managed to escape.

He scrambled south into neighboring Mississippi, running for some forty miles in all, until he arrived in the town of Corinth, which had fallen into the hands of the Union Army. By September 18, 1863, Jerry was offering his services to the Yankees. He enlisted that day and started preparing to fight the Confederate Army, to battle the white southerners who had stolen his freedom and torn him from his family. Years later, Jerry would cite that very month and day—September 18—as his date of birth. Technically, it wasn't accurate, of course. But when you think about it, it makes all the sense in the world. It was the day that Jerry was reborn as a free man.

He joined the Fifty-fifth Regiment of the United States Colored Infantry, Company E, less than nine months after President Abraham Lincoln finally agreed to put rifles in the hands of black men. The president and his generals and aides had agonized for years over whether to allow African Americans to fight. Lincoln worried that the prospect of black troops would so outrage white slaveholders in border states like Maryland and Kentucky that those states might decide to secede. Others debated whether blacks had the courage to serve, whether they could be trusted with guns, and whether they might turn those guns on their white commanding officers. In the end, the declining number of white volunteers and the pressing needs of the Union Army forced the president's hand. Lincoln's Emancipation Proclamation, which freed slaves in the South, also authorized the enlistment of black men in the Union forces.

Tens of thousands of black men, many of them runaway slaves like Jerry, volunteered. Frederick Douglass, the former slave turned abolitionist, urged them on. "Let the black man get upon his person the brass letters, U.S., let him get an eagle on his button, and a musket on his shoulder, and bullets in his pocket; there is no power on earth, or uder the earth, which can deny that he has earned the right to citizenship," he said. About 179,000 African Americans—about 10 percent of the entire corps—would ultimately serve in the Union Army. They were fighting for freedom and for respect, but they found that the latter was often in short supply. White commanders, who questioned the competence of black soldiers, made sure that many of them never saw combat. Black soldiers were forced into segregated units, denied the opportunity to become commissioned officers, and, at least initially, paid less than their white counterparts. Jerry and his fellow black compatriots were among the lucky ones: armed with rifles, muskets, and bayonets, they would have a rare chance to show their mettle. Only eight months after he enlisted, Jerry found himself in the thick of a deadly battle on a swelteringly hot day in northern Mississippi.

It was June 10, 1864, and Jerry's unit had been assigned to protect a train packed with supplies for the Union Army. But artillery blasts erupted as the train rumbled toward Brice's Cross-Roads, about six miles northwest of Guntown, Mississippi. The black men jumped into action when it became clear that their white colleagues were being overwhelmed in a blazing firefight with Confederate troops. Jerry and the other African Americans plunged into the front, holding the line with a fierce barrage of fire so that their white compatriots could retreat in safety. But they, too, were battered by the Confederate soldiers and forced to retreat. In the scramble, through dense woods, their white commander ended up surrounded by several hundred enemy soldiers. "My men, gathering around me, fought with terrible desperation," wrote the commander, Colonel Edward Bouton, describing the black soldiers who saved his life. "Some of them, having broken up their guns, in hand-to-hand conflict, unyielding, died at my feet, without a thing in their hands for their defense." Most of the white Union soldiers escaped capture thanks to the fierce fighting of the African American troops. The black men had proved their valor, but in so doing, many paid the ultimate price. African Americans accounted for half of the 223 Union soldiers killed on that blisteringly hot day in Mississippi.

The battle at Brice's Cross-Roads was a critical one for the Union Army because it distracted the Confederate Army's decorated cavalry corps and kept them out of Tennessee, where General Sherman was counting on the Nashville & Chattanooga Railroad to supply his troops during his march through Georgia. "The colored troops made for themselves on this occasion a brilliant record," Major General C. C. Washburn reported. "Their gallant and soldierly bearing, and the zeal and persistence with which they fought, elicited the warmest encomiums from all officers of the command. Their claims to be considered as among the very best soldiers of our army can no longer, in my opinion, be seriously questioned."

Jerry survived the battle and was promoted after that, from private to corporal and then from corporal to sergeant. Within a year of his enlistment, he had become a battle-hardened veteran, a black man who knew how to fight and survive in combat. It was an experience that would change his life.

Meanwhile, on the Shields farm, Henry and his son Charles did not appear to join the fighting until 1864, when Union soldiers were already beginning their march toward Atlanta. Henry was in his fifties by then, responsible for a wife, several young children, five slaves, and a farm. He certainly would have been worried about what might happen to his family and property in his absence. Charles's physical limitations—childhood polio had left him partly paralyzed on his right side—might have kept him from joining up sooner. Many people in the northern counties of Georgia also opposed the initial decision to secede from the United States. That opposition grew over the years as the casualties, desertions, and hardships of war mounted. The Shields men obviously supported slavery—it had brought them advantages and profits—but they may have been reluctant to fight in a war that they only halfheartedly supported.

In 1864, however, Henry and his sons had no choice but to take up arms. That year, the governor ordered all white men aged sixteen through sixty to join a reorganized militia tasked with supporting the Confederate forces that were defending the state as Sherman's army headed steadily toward nearby Atlanta. In Clayton County, the citizen-soldiers drilled for war behind the courthouse in Jonesboro. Henry, fifty-three, was still farming his land, as was his son Elisha. Charles was working as a schoolteacher. Charles could ride a horse, despite his bad right leg, and the authorities did not grant him an exemption from service. The militia—of about five thousand civilians—was inexperienced and ill-equipped, composed mainly of older men and young boys.

The men of the militia had little in the way of professional military armaments. Most carried flintlock muskets, ordinary rifles, and shotguns when they appeared for service. On the battlefield, two-thirds lacked cartridge boxes; there were virtually no ambulances or transportation of any kind. They endured a barrage of bullets from the Union soldiers, but their superiors praised their courage, particularly given their lack of military experience.

"Most of the reserves . . . never having been drilled at all, and the others but a few days, all performed well every service required of them during an arduous and dangerous campaign," their commander wrote. "They have been in service about one hundred days, during at least fifty of which they have been under close fire of the enemy mostly night and day." Some members of the militia ended up joining the Confederate forces, but others never actually fought in battle. There are indications that Charles did. As an older man, Charles was heralded in a local newspaper as one of his community's "honored Confederate veterans." Charles's descendants say that he didn't fight, but served as a messenger, carrying information across enemy lines. His wartime service took him away from the family farm for some time. His father and brother might have also been forced to leave. What that meant for Henry's wife and their other children remains unknown. But it may have had an impact on Melvinia. It would be years before she had another child.

For much of that sweltering summer of 1864, refugees fleeing the violence of war had poured into Jonesboro and the surrounding countryside where Melvinia and the Shields family lived. So many people were homeless that entire families took shelter in boxcars along the railroad tracks that traversed the city. Jonesboro was the heart of Clayton County, the bustling county seat, the place where local farmers and their wives went to shop at the grocery and general stores and consult with the doctor and the blacksmith. The community's white students attended school there. The Baptist and Methodist churches held Sunday services in town, and the local courthouse registered property deeds and mediated disputes. On market days, the streets and loading docks bustled with people. And in the fall, farmers brought countless bales of cotton, which were lined up along the railroad tracks awaiting shipment north. Henry, like the others, brought his cotton crop to the railroad depot there. Melvinia may well have visited Jonesboro, too, when she accompanied her mistress. It was the biggest town in the rural county, and public officials spoke of it with pride, noting the growing numbers of elegant homes, brick buildings, and the new courthouse. "We can state with pleasure that the society in Jonesboro and its vicinity are much improving," city officials said.

The encroaching war changed all that. Throughout the spring and summer of that year, bitter battles raged. On August 9, 1864, General W. T. Sherman ordered the bombardment of Atlanta, declaring that he planned to "make the inside of Atlanta too hot to be endured." His troops sent some three thousand shells raining down on the city, destroying its downtown and sending thousands of civilians fleeing. Jonesboro sat only twenty-one miles south of Atlanta, which had become the South's most important center of munitions and war supplies. Sherman, who had been unable to dislodge the Confederates from Atlanta, became convinced that capturing Jonesboro was the key to toppling Atlanta. He decided to destroy the Macon & Western Railroad, which ran through Jonesboro and provided a critical supply line to the Confederate forces defending Atlanta. On August 19, 1864, Sherman's blue-coated cavalry thundered into Jonesboro on horseback, routed a small Confederate detachment, and began the work of destroying the rail link to Atlanta. Even in the surrounding countryside, where Melvinia and the Shields family lived, people could hear the pounding of nearly twenty thousand hooves as the Northern soldiers swarmed the village.

It was just before dusk and the sun was falling in the sky. Once the Union soldiers had the town in their possession, they wasted little time. "The men went to work with a will," one observer reported.

The troops destroyed local stores and warehouses full of cotton. The soldiers torched the railway building and the courthouse and began to uproot about three miles of railroad track. A brisk wind sent the flames roaring through nearby stores and other buildings. Nearly two-thirds of the town burned to the ground that day. The following day, the soldiers withdrew from the area and, battling Confederate troops along the way, returned to Union positions near Atlanta. The commander of the Jonesboro raid claimed victory, declaring that the railroad would be unusable for at least ten days. But the Northern troops had in reality failed to complete their mission. The soldiers had pulled up the rails and tossed them to the side. But a driving rain prevented them from heating the rails to bend them out of shape. Within a day, a train was pulling into Atlanta from Jonesboro.

The white community in Jonesboro did not have much time to survey the extensive damage or to celebrate the town's resilience. Within days, Sherman's troops were on the move again. This time, he had ordered most of his infantry to head toward Jonesboro to finish the job of wrecking the rails. The pitched battles started up once again on August 31, 1864. The cannon roared and the earth shuddered and thundering horseman could be heard for miles around. Melvinia and the other residents of Clayton County, white and black, free and enslaved, huddled together as they listened to the boom of the big guns and the shelling of what remained of the city. The burning fields glowed in the darkness. By sundown on September 1 it was all over. The South lost 3,705 men. The Union lost some 3,237 men. But the supply lines to Atlanta were successfully destroyed. On September 2, 1864, Atlanta, Sherman's prize, finally fell into Union hands. He would leave Atlanta triumphant, beginning his march to the sea. So many enslaved women escaped from servitude to follow him and his troops that soldiers complained of the "helpless women and children" who trailed them and ate their rations.

The people of Jonesboro emerged from their homes to find their town shattered beyond recognition. Only about a dozen buildings were left standing, and many of those were damaged. Thousands of bodies filled the streets and the surrounding countryside. (According to the *New York Tribune* of September 1, 1864, "two-thirds of Jones-boro had been burned in Kilpatrick's raid of Aug. 19-20 and that was 12 days before the battle, in which additional buildings were blown away by shells.") Many people were left homeless and had to endure a particularly harsh winter that followed. Clayton County was bank-rupt. By 1865, the county's school fund had just $36 in Confederate money, which was worthless anyway. On April 9 of that year, the Confederate forces surrendered. The following day, Melvinia's son, Dolphus, celebrated his birthday. He was somewhere between the ages of six and eight. Melvinia and her two children had lived to see the end of war. Soon, the institution of slavery would crumble around them. Melvinia turned twenty-one that year and, for the first time in her life, she was free.

ALL ACROSS THE SOUTH, African Americans greeted Emancipation with a mix of jubilation, wonder, and disbelief. Impromptu celebra-tions erupted in Georgia, Virginia, South Carolina, and Illinois where Mrs. Obama's ancestors lived. "Negroes, you are free!" the Union soldiers called out as they marched through Georgia. "There are no more masters and mistresses." Some soldiers opened up the storehouses of white slave owners, telling former slaves to take all the meat and grain that they wanted. Others seized horses, livestock, and clothing and distributed them to African Americans. Gloria Baker of Georgia remembered how her fellow slaves responded when they heard the news. "Dey throwed down der hoes and jus' whooped and hollered 'cause dey was so glad," she said. The Yankee soldiers were heroes, the vanquishers of slavery. Hundreds of black people cheered the roaring thunder of their guns. "Freedom forever!" the slaves chanted. "Free-dom everymore!"

Caeser Cohen, the man who seems most likely to have been Mrs. Obama's great-great-grandfather, joined the army when the Union troops came marching through the Weymouth plantation in George-town, South Carolina. He said good-bye to his wife, Tira, and set

off. Maybe Caeser dreamed of becoming a legend in his community. Perhaps he figured he could finally earn some steady money,
away from the rice plantations. Caeser was about twenty-five years
old when he promised to serve for three years in Company A of the
128th Regiment, U.S. Colored Infantry. He lasted only six months.
It seems that he told his commanders that he had fallen ill and then
reported to a hospital for discharge. The hospital told him to return to
his company instead. Caeser duly left the hospital with an army-issued
knapsack and canteen, but he never returned to duty. "Dropped as
deserter," his military superiors wrote in his file.

Jerry Suter, whose company fought with such valor during the
war, stayed on with the Union Army. It wasn't until New Year's Eve
of 1865—twenty-five days after the states ratified the Thirteenth
Amendment, which abolished slavery—that Jerry finally shed his uniform. He was in Baton Rouge when he accepted his discharge papers
and a final cash payment of $36.31. And with some money in his pock-
ets and a rare view of his place in the world, he set off to begin the
rest of his life as a free man. He was just twenty-seven years old. Jerry
headed for Tennessee first, where he had been a slave and had been
separated from his family. Somehow, he managed to find his long-lost
father there. That reunion meant everything to Jerry, so much so that
he changed his name to commemorate it. Until then, he had gone by
the name of Jerry Sutton, carrying the surname of his white owner.
But in Tennessee, he learned that his father's last name was Suter, not
Sutton. And with that knowledge in hand, Jerry cast aside his master's
name and the last tangible vestige of his life in captivity. When he finally made his way to Illinois, where he met Mary, Phoebe's mother,
he introduced himself to his new neighbors as Jerry Suter.

Not everyone got the word right away. It took months for the
news to reach slaves on remote, rural farms and plantations and some
slave owners were determined to keep the Northern victory quiet for
as long as they could. Some slaves didn't find out until two months
after the war was over. The news was so stunning that some slaves
simply dismissed it outright. Martha Colquitt of Georgia said her

mother listened politely when a group of Union soldiers announced that she and her family were finally free. But once they left she decided that this crazy talk simply couldn't be true. " 'Sho' ain't no truf in what dem Yankees was a-sayin','" Ms. Colquitt recalled her mother saying. "Us went right on living just like us always done."

Former slaves and slave owners struggled to adjust to the new reality. Suddenly, Melvinia had to envision herself and her life in an entirely different way. She could come and go as she pleased. She could earn money for her labor. She could learn to read. She could try to reunite with her long-lost friends and family from South Carolina. Some slaves packed up their meager belongings and left their plantations as soon as they could. Some white owners wept as they watched their former servants, who represented much of their assets, walk off their farms to find work and long-lost relatives. John Davenport of South Carolina, who had been separated from his mother, finally found her. "She had been sold and sent away," he said. "I went to her and stayed two weeks."

Many other slaves stayed put for a while, persuaded by the pleas of their former owners who promised to pay them wages for the first time. Melvinia appears to have been one of those slaves. She slipped through those first years of Emancipation without leaving much of a mark, but historical records suggest that she decided to stay put in Clayton County. Maybe she thought it would be too hard to move with her young children in tow. Maybe she was reluctant to leave the white man who had fathered them. In any case, she looked at the hubbub around her and apparently cast her lot with the white family that had owned her since she was a little girl. When it came time to pick a surname for herself—her first as a free woman—she decided to take their name. Melvinia became a Shields.

TWENTY-EIGHT

Uneasy Freedom

T HE WHITE MEN CREPT TOWARD THE BUILDING, IGNITED the fire, and slipped back into the night. Hungry red flames erupted in the darkness, leaping and dancing and devouring the Freedmen's School House. The roaring inferno, with its clouds of swirling smoke and soot, shook the slumbering townsfolk from sleep just before midnight, but the blazing fury was unstoppable. By morning, onlookers could only shake their heads at the destruction. The building that had embodied the hopes and dreams of hundreds of former slaves had been completely decimated. Only charred wreckage remained of what was meant to be a school for black children in Jonesboro, Georgia. Melvinia was a twenty-three-year-old single mother at the time. Like most recently freed slaves, she must have prayed that she would send her children to study there one day. That dream died on the morning of May 4, 1867. Federal officials were outraged by the response of the town's prominent white citizens, who offered polite words of sympathy, but kept quiet when it came to identifying the arsonists. African Americans felt the wrenching loss more keenly. The consequences for them would reverberate for months to come. It would be years before Melvinia's oldest son, Dolphus, learned how to read and write.

How do you measure freedom? After the Civil War, African Americans savored, celebrated, and struggled to make sense of this utterly new state of being. For some, freedom was experiencing an existence without chains or shackles or whips. For others, it was wielding the power to decide whether to sweat all day in the fields—and receive the first wages of their lives—or to sleep until the burning sun was high. Some men relished that moment when they could tell their women that they no longer had to work for white men, that they could tend to their own homes and their own children. And some parents would never forget the day that they could finally send their sons and daughters to school or hear them sounding out their first words from the Bible. But the jubilation over newfound freedoms also came at a time of great turmoil and economic hardships, mounting violence and a steady erosion of the new rights that African Americans thought they had won. It became clear almost immediately that white southerners and blacks held very distinct visions about what freedom should be. Embittered by their defeat in battle and devastated by the financial loss of their human possessions, many white men began terrorizing former slaves who insisted on wages, education, and the right to vote. Melvinia soon learned that the freedom she had longed for came laced with hunger and fear.

Fire was one of the most potent weapons wielded by angry white men in Jonesboro. Between July 1866 and June 1867 alone, arsonists burned down two schools and two places of worship that served the community where Melvinia and her children lived. The first target was the white minister of a new Methodist Episcopal church who had invited blacks and whites to pray together, side by side, and promised to offer religious education to black children. His church viewed the teaching of illiterate former slaves as central to its mission, arguing that if "they could be elevated, enlightened and civilized, they will become a power for good." The minister, Rev. Richard Waters, built a rough brush arbor for the people who came together to call out to Jesus and to lament their continuing sufferings. The rustic refuge did not survive for long. "Our brush arbor has been burnt down where we preached to the colored people & some of the colored people have been badly beaten for asking men to pay them what they owed them & an attempt was made to kill one," Rev. Waters wrote to one of his church superiors on July 2, 1866. "This same crowd induced a low drunken wretch to attack & abuse me with his vile tongue."

The minister refused to let men of violence stand in the way of the good works of God. A week or so later, he bought a house in town for $320.50 and vowed to convert it into a new church for his parishioners. But white marauders burned that house down, too, and some citizens in town laughed openly at the minister's attempts to seek justice. Church leaders found themselves forced to beg for help from the federal government. "Do you think it would be possible for me to get military protection at one or two points where great outrages are being committed upon Freedmen and Union men, especially our preachers?" wrote Rev. James F. Chalfant, who headed the church's operations in Georgia. "The outrages at this point are beyond endurance."

The Freedmen's Bureau, the federal agency established to assist former slaves and to guide the South's transition from a system of slavery to one that embraced—or at least accepted—paid labor, decided to take matters into its own hands and opened up another school, which was also promptly burned to the ground. Undeterred, the officials found yet another place to serve as a school and even found a white widow who was willing to teach there. "The house is not as good as could be desired, but will do for the purposes," the teacher wrote on April 8, 1867. "Seats will have to be obtained. Do you furnish those? I think there will be a full school." One month later, the school was torched. Suspicion fell upon two white men who had been drinking heavily that night. But no one offered up any evidence, and federal authorities began to suspect that prominent members of Jonesboro's white establishment were complicit in the crime. One prominent citizen offered to house the school temporarily in one of his properties, and the white community at large raised a $200 reward for the capture of the arsonists. But federal officials began to doubt their sincerity. "I know that many, although they publicly condemn it, at heart rejoice in it," a federal official wrote of the schoolhouse arson in Jonesboro.

Melvinia struggled to make sense of this tenuous freedom during a period when drought had ravaged the fields and many people could barely feed their families. In one year alone, the Freedmen's Bureau fed 166 black adults and 252 black children. Whites were far from immune to the suffering: 115 white adults and 154 white children also received rations at that time. "The condition of some of the poor within my jurisdiction is very distressing," wrote J. L. H. Waldrop, the Freedmen's Bureau official responsible for the bureau's operations in Clayton County, which included the city of Jonesboro. He bitterly decried the intransigence of white officials there who repeatedly ignored the government's orders to provide assistance to former slaves. "The local authorities," Mr. Waldrop said, "have not made any provisions for the poor within my jurisdiction."

Melvinia may have been shielded from the worst of the hardships. After the Civil War, she had remained close to the Shieldses, the white family that had controlled her destiny during slavery. Her former owner, Henry, and several of his sons were still clinging to their farming lives in the countryside near Jonesboro, just like she was. The white man who had fathered her children might have shared the food from his own table and protected her from the racial violence flaring in town. Or Melvinia may have simply endured the difficult days of freedom just as she had endured the hard times of slavery. Maybe knowing that her children would never know the lash and would never be taken from her was enough, at least for a time.

Even in Illinois, where Mary and Nelson Moten, Mrs. Obama's paternal great-great-grandparents, were building new lives, the pace of progress seemed achingly slow. The Motens had run away from slavery in Kentucky to find freedom in Illinois sometime around 1863. But when it came to extending broad rights to African Americans after the Civil War, officials in the state took their time. In the late 1860s, Mary and Nelson and other blacks still found themselves barred from voting, from sitting on juries, from holding office, and from sending their children to integrated schools. Freedom only went so far. (Blacks were finally granted the right to vote there in 1870 when Illinois revised its constitution, in part, to reflect the provisions of the Fifteenth Amendment.) But for people who had lived through America's period of legalized bondage, even the tiniest slivers of liberty glittered like small gifts, like shiny precious stones. Mrs. Obama's forebears sidestepped the trials and tribulations and carefully collected as many of those stones as they could find.

It was that hunger for freedom that drew Dolly and Peter Jumper, Mrs. Obama's great-great-great-grandparents, to the courthouse in Henry County, Virginia, in 1866. Dolly and Peter had been free before the war, but the North's victory opened the doors to a kind of liberty they had never known. So on a winter day in February 1866, they joined hundreds of other African American couples in front of the two-story brick building. There were former slaves and people whose families had been free for generations, elderly couples with salt-and-pepper hair, and young lovers brimming with the giddiness of first-found romance. They were lining up because federal officials were legalizing the marriages of African Americans for the very first time. Dolly and Peter had lived together for thirty-five years by then. She was about fifty-three and he was about sixty-six. They may have been hobbled by arthritis, with graying hair and aching limbs, but they were determined to imbue their relationship with the formal recognition of the state. (Although as free people they had the right to marry even before the war, some free African Americans chose to cohabitate rather than to invite unwelcome attention from the white authorities responsible for handling marriage licenses.) So the Jumpers waited their turn amid the crowds. And when their moment came, they stood before a federal official who took up pen and paper and wrote down their names and ages, adding those of their children as well, and the year that they had first lived together as husband and wife. By the time the registration was through, 603 couples—12 of whom were free before the war—had enshrined their relationships in that courthouse, and Dolly and Peter were able to savor freedom's fullness in a way they never could before. They had never lived as slaves, but they had always been denied many of the basic rights that whites took for granted. For them, freedom meant finally receiving official acknowledgment of the precious and invisible bonds of their family, formal recognition as a committed couple and devoted parents.

No eyewitness accounts have emerged of that day in Henry County, but similar scenes played out across the country as African Americans wept and rejoiced as they turned up by the thousands to enshrine their relationships under the cloak of law. "I praise God for this day!" one black soldier declared after learning that Virginia would recognize the relationships between slaves. "I have long been praying for it." White missionaries and army officers, who had assumed that slavery had destroyed family ties among African Americans, watched with astonishment at the outpouring of enthusiasm for the institution of marriage. In one Mississippi military camp alone, a chaplain married 119 black couples in a single ceremony. "One of the most touching features of our work was the eagerness with which colored men and women availed themselves of the opportunities offered them to legalize unions already formed, some of which had been in existence for a long time."

Former slaves, then, were not the only African Americans who benefited from Emancipation. Blacks who had been free before the war—many of whom had experience working for wages, some education, and some means—were particularly well poised to seize the widening opportunities opening up for African Americans as they began taking their seats in county commissions, in state legislatures, and in Congress. This group accounted for only about 11 percent of the black population in 1860, but they would occupy a far larger share of political positions. Between 1869 and 1900, at least 10 of the 22 blacks who served in Congress had been free before the Civil War. In Virginia, where the Jumpers lived, 43 of the 102 blacks who held state office were free before Emancipation.

The Jumpers and the Motens illiterate and never became part of the African American elite. But when slavery ended, both families had some money on hand and some experience negotiating with whites for wages. Nelson Moten, who had escaped to freedom during the Civil War, had managed to acquire personal possessions worth $200 by the time he was in his forties, which made him one of the more prosperous black men in his rural community of Villa Ridge, Illinois. His daughter, Phoebe, would learn to read and write and would carry the family line to Chicago. In Virginia, Dolly and Peter Jumper, who were born free, could afford the help of a young woman who cooked for them as they settled into old age. Their son, Peter Jr., would exemplify the social changes rapidly transforming the postslave society. When it came time to marry, he picked a bride who had been born in servitude, bridging the long-standing divide between those who had been slaves and those who were born free.

Yet even as the Jumpers and Motens saw the world change in ways they could never have imagined before the Civil War, they still fell short of fulfilling the dream held so dearly by most African Americans. They never earned enough money to buy any land. Nelson Moten and Peter Jumper Sr. would both die as sharecroppers. Mary Moten died in Villa Ridge, Illinois, and Nelson probably died there, too, though no record of his death has survived. It appears that the Jumpers spent their last days amid the green hills of southern Virginia, the state where they were born free. Their final resting place has yet to be found.

In South Carolina, Mrs. Obama's ancestors also discovered that freedom brought mixed blessings. Caeser Cohen, who had joined the triumphant Union Army right after Emancipation, found himself at loose ends just six months later. By February 1866, he was right back where he had toiled as a slave, back at the Weymouth plantation. He had his wife, Tira, and several young children to feed. So he signed a labor contract with his former owner, promising to work ten-hour days, six days a week. In return, his master promised to provide him and his family a place to live, a quarter acre of land to farm, and a share of the corn, peas, potatoes, and rough rice grown on the plantation. Some former slaves never managed to escape this sharecropping existence, falling into an endless cycle of indebtedness.

But Caeser, the First Lady's paternal great-great-grandfather, found a way to thrive. His owner allowed his former slaves to raise their own poultry and livestock as well as growing vegetables. Some sharecroppers were able to earn a little money that way. Caeser managed to earn enough to buy a half an acre of land and to build a house on it for his family. He died there on July 16, 1904, at the age of eighty. Tira, his wife for nearly fifty years, died sometime afterward. Their daughter, Rosetta, also known as Rosella, would grow up to own a house of her own. And in her name, she would carry the long-lost clues to her family's past.

Jim Robinson, the young slave who developed a lifelong bond with his white overseer in Georgetown, South Carolina, moved away from the rice plantation where he grew up. He settled near the Black River and started a family with a woman named Louiser, which would include a son named Fraser. Jim was a free man. He could live where he wanted, work where he wanted, befriend who he wanted. Many former slaves chose to put some distance between themselves and their old plantation bosses. But Jim stayed close to William Nesmith, his former overseer. Slavery was over and gone, but the two men still lived near each other. Their sons—Fraser Robinson and Francis Nesmith—grew friendly over the years. They got to know each other so well, in fact, that Francis took young Fraser in when the boy started having trouble at home. (Jim remarried after his first wife died and young Fraser clashed with Jim's second wife.) Jim, who worked as a farm laborer, lived the rest of his life without leaving much of a trail. He didn't own any property; it appears he never learned how to read or write. But his descendants believe that his friendship with the Nesmiths, which took root on a rice plantation, changed the course of Fraser's life. Even after Jim's name was long forgotten, his descendants would still remember those Nesmiths.

In the countryside near Jonesboro, Georgia, the members of the white Shields family were still coming to terms with the devastated landscape around them. There is no way to know what they made of the changing times, whether they cheered on the arsonists who were burning black churches and schools or shook their heads in disgust. Some white businessmen had begun to abandon the place, moving to Atlanta and other big cities in the South. They looked around at the war-shattered buildings of Jonesboro, the fields ravaged by drought, and decided there was no future worth hanging on to. Many had been ruined by the war, left with little more than handfuls of worthless Confederate currency. "Within a few years, Jonesboro seemed to have more bar-rooms than anything else," filled with disillusioned farmers and Confederate veterans, wrote Alice Copeland Kilgore, a local historian. Henry Shields, Melvinia's former owner, could certainly understand their anguish. The value of his personal estate had plummeted from $3,475 in 1860 to $425 after the war. The staggering loss reflected the absence of his most valuable possessions, his human property, Melvinia, her two children, and two other slaves. Henry had spent nearly two decades building a life in Georgia and much of what he had prized was gone. He had lost his oldest son, David, in the Civil War. Moses, his second oldest, had married and was poised to move to another county.

In the face of such losses, Henry may have found comfort in the presence of his close-knit family. He still shared his farm with his wife and children, including one of his younger sons, Elisha. Another son, Charles, had returned from the war determined to establish a home of his own nearby. On January 15, 1867, Charles, who was twenty-seven by then, married Zipporah Robinson, whose parents had also moved to Georgia from South Carolina decades earlier. After so many years of war, tragedy, and turmoil, the family was finally settling into something akin to a stable life. Later that year, Henry and Charles signed an oath, pledging their allegiance to the United States. Any man who wanted to vote had to swear that they had never belonged to the Confederate leadership and vow that they would not support any insurrections or rebellions against the federal government. The Shields family had supported the Confederacy—Charles and Henry had served in the militia; Elisha, Moses, and David had served in the army—David had even given his life to the cause—but they seemed resigned to the new reality that defeat had delivered. They signed the pledge and went on with the business of rebuilding their lives.

Melvinia went on with her life, too, though she remained close to the Shields family. The fires had died down in Jonesboro. The Freedmen's Bureau was building yet another school for blacks, hiring a teacher and ordering up nails and lime to get the building ready. Yet tensions between blacks and whites still simmered in those years after the war. In Jonesboro, some African Americans were complaining that whites were still holding their children in unpaid servitude. In the state capital, white lawmakers were expelling the first black men elected to Georgia's legislature. The black legislators were ultimately returned to their seats, but nearly a quarter of them would be threatened, beaten, jailed, or killed by white men determined to keep blacks in their proper place and out of public office.

Melvinia could have packed up her belongings, gathered up her children, and joined some of the African Americans who were abandoning the farms and plantations that had dictated their lives for so long. She was no longer a slave. She was no longer a teenager. She was twenty-four years old, a mother of two, a free woman with the power to earn her own wages and to turn her back on the family that had owned her and the man who had fathered her children. And yet she knew, too, that black women, black people, were only so free in those years that followed the Civil War, that liberty was a fine word that rarely corresponded to the African American reality. Somehow, whether of her own accord or against her will, she found herself in a white man's arms again. Soon, Melvinia was pregnant again. In 1869, she gave birth to biracial twins, Alice and Talley.

Webs of open secrets, unspoken truths, and unsung sorrows often shroud the foundations of small southern towns. In such places, everyone knows everyone else. People often avert their eyes, but they see what can be seen. Melvinia was a black woman with four biracial children. There certainly would have been whispers, pained looks, and unkind comments. And many would have nodded knowingly, whether they were right or wrong in their assumptions, when they saw where Melvinia was living by the following year.

She was living next door to Charles Marion Shields, the thirty-one-year-old son of her former master, a man she had grown up with as a child. Charles, who had a sickly wife and a toddler, owned 122 acres of land. What Charles's wife, Zipporah, may have thought of the dark-eyed black woman and her children we will never know. Zipporah may have been too ill to care. She died of typhoid two years later, in 1872, and was buried in the Shields family cemetery under a white stone that read simply, "At Rest." Soon afterward, Charles married Zipporah's sister, Emma, who had come to help out during Zipporah's last days. But Emma was sickly, too, and died of typhoid herself in 1874. That year, Melvinia became pregnant again.

Charles, who was not a man inclined to live without female companionship, remarried two months after Emma's death. This time, he married Nancy Jane Porter, a strong-willed, healthy woman who would bear him at least seven children and would ultimately outlive him. In 1875, Charles and Nancy left the Jonesboro area and moved to neighboring Henry County. And Melvinia, who had given birth to another fair-skinned baby that year, finally decided to leave the Jonesboro area, too. No one knows if she ever returned to the place where she had found her freedom and met the white man who had fathered her children. She may have dreamed at some point that the end of slavery might have allowed her to spend the rest of her life at that man's side. Not as his wife, not as his equal, but in that amorphous space that African American mistresses sometimes occupied. But that was not to be. Melvinia had to consider a new future, a new life.

She reconnected somehow with a former slave, her dear friend Mariah from Spartanburg, South Carolina, who was establishing herself in Bartow County, a rural community in northern Georgia. Melvinia must have considered staying close to Charles and the rest of the Shields family. But she had to consider her children—Dolphus, who was about fifteen; Jane, who was about eleven; Alice and Talley, the twins who were about six; and Laura, her newborn—and she had to think hard about where they might have the best chance of living life to the fullest. We all know what she decided. Sometime around 1875, Melvinia cut her ties to the white family that had so defined her young life. And she started the trek north.

Melvinia's Secret

I PACKED THE TINY VIALS—FIVE IN ALL—INTO INDIVIDUAL Federal Express boxes and sent them on their way. The precious cargo flew from the FedEx Kinko's store near my house in Washington, D.C., to a ten-story building in Houston, Texas. The vials carried the cells that contained the strands of DNA from the descendants of Melvinia; her owner, Henry; and his son, Charles. All three had been dead for more than seventy years and the details of what had happened between them on that farm in Georgia in the 1800s had been lost ever since. But not irrevocably lost. The truth was always there, hidden within the microscopic makeup of their children and grandchildren, their great-grandchildren and great-great-grandchildren. It was secreted within the cells of descendants like Jewell Barclay and Joan Tribble, who had embarked on this quest. Melvinia and the man who impregnated her were silenced by shame and fear, circumscribed by the societal mores of the times in which they lived. But the country has changed enormously since then. Scientists have learned to unlock the mysteries of the double helix. Americans of all colors and stations have become increasingly willing to peel back the layers of the past, to examine and comprehend where we came from and how we came to be as a nation, no matter how agonizing the process, no matter how painful the find-ings. History is not simply stored in our archives or in the memories of our elders. It is also written in our cells. It was time to try to de-code those secrets.

In Houston, my packages landed in the eighth-floor offices of Family Tree DNA, which tests thousands of samples every year. Founded in 2000 by Bennett Greenspan, the company's chief execu-tive, the firm analyzes genetic materials for the National Geographic Society, which is trying to build the world's largest survey of DNA samples so that it can be used for mapping how humans populated the planet; for Harvard scholar Henry Louis Gates Jr., who employs gene-alogy and genetics to explore the family histories of renowned Ameri-cans in his documentaries on PBS; and for ordinary people searching for their roots. The company takes the cells that people like Joan and Jewell have scraped from the inside of their cheeks, extracts the DNA, and finds the genetic markers that distinguish the descendants of an individual. By comparing those markers, they can reveal if two people share a common ancestor. When my packages arrived at the Hous-ton headquarters, a company employee scanned the bar codes on each vial, placed each one into a green plastic rack, and sent them to the in-house laboratory. Then, as the team of technicians got to work, I waited at home for the results.

In the end, I would spend nearly two years digging through dusty courthouses and archives, poring over death certificates, marriage li-censes, property records, and maps that were more than a hundred years old. I had followed the First Lady's family trail across seven states and a dozen cities, feeling something like a modern-day detective rummaging through rusty old trunks for antebellum clues. But the DNA results, when they finally came some four weeks later, arrived in decidedly twenty-first-century fashion, with the ping of an incom-ing e-mail into my inbox. The subject line read: "New Family Finder Match." I was sitting in my home office on a brilliant, sunny October morning when I first saw it. For a moment, I just stared at the com-puter screen. I could barely breathe. Then I clicked on the note and opened it up. "A Family Finder match has been found," the e-mail told me. "Follow the link below to access your myFTDNA."

There it was: a hit between DNA samples, and a century-old mystery finally unraveled. The truth is what Joan and Jewell had long suspected: the black descendants of Melvinia and the white descendants of her owner are related. The DNA results suggest that the patriarch of the multiracial clan is Charles Marion Shields, who grew up with Melvinia when she was an enslaved little girl on his father's farm and later lived alongside her on his own land. The results suggest that he fathered Dolphus Shields, Melvinia's oldest son, and is the great-great-great-grandfather of Michelle Obama. (In the end, it was one of Charles's direct descendants, a person who requested anonymity, who turned out to be most closely related to the black Shields family. Joan, who is the great-granddaughter of one of Charles's younger brothers, has a much more distant genetic connection to Dolphus's descendants.) The First Lady is the descendant of both Irish immigrants who nurtured their dreams in a new land and of African Americans who triumphed over servitude and segregation. Michelle LaVaughn Robinson Obama is the inheritor of our nation's complex, often unspoken lineage.

The two women who offered their DNA to help unlock the doors to the First Lady's past, and their own, finally have some answers as well. Joan, who instinctively recognized Dolphus as kin the first time she saw his photograph, learned that she was right. He had inherited the bloodlines of her great-great-grandfather, Henry Shields. Jewell, who had heard whispers growing up that Dolphus, her great-grandfather, was the son of a white man, was right, too. Joan and Jewell are still strangers, two women who grew up on opposite sides of the American racial divide, who witnessed segregation as children and grew up to marvel at the sight of a black man becoming president of the United States. They have never met. But they know now that they both emerged from the same root. Their families are family.

For them, it is a remarkable discovery, and a connection to the White House that they had never dreamed possible. But science can take us only so far, and some of the most agonizing questions about this family's origins still linger, unsettled and unanswered. Was Melvinia raped? Did she and Charles feel any affection toward each other? Did Charles care for his biracial children? There is no way to know definitively, but we can try to glean some meaning from the scanty clues they left behind. After slavery ended, Melvinia chose to stay near Charles and his family for nearly a decade. She continued to have biracial children after the war, when she was a free woman, which suggests a liaison that was enduring, not transient or forced. Mrs. Obama's relatives—both black and white—like to think that this means that Melvinia cared for Charles and that he cared for her. They like to think that Charles privately accepted his son, Dolphus, even if he could not do so openly. Of all Melvinia's boys, Dolphus was the only one who ended up learning a trade, the craft of carpentry. He was also the only one of Melvinia's sons who spent his childhood in close proximity to his white father. Whoever taught him his craft gave him a gift that allowed him to climb heights that none of his other siblings would reach. Joan and Jewell like to think that Charles was the one who first put a hammer and nails in Dolphus's hands. It is not hard to imagine Charles as a man who cherished Melvinia, who watched over her and protected her, who cared for their children and chafed against the strictures of society that outlawed their affection. "Oh, it's a love story," said Jewell, with hope catching in her voice.

Some might call Jewell a romantic, an idealist, a naïf. True love between slave and master was exceedingly rare. But I understand Jewell's instinct. The alternatives are almost unbearable to think about. Try to visualize, for a moment, the image of Charles, about twenty at the time, preying on this young, teenage girl. Try to imagine Melvinia screaming and fighting with the horrifying knowledge that absolutely no one would come to save her. Try to imagine Melvinia pleading with Charles to recognize his own children and weeping when he turned his back. It is possible that Melvinia stayed, not because she was in love, but rather because she had been brutalized and was too frightened to leave. Or consider the possibility that Melvinia bore the pressure of Charles's body against hers, not out of fear and not out love, but out of hardship. In a time of drought and scarcity, tumult and racial violence, Charles might have provided food and clothing, shelter and protection. He could have offered Melvinia and her children the most essential gift of all, the gift of survival. Such scenes make all of us shudder and want to avert our eyes. But these things happened. They are part of our history, too. The truth is that we will never know which version of the past most mirrors Melvinia's experiences. But I remain struck by the fact that she never mentioned Charles, at least not to anyone who lived long enough to share her story. Some families took great pride in their white ancestors. They treasured the stories about their white forebears and passed them down through the generations. Melvinia stayed silent. That still keeps me awake some nights. Did he hurt her? Or did he fall in love with another woman, shattering her dreams? I find myself asking, "Melvinia, what happened to you?"

What we do know is that once Melvinia finally left Jonesboro, Georgia, around 1875 and moved north, Charles went on to live a full, productive life with his white family in Henry County. He and his third wife raised at least seven children and grew sweet potatoes, churned butter, and raised mules and horses on his farm. He taught in a one-room schoolhouse. He joined the Masons. In his later years, he ran a boardinghouse with his wife, who filled their home with the delicious aroma of her sweet, baking pies. He even appeared in the newspaper one year when a thief took off with two of his mules and his wagon. (Happily, the mules were recovered.) Whether he and Melvinia ever crossed paths again remains a tantalizing, unanswerable question. In 1882, about seven years after Melvinia and Charles parted ways, Melvinia gave birth to Henry. He was about twenty-two years younger than her oldest son, Dolphus. She was living in Cartersville at the time, about seventy-three miles north of Henry County, where Charles had moved with his third wife. Henry was much, much lighter than Melvinia. People who knew him described him as "high yellow." Was Henry also Charles's son? The people who might have known the answer to that question are long gone. Charles's father, Henry Wells Shields, who owned Melvinia and Dolphus when they were slaves, died on June 2, 1895, at the age of eighty-three. Charles died two decades later, on January 24, 1916. He was seventy-six. In an obituary that appeared on the front page of the *Henry County Weekly,* Charles was hailed as a Confederate veteran, "a useful and honorable citizen" who had devoted much of his life to teaching. There was no mention, of course, of his other family.

But it appears that some of the black and white members of the Shields family may have quietly kept in touch, at least for a time. One of Charles Shields's sons with his third wife was named McClellan Charles "Mack" Shields. That son made his way to Birmingham where his half brother, Dolphus, was already an established businessman and homeowner. The two brothers lived there for decades. At one point, Mack even lived within walking distance of Dolphus's carpentry shop. It's impossible to say for sure that Mack was the mysterious white visitor who often chatted with Dolphus on his front porch and the lone white man who took a seat at Dolphus's funeral. But it is also hard to believe that he wasn't. Dolphus, a carpenter and a well-known deacon, died around the age of ninety-one on June 3, 1950. Mack, a dairy manager and an insurance agent, died at the age of sixty-nine on May 29, 1961. If the brothers knew each other, they shared that knowledge only with their closest friends and relatives. On both sides of the color line, the Shields family learned to keep their mouths shut.

In the end, though, Mrs. Obama's family saga is as much about the living as it is about the dead. The legacy of slavery and segregation still reverberates in our contemporary political discourse, in the raw debate over affirmative action, in the periodic calls for reparations for African Americans, in the simmering questions over how to atone in modern times—and whether there is any need to atone—for one of the darkest stains on the nation's conscience. Slavery ended in this country more than 145 years ago. Yet waves of shame and guilt, fear and great sadness, still spill into the living rooms of the descendants of some slaves and slave owners. Some of Charles's descendants asked me to keep their names and photographs out of these pages, fearful that their lives, their children, and their careers would be indelibly tainted by the history they have inherited. A decades-old black-and-white photograph of Charles Marion Shields has survived—I have seen it—but his descendants, after wrestling for weeks over the matter, decided that they did not want it published. I explained to them that Mrs. Obama has publicly embraced her mixed heritage, that she is fascinated by her family history, and that she knows that the blood of slaves and slave owners runs through her veins. One of Charles's great-grandchildren smiled sadly at that. Some of the white Shields descendants say it is naive to believe that the white and black members of the family could ever have an open and meaningful discussion about the past. The scar tissue that hides so many of our old, ugly wounds remains tender and sore. "They are on the right side of history and we are not," the descendant said of the First Lady and her family. "I don't think there's going to be a Kumbaya moment here."

Joan and Jewell do not expect the DNA results or their newfound connection to the First Lady to transform their lives either. But they do hope to meet each other someday. "Some people would say, 'I don't want to meet them white people,'" Jewell said. "But I'm not like that. This happened years and years ago. Why hold grudges? We got the same blood. I'm glad we're in the same family. I'll probably give her a hug, if she'll hug me." The two women are both mostly retired now, focused on their children and grandchildren and on praising God at church on Sunday mornings. Even so, they cannot help but marvel at their family's journey, which in so many ways mirrors the evolution of this country. Mrs. Obama's family tree bloomed in barren soil, amid poverty and servitude, violence and hard times. Yet her melting-pot ancestors kept pushing forward, finding love, cherishing family and education, and vaulting—and sometimes stumbling—over the obstacles in their way. Americans are famously focused on the here and now. We keep our eyes fixed on the winding road ahead, not on the rearview mirror. But looking back can sometimes give us clearer vision. Had it not been for this nation's singular history and its singular mix of people—Irish Americans like Moses Shields, rice-planting slaves like Jim Robinson, and mixed-race wanderers like Phoebe Moten Johnson—the First Lady would never have been born.

The laws that once barred men and women like Melvinia and Charles from dating or marrying across the color line are memories now. Mrs. Obama's brother, Craig Robinson, the head basketball coach at Oregon State University, has a white wife and two biracial sons. Charles's white descendants have dated, married, and adopted across racial and ethnic lines, too. Henry, Melvinia's owner and Joan's great-great-grandfather, might have been astonished, but Joan was not when her daughter decided to marry a black man. Sometimes in life, history comes full circle. Joan's grandsons, who are eleven and eighteen, are her companions at church, amusement parks, school football games, and at her home. They fill her days with joy and delight and, at times, no small measure of aggravation. The day we met at the Georgia Archives, before we dove into my stack of historical records, Joan pushed a handful of snapshots across the table. There, in Technicolor, were her handsome, impish, caramel-colored boys. Joan Tribble, the great-great-granddaughter of the man who had owned the great-great-great-grandmother of Michelle Obama, could not have been more proud. We had centuries of history to discuss, but this came first. "They are the light of my life," she said. Only in America, as President Obama likes to say, would such a story be possible.

ACKNOWLEDGMENTS

I still remember trekking for nearly two hours through the tall, sway-ing grass in that vast, neglected cemetery in Birmingham, Alabama. It was a breezy afternoon in September 2009, and I was searching for the tombstone of Dolphus Shields. I never found his grave, but I vividly remember stopping short in the middle of that solemn place. In that moment, I realized that there was nothing I'd rather be doing than hunting through the nation's history. This has been a labor of love since then. There is no way that I could have done it alone.

This book grew out of an article that I wrote with a colleague for the *New York Times* in October 2009. Megan Smolenyak, the genealo-gist who discovered Melvinia and Dolphus Shields and many other ancestors of Michelle Obama, collaborated with us on that article and fired my fascination for the First Lady's family history. At the *Times,* Rebecca Corbett, my editor in the Washington bureau, and Jodi Kan-tor, my colleague and cowriter, were invaluable partners in the report-ing, writing, and editing of the story. After the article appeared in the newspaper, Jill Abramson and Dean Baquet encouraged me to embark on this journey, even at a time when I didn't think a book was possi-ble, and Bill Keller gave this project his blessing. Janet Elder urged me to cover the First Lady in the first place, setting all of this in motion.

Flip Brophy, my agent, offered wise counsel, warm hugs, and nerves of steel. She believed in this book before I did. Dawn Davis, my editor at HarperCollins, believed in it, too. She emailed me the day after the article appeared in the *New York Times* and since then has offered constant encouragement and her fine eye to the manuscript.

I would also like to thank Dawn's assistant, Shanna Milkey, for her thoughtful and meticulous attention to detail and her warm and welcoming spirit.

I spent more than two years researching the First Lady's family and benefited from the assistance and counsel of many genealogists, historians, and researchers. There are more people to thank than I can name, but here are a few. Jim Sherling fell in love with Melvinia and her family and spent hours digging through records and finding people who knew them. There are few people who know the First Lady's ancestors in Georgia and South Carolina better than Jim does. Johni Cerny, a master of the online universe of genealogical records, found documents for me and offered a wealth of advice as I began searching for records in courthouses, archives, and libraries around the country. Elizabeth Wolff generously shared the research she had done on the white descendants of Henry Wells Shields, Melvinia's owner.

Professor Henry Louis Gates Jr. of Harvard University graciously helped me to navigate the world of DNA testing and genealogical research and introduced me to Johni Cerny and Bennett Greenspan of Family Tree DNA. Bennett helped me from the very beginning, as I searched for descendants of Melvinia and her owner, Henry, who were willing to be tested. He walked me through the DNA testing process and the analysis of the results. Professor Charles Ogletree of Harvard, who believed there was a book in me before I did, was a wonderful sounding board and supporter. Reginald Washington of the National Archives was a wise and patient guide who introduced me to the Freedmen's Bureau records, Southern Claims Commission records, and the Civil War service and pension records, which helped illuminate the nineteenth-century lives of Mrs. Obama's ancestors.

Jim Baggett of the Birmingham Public Library provided me with maps, articles, and photographs that brought nineteenth-century and early-twentieth-century Birmingham to life. Elizabeth Wells of Samford University's library found a rare profile of Dolphus, offering a precious glimpse of an early part of his life. Wilson Fallin Jr. shared his vast knowledge of the first black Baptists in Birmingham and helped me to find the very first person I encountered who actually knew Dolphus Shields. Jim Grossman, the president of the American Historical Association and the former vice president for research at Chicago's Newberry Library, read sections of my manuscript, gave me my first tour of Hyde Park, and was the first to tell me about Sanborn Fire Insurance maps, which brought the neighborhoods where Mrs. Obama's ancestors dwelled to life for me. I cannot thank his staff at the Newberry, particularly Matt Rutherford and Grace Dumelle, enough for their help. Lesley Martin of the Chicago History Museum and Delilah Smith of the Chicago Board of Elections met with me and fielded my countless queries via e-mail and phone. I am grateful to both of them. Timuel Black, that historian and sage of the South Side, pored over the addresses of Mrs. Obama's ancestors and regaled me with stories of that community's history. Karen Cullotta kindly assisted during those stretches when I could not be in Chicago, hunting for records for me there and in Evanston.

Pat Ross and Anne Copeland of the Bassett Historical Center in Virginia helped me re-create the lives of Mrs. Obama's ancestors who were free long before the Civil War. Nicholas Lemann of Columbia University introduced me to the congressional investigations that examined the violent attacks on blacks that erupted across Georgia, South Carolina, and elsewhere after the Civil War. Bob Carter at Rockingham Community College directed me to articles and city directories about the fledgling black communities in Rockingham, North Carolina, in the early 1900s. Rod Sievers at Southern Illinois University in Carbondale and Darrel Dexter, a local historian there, helped me to learn more about the First Lady's roots in southern Illinois. Steven F. Miller of the University of Maryland's Freedmen and Southern Society Project guided me through their records, where I found details about the early years after Emancipation in Jonesboro, Georgia. Toni Carrier, who researched Mrs. Obama's paternal ancestors, shared her insights into the early life of the young Fraser Robinson Sr. Professor Kate Masur of Northwestern University read my manuscript in warp speed, and I benefited greatly from her expertise and her suggestions. Professor Steven Hahn of the University of Pennsylvania also took time to read these pages and I am grateful for his thoughtful comments.

Several people offered me a quiet place to work while I was on leave from the *New York Times* and supported my research and writing in other ways. Professor Stephen Schneck, Dean Larry Poos, and Professor John White of the Catholic University of America offered their assistance even before I had begun my research, providing me with an office, a research assistant—the warm and capable Patricia Murphy—and constant encouragement throughout this entire process. Professor Stephen West of Catholic University provided insight into nineteenth-century Spartanburg, South Carolina, and kindly offered corrections to my manuscript. I cannot thank them enough.

Lonnie Bunch of the Smithsonian's National Museum of African American History and Culture gave me an office and space for my burgeoning files as well as insight into the nineteenth-century South and early-twentieth-century Chicago. Fleur Paysour, his wonderful director of communications, brought us together and made it all happen. The Wilson International Center for Scholars provided funding, an office, and a warm and welcoming place to mix and meet with others engaged in intellectual pursuits. I'd like to thank Robert Litwak for bringing me in and the other members of the staff, particularly Sonya Michel and Lucy Jilka. I'd also like to thank the library's amazing staff: Janet Spikes, Michelle Kamalich, and Dagne Gizaw. The Wilson Center staff also introduced me to the delightful and tireless Natasha Escobar, who exceeded all of my expectations for a research assistant as she dived headlong into the world of African American history. She relied greatly on the helpful staff at the Library of Congress who offered research advice and resources. Charlie Wilson and Robert Liguori pored over many sections of the manuscript to help ensure its accuracy. And Alphonse Fletcher Jr., who created and endowed the Fletcher Fellowship program, also supported this project with a generous stipend, which kept me going when my research and writing ended up taking longer than I had expected.

I am also indebted to many wonderful friends. First to Dana Canedy, who encouraged me to cover Michelle Obama and, once I agreed, told me over and over again that she knew I would write a book. She and my dear friend Lynette Clemetson kept me going with countless phone calls, e-mails, and coffees. Teresa Wiltz, Marjorie Valbrun, Evelyn Larrubia, and Joao Silva always offered support and inspiration. Thank you all: your friendship means the world to me. Brad Snyder offered legal and publishing advice—often on a few hours notice—and much encouragement. Teddy and Nori Greenstein offered me their guest bedroom in Chicago, their gracious company, and many fabulous dinners. Peter Baker and Nadine Duplessy Kearns took the time to read my manuscript on very short notice, and shared their wise thoughts and suggestions. And Christine Kay, one of the best journalists on the planet, read every word of this manuscript, several times over, and cheered me on, day in and day out. She never doubted the power of this story, even when I was unsure myself, and she pushed and prodded me forward. I am so grateful for her support and counsel.

This is a book about family and as I wrote I was constantly reminded of how grateful I am to my own family. My parents, Joseph and Lucille Swarns, taught me to care about history and all of the journeys that carry us from the past to the present. They offered constant phone calls, e-mails, prayers, and occasional babysitting. My mother learned to know and love the complex characters in this book as much as I did. My husband, Henri Cauvin, was a steadfast supporter during the long days and nights that it took to pull this book together. He urged me to pursue this project and held everything together during my travels away from home and the countless weekends that I had to work. My sister, Christina Swarns, offered me her couch and her company during my sojourns in New York. My sister, Jessica Swarns; my in-laws, Anne and Louis Cauvin; and my brother-in-law, Jean-Louis Cauvin, helped to entertain my children on many weekends while I worked. Amanda Eduful, so warm and conscientious, kept our boys safe and happy and our lives running smoothly, even in the most difficult of times. My little boys, Gabriel and Julian, loved me without question, even when I had to be away, and absorbed the project into their psyches. ("Will you still be working for Mr. Dolphus?" Julian asked when I told him I was finally returning to work at the *Times*.)

I would also like to thank the members of Mrs. Obama's family who so graciously shared their stories with me. In Illinois, Francesca Gray, Nomenee Robinson, and Mary Lang shed light on the Johnson and Robinson clans. Johnny D. Johnson, who started studying his family's roots long before the Obamas moved into the White House, was a remarkable family historian and an inspiration in his own right. I will never forget his passion for history or his phone calls, urging me to keep digging.

In Georgia, Nellie Margaret Applin, and her husband, David, introduced me to Ruth Wheeler Applin and Harold Wise Sr., who knew Melvinia, Dolphus, and Henry. Nellie, who is a remarkable community historian in her own right, was an ideal guide during my visits to Kingston, Georgia. In Cleveland, the lovely Jewell Barclay and her cousin, Tony Allmond, shared their remembrances of the Shields family. In Georgetown, South Carolina, Harolyn Siau and Connie Jones described their family recollections. I would be remiss if I failed to mention Helen Heath, the daughter of Dolphus's last pastor, who described Dolphus's later years. She also introduced me to Bobbie Holt, whose love for Dolphus and Lucy, the old man and woman who raised her, has endured through the decades.

The descendants of Melvinia's owners also generously shared their memories and family stories and records. They include Sherry George and Greg Shields in Georgia and Aliene Shields in South Carolina, as well as the remarkable Joan Tribble, who so openly confronted the past. I would also like to thank those descendants who chose to remain anonymous in these pages, yet still took the time to help guide my research.

Most of all, I'd like to thank Phoebe and Melvinia, two remarkable women who continue to inspire me. They are long gone, but I like to think that they have been watching over me over the past few years, praying for me and guiding me from the other side. It has been an honor to tell their family's story.

NOTES

PROLOGUE:
THE MYSTERY OF MICHELLE OBAMA'S ROOTS

1 *hardest of hard times:* Several sources describe the drought in Georgia at the time, including Kennett, *Marching Through Georgia*, 83, 315. Also, Brooks, "The Agrarian Revolt," 10, describes the "almost total failure of crops" in Georgia in 1865 and 1866.

1 *The town was in ruins:* The devastation of Jonesboro is described in Kilgore, *History of Clayton County*, 34, 35, 41.

1 *Everywhere southerners turned, people were moving:* Historians believe that many newly freed slaves moved after Emancipation, though "a majority did not abandon their home plantations in 1865." See Foner, *Reconstruction,* 81. The situation was different, however, in northern Georgia, where the drought and crop failures appear to have pushed thousands of blacks to move. See Brooks, "The Agrarian Revolt," 10; and Drago, *Black Politicians and Reconstruction in Georgia*, 122. Former slaves, who were typically a minority in upcountry Georgia, also moved to find family and to settle in communities with larger black populations. Between 1865 and 1870, the black population of the largest cities in the South doubled, while the white population increased only by 10 percent. See Foner, *Reconstruction*, 81–82.

1 *Melvinia, a dark-eyed young woman:* The physical description of Melvinia comes from interviews with Ruth Wheeler Applin and Harold Wise Sr., who knew her. Interviews by author, in Kingston, Georgia, February 3, 2010, and June 3, 2010.

2 *A census taker would record:* The details of Melvinia's life after Emancipation come from the 1870 census; the death certificate of her daugh-

ter Laura Shields, which indicates that Melvinia moved to Atlanta in 1875; and the reminiscences of her son, Dolphus Shields, who said he and his family were living in Cartersville, Georgia, in 1880. His reminiscences are recounted in Reid, *History of Colored Baptists in Alabama*, 291–292.

3 *lived together on a two-hundred-acre farm near Jonesboro:* The details about the farm where Melvinia and Henry lived come from the U.S. Census agricultural survey of the farm, which was conducted in 1850. The 1850 and 1860 censuses describe the value of Henry's land and possessions.

7 *Rumors about Sally Hemings:* See Reed, *The Hemingses of Monticello*, 24.

8 *day-to-day life in the antebellum South:* The description of slavery in Clayton County, Georgia, comes from Kilgore, *History of Clayton County*, 11, 16–20.

10 *Her forebears would witness:* Insights into life on the small slave estate can be found in Kolchin, *American Slavery*, 101–102, and Hahn, *Roots of Southern Populism*, 15–18, 25–32.

11 *"Their American dream was . . .":* Francesca Gray, interview by author, in Chicago on October 21, 2010, and several times afterward by telephone.

12 *Mr. Robinson remembers discussing slavery and segregation:* See Robinson, *A Game of Character*, 58, 59.

12 *He and his sister watched:* See ibid., 59. Also, on September 28, 2011, a senior aide to Mrs. Obama, who spoke on condition of anonymity, confirmed to the author that the First Lady had watched the miniseries *Roots* with her family.

12 *Mrs. Obama, meanwhile, recalls being transfixed:* Mrs. Obama described her passion for Toni Morrison's *Song of Solomon* in response to a question from a child at a "Take Your Son and Daughter to Work" event at the White House on April 28, 2011.

12 *but "we didn't talk about that":* Shailagh Murray, "A Family Tree Rooted in American Soil," *Washington Post,* October 8, 2008. This article was the first to describe Mrs. Obama's slave roots in Georgetown, South Carolina.

13 *"We were aware that most [African American] families . . .":* Craig Robinson, unpublished interview conducted by Jodi Kantor, *New York Times,* January 2009.

13   *". . . What I think is that they blocked it out"*: Author telephone interviews of Nomenee Robinson on November 10, 2010, and August 12, 2011.

14   *"They were visibly shaken"*: Author telephone interview of Fritz Baffour in July 2009.

ONE: PHOEBE, THE WANDERER

19   *Her name was Phoebe Moten:* In the historical records that I examined, Phoebe's surname is spelled several different ways. In the 1870 census, her parents appear as Nelson and Mary Morten. In the 1880 census, her parents appear as Nelson and Mary Moulton. But in 1899, when Phoebe married for the first time, her maiden name appears as Mary Moten on her wedding license. (It appeared as Morton when she married for the second time, two years later.) Phoebe's grandson, Johnny D. Johnson, who knew Phoebe and some of her sisters said that Moten was the way the family spelled their name. So that is the spelling that I use in this book.

Phoebe's year of birth appears variously as 1879 and 1880 in the historical record. The earliest records available—her marriage licenses and the 1900 census—indicate that she was born in 1879, and that is the year accepted by her family, according to her son, Johnny D. Johnson. I rely on that year in this book.

19   *Phoebe would take her first steps:* The descriptions of Villa Ridge and Pulaski County, Illinois, in terms of the landscape and black settlers, come from several sources, including: Perrin, *History of Alexander, Union and Pulaski Counties,* 581, 582; Carlson, "Black Migration to Pulaski County," 37–46; Jones, "Black Land Tenancy," 41–51; and White *Cache Area River Assessment,* 2–74.

22   *In 1880, about five hundred:* See Carlson, "Black Migration to Pulaski County," 42, and Jones, "Black Land Tenancy," 4.

22   *A small but growing number of blacks:* Carlson, "Black Community in the Rural North," 141, has a description of the occupations of black residents at the time.

23   *"Just now our town . . .":* Carlson, "Black Migration to Pulaski County," 45, describes the black community that blossomed in southern Illinois, beginning in the 1860s, when runaway slaves began pouring into the state during the Civil War. Illinois, which was bordered by

slave states, was a destination for many African Americans yearning to be free.

23   *"Our newly instituted . . .":* Ibid., 36.

24   *Still, Phoebe somehow learned:* Author telephone interview of Johnny D. Johnson on November 11, 2010, and interview in Idlewild, Michigan, on December 1, 2010; also see "Negroes in the United States: 1910," 27, which refers to 1900 data.

24   *Phoebe's accomplishments suggest:* The details of Phoebe's life and her parents' lives emerged from her mother's marriage record; Jerry Suter's Civil War pension file, application file no. 897, 567; and the 1880 and 1900 censuses.

25   *Carbondale had a university:* "Population by Sex, General Nativity, and Color for Places Having 2,500 Inhabitants or More: 1900," 613; City of Carbondale website, www.ci.carbondale.il.us/node/110 (accessed 2010).

25   *Phoebe might have left:* Green, *Traces in the Dust,* 64. Death certificate of Ibby Bowers, who died on August 1, 1942; and author interview with Johnny D. Johnson in Idlewild, Michigan, on December 1, 2010.

25   *They exchanged wedding vows:* The details about Phoebe and her first husband, Elbert, and their families come from their marriage license and the 1880 and 1900 censuses; and Green, *Traces in the Dust,* 64.

26   *Phoebe decided on a December wedding:* Phoebe's older sister, Coria, married A. M. Armstrong on December 24, 1874. Pulaski County, Illinois, Marriage Register 1, 49. Phoebe's mother, Mary Moten, remarried after her first husband, Nelson, died. She married Jerry Suter on December 26, 1887. Pulaski County, Illinois, Marriage Register 1, 122.

26   *It was a custom that dated back:* Mays, *Women in Early America,* 253.

26   *Phoebe was only twenty:* Information is from the 1900 census.

26   *State law at the time:* State of Illinois, "Illinois Statewide Death Index: Pre-1916: Recordation of Deaths in Illinois," www.cyberdrive illinois.com/departments/archives/death.html (accessed 2010).

27   *Jeff had already made the break:* The information about Phoebe's life with her in-laws, after Elbert's death, comes from the 1900 census.

28   *African American women who worked as domestics:* Carlson, "Black Community in the Rural North," 142.

28   *a "black angel in calico":* Hays, "The African American Struggle,"

270–273. I relied heavily in this section on Hays's article, which describes in some detail the situation encountered by black domestics in Cairo, Illinois, in the late nineteenth century. I relied on his article for the quotes from the Cairo newspaper, black domestics, and white employers.

TWO: ST. LOUIS

29 *Between her nineteenth and twenty-second birthdays:* Details about Phoebe's wedding, her new husband, James, and her time in Edwardsville come from their marriage license, dated April 9, 1901. They married on April 20, 1901. Phoebe's son, Johnny D. Johnson, provided me with a copy of the wedding license in December 2010 when I visited him in Idlewild, Michigan.

30 *James also had white ancestry:* Details about James and his parents come from his marriage license, the 1870 census, and the 1880 census.

31 *By 1878, with the last of federal troops:* Jack, *St. Louis African American Community,* 4.

32 *Only in Baltimore:* Corbett and Seematter, "Black St. Louis," 42.

33 *Phoebe and James joined:* Rumbold, *Housing Conditions in St. Louis,* 65 67, 78 84.

33 *The newlyweds unpacked:* The details about the building and the neighborhood where Phoebe and James lived comes from the birth record of their son, Preston; also from Sanborn Insurance Company, St. Louis, fire insurance map, 1909.

33 *The couple could stroll about a dozen blocks:* Sanborn Insurance Company, St. Louis, fire insurance map, 1909.

33 *the most dilapidated houses:* The description of the poverty in St. Louis, particularly in the black community, comes from Rumbold, *Housing Conditions in St. Louis,* 54.

34 *There were some luxuries:* Ibid., 8.

34 *Roy Wilkins, one of the leaders:* Roy Wilkins describes his childhood in St. Louis in his memoir with coauthor Tom Mathews, *Standing Fast,* 17–23.

34 *The city was almost completely divided:* Christensen, "Black St. Louis: A Study in Race Relations," 134.

34 *James found a job as a laborer:* Birth record of James Preston Johnson Jr.

34 *About a third of the black men:* A description of the occupations of black

men and women at the time can be found in Corbett and Seematter, "Black St. Louis," 40, 41.

35 *women typically cared for children:* Rumbold, *Housing Conditions in St. Louis,* 72.

35 *John W. Wheeler, the prominent owner:* Jack, *St. Louis African American Community,* 153.

35 *St. Louis hosted the World's Fair:* Bourgois, "If You're Not Black," 119.

36 *Her fourth son, Charlie:* The details of the death of Phoebe's child Charlie come from family records, provided by Johnny D. Johnson, interview by author, in Idlewild, Michigan, on December 1, 2010; also Charlie's death certificate/record, accessed on ancestry.com, in 2010.

37 *The Illinois Central Railroad ran several trains:* Railroad Guide, 972. *The Official Guide of the Railways and the Steam Navigation Lines of the United States,* 133, 790.

THREE: SIREN SONG OF THE NORTH

38 *Historians describe it:* Lemann, *The Promised Land,* 6.

39 *The vast majority of blacks:* ibid.

39 *By 1900, Carrie's family had moved:* The details about Carrie and her family's migration from Virginia to North Carolina come from the 1880 and 1900 census; and Carrie's death certificate. Descriptions of Leaksville come from Butler, *Rockingham County: A Brief History,* 57–60, 62.

40 *stripped blacks from the voting rolls:* North Carolina History Project, www .northcarolinahistory.org/encyclopedia/ (accessed summer 2011).

40 *Their destination was forty miles north:* Carrie's move to Baltimore is captured by the 1910 census. She and John appear in the city that year.

40 *More foreign immigrants:* See Power, "Apartheid Baltimore Style," 290.

40 *By the time Carrie arrived:* Gibson, *Population of the 100 Largest Cities and Other Urban Places in the United States: 1790–1900,* Table 13.

40 *Striving, impoverished blacks:* Pietila, *Not in My Neighborhood,* 10, 14.

41 *"There is not one house on Biddle Alley . . .":* Power, "Apartheid Baltimore Style," 295.

41 *They settled on the east side of town:* Sanborn Insurance Company, Baltimore, fire insurance map, 1915.

41 *By 1910, Carrie was washing clothes:* The 1910 census.

41 *"Negroes Encroaching" warned a headline:* Pietila, *Not in My Neighborhood,* 21.

41 *restaurants, which once allowed:* Ibid., 14.

41 *riots broke out across the country:* Ibid., 6.

42 *White citizens had already been up in arms:* I relied on Pietila's detailed study of the efforts of whites in Baltimore to prevent blacks from moving into white neighborhoods. Baltimore's attempts at residential segregation inspired many other cities; Ibid., 6, 8, 22.

42 *"a great public moment":* Ibid., 22.

43 *Carrie and John remained childless:* Details about Carrie's childbearing come from the 1900, 1910, and 1920 censuses.

43 *an unmerciful plague had descended:* Details about the influenza epidemic in North Carolina can be found in these articles: McKnown, "This Month in North Carolina History," and the U.S. Department of Health and Human Services, "The Great Pandemic."

44 *Perhaps they were drawn by:* Grossman, *Land of Hope,* 113.

44 *Or maybe they heard the call:* The quotations from letters written by African American migrants eager for opportunities in the north come from Scott, "Letters of Negro Migrants," 298.

45 *She became so close:* The death certificate of Rebecca's husband, Purnell Shields, describes her maiden name as Coleman.

FOUR: A FAMILY GROWS IN CHICAGO

46 *The house at 5037 Dearborn Street:* I found Phoebe's addresses in Chicago on the death certificates and birth certificates of her children; in the 1910, 1920, and 1930 censuses; and in her husband's World War I draft record.

47 *Between 1900 and 1910, the number of blacks:* Gibson and Jung. "Historical Census Statistics on Population Totals by Race," Table 14.

47 *the city's most menial and low-paying jobs:* Chicago Commission on Race Relations, *The Negro in Chicago,* 80, 84.

47 *In the summer of 1909:* The details about the births and deaths of Phoebe's children come from birth and death certificates; census and family records.

48 *"Is it the corsets we wear? . . .":* Blake Smith and Dye, "Mother Love and Infant Death," 351–352.

48 *There were only two black churches:* Perrin, *History of Alexander, Union and Pulaski Counties,* 582.

48 *By 1910, James had found employment:* The 1910 census records James's occupation as a laborer in the asphalt business that year. Francesca Gray, Phoebe's granddaughter, recalls the stories she heard growing up about how Phoebe did domestic work, interview by author in Bellwood, Illinois, on October 21, 2010.

49 *"When one treats these dear little children, . . .":* Homel, *Down from Equality,* 7.

49 *"When I got here . . .":* Chicago Commission on Race Relations, *The Negro in Chicago,* 99.

49 *"Pull off your coat . . .":* Chicago Defender, April 2, 1910.

50 *The South Side was still 90 percent white:* Chicago Commission on Race Relations, *The Negro in Chicago,* 107; 1910 census.

50 *She had only one white neighbor:* The information about Phoebe's neighbors and her family's racial designation as "mulatto" comes from the 1910 census.

50 *Employers—both black and white—openly professed:* Cayton and Drake explore the color preferences of employers—white and black—and among African Americans more generally in *Black Metropolis,* 498, 499.

51 *The* Chicago Defender *reinforced the bias:* The *Chicago Defender*'s pages during this period often included advertisements for face lightening creams, including "Why Be Dark and Swarthy?" *Chicago Defender,* November 12, 1910, 4; and "Do You Want to Be Beautiful?" *Chicago Defender,* December 19, 1914, 4.

51 *In this color-conscious society:* Black sociologists like Samuel M. Strong echoed the thinking of many professional blacks when he claimed that "lower class churches" in Chicago were "frequented by the darker Negroes who constitute the largest number of the lower class groups." Middle-class churches, he said, were frequented by the "brown varieties of Negroes" while "Pale Negroes" attended upper-class churches. See Best, *Passionately Human, No Less Divine,* 29.

52 *James had found work as a Pullman porter:* See Tye, *Rising from the Rails,* 32, 34, 82, 88, 89; and Grossman, *Land of Hope,* 78, 129, for the description of Pullman porters in the early twentieth century.

54 *James was far from the only ancestor:* Mrs. Obama mentioned the Pull-

man porters sprinkled in her family tree in a speech to the employees of at U.S. Department of Transportation on February 20, 2009.

54 *The temperature dipped:* The descriptions of the weather on notable dates in Mrs. Obama's family history come from Jeffrey Robel, of the National Climatic Data Center of the National Oceanic and Atmospheric Administration, e-mails, May 12, 2011, May 10, 2011, October 7, 2010, September 29, 2010; and from the *Chicago Tribune,* which recorded the day's temperature on the front page of its newspaper for many years.

55 *lives circumscribed by racism and discrimination:* I relied on several sources for a description of the discrimination that African Americans encountered at the time, including Chicago Commission on Race Relations, *The Negro in Chicago,* 391; Grossman, *Land of Hope,* 33, 127, 128; and *Chicago Defender,* December 19, 1914, 4.

56 *"declared that their economic situation had improved in Chicago":* Chicago Commission on Race Relations, *The Negro in Chicago,* 165, 166.

56 *The* Chicago Defender *issued the rallying cry:* Grossman, *Land of Hope,* 82–85.

57 *Housing was so scarce:* See Chicago Commission on Race Relations, *The Negro in Chicago,* 93; and Hughes, *The Big Sea,* 33. Both sources describe the housing shortages on the South Side.

57 *They were "Old Settlers":* Cayton and Drake, *Black Metropolis,* 66, 543.

57 *James had found a new job:* The family's move to Hyde Park is documented in James's World War I draft record and the 1920 census. James also described his job at the Consumers Company in his draft application.

58 *"That was a big jump . . .":* Timuel Black, interview by author, in Chicago on September 20, 2010.

58 *The neighborhood was a natural destination:* A description of the black migration to Hyde Park can be found in Chicago Commission on Race Relations, *The Negro in Chicago,* 118, 122.

58 *Phoebe's home no longer stands today:* The description of Phoebe's neighbors in Hyde Park and the neighborhood come from the 1920 census and the Sanborn Insurance Company, fire insurance map, Chicago, 1925.

FIVE: EXPLODING DREAMS

60 *Phoebe and her family had moved:* Chicago Commission on Race Relations, *The Negro in Chicago,* 115–129, 133.

61 *The Great Fire of 1871:* Karen Sawislak, "Fire of 1871," *Encyclopedia of Chicago,* http://encyclopedia.chicagohistory.org/pages/1740.html (accessed spring 2011).

61 *Racial violence gripped:* The *New York Times,* October 6, 1919, describes the riots and the lynchings that took place around that time in considerable detail.

61 *Seven black World War I veterans:* Johnson, *Along This Way,* 341; Peter Perl, "Race Riot of 1919 Gave Glimpse of Future Struggles," *Washington Post,* March 1, 1999, A1.

62 *Nine people were killed:* Ibid.

62 *None of the riots that summer:* Chicago Commission on Race Relations, *The Negro in Chicago,* 1, 5–7, 45–46, 126, 481.

63 *"She talked about how terrible it was":* Author telephone interviews of Mary Lang, daughter of Phoebe Moten, on February 4, 2011, and March 30, 2011.

64 *Four days after the riots began:* Cayton and Drake, *Black Metropolis,* 69.

65 *in the face of high unemployment:* Chicago Commission on Race Relations, *The Negro in Chicago,* 105.

66 *Evanston, the home of Northwestern University:* The portrait of the family's life in Evanston emerged from the recollections of Johnny D. Johnson, in a telephone interview by author on November 11, 2010, and in Idlewild, Michigan, on December 1, 2010. Francesca Gray, interview by author, in Bellwood, Illinois, on October 21, 2010; the birth certificates of Phoebe's children, Johnny Johnson and Mary Lang, who were both born in Evanston; Evanston city directories from the years 1921, 1922–23, 1925, 1927; and the Sanborn Insurance Company, fire insurance map, Evanston, 1920.

67 *Hundreds of other African Americans:* The description of black migration to Evanston and the details about the lives, businesses, and institutions came from several sources, including Bruner, "Survey of the Negro Population of Evanston," 1–8, 24–28, 30–31, 35, 37, 42, 49–50, 52, 60; Robinson, *A Place We Can Call Our Home,* 26–48.

67 *Howard, flourished:* The description of the accomplishments of James Johnson, Phoebe's husband, came from the recollections of his son,

Johnny D. Johnson, telephone interview by author on November 11, 2010, and in Idlewild, Michigan, on December 1, 2010; news articles.

68 *"The hotels and the big places . . .":* "Through the Eyes of Us," Evanston oral histories of early black settlers. Pauline Elizabeth Lewis Williams was sixteen when she moved to Evanston in the 1920s.

SIX: A CHILD OF THE JAZZ AGE

72 *Fats Waller was pounding on the ivories:* University of Chicago, "Key to Map of Chicago South Side Jazz, c. 1915–1913," University of Chicago Library, www.lib.uchicago.edu/e/su/cja/mapkey.html (accessed 2011).

72 *"We cracked down on the first note . . .":* Armstrong, *In His Own Words,* 51.

72 *Purnell Shields, just eleven:* Information about Purnell's arrival in Chicago and his early life there come from his voter registration records and the 1920 and 1930 census.

73 *His father, Robert Lee Shields:* I found information about Purnell's parents, Anna and Robert Shields, from their marriage license; the 1910, 1920, 1930 censuses; and Chicago city directory, 1923.

73 *"There is nothing here . . .":* Scott, "Letters of Negro Migrants," 329.

74 *Five black lawmakers:* Cayton and Drake, *Black Metropolis,* 349.

74 *members of the Ku Klux Klan:* The account of the Klan's activities in Birmingham came from several sources, including Snell, "Fiery Crosses in the Roaring Twenties," 261, 272, 273, 312, 317; and Feldman, *A Sense of Place* 21, 22.

75 *Every day, Purnell and the other newcomers:* Craig Robinson, the brother of Michelle Obama, described his memories of his grandfather, Purnell Shields, in his memoir, *A Game of Character,* 16.

75 *for a jazz lover:* The Encyclopedia of Chicago, "Jazz," by William Howland Kenney, http://encyclopedia.chicagohistory.org/pages/665.html (accessed spring 2011).

75 *To newcomers like Purnell:* Kenney, *Chicago Jazz,* 14, 38.

75 *In 1927, the Savoy Ballroom:* Ibid., 14.

76 *The place became a must-stop:* From http://chicago.urban-history.org/ven /dhs/savoy.shtml (accessed spring 2011).

76 *"He would play jazz 24 hours a day":* Laura Brown, "Michelle Obama: America's Got Talent," *Harper's Bazaar,* November 2010, 282.

SEVEN: A MAN OF PROMISE

77 *His parents welcomed him:* Information about Fraser Robinson Jr.'s early years in Georgetown, South Carolina, and Chicago, Illinois, come from the 1920 and 1930 censuses; his funeral program; author's telephone interviews with Nomenee Robinson on November 10, 2010, and August 16, 2010; and author's interview with Francesca Gray in Bellwood, Illinois, on October 21, 2010.

78 *The Boy Scouts refused:* "Allen Life Guard Supplants Scouts," *Afro-American,* September 12, 1924.

78 *An old, undated black-and-white photo:* Author telephone interview with Toni Carrier, director of Lowcountry Africana, on August 19, 2011.

80 *Before long, he was attending services:* Author telephone interviews with Mary Lang, sister of LaVaughn Robinson, on February 4, 2011, and March 30, 2011.

80 *the minister, Mother Ella Allensworth:* Author telephone interview with Bishop Sylvester Brinson, who served as pastor of Full Gospel Church between 1973 and 2000, on December 14, 2010. The information about Full Gospel Church that appears in this chapter and the following chapter come from Bishop Brinson and Francesca Gray, the daughter of Fraser and LaVaughn Robinson, who also described the church rules and practices in an interview with the author in Bellwood, Illinois, on October 21, 2010. The following newspaper article was also very helpful: "Full Gospel Mission 8th Anniversary," *Chicago Defender,* September 12, 1936.

80 *"People used to joke . . .":* Fraser Jr.'s son, Nomenee Robinson, also described his father's churchgoing at Full Gospel. Author telephone interviews with Nomenee Robinson on November 10, 2010, and August 16, 2010.

EIGHT: STUMBLING BACKWARD

81 *After leaving Evanston:* Johnny D. Johnson, interview by author in Idlewild, Michigan, on December 1, 2010. He also described the family's time in Chicago during the Depression.

81 *"Something is happening in Chicago . . .":* Cayton and Drake, *Black Metropolis,* 83.

82 *How does a marriage come undone?:* I relied on the 1930 census, which

showed Phoebe and James living at separate addresses in Chicago that year.

83 *Jesse Binga, the black banker:* Cayton and Drake, *Black Metropolis,* 84–87, which also describes the evictions and protests at the time.

83 *This time, she was scrubbing floors:* Interview with Francesca Gray, interview by author, in Chicago, on October 21, 2010. She described how her grandmother, Phoebe, and her mother, LaVaughn, cleaned houses in Hyde Park.

84 *Phoebe began traveling back to southern Illinois:* Author interview of Phoebe's son Johnny D. Johnson in Idlewild Michigan, on December 1, 2010, and author telephone interviews of Phoebe's daughter Mary Lang on February 4, 2011, and March 30, 2011.

86 *Something about that church:* Francesca Gray, interview by author in Bellwood, Illinois, on October 21, 2010.

NINE: LOVE IN HARD TIMES

87 *Purnell was a gregarious charmer:* Robinson, *A Game of Character,* 16. In his book, Mr. Robinson also describes how the couple ultimately split up.

88 *He was nineteen and she was about twenty:* The 1930 census.

89 *Fraser was soon taken:* Francesca Gray described this and the courtship between her parents, LaVaughn and Fraser Robinson Jr., in an interview by author in Bellwood, Illinois, on October 21, 2010.

90 *In February 1934, she graduated:* Englewood High School graduation records.

90 *James died at the hospital:* Death certificate of James Preston Johnson. James's children, Mary Lang and Johnny D. Johnson, described his illness, death, and burial in interviews. Author telephone interview of Johnny D. Johnson on November 11, 2010, and in Idlewild, Michigan, on December 1, 2010; author telephone interviews of Mary Lang on February 4, 2011, and March 30, 2011.

91 *LaVaughn, nineteen, became the first:* Marriage license of LaVaughn Johnson and Fraser Robinson Jr. LaVaughn's sister, Mary Lang, and her daughter, Francesca Gray, also described what they knew about the wedding. Francesca Gray, interview by author, in Bellwood, Illinois, on October 21, 2010; author telephone interviews of Mary Lang on February 4, 2011, and March 30, 2011.

92 *the golden boy from Georgetown:* Nomenee Robinson and Francesca

Gray, the children of Fraser Robinson Jr., described their father's struggles during the Depression. Author interview of Francesca Gray in Bellwood, Illinois, on October 21, 2010; author telephone interviews of Nomenee Robinson on November 10, 2010, and August 16, 2010.

93 " . . . there weren't no jobs to be found": Black, Bridges of Memory, 26.

93 Fraser's father was out of work: Death certificate of Fraser Robinson Sr. describes him as unemployed; Harolyn Siau, niece of Fraser Robinson Jr., described the struggles of the family in South Carolina during the Depression. Author telephone interview of Harolyn Siau on November 9, 2010.

93 Fraser finally started earning: Fraser's marriage license describes him as working on city relief. Cayton and Drake, Black Metropolis, 512, describes the salary those jobs typically paid in Chicago.

93 Soon LaVaughn, with a new baby: LaVaughn's son, Nomenee Robinson, described her work as a domestic. Author telephone interviews of Nomenee Robinson on November 10, 2010, and August 16, 2010.

94 That may be one reason: The children of Fraser and LaVaughn described their parents' passion for voting. Francesca Gray, interview by author in Bellwood, Illinois, on October 21, 2010. Author telephone interviews of Nomenee Robinson on November 10, 2010, and August 16, 2010.

94 "I had a father . . .": Marian Robinson, unpublished interview conducted by Michael Powell, New York Times, in Chicago, in the spring of 2008.

95 Purnell soon learned that segregation: Cayton and Drake, Black Metropolis, 102, 105.

95 Accidentally stumbling across: Black, Bridges of Memory, 304.

95 Fraser's father died of tuberculosis: Death certificate of Fraser Robinson Sr.

96 Rebecca's uncle, John Coleman: U.S. World War II Draft Registration Card for John Dan Coleman, April 27, 1942.

97 Fraser enlisted in the army: U.S. World War II Army Enlistment Records, 1938–1946.

TEN: STRUGGLING AND STRIVING

98 They prayed together at church: Mary Lang, Phoebe's daughter, described the relationship between her mother and her older sister,

LaVaughn, in telephone interviews by author on February 4, 2011, and March 30, 2011.

100 *She felt ashamed:* LaVaughn's daughter, Francesca Gray, did not learn of her parents' separation until she was an adult. Author interview of Francesca Gray in Chicago on October 21, 2010.

100 *Fraser Robinson III, Mrs. Obama's father:* Author telephone interviews of Mary Lang on February 4, 2011, and March 30, 2011; author telephone interviews of Nomenee Robinson on November 10, 2010, and August 16, 2010.

101 *"I think the only man . . .":* Moore, *Fighting for America,* xvii.

102 *Fraser got a night job:* Author telephone interviews of Mary Lang on February 4, 2011, and March 30, 2011; author telephone interviews of Nomenee Robinson on November 10, 2010, and August 16, 2010.

102 *he began to inch his way back:* Nomenee Robinson described his parents' reconciliation. Ibid.

103 *Phoebe died on June 19, 1946:* Death certificate of Phoebe Moten Johnson.

103 *Her children honored her:* I visited Phoebe's grave at Lincoln cemetery in Chicago in September 2010.

104 *her youngest son, Johnny:* Author interviews of Johnny D. Johnson, by telephone on November 11, 2010, and in Idlewild, Michigan, on December 1, 2010; author telephone interviews of Nomenee Robinson on November 10, 2010, and August 16, 2010.

104 *He and LaVaughn had three children:* Francesca Gray, interview with author, in Chicago, on October 21, 2010; author telephone interviews of Nomenee Robinson on November 10, 2010, and August 16, 2010; e-mail November 15, 2011.

104 *urged his two oldest sons to tread carefully:* Author telephone interviews of Fraser's son Nomenee Robinson on November 10, 2010, and August 16, 2010.

105 *Fraser saved up enough money:* Ibid.

106 *As the years passed:* Ibid.

106 *Fraser's artistic firstborn child:* Author telephone interview of Nomenee Robinson on August 16, 2011.

106 *He worked as a lifeguard:* Ibid.

106 *Diddley was something of a man about town:* Robinson, *A Game of Character,* 6.

106   *But he fell hard for Marian:* Ibid.

106   *On October 27, 1960:* Marriage license for Marian Shields and Fraser Robinson III; author telephone interview of Nomenee Robinson, August 2011.

107   *Some fifty years after:* Fraser's daughter, described her father's return to Georgetown, South Carolina. Author interview of Francesca Gray in Chicago, on October 21, 2010.

107   *During the funeral:* Funeral program for Fraser Robinson Jr.

107   " . . . *He was proud of his lineage":* Shailagh Murray, "A Family Tree Rooted in American Soil," *Washington Post,* October 8, 2008.

107   *When she died of a heart attack:* Death certificate of LaVaughn Robinson.

108   *"He did not let it carry over":* Marian Robinson, unpublished interview conducted by Michael Powell, *New York Times,* in Chicago, in the spring of 2008.

108   *His mother, Annie:* Robinson, *A Game of Character,* 17.

108   " . . . *my grandparents had separated . . .":* Ibid., 16.

109   *He died of cardiac arrest:* Death certificates for Purnell and Rebecca Shields.

109   *Purnell passed on many things:* Robinson, *A Game of Character,* 16, 32, 132; Laura Brown, "Michelle Obama: America's Got Talent," *Harper's Bazaar,* November 2010, 282.

110   *But Mrs. Obama had never:* Former aide to Mrs. Obama, who spoke on condition of anonymity. Telephone interview by author, November 2011.

ELEVEN: THE SEARCH FOR THE TRUTH: CLEVELAND

111   *Jewell Barclay, the long-lost cousin:* The interviews that form the basis of this chapter were conducted with Jewell Barclay, the great-granddaughter of Dolphus Shields and the great-great-granddaughter of Melvinia Shields. Interviews were conducted by author in Cleveland, Ohio, May 6, 2010, and May 20, 2010; and by telephone on February 8, 2011, and November 22, 2011.

112   *The children of his son, Robert Lee:* Robert Lee's widow, Annie, appears in the Chicago city directory in 1923, but she may have been there even earlier. In a voting registration record, dated October 13, 1961, her son, Purnell Shields, said that he had moved to Chicago in 1921.

112 *His daughter, Pearl, moved:* I can't say precisely when Pearl ended up in Cleveland, but her son James had a child there in 1927, according to the 1930 census. Jewell Barclay, Pearl's granddaughter, says that Pearl also lived in Detroit for a while, but I have not been able to find any records that document her time there. Telephone interview, November 22, 2011.

113 *She found work as a seamstress:* Jewell Barclay provided this information as well as the rest of the information in this chapter. Interviews by author in Cleveland, Ohio, on May 6, 2010 and May 20, 2010; and by telephone on February 8, 2011, and November 22, 2011. Jewell's cousin, Tony Allmond, also remembered the packages of sugarcane and pecans that came in the mail. Tony Allmond, interview by author, in Cleveland, Ohio, May 6, 2011.

115 *So she agrees to take a DNA test:* I bought the DNA collection kits used by Jewell Barclay and the others in this book from Family Tree DNA, a DNA testing company based in Houston, Texas. The testing is typically done over a period of two days, though it can be done in one day. I consulted extensively with Bennett Greenspan, the founder and chief executive of the company, who guided me through the testing process and helped to analyze the results.

TWELVE: A MAN ON THE RISE

119 *His full name was Dolphus Theodore Shields:* For details about Dolphus's life in Georgia, I relied on the 1870 census; and Reid, *History of Colored Baptists in Alabama,* 291–292. I also relied on the death certificates of his brother, Henry Shields, who died on November 10, 1945; his first wife, Alice Easley Shields, who died on April 26, 1915; and his son Willie Arthur Shields, who died on December 31, 1962. These records indicate the birth dates in Georgia of these relatives and, in some instances, the identities of their parents.

120 *Instead, blacks found themselves:* Foner, *Reconstruction,* 424.

121 *Dolphus had an epiphany:* Reid, *History of Colored Baptists in Alabama,* 291–292. Reverend Sebastian Holley, pastor of Pleasant Grove Baptist Church, described the history of the church in a telephone interview by author on December 15, 2010; also the website of Pleasant Grove Baptist Church, www.pleasantgrovecv.org (accessed December 15, 2010).

122   *They made sure that religious services:* Foner, *Reconstruction,* 88–89.

122   *Unsurprisingly, African Americans emerged:* Ibid., 89.

122   *former slaves called out to Jesus:* Ibid., 90.

122   *they prayed in a half-built structure:* Lemann, *Redemption,* 57.

122   *The emptying of the pews:* Foner, *Reconstruction,* 91.

123   *"You know those who . . .":* Ibid., 93.

123   *Dolphus took another step:* Reid, *History of Colored Baptists in Alabama,* 291–292.

123   *His bride was only about fourteen:* Information about Alice Easley, Dolphus's first wife, comes from the city directories of Birmingham, 1893, 1896, 1897, 1898, 1900; the 1900 and 1910 censuses; her death certificate; and Reid, *History of Colored Baptists in Alabama,* 291–292.

123   *At a time when many blacks:* U.S. Bureau of the Census, *Negroes in the United States,* 27.

123   *He grew up on a farm:* Reid, *History of Colored Baptists in Alabama,* 291.

124   *His younger brother, Henry:* Information about Henry comes from the 1900 census; his death certificate; and Ruth Wheeler Applin, who married his nephew. Interview by author in Kingston, Georgia, on February 3, 2010, and June 3, 2010.

124   *Later in life, Dolphus would refer:* Reid, *History of Colored Baptists in Alabama,* 291–292.

124   *The mothers of Dolphus and Alice:* The story of Melvinia Shields and Mariah Easley emerges from various records, including the estate inventory of David Patterson of Spartanburg, South Carolina, where both were listed as slaves. Various records document their presence in Bartow County, Georgia, in the 1880s: Mariah Easley, her husband, Bolus, and their daughter, Alice, appear in the 1880 census in the county. Bolus Easley also appears in the Cartersville City Directory of 1883–1884, "Colored Department," 2. Reid, who profiles Dolphus in his book, says that Dolphus's entire family lived in Cartersville, the Bartow county seat, that year. Reid, *History of Colored Baptists in Alabama,* 291–292.

125   *"In their eyes," wrote one federal official:* Foner, *Reconstruction,* 82.

126   *One couple, unwilling to give up hope:* Ibid., 84.

126   *"I wish you could see this,":* Ibid.

126   *Cartersville was becoming a hub:* Cunyus. *The History of Bartow County,* 36; Cartersville city directory, 1883–1884, "Colored Department," 2.

127 *Poor tenant farmers:* Hahn, *The Roots of Southern Populism,* 258.

127 *In 1880, only 39 percent:* Kousser, *The Shaping of Southern Politics,* 68.

127 *The poll tax, devised by white legislators:* Coleman, *A History of Georgia,* 270.

128 *It required African Americans:* Legal restrictions imposed on recently freed slaves are described in detail in Foner, *Reconstruction,* 424.

128 *fifty-one African Americans were lynched:* Brundage, *Lynching in the New South,* 8, 38, 263.

128 *During Reconstruction, only two schools:* Hebert, "Civil War and Reconstruction Era," 329–331.

128 *public education for blacks:* Rodgers, *Bartow County, Georgia,* 7.

129 *While most whites owned:* U.S. Bureau of the Census, *Negroes in the United States,* 8, 15.

129 *Sometime around 1888:* Reid, A *History of Colored Baptists in Alabama,* 291–292.

THIRTEEN: LEFT BEHIND

130 *Dolphus had chosen a place:* I relied on several sets of records to piece together the story of Dolphus's life during this time period in Birmingham: the Birmingham city directories, in which he appears in 1893, 1895, 1897, 1898, 1899, and 1900; his marriage license to Mattie Hallie; the 1900, 1910, and 1930 censuses; and the Sanborn Insurance Company, fire insurance map, Birmingham, 1893. I also relied on the recollections of people who knew Dolphus: Jewell Barclay, interviews by author in Cleveland, Ohio, on May 6, 2010 and May 20, 2010, and by telephone on February 8, 2011; Helen Heath, interview by author in Birmingham, Alabama, in September 2008; Ruth Wheeler Applin and Harold Wise Sr., interviews by author in Kingston, Georgia, on February 3, 2010, and June 3, 2010; and Bobbie Holt, interview by author in New York on September 2009 and January 27, 2010.

131 *the city's* Weekly Iron Age *reported:* Atkins, "Birmingham: The Magic City."

131 *43 percent of Birmingham's population:* Feldman, *A Sense of Place,* 7.

131 *He joined Tabernacle Baptist Church:* Reid, *A History of Alabama Baptists,* 291. Also see Fallin, *The African American Church in Birmingham, Alabama,* 32.

131 *In the 1880s, about 45 percent:* Feldman, *A Sense of Place,* 9.

132 *Dolphus and Alice split up:* The Birmingham City Directory of 1893 shows Dolphus and Alice living at different addresses. Dolphus's marriage license shows that he married Mattie Hallie in Birmingham on October 31, 1893.

132 *He found a one-story wooden house:* Sanborn Insurance Company, fire insurance map, Birmingham, 1893.

133 *By 1900, Dolphus had managed:* The 1900 census.

133 *While nearly half of all whites:* U.S. Bureau of the Census, *Negroes in the United States,* 29; Collins and Margo, "Race and Homeownership," 17.

133 *"The city tax collector . . .":* Feldman, *A Sense of Place,* 27.

133 *She moved at least three times:* Birmingham City Directories of 1893, 1896, 1897, and 1900; also 1900 census.

133 *Mariah, who was so close:* Mariah appears in the 1900 Census in Birmingham.

134 *he was told she was a widow:* The 1900 census.

135 *Melvinia moved with her remaining children:* The information about Melvinia's life in Kingston, Georgia, comes from a variety of sources, including the 1900, 1910, 1920, and 1930 censuses; her death certificate; and property records for the house she lived in. Ruth Wheeler Applin and Harold Wise Sr., interviews by author in Kingston, Georgia, on February 3, 2010, and June 3, 2010.

137 *Blacks could still participate:* Coleman, *A History of Georgia,* 279. Coleman offers a detailed description of the efforts to disenfranchise blacks in Georgia.

137 *Henry and other blacks were effectively barred:* Ibid., 280.

137 *"If it takes lynching . . .":* Parker, "Rebecca Latimer Felton, 1835–1930."

138 *Five years later, a mob:* Bostick, "Lynchings in Bartow County," 4, 5.

139 *As Melvinia approached:* For information about Henry, I relied on the 1910, 1920, and 1930 censuses; the license for his marriage to Ida Houston on July 2, 1901; the license for his marriage to Onie Lee White on October 17, 1915; his World War I Draft Registration Card, dated September 19, 1915; the property records for the little house on Shaw Street, Bartow County, Illinois, Book ZZ, page 507; and interviews with people who knew him. Ruth Wheeler Applin and Harold Wise Sr., interviews by author in Kingston, Georgia, on February 3, 2010, and June 3, 2010.

139 *Tragedy struck again:* Death certificate of Henry's nephew, Sylvester Shields.

FOURTEEN: NEITHER BLACK NOR WHITE

141 *His name was Jerry Suter:* Information about Jerry Suter comes from various sources, including the 1870, 1880, 1900, and 1910 censuses. Also, his marriage record from December 26, 1887; his Civil War pension file; his death certificate; and the inventory of his estate: Pulaski County, Illinois, Estate Box S-4. Johnny D. Johnson, interview by author in Idlewild, Michigan, on December 1, 2010.

141 *He had dark eyes:* The description of Jerry Suter comes from his Civil War pension file, which is located in the National Archives in Washington, D.C. File No. 897,567.

142 *he had escaped from slavery* The story of Jerry's birth, his time in slavery, his escape from slavery, and his time in the military is recounted in affidavits that appear in his Civil War pension file.

142 *he was one of only two black landowners:* See the 1870 census; and Jones, "Black Land Tenancy," 42.

142 *"The people are thrifty, . . .":* Perrin, *History of Alexander, Union and Pulaski Counties,* 582, 585, 586.

143 *Photographs that have survived*: Photographs came courtesy of Johnny D. Johnson, grandson of Mary Moten; and Francesca Gray, great-granddaughter of Mary Moten.

143 *Mary was born in Missouri:* Information about Mary Moten, the great-great-grandmother of Mrs. Obama, and her husband, Nelson, comes from various records, the 1870 and 1880 census; from the Pulaski County marriage index that lists her marriage to Jerry Suter; from Jerry Suter's pension file, which mentions his marriage to her and her death. Mary's grandchildren also shared what they knew of her. Author telephone interview of Johnny D. Johnson on November 11, 2010, and interview in Idlewild, Michigan, on December 1, 2010; Francesca Gray, interview by author in Chicago on October 21, 2010.

143 *most black tenant farmers:* Jones, "Black Land Tenancy," 44.

146 *"Mulatto" forebears pop up:* The following forebears of Mrs. Obama were described as mulatto in the census or other records: Phobe Moten Johnson and James Preston Johnson, her paternal great-

grandparents, in the 1910 census in Chicago; Ruby Johnson, her paternal great-great-grandfather, in the 1870 census in Madison County, Louisiana; Dolphus Shields, her maternal great-great-grandfather, in the 1870 census in Clayton County, Georgia; Jim Jumper, her maternal great-grandfather, in the 1880 census in Virginia; Peter Jumper Jr., her maternal great-great-grandfather, in the 1880 census in Virginia; Dolly and Peter Jumper Sr., her maternal great-great-great-grandparents, in the 1870 census in Virginia. Mary Moten, her paternal great-great-grandmother, was never described in the census as mulatto, but she clearly appears to be of mixed race in the photographs of her that have survived. Her descendants say that she had Cherokee ancestry. Johnny D. Johnson, telephone interview by author on November 11, 2010, and interview in Idlewild, Michigan, on December 1, 2010; Francesca Gray, interview by author in Chicago on October 21, 2010.

147 *The racial designation of mulatto:* Information about Jim Jumper and his family comes from the 1850, 1870, 1880, 1900, and 1910 censuses; and marriage records for Jim and his father, Peter Jr.

147 *everyone was intimately aware:* Information about the mixed-race people in the county comes from the Henry County Bicentennial Commission, *Bicentennial Collection,* Volume 13, 82–103.

148 *"the blacks were arrayed against . . .":* Foner, *Reconstruction,* 100, 101.

149 *Uniquely positioned among African Americans:* Foner, *Freedom's Lawmakers,* xvi.

149 *Fair skinned and bearded:* Dray, *Capitol Men,* 103.

149 *Over the years, Esau managed:* Real Estate, Henry County, Virginia. Book 18, page 473. Book 19, page 452 .

150 *Jim met a young black woman:* Information about Eliza Tinsley comes from the 1880, 1900, and 1910 censuses; also her marriage record to Jim Jumper.

151 *Black entrepreneurs were thriving:* "Successful Colored Citizens Who Believe That Reward Awaits Industry, Sobriety and Perseverance to a Definite End." *Reidsville Review,* September 3, 1909.

151 *In 1910, Booker T. Washington:* "Booker Washington Here," *Webster's Weekly,* November 1, 1910.

152 *Jim's half brother, Julius:* Julius Jumper appears in the 1920 census, living in Marion County, West Virginia.

FIFTEEN: THE RECKONING

153 *a powerful patriarch:* Information about Fraser Robinson Sr. and his family in this chapter comes from various records, including the 1880, 1900, and 1910 census. I also relied on interviews with his descendants, including his grandson Nomenee Robinson, interviewed by telephone on November 10, 2010, and August 16, 2011.

153 *Born on March 24, 1884*: Fraser's birth date appears on his death certificate.

154 *His father remarried:* The details of Fraser's troubled early life, his childhood injury, and his rescue by the white Nesmith family come from Murray, "A Family Tree Rooted in American Soil."

154 *But Fraser was growing up:* Rodgers, *The History of Georgetown County, South Carolina,* 474.

155 *After the Civil War:* Edgar, South Carolina, 387.

155 *Georgetown, where blacks accounted for 82 percent:* Edgar, *South Carolina: A History,* 412.

155 *Democrats picked the sheriff:* Ibid.

155 *He would have seen black men:* Rodgers, *The History of Georgetown County, South Carolina,* 476.

156 *"He said he would take good care . . .":* Details of Fraser's relationship with the Nesmiths came from Murray, "A Family Tree Rooted in American Soil"; and the 1900 and 1910 censuses.

156 *"They pushed their kids . . .":* Murray, "A Family Tree Rooted in American Soil."

156 *Fraser could not read or write:* He is described as illiterate in the 1900 census.

156 *One hundred thousand African Americans*: Edgar, *South Carolina: A History,* 447.

156 *In 1900, more than half:* Rubillo, *Trial and Error,* 109.

157 *The gunshots rang out:* The details of the shooting, the protest, and the crackdown that followed come from ibid., 91, 92; and Rodgers, *The History of Georgetown County, South Carolina,* 481–484.

157 *But the number of lynchings:* Edgar, *South Carolina: A History,* 417.

158 *His own church, Bethel AME:* Rubillo, *Trial and Error,* 108.

159 *nearly three hundred armed troops:* Ibid., 105.

159 *residents formed a "White Supremacy Club":* White efforts to disenfranchise blacks in Georgetown is recounted in detail in ibid., 150–154.

160 *only voters could serve on juries:* Edgar, *South Carolina: A History,* 448.

160 *"The slave went free; . . .":* Foner, *Reconstruction,* 602.

SIXTEEN: BIRMINGHAM, THE MAGIC CITY

161 *Somehow, Dolphus became acquainted:* Reverend Kennedy is described in Boothe, *The Cyclopedia of the Colored Baptists of Alabama.* Dolphus's description as an early founder of Trinity Baptist Church is mentioned on the church's website, www.tbcgraymont.org/page21.shtml (September 2008); his connection to the church is also mentioned in his funeral program, which was given to me by Helen Heath, interview by author, Birmingham, Alabama, September 2008. Fallin, *The African American Church in Birmingham,* 38, describes the founding of the church.

162 *"The people of Smithfield . . .":* Feldman, *A Sense of Place,* 68, 72.

162 *number of black churches:* Fallin, *The African American Church in Birmingham,* 37.

162 *Dolphus's third wedding:* The description of Dolphus's serial marriages in Birmingham comes from his marriage licenses. He married Mattie Hallie on October 31, 1893. He married Melissa Wilcox on June 11, 1902, and he married Lucy Ellis on April 1, 1906. Rev. Kennedy presided over the wedding between Dolphus and Melissa Wilcox.

163 *In churches like Trinity and Tabernacle:* Fallin, *The African American Church in Birmingham,* 49.

163 *In African American circles:* Ibid., 87.

163 *"These were churches . . .":* Author telephone interview of Wilson Fallin on December 21, 2010.

164 *white Democrats campaigned:* The disenfranchisement of blacks in Birmingham is described in Feldman, *A Sense of Place,* 10; Harvey H. Jackson III, "Stolen Vote," *Mobile Register,* December 11, 1994.

164 *steps to eliminate integrated neighborhoods:* Feldman, *A Sense of Place,* 11, 15; Fallin, *The African American Church in Birmingham,* 55.

164 *"We advise Afro-Americans . . .":* Feldman, *A Sense of Place,* 12.

165 *they were all living under one roof:* Jewell Barclay, interview by author in Cleveland, Ohio, on May 6, 2010, and May 20, 2010, and interviewed by telephone on February 8, 2011; Bobbie Holt, interview by author in Queens, New York, on January 27, 2010. Property records 850–854 Lomb Avenue, Birmingham Public Library, Archives.

166   *any African American who dared to move:* Feldman, *A Sense of Place,* 27

166   *By 1911, he had opened:* Birmingham city directory, 1911; Bobbie Holt, interview by author in New York on January 27, 2010.

166   *He could certainly look with pride:* Information about Robert Lee Shields comes from various records, including the 1900 and 1910 censuses and his marriage license. He married Annie Lawson on June 24, 1906. Also, Birmingham city directories, 1907, 1908, 1911.

167   *the deaths of four of his children:* Death certificates of Dolphus's children. A death certificate for Robert Lee Shields has yet to be found, but the 1920 census lists his wife, Annie, as a widow.

167   *Alice had moved once again:* Death certificate for Alice Easley Shields.

168   *Robert Lee died:* There is very little information available about the death of Robert Lee Shields. I relied on the 1920 census, which described his wife, Annie, as a widow; and the recollection of Jewell Barclay, who recalled her grandmother, Pearl, saying that one of her brothers had died. Pearl was Robert Lee's sister. Jewell Barclay, interview by author, in Cleveland, Ohio, on May 6, 2010, and May 20, 2010, and interviewed by telephone on February 8, 2011.

SEVENTEEN: TWO BROTHERS, TWO DESTINIES

171   *"Like men we'll face . . ."*: Claude McKay poem, McKay, *Claude McKay: Selected Poems,* 43.

171   *Billie Holiday sang of it:* Billie Holiday, "Strange Fruit," David Nasaw, "Show-Stopper," *New York Times,* May 21, 2000.

172   *he never measured up to his big brother:* Information about Henry came from various records, including the 1900, 1910, 1920, and 1930 censuses; U.S. World War I Draft Registration Card, September 12, 1915; property records for the house on Shaw Street, 1925; Ruth Wheeler Applin and Harold Wise Sr., interviews by author in Kingston, Georgia, on February 3, 2010, and June 3, 2010.

172   *The house that Henry had bought:* Recollections of Ruth Wheeler Applin, interview by author in Kingston, Georgia, on February 3, 2010, and June 3, 2010.

172   *another black man was lynched:* Bostick, "Lynchings in Bartow County," 7.

173   *The house was valued:* The 1930 census.

174   *The brothers feuded:* Ruth Applin and Harold Wise Sr. described the strained relationship between Henry and his brother, Dolphus, in

interviews with author in Kingston, Georgia, on February 3, 2010, and June 3, 2010.

175 *On June 4, 1938, Melvinia:* The description of Melvinia's death came from her death certificate and from Ruth Wheeler Applin, interviews by author in Kingston, Georgia, on February 3, 2010, and June 3, 2010.

EIGHTEEN: THE ONE-ARMED PATRIARCH

179 *In the only surviving photo:* Information about Fraser Robinson Sr. in this chapter comes from various records, including the 1910, 1920, and 1930 censuses.

179 *He lounges in a convertible:* The photograph of Fraser Robinson Sr. and his wife, Rosella Cohen, was provided by Francesca Gray, interview by author in Chicago on October 21, 2010.

180 *By the time he registered:* Fraser Robinson's draft registration card, dated September 23, 1918, mentions his employment at Atlantic Coast Lumber Company; it also describes his missing left arm; ancestry.com (accessed on July 13, 2010).

180 *By the early 1920s:* The description of Atlantic Coast Lumber company at the time comes from Circa Inc., "City of Georgetown Historic Resources Survey, Final Report," 8, www.nationalregister.sc.gov/SurveyReports/HC22002.pdf (accessed spring 2011).

181 *"He was a charmer . . .":* Francesca Gray, interview by author in Bellwood, Illinois, on October 21, 2010.

182 *"There's no doubt . . .":* Author telephone interview of Nomenee Robinson on November 10, 2010.

182 *he found great comfort:* Information about the history of Bethel AME Church comes from the following sources: Bill Steiger, "Historic Bethel AME Church to Honor Its Founders Today," *Post and Courier,* July 3, 1988; "Bethel Church Rich in History," *Georgetown* (South Carolina) *Times,* April 7, 1977. Also, "A Condensed Historical Sketch of Bethel African Methodist Episcopal Church," an unpublished history produced by the church and obtained by author in the fall of 2009.

183 *He sold newspapers:* Author telephone interview of Harolyn Siau on November 9, 2010; Murray, "A Family Tree Rooted in American Soil."

183 *He read those newspapers:* Francesca Gray, interview by author in Chicago on October 21, 2010.

183 *"It was the belief . . .":* Murray, "A Family Tree Rooted in American Soil."

183 *By 1930, Fraser Sr., forty-six:* Information about the house on Prince Street comes from the 1930 census; property records; author telephone interview of Harolyn Siau on November 9, 2010; and author telephone interview of Nomenee Robinson on November 10, 2010.

184 *the man who prided himself:* Fraser's death certificate described him as unemployed. In a telephone interview with the author on November 9, 2010, Harolyn Siau described the struggles of Fraser's children during the Depression after his death.

184 *Fraser Sr. contracted tuberculosis:* Fraser's death certificate; it also describes his burial at Bethel AME church.

186 *She started visiting the house:* Murray, "A Family Tree Rooted in American Soil."

186 *Campaign aides for then senator:* Author telephone interview of Toni Carrier on August 19, 2011.

186 *"A lot of the time these stories . . .":* Murray, "A Family Tree Rooted in American Soil."

NINETEEN: TWILIGHT

188 *Dolphus was a familiar figure:* Bobbie Holt, interview by author in New York on January 27, 2010; Helen Heath, interview by author in Birmingham, Alabama, in September 2009.

189 *He was so well regarded:* A copy of the flyer was given to me by Mrs. Heath in September 2009.

190 *Ku Klux Klan did its part:* Feldman, *A Sense of Place,* 21–22.

190 *city had barred blacks and whites:* Connerly, "The Most Segregated City in America," 37.

190 *His carpentry shop stood:* Birmingham city directory, 1942. Bobbie Holt, interview by author in Queens, New York, on January 27, 2010; Helen Heath, interview by author in Birmingham, Alabama, in September 2009.

190 *Birmingham's zoning code:* Connerly, "The Most Segregated City in America," 79.

191 *Angry whites hurled rocks:* Ibid., 80.

191 *Lucy, who worked as a laundress:* Bobbie Holt, interview by author in Queens, New York, on January 27, 2010.

192 *whites threw seven bombs:* Connerly, *"The Most Segregated City in America,"* 85. Also, "Houses in Zoning Dispute Blown Up," *Birmingham News,* August 19, 1947. "Midnight Blast Rips Three Houses," *Birmingham News,* March 25, 1949. "Dynamite Explosions Rock Houses of Negro Ministers," *Birmingham News,* August 13, 1949.

192 *the man who came to sit a spell:* Bobbie Holt, interview by author in New York on January 27, 2010.

193 *McClellan "Mack" Shields:* Mack Shields's U.S. World War I Draft Registration Card, June 5, 1917. The card also contains a physical description of him. His granddaughter, Sherry George, also provided a photograph of him and was interviewed by phone on February 8, 2011.

193 *Mack lived only eight blocks:* Birmingham city directory, 1923.

193 *both members of Baptist churches: Birmingham News,* May 30, 1961.

193 *Mack moved frequently:* Birmingham city directories, 1923, 1924, 1925, 1929, 1930, 1931, 1934–35, 1937, 1938, 1939, 1940, 1941, 1942, 1944, 1946, 1947–48, 1950–51.

195 *Dolphus could take pride:* His patents can be found online at the United States Patent and Trademark Department, http://patft.uspto.gov/ (accessed in fall 2010).

195 *carried the Shields name:* Birmingham city directories; his obituary.

195 *He had two sons:* The news of the death of Charles McClelland Shields's son, Mack Shields, who was killed on D-Day in World War II, appeared in the *Birmingham News* on July 7, 1944, and on December 12, 1947. His son, Charles Elliott Shields, also served in the army, according to his army discharge papers.

195 *Dolphus suffered a stroke:* Death certificate. Bobbie Holt, interview by author in New York on January 27, 2010.

196 *Lucy paid $50 for a funeral plot:* Order for Internment for D. T. Shields, Birmingham Public Library, Archives.

196 *At Dolphus's funeral:* Funeral program provided by Helen Heath, interview by author in Birmingham, Alabama, on September 2008.

197 *On the day his obituary appeared:* "Shields Rites Set for Sunday," *Birmingham World,* June 9, 1950.

TWENTY: THE SEARCH FOR THE TRUTH: ATLANTA

198 *Joan Tribble still remembers:* Joan Tribble, interview by author in Morrow, Georgia, on August 20, 2010, and interviewed by telephone on December 21, 2010; Joan Tribble, e-mail to author, November 18, 2011.

200 *Sherry George, whose great-grandfather:* Author telephone interview of Sherry George on February 8, 2011.

201 *One member of the Shields family provided:* I interviewed three members of the white Shields family, who shared information with me but declined to be identified in this book.

201 *Aliene Shields, a descendant:* Author telephone interview of Aliene Shields on December 1, 2009.

204 *declined to undergo DNA testing:* Three members of the white Shields family took DNA tests. Two members of the black Shields family took DNA tests. (Three members of the white Shields family declined.) One member of the Robinson family also took a DNA test.

TWENTY-ONE: A SLAVE GIRL NAMED MELVINIA

209 *Patrician landowners:* Simms, *The Geography of South Carolina,* 128, 131; West, *From Yeoman to Redneck,* 19, 20.

209 *She lived near:* Simms, *The Geography of South Carolina,* 128–129.

210 *Melvinia was born:* In his will, Melvinia's owner, David Patterson, said that she was six years old in 1850, which would suggest that she was born in 1844. She is described as twenty-six years old in the 1870 census, which also supports that birth year. But in her sixties and seventies, she gave census takers different dates, sometimes offering her birth year as 1842 or 1838. Many former slaves, whose births were not formally documented, did not know their birth dates. I give more credence to 1844 because she was younger when she provided the information and may have had a better memory for what she was told about her birth date by her master, relatives, and friends.

210 *By 1850, her home state:* Virginia had 472,528 slaves. "The Progress of Population," *New York Times,* May 5, 1861.

210 *In his house, Melvinia:* Melvinia's owner, David Patterson, died in 1952. The inventory of his estate listed a coffee grinder, calico curtains, books, and beehives among his many possessions.

210 *He owned twenty-one slaves:* West, *From Yeoman to Redneck,* 20, offers a fascinating glimpse of slavery in up-country South Carolina.

211 *he took pen in hand:* David Patterson's first will is dated April 15, 1846. He amended that will on August 1, 1850, which is when he mentioned Melvinia.

211 *She had chocolate-colored skin:* Author interviews of Ruth Wheeler Applin in Kingston, Georgia, on February 3, 2010, and June 3, 2010.

211 *Melvinia would tell census takers:* The 1900 census.

211 *Her owner, Mr. Patterson:* His marriage license, dated April 6, 1793, describes him as a bachelor from Bedford, Virginia. In the 1800, 1810, and 1820 censuses he is living in North Carolina. By 1830, he is living in Spartanburg, South Carolina, according to the census of that year.

213 *The scattered fragments:* The 1850 census indicates that Patterson owned twenty-one slaves and that only two of them were female. (Both were described as adults.) But Patterson's will suggests that that census count was inaccurate because it does not include Melvinia, who was around six years old at the time.

213 *Several young children:* The names of several other children appear in the inventory of his estate, which was put together after Patterson's death in 1852.

213 *children entertained themselves:* Spartanburg slave narratives.

213 *Mariah was born in South Carolina:* The 1880 census.

213 *There were four cows:* The 1850 agricultural census for David Patterson's farm.

213 *In the day-to-day lives:* Kolchin, *American Slavery,* 162.

214 *Mr. Patterson was a religious man:* On December 6, 1841, David Patterson appears in a land deed as a trustee for McKindrals or Cannons Chapel ("being a church under the Methodist Episcopal Church"). Larry Vehorn, "Spartanburg District, S.C. Deed Abstracts, Books X-Z, 1839–1848."

214 *whites outnumbered blacks:* Eelman, *Entrepreneurs in the Southern Up-country,* 15.

215 *"rare the slave that escaped the lash":* Kolchin, *American Slavery,* 121.

215 *David Harris, a Spartanburg slave owner:* West, *From Yeoman to Redneck,* 27, 28.

215 *they determined who would marry:* Kolchin, *American Slavery,* 118.

215 *Mr. Harris viewed his slaves:* West, *From Yeoman to Redneck,* 28.

216 *It would take most:* Ibid., 33.

216 *Mr. Patterson died in 1852:* The inventory of Patterson's estate is dated 1852.

216 *There were cows and steers:* Inventory of Patterson's estate.

216 *What we do know:* The valuation of his individual slaves also appeared in the inventory of Patterson's estate.

217 *Historian Michael Tadman estimates:* Kolchin, *American Slavery,* 126.

217 *Laura Clark, a former slave:* Ibid., 97.

TWENTY-TWO: JOURNEY TO GEORGIA

218 *Some conjure up visions:* Thomas Jefferson's Monticello, "Monticello," Thomas Jefferson Foundation, www.monticello.org (accessed spring 2011).

218 *That fabled mansion:* Margaret Mitchell, *Gone with the Wind* (New York: Scribner, 2011).

218 *Only a tiny fraction:* Kolchin, *American Slavery,* 101.

219 *Wealthy slave owners in Spartanburg:* South Carolina Department of Archives and History, National Register Properties in South Carolina, Price's Post Office, www.nationalregister.sc.gov/spartanburg/S10817742001/index.htm (accessed spring 2011).

219 *Melvinia's new home:* Information about Henry Shields in this chapter comes from several records, including the 1840, 1850, and 1860 censuses.

219 *Henry County, a sleepy town:* White, *Statistics of the State of Georgia,* 325.

219 *Archibald T. Burke, a slave owner:* Hahn, *The Roots of Southern Populism,* 15.

220 *Melvinia's and Henry's lives intersected:* The 1850 census.

220 *The first recorded arrival:* Goodheart, "How Slavery Really Ended in America," *New York Times,* April 1, 2011.

221 *a small group of abolitionists:* Kolchin, *American Slavery,* 3.

221 *the descendant of Irishmen:* Interview by author of two white Shields descendants, who spoke on condition of anonymity, May 18, 2008.

221 *According to family lore:* White Shields descendant, who prefers to remain anonymous, interview by author on May 18, 2010.

221 *In return, his descendants say:* Candler, *The Revolutionary Records of the State of Georgia,* 312, 685, 686.

222 *Moses was landless and slaveless:* The 1810 census.

222 *Henry was born a year later:* Henry's birth date is inscribed on his tombstone in Clayton County, Georgia. I visited his grave in February 2010.

222 *the daughter of a wealthy farmer:* Vehorn, "Spartanburg District, S.C. Deed Abstracts," 275–276.

222 *Moses inherited his very first slave:* Holcomb, *Spartanburg County, South Carolina Will Abstracts, 1787–1840,* 141–143. Also, see will of Vincent Wyatt, Moses' father-in-law, South Carolina Will Transcripts (Microcopy No 9), South Carolina Department of Archives and History, http://www.archivesindex.sc.gov/onlinearchives/ViewImage.aspx? imageNumber=S108093002400423000a.jpg&recordId=303463 (accessed spring 2010).

222 *Henry did not own any land:* I did not find any records that suggested Henry owned any property in South Carolina.

222 *In up-country South Carolina:* West, *From Yeoman to Redneck,* 28, 30.

223 *David Golightly Harris, a Spartanburg farmer:* Ibid., 26.

223 *In 1842, the sheriff of Spartanburg:* Vehorn, *Spartanburg District, S.C. Deed Abstracts, Books X–Z, 1839–1848,* 157.

223 *the state's* Camden Journal *reported:* Edgar, *South Carolina: A History,* 276.

223 *Moses Shields's children scattered:* The 1850 census; his sister-in-law, Mary Patterson, married Lewis Peebles; they both appear next door to Henry in the 1850 census. Author interview with Gregory Shields, June 2011.

223 *his first piece of property:* The 1850 census.

224 *A recently established railroad:* Kilgore, *History of Clayton County,* 8.

224 *A new post office:* White, *Historical Collections of Georgia,* 451.

224 *In that part of Georgia:* Hahn, *The Roots of Southern Populism,* 54.

224 *Melvinia shared a single house:* The 1860 slave schedule.

224 *In such close quarters:* Kilgore, *History of Clayton County,* 19.

224 *social interactions across the color line:* Hahn, *The Roots of Southern Populism,* 30.

225 *Daniel Robinson Hundley grumbled:* Ibid., 108.

225 *"For a long time, historians":* Steven Hahn, interview by author, interviewed by telephone, in spring 2010.

226 *Henry and his wife believed:* The 1860 census.

226 *but Melvinia was not taught:* She is described as illiterate in the 1870 census.

226 *Georgia was one of four states:* Kolchin, *American Slavery,* 129.

226 *In Georgia, teaching a slave:* Logan-Alexander, *Ambiguous Lives,* 49, 60.

226 *Henry had eight children:* The 1850 and 1860 censuses.

TWENTY-THREE: SOUTH CAROLINA GOLD

228 *South Carolina gold:* www.nps.gov/ethnography/aah/aaheritage/low CountryD.htm (accessed spring 2011).

228 *thousands of enslaved African Americans:* Edgar, *South Carolina: A History,* 267.

228 *Over the next months:* Ibid., 268.

229 *"All dem rice field . . .":* Joyner, *Down by the Riverside,* 42.

229 *One startled Northern visitor:* Ibid., 10.

229 *One local historian described:* Sims, *The Geography of South Carolina,* 81.

230 *Another Southern planter warned:* Joyner, *Down by the Riverside,* 35.

230 *Tira was born:* Affidavit of Tira Cohen, dated November 1, 1904, which is included in her application for the military pension entitled to widows of Civil War veterans. This file can be found in the National Archives in Washington, D.C., application file 878010; 1880 census.

230 *a sprawling estate:* Linder and Thacker, *Historical Atlas of the Rice Plantations,* 285. And the 1860 slave schedules in the census.

231 *slaves produced 1.2 million pounds:* Linder and Thacker, *Historical Atlas of the Rice Plantations,* 285.

231 *Educated in Europe:* Ibid.

231 *She met the man:* Affidavit of Tira Cohen, dated November 1, 1904, which is included in her application for the military pension entitled to widows of Civil War veterans. Application file number 878010.

232 *Moises Cohen, who emigrated:* The censuses for the years of 1790, 1810, 1820, and 1850 document the slave holdings of various members of the Cohen family. Articles in the *Georgetown Gazette* and *Winyaw Intelligencer* chronicle the social happenings in the family, mostly weddings and deaths: *Georgetown Gazette*—December 26, 1803, October 6, 1819; *Winyaw Intelligencer*—February 20, 1819;

June 5, 1819; June 27, 1832; July 25, 1848; and February 8, 1851. Rabbi Cohen's advertisement for the runaway indentured servant appeared in the *South Carolina Gazette* on August 15, 1753.

232 *"Behind them came . . .":* West, *Chains of Love,* 87.

233 *Young people also courted:* Ibid., 37.

233 *"I wanted a friend . . .":* The Experience of Thomas H. Jones, http://books.google.com/books/about/The_experience_of_Thomas_H_Jones.html?id=R6aK--f6p6kC (accessed spring 2011).

233 *When Caeser, who was in his twenties:* This description of Caeser comes from his military and pension records. Civil War service record of Caeser Cohen, who served in Company A of the U.S. 128th Colored Infantry. Microfilm number: M589, roll 18. National Archives, Washington, D.C.

234 *Mr. Izard married the living:* Schwalm, *A Hard Fight for We,* 53.

234 *"There is no record . . .":* Affidavit of Tira Cohen, dated November 1, 1904, which is included in her application for the military pension entitled to widows of Civil War veterans. Application file number 878010.

234 *One of their fellow slaves:* Affidavit in Civil War pension file.

234 *they named her Rose:* The records that suggest that Tira and Caeser Cohen were the parents of Rosella/Rosetta Cohen and the paternal great-great-grandparents of Mrs. Obama are persuasive, though not conclusive. The 1900 census in Georgetown, South Carolina, shows a Rosetta Cohen living with her twenty-three-year-old married sister, Louisa Poinsette. The 1880 census from Georgetown shows Tira and Caeser Cohen living with several children, including a three-year-old girl named Louisa. Rosella Cohen's children also happen to bear the names of many of Tira and Caeser's children, who would have been her siblings, including Thomas, Janie, and Nehemiah. Mrs. Cohen's descendants don't believe that that is happentance. It was common at the time for people to name their children after their brothers and sisters.

234 *Jim Robinson, Mrs. Obama's:* The 1880 census.

235 *Gullah emerged from:* Opala, *The Gullah,* http://yale.edu/glc/gullah/links.htm.

235 *When Fraser Jr. died:* Author telephone interviews of Nomenee Robinson on November 10, 2010, and August 16, 2010.

236 *"My Pa sister, Ritta One . . ."*: Born in Slavery: Slave Narratives from the Federal Writers' Project, 1936–1938, Library of Congress, Washington, D.C.

236 *The Georgetown region:* Joyner, *Down by the Riverside*, 37.

236 *Hagar Brown, who was enslaved:* Born in Slavery: Slave Narratives from the Federal Writers' Project, 1936–1938, Library of Congress, Washington, D.C.

237 *They hired Toni Carrier:* Author telephone interview of Toni Carrier on August 19, 2011.

237 *Friendfield was owned:* Lachicotte, *Georgetown Rice Plantations*, 135.

237 *His slaves lived in:* Dahleen Glanton and Stacy St. Clair, "Michelle Obama's Family Tree Has Roots in a South Carolina Slave Plantation," *Chicago Tribune*, December 1, 2008.

237 *In 1860, 273 slaves:* Slave schedule 1860.

237 *Several of the First Lady's cousins:* Author telephone interview of Connie Jones on November 6, 2010; and of Harolyn Siau on November 9, 2010.

237 *nothing that directly links:* Census records indicate that a man by the name of Jim Robinson lived quite close to the Friendfield plantation five years after the Civil War. But that Jim Robinson was several decades older than Mrs. Obama's ancestor. (Other Jim Robinsons also appear in the census in 1870, but none can be conclusively linked to the man who was Mrs. Obama's great-great-grandfather.)

238 *"This is what these documents suggest, . . .":* Author telephone interview of Toni Carrier on August 19, 2011.

238 *Maryville was owned in the 1800s:* Lachicotte, *Georgetown Rice Plantations*, 139–142.

238 *Slaves on the plantation:* The 1850 agricultural survey.

238 *One of those overseers:* The 1860 census shows the Nesmiths living close by Maryville plantation, where they worked. The Nesmith and Robinson families both lived along the Black River in the 1880 census.

238 *The First Lady's relatives say:* Murray, "A Family Tree Rooted in American Soil."

TWENTY-FOUR: A CHILD IS BORN

240 *In 1860, Henry Shields:* The 1860 census; his age was derived from the date of birth etched into his tombstone in Rex, Georgia.

240 *As he strode across his property:* The 1860 agricultural census describes in great detail the crops and livestock on Henry's farm that year.

240 *he acquired more land:* The 1850 and 1860 censuses.

241 *Only 117 people:* Kilgore, *History of Clayton County,* 11.

242 *Harriet Jacobs, who was a slave:* Jacobs, *Incidents in the Life of a Slave Girl,* 27, 44.

243 *Masters and their young sons:* Kolchin, *American Slavery,* 125.

243 *David Dickson set his sights:* Logan-Alexander, *Ambiguous Lives,* 65.

243 *Georgia had instituted:* Ibid., 36.

243 *his younger brother, Moses:* The photograph of Moses was provided courtesy of Greg Shields, the great-grandson of Moses Shields.

244 *farmers in their own right:* The 1860 census.

244 *Charles Marion Shields:* Interview with great-grandchild of Charles, who spoke on the condition of anonymity, spring 2009.

244 *Elisha Shields, nineteen:* The 1860 census.

244 *white man had sex with Melvinia:* I determined when Melvinia was pregnant based on the birth dates of her son Dolphus. Dolphus was born either in 1859 or 1861.

246 *"lustful entrapments":* Bradley and Leslie, "White Pain Pollen," in *Sex, Love, Race,* 213.

247 *"Which of us has not . . .":* Ibid.

247 *newly established Clayton County:* Kilgore, *History of Clayton County, Georgia,* 11.

247 *Georgia law attempted:* Logan-Alexander, *Ambiguous Lives,* 89.

247 *Jesey Wade, a sixty-year-old:* The mixed-race slaves who lived in the community where the Shieldses lived were listed in the 1860 slave schedule for the area.

247 *"In them times . . .":* Louise Oliphant, Compilation of Richmond County ex-slave interviews, *Born in Slavery: Slave Narratives from the Federal Writers' Project, 1936–1938,* Library of Congress, Washington, D.C.

248 *Newman Roane of Virginia:* Rothman, *Notorious in the Neighborhood,* 189–190.

248 *John C. Clark of Texas:* Gillmer, "Base Wretches and Black Wenches," 1534.

248 *"Before my old marster died . . .":* Compilation of slave narratives from

Georgia, *Born in Slavery: Slave Narratives from the Federal Writers' Project, 1936–1938,* Library of Congress, Washington, D.C.

249 *"Neither color, caste . . .":* Bradley and Leslie, "White Pain Pollen," 213.

250 *But they painstakingly recorded:* Interview with a great-great-grandchild of Henry Shields, who chose to remain anonymous, but shared with me photocopies of the old Shields family Bible, spring 2010.

TWENTY-FIVE: BORN FREE

251 *simple, handwritten record:* Library of Virginia, Richmond, Virginia. Microfilm: Henry County, Reel 104, 98 (accessed April 9, 2010).

251 *In 1860, only 11 percent:* Berlin, *Slaves Without Masters,* offers a fascinating, comprehensive portrayal of the lives of free blacks before Emancipation.

252 *a life like Dolly Jumper's:* Information about Dolly Jumper and her husband, Peter Jumper, emerge from various records, including the 1850, 1870, and 1880 censuses.

252 *She was born free:* Her year of birth appears in the "Register of Colored Persons . . . Cohabitating Together . . ." in the archives of the Library of Virginia. Microfilm: Henry County, Reel 55, 129 (accessed April 9, 2010).

252 *Her hometown prided itself:* Hill, *A History of Henry County Virginia.*

253 *Patrick Henry was a slave owner:* Mayer, *A Son of Thunder,* 170.

253 *"No other combination . . .":* Hill, *A History of Henry County Virginia.*

253 *During her lifetime:* Henry County Bicentennial Commission, *The Bicentennial Collection,* Volume 13, 82–103.

253 *Slave traders routinely auctioned:* Ibid.

254 *Because so many free blacks:* Berlin, *Slaves Without Masters,* 178.

254 *"We had no more privileges . . .":* Southern Claims Commission, I-667, Freedmen and Southern Society Project, University of Maryland, College Park. Testimony of Benjamin Dabney, 22 February 1873, Claim of Benjamin Dabney, Dinwiddie County, Virginia case files, Approved Claims, *series 732,* Southern Claims Commission, 3rd Auditor, Records of the United States General Accounting Office, *Record Group 217,* National Archives, Washington, D.C. [I-667: Freedmen and Southern Society Project, University of Maryland, College Park, Md.]

254 *light enough skin:* Henry County Bicentennial Commission, *The Bicentennial Collection,* 82–103, describes some mixed race people who were formally declared white.

254 *Only about 6 percent:* Unpublished manuscript John B. Harris, courtesy of Bassett Historical Center in Martinsville, Virginia.

255 *John Lawson, the surveyor general:* Hodge, *The Handbook of American Indians North of Mexico.*

255 *a group of Tuscarora Indians:* Heinegg, *Free African Americans of North Carolina, Virginia and South Carolina from the Colonial Period to about 1820,* 729.

255 *Her name was Hagar Jumper:* Ibid.

255 *she belonged to a white man:* The William and Mary Quarterly, vol. 26. Williamsburg, Va.: College of William and Mary, Earl Gregg Swem Library, Institute of Early American History and Culture (Google e-book).

255 *Hagar was joining:* Kolchin, *American Slavery,* 81.

255 *One Maryland woman said:* Berlin, *Slaves Without Masters,* 30.

256 *"Whole families" . . .:* Ibid., 33.

256 *It was not uncommon:* Henry County Bicentennial Commission, *The Bicentennial Collection,* 82–103.

256 *free blacks in the United States:* Kolchin, *American Slavery,* 81.

256 *free black population more than doubled:* Ibid.

256 *Most free blacks:* Henry County Bicentennial Commission, *The Bicentennial Collection,* 82–103.

257 *They were forced to register:* Berlin, *Slaves Without Masters,* 93.

257 *a shoulder patch inscribed:* Ibid.

257 *They were barred:* Restrictions described in detail in ibid., 97, 350.

257 *Indeed, many free African Americans:* Henry County Bicentennial Commission, *The Bicentennial Collection,* 82–103.

258 *Dolly and Peter turned to each other:* The 1850 census; "Register of Colored Persons . . . Cohabitating Together . . ." in the archives of the Library of Virginia. Microfilm: Henry County, Reel 55, 129 (accessed April 9, 2010).

258 *Everyone was talking:* Aaron, *Pittsylvania County, Virginia: A Brief History,* 105.

258 *The family quietly blended:* Ibid.

258 *Peter found work:* The 1850 census.

258 *In 1850, they lived next door:* Ibid.

258 *Richard Jumper, who registered:* Ibid.

259 *The advent of the 1850s:* Berlin, *Slaves Without Masters,* 344, 345, 346.

260 *Legislators in Virginia debated:* Ibid., 370–372.

260 *technical violations of the law:* Henry County Bicentennial Commission, *The Bicentennial Collection,* 82–103.

260 *"he suffer[ed] more abuse . . .":* Henry County Bicentennial Commission, *The Bicentennial Collection;* Berlin, *Slaves Without Masters,* 57, 273.

260 *Some free blacks had relatives:* Berlin, *Slaves Without Masters,* 269.

261 *Elizabeth Wingfield, a black woman:* Testimony of Elizabeth Wingfield, 20 February 1873, Claim of Elizabeth Wingfield, Dinwiddie County, Virginia case files, Approved Claims, *series 732,* Southern Claims Commission, 3rd Auditor, Records of the United States General Accounting Office, *Record Group 217,* National Archives, Washington, D.C. [I-669: Freedmen and Southern Society Project, University of Maryland, College Park, Md.]

261 *enslaved common-law spouses:* Harris, unpublished.

261 *In 1859, Peter took care:* Henry County records; Henry County Bicentennial Commission, *The Bicentennial Collection,* 82–103.

262 *William Henry Brisby, who worked:* Miles M. Jackson, *A Free Black in 19th Century New Kent County, Virginia,* 4. Accession 44081. Personal papers collection, The Library of Virginia, Richmond, Virginia.

262 *"able-bodied male free negroes":* Henry County (Va.) Circuit Court, Free negro and slave records, 1838–1900, Accession 34440, The Library of Virginia, Richmond, Virginia, 23219

262 *medical director and surgeon:* Ibid.

262 *One Confederate document:* Ibid.

263 *People were forced:* Hill, *A History of Henry County Virginia,* 23.

263 *"Times are very hard here; . . .":* University of Virginia Library, "Hearts at Home: Southern Women in the Civil War," University of Virginia, www2.lib.virginia.edu/exhibits/hearts/hard.html (accessed summer 2011).

TWENTY-SIX: EXODUS

264 *The runaways from Kentucky:* Carlson, "The Black Community in the Rural North," in Carlson, *Black Migration to Pulaski County, Illinois 1860–1900,* 37, 40.

264 *Mary Moten was a young mother:* I pieced together the story of the Motens and their escape from freedom with information from the 1870 census, which shows that the Motens moved to Illinois, a free state, from Kentucky, a slave state, between 1859 and 1863. Additional information came from interviews with Johnny D. Johnson, the grandson of Mary Moten. Mr. Johnson said that when his mother talked about her family, she talked about how they escaped from slavery. Author telephone interview of Johnny D. Johnson on November 11, 2010, and interview in Idlewild, Michigan, on December 1, 2010.

265 *James and Matilda Busey:* Schwalm, *Emancipation's Diaspora,* 43.

265 *Chambliss took his chances:* Carlson, "The Black Community in the Rural North," 1.

265 *Henry Bibb, a Kentucky slave:* Bibb, *Narrative of the Life and Adventures of Henry Bibb.*

265 *"The arrival among us . . .":* Goodheart, "How Slavery Really Ended in America."

266 *She was born around 1835:* Francesca Gray, interview by author in Bellwood, Illinois, on October 21, 2010. Mrs. Gray said that her mother, LaVaughn Robinson, the granddaughter of Mary Moten, described Mary's lineage to her.

266 *straight, prominent nose:* The physical description comes from a black-and-white photograph of Mary Moten, which was provided to me by Francesca Gray.

266 *Later in life, Mary said:* The 1870 census.

266 *But she was still a slave:* Ibid.

267 *a baby girl named Cora:* Ibid.

267 *their owner remains unknown:* The 1850 or 1860 slave schedule.

267 *"I proclaimed . . .":* Washburne, *Sketch of Edward Coles,* 44.

267 *The state's "Black Laws":* Bridges, "Equality Deferred," 83, 84.

267 *"catching and returning . . .":* Raines, "The American Missionary Association in Southern Illinois, 1856–1862," 264.

268 *A year later, a mob formed:* Ibid., 258, 267.

268 *Abolitionists in southern Illinois:* Ibid., 258.

268 *"Cairo now begins . . .":* Schwalm, *Emancipation's Diaspora,* 74.

268 *the* New York Times *reported:* Ibid., 75.

268 *Some were victimized:* Ibid., 76.

269 *They ultimately settled:* The 1870 census.

269 *In 1860, only about 40:* Carlson, "The Black Community in the Rural North," 15.

269 *a baby girl named Aby:* The 1870 census.

269 *Toward the end of the war: Report of the adjutant general of the state of Kentucky,* Frankfort, Ky.: Printed at the Kentucky Yeoman Office, J.H. Harney, public printer, 1866–1867, 23. www.ancestry.com (accessed summer 2010).

TWENTY-SEVEN: THE CIVIL WAR

271 *Throngs of flag-waving:* McPherson, *Battle Cry of Freedom.*

271 *Alexander Stephens, the vice president:* Ibid., 244.

271 *white Southern men rallied:* Hahn, *The Roots of Southern Populism,* 117.

272 *In up-country Georgia:* Hahn, *The Roots of Southern Populism,* 117; Historical Jonesboro/Clayton County Inc., *Images of America: Jonesboro.*

272 *The first to go:* Confederate service record of David T. M. Shields, Co. B, 30 Georgia Infantry. www.footnote.com/image/48611228 (accessed April 22, 2011).

272 *The next year:* Confederate service record of Elisha S. Shields, Co. K, 41 Georgia Infantry, www.footnote.com/image/51681080 (accessed September 11, 2011), Confederate service record of Moses A. Shields, Co. K, 41 Georgia Infantry, www.footnote.com/51681104 (accessed September 14, 2011).

272 *morale began to plummet:* Hahn, *The Roots of Southern Populism,* 123, 124.

272 *"Died of disease":* Confederate service record of David T. M. Shields, Co. B, 30 Georgia Infantry, www.footnote.com/image/48611228 (accessed April 22, 2011)

273 *A severe drought battered:* Hahn, *The Roots of Southern Populism,* 124, 125, 128.

273 *A smallpox epidemic:* Kilgore, *History of Clayton County,* 32, 33.

273 *Nancy Boudry remembered: Born in Slavery: Slave Narratives from the Federal Writers' Project, 1936–1938,* Library of Congress, Washington, D.C.

273 *The Confederate Army repulsed:* "Battle of Chickamauga," *New Georgia Encyclopedia,* www.georgiaencyclopedia.org/nge/Article.jsp?id=h-642, (accessed in Spring 2011).

273 *the man who impregnated her:* The 1870 census.

275 *Of the 1,217 blacks:* Kilgore, *History of Clayton County,* 11.

275 *But secretly, African Americans:* Kolchin, *American Slavery,* 204.

275 *So many men had been called up:* Ibid.

275 *"All de white folks . . .":* Born in Slavery: Slave Narratives from the Federal Writers' Project, 1936–1938, Library of Congress, Washington, D.C.

278 *on the Shields farm:* Cornell, *1864 Census for Re-Organizing the Georgia Militia,* 135, includes Charles Shields, Elisha S. Shields, and Henry Wells Shields on a list of men who were enrolled in the Georgia militia. In addition, service records for the Georgia militia indicate that Charles Shields served in the Thirty-fifth Senatorial District Georgia Militia, #1088 District, Clayton County.

278 *opposed the initial decision:* Hahn, *The Roots of Southern Populism,* 114, 115.

278 *Henry and his sons had no choice:* Cornell, *1864 Census for Re-Organizing the Georgia Militia,* 135; interview with great-great-grandchild of Henry Shields, spring 2010.

278 *Charles was working:* "1864 Census for Re-Organizing the Georgia Militia," abstracted and compiled by Nancy J. Cornell; interview with great-great-grandchild of Henry Shields.

279 *The men of the militia:* Smith, *Georgia Militia About Atlanta,* 335.

279 *"Most of the reserves . . .":* Ibid.

279 *So many people were homeless:* Kilgore, *History of Clayton County,* 10.

280 *"We can state with pleasure . . .":* "City History," City of Jonesboro website http://jonesboroga.com/site/VisitingJonesboro/CityHistory/tabid/90/Default.aspx (accessed summer 2011).

280 *He decided to destroy:* "Civil War Sites Advisory Commission Battle Summaries: Jonesborough," http://www.nps.gov/history/hps/abpp/battles/ga022.htm (accessed summer 2011). Also, Hoehling, *Last Train from Atlanta,* 388, 391, 393.

280 *"The men went to work with a will":* More, *The Rebellion Record,* 270.

281 *A brisk wind sent the flames:* Ibid.

281 *The people of Jonesboro emerged:* Kilgore, *History of Clayton County,* 34.

282 *Clayton County was bankrupt:* Ibid., 35.

282 *for the first time in her life, she was free:* The 1870 census.

282 *"Dey throwed down der hoes . . .":* Gloria Baker, *Born in Slavery: Slave Narratives from the Federal Writers' Project, 1936–1938,* Library of Congress, Washington, D.C.

282 *The Yankee soldiers were heroes:* Aunt Ellen Godfrey, *Born in Slavery: Slave Narratives from the Federal Writers' Project, 1936–1938,* Library of Congress, Washington, D.C.

283   *Caeser was about twenty-five:* Civil War service record of Caeser Cohen, who served in Company A of the U.S 128th Colored Infantry. Microfilm number: M589, roll 18. National Archives, Washington, D.C.

283   *Some slaves didn't find out:* Martha Colquitt, *Born in Slavery: Slave Narratives from the Federal Writers' Project,* 1936–1938, Library of Congress, Washington D.C.

284   *Some slaves packed up:* Foner, *Reconstruction,* 81, 82; Brooks, *The Agrarian Revolt,* 10; Drago, *Black Politicians and Reconstruction in Georgia,* 122.

284   *"She had been sold and sent away":* John Davenport, *Born in Slavery: Slave Narratives from the Federal Writers' Project, 1936–1938,* Library of Congress, Washington, D.C.

TWENTY-EIGHT: UNEASY FREEDOM

286   *arsonists burned down:* Bvt. Major Fred. Mosebach to Col. C. C. Sibley, 13 May 1867, enclosed in Bvt. Major Fred. Mosebach to Col. C. C. Sibley, 14 May 1867, M-321 1867, Letters Received, *series 631,* Georgia Assistant Commissioner, Records of the Bureau of Refugees, Freedmen, and Abandoned Lands, *Record Group 105,* National Archives, Washington, D.C. [FSSP A-104]

286   *His church viewed:* Inscoe, *Georgia in Black and White,* 67.

286   *"Our brush arbor . . .":* Daniel W. Stowell, e-mail to author, September 4, 2011.

287   *"Do you think . . .":* Jas S Chalfant to Genl Clinton B. Fisk, 4 August 1866, C-131 1866, Registered Letters Received, *series 3379,* Tennessee Assistant Commissioner, Records of the Bureau of Refugees, Freedmen, and Abandoned Lands, *Record Group 105,* National Archives, Washington, D.C. [A-104: Freedmen and Southern Society Project, University of Maryland, College Park, Md.]

287   *"The house is not . . .":* Mary F. Fuller to Col G. L. Eberheart [sic, his name was Eberhart], 8 April 1867, Letters Received, *series 657,* Georgia Superintendent of Education, Records of the Bureau of Refugees, Freedmen, and Abandoned Lands, *Record Group 105,* National Archives, Washington, D.C. [A-104: Freedmen and Southern Society Project, University of Maryland, College Park, Md.]

287   *But federal officials began:* Bvt Major Fred. Mosebach to Col. C. C. Sibley, 13 May 1867, enclosed in Bvt. Major Fred. Mosebach to Col. C. C. Sibley, 14 May 1867, M-321 1867, Letters Received, *se-*

ries 631, Georgia Assistant Commissioner, Records of the Bureau of Refugees, Freedmen, and Abandoned Lands, *Record Group 105,* National Archives, Washington, D.C. [A-104: Freedmen and Southern Society Project, University of Maryland, College Park, Md.].

288 *Freedmen's Bureau fed:* Records of the field offices for the state of Georgia, Bureau of Refugees, Freedmen, and Abandoned Lands, 1865–1872. M1903, Roll 66. National Archives, Washington, D.C.

288 *"The condition of some . . .":* Ibid.

288 *barred from voting:* Blacks were granted the right to vote in 1870.

289 *So on a winter day:* Henry County (Va.) Circuit Court, Free negro and slave records, 1838-1900, Accession 34440, The Library of Virginia, Richmond, Virginia. Also, Ruth Brown, Curtis Price, and Michael Stowe, "Transcriptions from the John B. Harris Collection," unpublished, Bassett Historical Center, Bassett, Virginia.

290 *"I praise God for this day!":* Eaton, *Grant, Lincoln and the Freedmen,* 34, 35.

290 *Between 1869 and 1900:* Berlin, *Slaves Without Masters,* 385.

291 *Nelson Moten, who had escaped:* The 1870 census.

291 *Dolly and Peter Jumper, who were born free:* Ibid.

291 *Their son, Peter Jr.:* Peter Jumper Jr., who was born free, married Eliza Wade, who was born into slavery, on April 18, 1870.

291 *So he signed a labor contract:* Signed labor contract between Caeser Cohen and R. S. Izard, dated February 28, 1866, Georgetown, South Carolina. National Archives. Microfilm Roll 76, Target 3. Register of Contracts, Volume 197, December 1865–April 1866.

292 *Caeser managed to earn enough:* Caeser Cohen's wife, Tira, applied for a military pension after his death. The Civil War pension application file, which is housed at the National Archives in Washington, D.C., file number 878, 010, describes the land that he owned.

293 *Some white businessmen had begun:* Kilgore, *History of Clayton County,* 41.

293 *The value of his personal estate:* The 1870 census, agricultural census.

293 *Charles . . . married Zipporah Robinson:* Shields family Bible.

293 *Henry and Charles signed an oath:* Oaths of allegiance, Clayton County, Georgia, 1867.

294 *white lawmakers were expelling:* Drago, *Black Politicians and Reconstruction in Georgia,* 146.

294 *biracial twins, Alice and Talley:* The 1870 census.

295 *She was living next door:* Ibid.

295 *Charles, who had a sickly wife:* Tax records from 1869 show that Charles owned 122 acres of land in the Jonesboro district of Clayton County, Georgia. The records also indicate that he had one hired farm laborer.

295 *She died of typhoid:* Visit by author to Shields family graveyard in Rex, Georgia, in February 2010; interview with great-great-grandchild of Henry Shields in spring 2010.

295 *Soon afterward, Charles married:* Visit by author to Shields family graveyard in Rex, Georgia, in February 2010; interview with great-great grandchild of Henry Shields in spring 2010.

295 *he married Nancy Jane Porter:* Charles Shields married Nancy Jane Porter in June 1874. Clayton County, Georgia Marriage Book "B," 1870–1876. Shields family Bible.

295 *And Melvinia, who had given birth:* Death record of Melvinia's daughter, Laura, indicated that she was born in Fulton County, Atlanta, in 1875.

EPILOGUE: MELVINIA'S SECRET

Six people agreed to do DNA testing to assist me with my research. Five were members of the white and black Shields samilies. The sixth was a descendant of Phoebe Moten who hoped to confirm whether Phoebe had Native American ancestry. Unfortunately, the test was unable to prove conclusively whether Phoebe did or not.

301 *once Melvinia finally left Jonesboro:* The 1880, 1900, and 1910 censuses; interview by author of two descendants, who spoke on condition of anonymity, spring 2010.

301 *He even appeared:* "Stole Team and Cotton," *Atlanta Journal,* November 28, 1896.

302 *Charles's father, Henry Wells Shields:* I visited their graves—Henry's in Rex, Georgia, and Charles's in Henry County, Georgia, in February 2010.

302 *Charles was hailed:* "Three Aged Citizens Pass to Beyond," *Henry County Weekly,* January 28, 1916.

302 *Mack, a dairy manager:* Obituary for Mack C. Shields, "Deaths in Birmingham," *Birmingham News,* May 30, 1961.

BIBLIOGRAPHY

Aaron, Larry G. *Pittsylvania County, Virginia: A Brief History.* Charleston, SC: The History Press, 2009.

Armstrong, Louis. *In His Own Words: Selected Writings.* Edited by Thomas Brothers. New York: Oxford University Press, 2001.

Arnold, Edwin T. *What Virtue There Is in Fire: Cultural Memory and the Lynching of Sam Hose.* Athens: University of Georgia Press, 2009.

Atkins, Leah Rawls. "Birmingham: The Magic City." Society of American Archivists. www.archivists.org/conference/birm2002/magiccity.asp (accessed November 24, 2010).

Bardaglio, Peter W. " 'Shamefull Matches': The Regulation of Interracial Sex and Marriage in the South Before 1900." In *Sex, Love, Race: Crossing Boundaries in North American History,* ed. Martha Hodes, 112–138. New York: New York University Press, 1999.

Berlin, Ira. *Slaves Without Masters: The Free Negro in the Antebellum South.* New York: The New Press, 2007.

Bernet, Eleanor H., and Louis Wirth, eds. *Local Community Fact Book, 1938.* Chicago: Chicago Recreation Commission, 1949.

Best, Wallace D. *Passionately Human, No Less Divine: Religion and Culture in Black Chicago, 1915–1952.* Princeton: Princeton University Press, 2005.

Bibb, Henry. *Narrative of the Life and Adventures of Henry Bibb, An American Slave, Written by Himself.* 1849. http://docsouth.unc.edu/neh/bibb/bibb.html (accessed spring 2011).

Black, Timuel D., Jr. *Bridges of Memory: Chicago's First Wave of Black Migration.* Evanston, IL: Northwestern University, 2005.

Blake Smith, Daniel, and Nancy Schrom Dye. "Mother Love and Infant Death, 1750–1920." *Journal of American History* 73, no. 2 (September 1986): 329–353.

Boothe, Charles Octavius. *The Cyclopedia of the Colored Baptists of Alabama: Their Leaders and Their Work*. First electronic edition. University of North Carolina, Chapel Hill, 2001. http://docsouth.unc.edu/church/boothe/boothe.html (accessed June 2011).

Bostick, Ed. "Lynchings in Bartow County." *Etowah Valley Historical Society* 69 (October 2008): 4–7.

Bourgois, Philippe. "If You're Not Black, You're White: A History of Ethnic Relations in St. Louis." *City and Society* 3, no. 2 (December 1989): 106–131.

Bradley, Josephine Boyd, and Kent Anderson Leslie. "White Pain Pollen: An Elite Biracial Daughter's Quandary." In *Sex, Love, Race: Crossing Boundaries in North American History*, ed. Martha Hodes, 213–236. New York: New York University Press, 1999.

Bridges, Roger D. "Equality Deferred: Civil Rights for Illinois Blacks, 1865–1885." *Journal of the Illinois Historical Society* 74, no. 2 (Summer 1981): 82–108.

Brooks, Robert Preston. "The Agrarian Revolt in Georgia: 1865–1912." *Bulletin of the University of Wisconsin* 3, no. 3 (1914): 393–524.

Brundage, W. Fitzhugh. *Lynching in the New South: Georgia and Virginia, 1880–1930*. Chicago: University of Illinois Press, 1993.

Bruner, David K. "Survey of the Negro Population of Evanston." Master's thesis, Northwestern University, 1924.

Buckley S.J., Thomas E. "Unfixing Race: Class, Power, and Identity in an Interracial Family." In *Sex, Love, Race: Crossing Boundaries in North American History*, ed. Martha Hodes, 164–190. New York: New York University Press, 1999.

Butler, Lindley S. *Rockingham County: A Brief History*. Raleigh, North Carolina: Division of Archives and History, 1982.

Candler, Allen D. *The Revolutionary Records of the State of Georgia*. Volume II. Atlanta: The Franklin-Turner Company, 1908.

Candler, Allen D., and General Clement A. Evans, eds. *Georgia: Comprising Sketches of Counties, Towns, Events, Institutions, and Persons, Arranged in Cyclopedic Form*. Vol. 2. Atlanta: Georgia State Historical Association, 1906.

Carlson, Shirley J. "Black Migration to Pulaski County, Illinois: 1860–1900." *Illinois Historical Journal* 80, no. 1 (Spring 1987): 37–46.

―――――. "The Black Community in the Rural North: Pulaski County, Illinois, 1860–1900." Ph.D. diss., Washington University, 1982.

Cayton, Horace, and St. Clair Drake. *Black Metropolis: A Study of Negro Life in a Northern City.* Rev ed. Chicago: University of Chicago Press, 1993.

Chicago Commission on Race Relations. *The Negro in Chicago: A Study of Race Relations and a Race Riot in 1919.* Chicago: University of Chicago Press, 1922.

Christensen, Lawrence O. "Black St. Louis: A Study in Race Relations, 1865–1916." Ph.D. diss., University of Missouri, 1972.

―――――. "Race Relations in St. Louis: 1865–1916." *Missouri Historical Review* 78, no. 2 (January 1984): 123–136.

Circa Inc. "City of Georgetown Historic Resources Survey, Final Report." Durham, NC: May 2002. www.nationalregister.sc.gov/Survey-Reports/IIC22002.pdf (accessed Spring 2011).

Coleman, Kenneth, ed. *A History of Georgia.* Athens: University of Georgia Press, 1977.

Collins, William J., and Robert A. Margo. "Race and Homeownership from the Civil War to the Present." *American Economic Review* 101, no. 3 (May 2011): 355–359.

Comstock, Alzada P. "Chicago Housing Conditions, IV: The Problem of the Negro." *American Journal of Sociology* 18, no. 2 (September 1912): 241–57.

Connerly, Charles E. *"The Most Segregated City in America": City Planning and Civil Rights in Birmingham, 1920–1980.* Charlottesville: University of Virginia Press, 2005.

Corbett, Katharine T., and Mary Seematter. "Black St. Louis at the Turn of the Century." *Gateway Heritage* 7, no. 1 (1986): 40–48.

Cornell, Nancy Jones. *1864 Census for Re-Organizing the Georgia Militia.* Baltimore, MD: Genealogical Publishing Company, 2000.

Cunyus, Lucy Josephine. *The History of Bartow County, Formerly Cass.* Cartersville, GA: Tribune Publishing Co., Inc., 1933.

Dray, Philip. *Capitol Men: The Epic Story of Reconstruction Through the Lives of the First Black Congressmen.* Boston-New York: Houghton Mifflin Company, 2008.

DuBois, W. E. B. *The Souls of Black Folk.* New York: Penguin Classics, 1996.

Dwight, Margaret L. "A Socio-Economic History of Blacks in Pulaski

County, 1850–1900." Master of Science thesis, Southern Illinois University, Carbondale, 1972.

Early, Gerald, ed. *"Ain't But a Place": An Anthology of African American Writings about St. Louis*. St. Louis: Missouri Historical Society Press, 1998.

Eaton, John. *Grant, Lincoln and the Freedmen: Reminiscences of the Civil War.* 1907.

Edgar, Walter B. *South Carolina: A History*. Columbia: University of South Carolina Press, 1998.

Eelman, Bruce W. *Entrepreneurs in the Southern Upcountry: Commercial Culture in Spartanburg, South Carolina: 1845–1880*. Athens: University of Georgia, 2008.

Fallin, Wilson, Jr. *The African American Church in Birmingham, Alabama, 1815–1963: A Shelter in the Storm*. New York: Garland Publishing Inc., 1997.

Farmer-Kaiser, Mary. *Freedwomen and the Freedmen's Bureau*. New York: Fordham University Press, 2010.

Feldman, Lynne B. *A Sense of Place: Birmingham's Black Middle Class Community, 1890–1930*. Tuscaloosa: University of Alabama Press, 1999.

Foner, Eric. *A Short History of Reconstruction*. New York: Harper Perennial, 1990.

―――. *Freedom's Lawmakers: A Directory of Black Officeholders During Reconstruction*. Baton Rouge: Louisiana State University Press, 1996.

―――. *Reconstruction: America's Unfinished Revolution, 1863–1877*. New York: Harper Perennial Classics, 2002.

Foster, Clyde D. *Evanston's Yesterdays: Stories of Early Evanston and Sketches of Some of Its Pioneers*. Evanston, IL: Self-published, 1956.

Furez, Margaret, and Louis Wirth, eds. *Local Community Fact Book, 1938*. Chicago: Chicago Recreation Commission, 1938.

Gibson, Campbell. "Population of the 100 Largest Cities and Other Urban Places in the United States: 1790 to 1990." Population Division Working Paper No. 27. Washington, DC: Population Division, U.S. Bureau of the Census, June 1998.

Gibson, Campbell, and Kay Jung. "Historical Census Statistics on Population Totals by Race, 1790 to 1990, and by Hispanic Origin, by 1790 to 1990, for Large Cities and other Urban Places in the United States." Population Division, Working Paper No. 76, U.S. Census Bureau, February 2005, Table 14.

Gillmer, Jason A. "Base Wretches and Black Wenches: A Story of Sex and Race, Violence and Compassion, During Slavery Times." *Alabama Law Review* 59 (2008): 1501–1555.

Goodheart, Adam. "How Slavery Really Ended in America." *New York Times Magazine,* April 1, 2011.

Gordon-Reed, Annette. *The Hemingses of Monticello: An American Family.* New York: W.W. Norton & Co., 2008.

Green, LeRoy Melvin. *Traces in the Dust: Carbondale's Black Heritage 1852–1964.* Elizabeth I. Mosley-Lewin, ed. Magnolia, TX: Ingenuity Press, 2001.

Grieve, Victoria Maria. "Any Perceptible Trace: Representations of the 'Mulatto' in the United States Census 1850–1920." Master's thesis, University of Georgia, 1996.

Griffith, Alva H. *Pittsylvania County, Virginia: Register of Free Negroes and Related Documentation.* Bowie, MD: Heritage Books, Inc., 2001.

Grossman, James R. *Land of Hope: Chicago, Black Southerners, and the Great Migration.* Chicago: University of Chicago Press, 1991.

———. "The White Man's Union: The Great Migration and the Resonance of Race and Class in Chicago, 1916–1922." In *The Great Migration in Historical Perspective: New Dimensions of Race, Class, and Gender,* ed. Joe William Trotter, 83–99. Bloomington: Indiana University Press, 1991.

Gutman, Herbert G. *The Black Family in Slavery and Freedom: 1750–1925.* New York: Pantheon Books, 1976.

Hahn, Steven. *The Roots of Southern Populism: Yeoman Farmers and the Transformation of the Georgia Upcountry, 1850–1890.* New York and Oxford: Oxford University Press, 2006.

Halliburton, R., Jr. "Origins of Black Slavery Among the Cherokees." *Chronicles of Oklahoma* 52 (Winter 1974–75): 483–496.

Hargrove, Hondon B. *Black Union Soldiers in the Civil War.* Jefferson, NC: Mcfarland & Company Inc., 2003.

Hays, Christopher K. "The African American Struggle for Justice and Equality in Cairo, Illinois, 1865–1900." *Illinois Historical Journal* 90, no. 4 (Winter 1997): 265–284.

Hebert, Keith. "Civil War and Reconstruction Era Cass/Bartow County, Georgia." Ph.D. diss., Auburn University, 2007.

———. "The Bitter Trial of Defeat and Emancipation: Reconstruction in

Bartow County, Georgia, 1865–1872." *Georgia Historical Quarterly* 92, no. 1 (Spring 2008): 65–92.

Heinegg, Paul. *Free African Americans of North Carolina, Virginia and South Carolina from the Colonial Period to About 1820*, Vol. II. Fifth edition. Baltimore: Genealogical Publishing Company, 2005.

Henry County Bicentennial Commission. *The Bicentennial Collection: Abstracts of Henry County and Martinsville Order Books, Minute books, and Loose Papers, 1777–1904*. Martinsville, VA: Bassett Public Library, 1991.

Hill, Judith Parks America. *A History of Henry County Virginia*. Baltimore: America Hill Regional Publishing Company, 1976.

Historical Jonesboro/Clayton County Inc. *Images of America: Jonesboro*. Charleston, SC: Arcadia Publishing, 2007.

Hochschild, Jennifer L., and Brenna M. Powell. "Racial Reorganization and the United States Census 1850–1930: Mulattoes, Half-Breeds, Mixed Parentage, Hindoos, and the Mexican Race." *Studies in American Political Development* 22 (Spring 2008): 59–96.

Hodge, Frederick Webb, ed. *The Handbook of American Indians North of Mexico*. Washington, DC: Government Printing Office, 1907.

Hoehling, A. A. *Last Train from Atlanta*. Harrisburg, PA: Stackpole Books, 1992.

Holcomb, Brent. *Spartanburg County, South Carolina Will Abstracts, 1787-1840*. Columbia, SC, 1983.

Homel, Michael W. *Down from Equality: Black Chicagoans and the Public Schools, 1920–1941*. Chicago: University of Illinois Press, 1984.

———. "The Politics of Public Education in Black Chicago, 1910–1941." *Journal of Negro Education* 45, no. 2 (Spring 1976): 179–191.

Hughes, Langston. *The Big Sea: An Autobiography*. 1940. Reprint. New York: Hill and Wang, 1993.

Inscoe, John C., ed. *Georgia in Black and White: Explorations in Race Relations of a Southern State, 1865–1950*. Athens: University of Georgia Press, 2009.

Jack, Bryan M. *The St. Louis African American Community and the Exodusters*. Columbia: University of Missouri Press, 2007.

Jacobs, Harriet. *Incidents in the Life of a Slave Girl*. 1861. Reprint, edited by Nellie Y. McKay and Frances Smith Foster. New York: W.W. Norton & Company, 2000.

Johnson, James Weldon. *Along This Way: The Autobiography of James Weldon Johnson.* New York: Da Capo Press, 2000.

Jones, Johnetta Y. "Black Land Tenancy in Extreme Southern Illinois, 1870–1920." In *Selected Papers in Illinois History, 1980,* 41–51. Springfield: Illinois State Historical Society, 1982.

Joyner, Charles. *Down by the Riverside: A South Carolina Slave Community.* Chicago: University of Illinois Press, 1984.

Kennett, Lee. *Marching Through Georgia: The Story of Soldiers and Civilians During Sherman's Campaign.* New York: HarperCollins, 1995.

Kenney, William Howland. *Chicago Jazz: A Cultural History, 1904–1930.* New York: Oxford University Press, 1993.

Kilgore, Alice Copeland, Edith Hanes Smith, and Frances Partridge Tuck, eds. *History of Clayton County, Georgia: 1821–1983.* College Park, GA: Ancestors Unlimited, 1983.

Kolchin, Peter. *American Slavery: 1619–1877.* New York: Hill and Wang, 2003.

Kousser, J. Morgan. *The Shaping of Southern Politics: Suffrage Restriction and the Establishment of the One-Party South, 1880–1910.* New Haven: Yale University Press, 1974.

Lachicotte, Alberta Morel. *Georgetown Rice Plantations.* Georgetown, SC: Georgetown County Historical Society, 1993.

Lemann, Nicholas. *The Promised Land: The Great Black Migration and How It Changed America.* New York: Vintage Books, 1992.

———. *Redemption: The Last Battle of the Civil War.* New York: Farrar, Straus and Giroux, 2007.

Leonard, Kevin Barry. "Paternalism and the Rise of a Black Community in Evanston, Illinois: 1870–1930." Master's thesis, Northwestern University, 1982.

Linder, Suzanne Cameron, and Marta Leslie Thacker. *Historical Atlas of the Rice Plantations of Georgetown County.* Columbia, South Carolina: Department of Archives and History, 2001.

Littlefield, Daniel F., Jr., and Lonnie E. Underhill. "Slave 'Revolt' in the Cherokee Nation, 1842." *American Indian Quarterly* 3, no. 2 (Summer 1977): 121–131.

Logan-Alexander, Adele. *Ambiguous Lives: Free Women of Color in Rural Georgia, 1789–1879.* Fayetteville: University of Arkansas Press, 1991.

Martin, Valerie. *Property.* New York: Nan A. Talese/Doubleday, 2003.

Mayer, Henry. *A Son of Thunder: Patrick Henry and the American Republic.* New York: Grove Press, 1991.

Mays, Dorothy. *Women in Early America: Struggle, Survival and Freedom in a New World.* Santa Barbara, CA: ABL-CLIO, 2004.

McCurry, Stephanie. *Confederate Reckoning: Power and Politics in the Civil War South.* Cambridge: Harvard University Press, 2010.

McKay, Claude. *Claude McKay: Selected Poems,* ed. Joan R. Sherman. New York: Dover Publications, 1999.

McKnown, Harry. "This Month in North Carolina History: October 1918—North Carolina and the Blue Death." University of North Carolina Libraries. www.lib.unc.edu/ncc/ref/nchistory/oct2008/index.html (accessed Spring 2011).

McLoughlin, William G. "Red Indians, Black Slavery, and White Racism: America's Slaveholding Indians." *American Quarterly* 26, no. 4 (October 1974): 367–385.

McPherson, James M. *Battle Cry of Freedom: The Civil War Era.* New York: Oxford University Press, 1988.

Moore, Christopher Paul. *Fighting for America: Black Soldiers—The Unsung Heroes of World War II.* New York: Presidio Press, 2005.

Moore, Frank, ed. *The Rebellion Record: A Diary of American Events with Documents, Narratives, Illustrative Incidents, Poetry, Etc.* Vol. 11. 1868.

National Archives. "Teaching with Documents: The Fight for Equal Rights: Black Soldiers in the Civil War." http://www.archives.gov/education/lessons/blacks-civil-war/ (accessed Spring 2011).

National Park Service. "Brices Cross Roads: The Battle." www.nps.gov/brcr/the-battle.htm (accessed Spring 2011).

North Carolina History Project. "North Carolina History Project Encyclopedia." John Locke Foundation. http://www.northcarolinahistory.org/encyclopedia/ (accessed Summer 2011).

Norton, Wilbur T., ed. *Centennial History of Madison County Illinois and Its People: 1812–1912.* Vol. 1. Chicago: The Lewis Publishing Company, 1912.

Official Guide of the Railways and Steam Navigation Lines of the United States, Porto Rico, Canada, Mexico and Cuba. New York: The National Railway Publication Company, Publishers and Proprieters, 1908.

Opala, Joseph A. "The Gullah: Rice, Slavery and the Sierra Leone-

American Connection." New Haven: The Gilder Lehrman Center for the Study of Slavery, Resistance, and Abolition, Yale University, http://yale.edu/glc/gullah/index.htm (accessed Spring 2011).

Parker, David B. "Rebecca Latimer Felton, 1835–1930." *The New Georgia Encyclopedia*. http://www.georgiaencyclopedia.org/nge/Article.jsp?id=h-904&hl=y (accessed Spring 2011).

Perkins-Valdez, Dolen. *Wench*. New York: Amistad, 2010.

Perrin, William Henry, ed. *History of Alexander, Union and Pulaski Counties, Illinois*. Chicago: O. L. Baskin and Co., 1883.

Pietila, Antero. *Not in My Neighborhood: How Bigotry Shaped a Great American City*. Lanham, MD: Ivan R. Dee, 2010.

Power, Garrett. "Apartheid Baltimore Style: The Residential Segregation Ordinances of 1910–1913." *Maryland Law Review* 42 (1983): 289–328.

Raines, Edgar F., Jr. "The American Missionary Association in Southern Illinois, 1856–1862: A Case History in the Abolition Movement." *Journal of the Illinois Historical Society* 65, no. 3 (Autumn 1972): 246–268.

Reid, Stevenson Nathaniel. *History of Colored Baptists in Alabama: Including Facts About Men, Women and Events of the Denomination Based upon the Careful Study of the Highest Recognized Authority Within Reach*. Birmingham: Forniss Printing Company, 1949.

Robinson, Craig. *A Game of Character: A Family Journey from Chicago's Southside to the Ivy League and Beyond*. New York: Gotham Books, 2010.

Robinson, Morris E., Jr. *A Place We Can Call Our Home: The Emerging Evanston Black Community Circa 1850–1930*. Evanston, IL: Shorefront, 2010.

Rogers, George C., Jr. *The History of Georgetown County, South Carolina*. Columbia: University of South Carolina Press, 1970.

Rodgers, Michele. *Bartow County, Georgia*. Charleston, SC: Arcadia Publishing, 1996.

Rothman, Joshua D. *Notorious in the Neighborhood: Sex and Families Across the Color Line in Virginia, 1787–1861*. Chapel Hill: University of North Carolina Press, 2003.

Rubillo, Tom. *Trial and Error: The Case of John Brownfield and Race Relations in Georgetown, South Carolina*. Charleston: History Press, 2005.

Rumbold, Charlotte. *Housing Conditions in St. Louis: Report of the Housing Committee of the Civic League of St. Louis*. St. Louis: Civic League of St. Louis, 1908.

Russell, John H. *The Free Negro in Virginia: 1619–1865*. Baltimore: Johns Hopkins Press, 1913.

Sandweiss, Martha A. *Passing Strange: A Gilded Age Tale of Love and Deception Across the Color Line*. New York: Penguin Press, 2009.

Schwalm, Leslie A. *Emancipation's Diaspora: Race and Reconstruction in the Upper Midwest*. Chapel Hill: University of North Carolina Press, 2009.

———. *A Hard Fight for We: Women's Transition from Slavery to Freedom in South Carolina*. Chicago: University of Illinois Press, 1997.

Schwartz, Marie J. *Born in Bondage: Growing Up Enslaved in the Antebellum South*. Cambridge: Harvard University Press, 2000.

Scott, Emmett J. "Letters of Negro Migrants of 1916–1918." *Journal of Negro History* 4, no. 3 (July 1919): 290–340.

Simms, William Gilmore. *The Geography of South Carolina*. Charleston: Babcock & Co., 1843.

Smith, Gustavus W. *"Georgia Militia about Atlanta,"* in *Battles and Leaders of the Civil War*. Vol. IV. New York: Century Company, 1884.

Snell, William R. "Fiery Crosses in the Roaring Twenties: Activities of the Revised Klan in Alabama, 1915–1930." *Alabama Review* 23, no. 4 (October 1970): 256–276.

Stowell, Daniel. "The Negroes Cannot Navigate Alone: Religious Scalawags and the Biracial Methodist Episcopal Church in Georgia, 1866–1876." In *Georgia in Black and White: Explorations in the Race Relations of a Southern State: 1865–1950*, ed. John C. Inscoe, 65–90. Athens: University of Georgia Press, 1994.

Thomas Jefferson's Monticello. "Monticello." Thomas Jefferson Foundation. www.monticello.org (accessed Summer 2011).

The Experience of Thomas H. Jones Who Was a Slave for Forty-three Years. Worcester: Henry J. Howland, 1857.

Tye, Larry. *Rising from the Rails: Pullman Porters and the Making of the Black Middle Class*. New York: Henry Holt and Company, 2004.

University of Chicago. "Key to Map of Chicago South Side Jazz, c. 1915–1913." University of Chicago Library. www.lib.uchicago.edu/e/su/cja/mapkey.html (accessed Fall 2010).

University of Virginia Library. "Hearts at Home: Southern Women in the Civil War." University of Virginia. www2.lib.virginia.edu/exhibits/hearts/hard.html (accessed Summer 2010).

U.S. Bureau of the Census. *Negroes in the United States, Bulletin 129*, by William J. Harris. Washington, DC: Government Printing Office, 1915.

———. *Negro Population: 1790–1915*, by Sam L. Rogers. Washington, DC: Government Printing Office, 1918.

U.S. Department of Health and Human Services. "The Great Pandemic: The United States in 1918–1919: North Carolina." http://1918.pandemicflu.gov/your_state/north_carolina.htm (accessed Spring 2011).

Vehorn, Larry. *Spartanburg District, S.C.: Deed Abstracts*. Books X–V. Greenville, SC: Southern Historical Press, 2001.

Washburne, Elihu Benjamin. *Sketch of Edward Coles, Second Governor of Illinois, and of the Slavery Struggle of 1823–4*. Chicago: James, McClurg & Company, 1882.

West, Emily. *Chains of Love: Slave Couples in Antebellum South Carolina*. Champaign: University of Illinois Press, 2004.

West, Stephen A. *From Yeoman to Redneck in the South Carolina Upcountry, 1850–1915*. Charlottesville: University of Virginia Press, 2008.

White, George. *Historical Collections of Georgia: Containing the Most Interesting Facts, Traditions, Biographies, Sketches, Anecdotes, Etc., Relating to Its History and Antiquities from Its First Settlement to the Present Time*. 3rd ed. New York: Pudney & Russell, Publishers, 1855.

———. *Statistics of the State of Georgia: including an account of its natural, civil, and ecclesiastical history; together with a particular description of each county, notices of the manners and customs of its aboriginal tribes, and a correct map of the state*. Savannah: W.T. Williams, 1849.

White, John. *Cache Area River Assessment, Vol. II. Socioeconomic Profile, Early Accounts of the Ecology of the Cache River Area*. Urbana: Illinois Department of Natural Resources, Ecological Services, March 1997.

Wilkins, Roy, with Tom Mathews. *Standing Fast: The Autobiography of Roy Wilkins*. New York: Da Capo Press, 1994.

Wright, Richard. *Black Boy (American Hunger): A Record of Childhood and Youth*. 1945. Reprint. New York: HarperCollins, 2005.

INDEX

About the author

About the book

Insights,
Interviews
& More...

Read on

Meet Rachel L. Swarns

© 2011 SCOTT ROBINSON

RACHEL L. SWARNS has been a correspondent for the *New York Times* since 1995. She has written about domestic policy and national politics, reporting on immigration, the presidential campaigns of 2004 and 2008, and First Lady Michelle Obama and her role in the Obama White House. She has also worked overseas for the *New York Times*, reporting from Russia, Cuba, and southern Africa, where she served as the Johannesburg bureau chief. She currently writes about demographics, social trends, and the modern American family. Prior to joining the *New York Times*, Ms. Swarns worked for the *Miami Herald*, where she reported from Haiti and from Guantanamo Bay, Cuba, and covered the L.A. riots and the aftermath of Hurricane Andrew. She started her journalism career at the *St. Petersburg Times*. Born in New York City, she received her BA in Spanish from Howard University, summa cum laude, Phi Beta Kappa. She received her MA in international relations, with distinction, from the University of Kent in Canterbury, England. She lives in Washington, D.C., with her husband and two children. You can keep up with her book events on www.facebook.com/rachel.l.swarns and rachelswarns .com. Follow her on Twitter at @rachelswarns.

A Family Expands

ONE WEEK after the first edition of this book was published, officials in Clayton County, Georgia, unveiled a granite monument in Melvinia's honor. It was erected in the village of Rex, not far from where Melvinia was enslaved in the 1850s and 1860s.

Hundreds of people gathered for the occasion, on a searing afternoon in June of 2012. Among them were the descendants of Melvinia, and the white descendants of Melvinia's owner, Henry, who met for the very first time.

County officials, who began planning the memorial after learning about Melvinia in the 2009 article that I wrote with my colleague Jodi Kantor for the *New York Times,* had invited Melvinia's great-grandson to the ceremony. He drove in with his family from Kingston, Georgia. With the county's blessings, I also invited Henry's great-great-grandchildren and great-great-great-grandchildren, who traveled from other towns in Georgia and Alabama.

At the ceremony, Eldrin Bell, the chairman of the county commission, urged those in the crowd to learn more about their roots. "Let the stories of our past draw us closer together," he said. And then he asked the family to come forward. One by one, they left their seats to take their places before the crowd. There was David Applin, Melvinia's great-grandson, and Joan Tribble, Henry's great-great-granddaughter, and the members of their extended families.

When I first started digging into Michelle Obama's family tree, I never imagined that my research might bring the black and white branches ▶

3

of her family together. But there they were, for the very first time, the contemporary descendants of slave and slave owner standing side by side. It was something to see.

"There were tears in my eyes," Mr. Applin said afterward.

Joan Tribble is standing with a cane on the right. Her cousin Jarrod Shields is standing behind her in the collared shirt. David Applin is the bald, bearded man standing next to Joan. (© Damon Wood)

Among the white descendants attending the ceremony that day was Jarrod Shields, the great-great-great-grandson of Melvinia's owner, and one of Joan Tribble's cousins. He shared what he knew about his ancestors with the Applins and showed them a rare black-and-white photograph that provided the Applins with the first glimpse of two key figures in the First Lady's family and their own: Henry Wells Shields, the white man who owned Melvinia, and his son Charles Marion Shields, who most likely fathered Melvinia's son, Dolphus.

Henry is the man with the white beard. His wife, Christian Patterson Shields, sits to his right. Charles is the third man standing from the right. (Courtesy of Jarrod Shields)

The photograph, which Jarrod believes was taken in Georgia sometime around 1884, was passed down in his family from one generation to the next. Jarrod had grown up knowing that his family had once owned slaves and had always wondered what happened to their descendants.

He said he was grateful to finally meet them.

"I always really wanted to say I was sorry," he said. "I also wanted to let them know that we're glad that you're part of our family, however it came about."

—*Rachel L. Swarns* ❦

Nine Tips for Researching Your Family Tree

DURING MY conversations with readers of *American Tapestry*, one question has popped up over and over again. People want to know: How do I research *my* family tree? Below is an excerpt from a piece that appeared on GoodHousekeeping.com, in which I lay out a solid plan for anyone hoping to unearth the stories of their ancestors.

* Get started by interviewing your parents, grandparents, aunts, uncles—all of your oldest relatives. With their help, you can start to put together what is known about your family tree. Important details to ask about? Names (including maiden names of female relatives), dates of birth and death, marriage, and military service.

* Once you've collected the basics, conduct more interviews, but this time dig deeper. Use your video camera or tape recorder to document your conversations if you can. Talk to your oldest relatives to find out everything they know about your family's origins. Ask them what they remember most about their childhood and about the key moments in their lives. You should also find out if your family emigrated from one country to another, or even from one state to another.

* Create a diagram of your family tree and include the names and dates that you've collected. FamilyTreeMaker.com and Lineages.com are great websites to use to get started on this.

* Collect copies of any records that your family has: birth certificates, marriage licenses, baptismal certificates, death certificates. You can use these to help confirm the accuracy of the family stories you've collected.

* If you live in the area where your parents or grandparents lived, check out what records are available from city agencies, courthouses, and local libraries. You can often find marriage and birth and death records, if you don't have them, as well as old wills and property records.

* Find out where the closest regional office of the National Archives is located. There you'll be able to search for your ancestors in the census, uncover immigration and military records, and more. Bonus. The National Archives also offers tips on how to get started researching your family tree, free online access to some historical records, and a calendar of genealogical workshops around the country.

* Think about using an online genealogical service that provides access to historical records on your computer. For example, FamilySearch.org offers free online access to historical records, including birth, marriage, death, probate, land, military, and more from the United States and other countries. Ancestry.com is another great site—paid subscribers get access to genealogical records from all over the world.

* Consider DNA testing. There are several companies that can help you find out more about your ancestry and your ▶

ethnic heritage this way. Two sites worth checking out?
FamilyTreeDNA.com and 23andMe.com.

* Most important, get together with the members of your
  family and share what you've found. You might inspire others
  to join in your search! ∾

*From "9 Tips for Researching Your Family Tree" from
GoodHousekeeping.com, written by Rachel Bowie.
Copyright 2012 by Hearst Communications, Inc.*